T0243420

THE SILVER BULLET SOLUTION

Is It Time to End the War on Drugs?

Violence, Gangs, Guns, Drugs, Policing, Mass Incarceration, Racism, Immigration, Human Rights, Healthcare, AIDS, and Corruption

James E. Gierach

THE SILVER BULLET SOLUTION

Is It Time to End the War on Drugs?

Foreword by Brian A. Ford

GAUDIUM

Gaudium Publishing

Las Vegas ◊ Chicago ◊ Palm Beach

Published in the United States of America by
Histria Books
7181 N. Hualapai Way, Ste. 130-86
Las Vegas, NV 89166 USA
HistriaBooks.com

Gaudium Publishing is an imprint of Histria Books. Titles published under the imprints of Histria Books are distributed worldwide.

Library of Congress Control Number: 2023939519

ISBN 978-1-59211-338-5 (hardcover)
ISBN 978-1-59211-351-4 (eBook)

Contents

Dedicated to my wife, Melissa; my parents,
Will and Dorothy Gierach; and family,
Julie, Laura and Billy.

Foreword

This book is important because drug policy is a choice. Prohibition is a choice. Therefore, undoing prohibition is also a choice, and it is a choice we must make with urgency.

When I grew up, I did not know we had a choice — the war on drugs was a given. Born in California in 1984, I was firmly in the D.A.R.E. generation and the common cultural refrain was "Just say no to drugs!" The act of smoking pot in high school was rebellious, punk rock. It also carried the risk of life destroying criminal penalties, more so if you were poor or a person of color. These were policies that I inherited; they predated my existence.

But being raised in California at the turn of the century also meant that I grew up in a state that found a way to start cracking the war on drugs. I was 12 years old when California decriminalized "medical marijuana" in 1996. I was 32 years old when California legalized recreational use of cannabis for adults in 2016, four years after the states of Colorado and Washington had done the same in 2012. Now, in 2023, medical use of cannabis is legal in 37 U.S. states, and recreational use for adults is legal in 21 states and decriminalized in another 10. So I have seen change, and therefore I know that change is possible.

Nonetheless, marijuana is still illegal and prohibited in all of those states by Federal law under the Controlled Substances Act of 1970. Meaning, no matter what California says, the Feds are still locking Californians up for pot. And despite the inroads we have made with marijuana, there has been little to no similar progress pushing back on prohibition of any other scheduled, listed, or prohibited substance in any state or federal law.

To the contrary, the standard is still prohibition, and the consequence is still prison for people involved with drugs. A child born in the U.S. today may not know a world where marijuana use is strictly prohibited, but they will know a world that continues to suffer under the yoke of an unwinnable war on drugs, a war which has lasted longer and which consumes more resources and human lives than any other war in human history. They may be raised to believe, as many do, that marijuana is ok but other drugs are not, and so inherit the same morally corrupted philosophy of prohibition that continues to dictate global drug policy. So I also know that there remains much to be done in the work of fighting against the prohibitionist war on drugs.

James Gierach has been fighting against the prohibitionist war on drugs almost as long as I have been alive. His journey begins as an agent of the prohibitionists, as a prosecutor, and continues through his political endeavors and activism all the way through his efforts at the United Nations to amend the foundational international treaties underlying the prohibitionist global order. This text contains many of the invaluable insights and lessons learned that he has collected in those decades. As a criminal defense attorney and an advocate for both Black Lives Matter and ANTIFA, there is plenty that Mr. Gierach and I may disagree about concerning current events and political actors, but we do agree that prohibition is the greatest man-made contributor to global violence against civilians, poverty, mass incarceration, systemic racism, corruption of government and police, accidental overdoses, and much much more. Spoiler alert, the silver-bullet solution to these societal ills and many more is simple: legalize drugs.

Mr. Gierach's text, however, does not just give life and animation to these harms of the war on drugs. His text also provides multiple roadmaps to actionable ways we can address the problem and end prohibition. The reality is that the solution may be simple, but the means of getting to the solution is more complicated. Efforts have to be sustained at all levels of government, from local towns and cities, all the way up to the highest echelons of the international order.

Before I was an attorney, I was an academic studying international law with a focus on the war on drugs. My initial point of entry into drug policy was through the lens of the Latin American experience, and I quickly learned of the massive levels of human carnage suffered in so-called "producer" nations. Through my research, I also quickly learned that there were two broad but opposing areas of consensus in the existing literature at that time: Economic-based perspectives that understood the futility of the prohibitionist model; and political-based perspectives which noted the extreme costs (or destruction) of the war on drugs, often times recognized the superiority of harm-reduction models, but inevitably seemed to call for a doubling down on or an intensifying of the prohibitionist model of the war on drugs. In other words, between these two spheres there seemed to be an objective consensus that prohibition was fundamentally doomed to failure, and a subjective consensus that the only answer to this certain failure was to increase our investment in this failed experiment. In short, there was nothing but insanity underpinning the belief that the international war on drugs was either necessary or effective.

As I began to produce more research papers examining drug policies and their outcomes in various nations, I came to learn more about international treaty law and the laws of nations. Similar to Mr. Gierach, I discovered that it is possible to trace the global war on drugs back to the formation and near-universal adoption of the three international treaties related to narcotics control. Notably, if we measure international consensus in terms of parties to a treaty, the international treaties prohibiting drugs have reached more consensus at the time of this writing than the 1969 International Convention on the Elimination of All Forms of Racial Discrimination (180 parties), the 2000 Protocol to Prevent, Suppress and Punish Trafficking in Persons, especially Women and Children (179 parties), the 1930 Forced Labor Convention (179 parties), the 1996 Comprehensive Nuclear Test-Ban Treaty (174 parties), the 1956 Statute of the Atomic Energy Agency (175 parties), the 1957 Abolition of Forced Labour Convention (175 parties), the International Convention against the Taking of Hostages (175 parties), the 1966 International Convention on Civil and Political Rights (172 parties), the 1984 Convention against Torture and Other Cruel, Inhuman, or Degrading Treatment or Punishment (171 parties), and the 1976 International Covenant on Economic, Social and Cultural Rights (170 parties).

More than that, parties to the international treaties prohibiting drugs have *implemented* those treaty obligations through myriads of criminal laws and punishments, in some cases including death. There is simply no other subject of international law that has been so successfully implemented across the world. By comparison, consider the International Criminal Court (ICC), tasked under the 2002 Rome Statute with adjudicating "the most serious crimes of concern to the international community as a whole" including genocide, crimes against humanity, war crimes, and the crime of aggression." There are presently only 123 parties to the Rome Statute establishing the ICC, and thus only 123 nations subject to its jurisdiction, whereas there are 186 parties to the 1988 UN Convention Against Illicit Traffic in Narcotic Drugs and Psychotropic Substances. Stated another way, approximately a third of the United Nations' Member States are more obliged to prosecute a person for drug trafficking than they would be to execute an ICC warrant for an international war criminal, given the opportunity.

Clearly, the current state of affairs makes no sense and meets no rational moral standard. That same child, spoken of earlier who was born today, might also grow to see a world that changes back towards the prohibitionist policies we have recently stepped away from. Today in San Francisco, for instance, there has been an undoing of criminal justice reforms that had largely decriminalized hand-to hand street sales of narcotics. In the name of the war on fentanyl, law enforcement officers previously identified in corrupt policing have been put back on the streets to police in the same manner as before. Access to drug courts and diversion programs has been cut short for persons charged with possessing fentanyl for sale. Pre-trial release, even under conditions of electronic monitoring or home confinement, have been denied to persons accused of distributing fentanyl. This harsher prosecutorial treatment has been extended to all classes of what Mr. Gierach classifies as "Addict crime" and is motivated by the same defunct moralistic underpinnings of the prohibitionist war on drugs. It was crack cocaine in the '80s, PCP in the '90's, "bath salts" in the aughts, today it is fentanyl, and who knows what it will be next tomorrow, but the prohibitionist approach of "lock 'em up" will always be the same failed policy.

It is clearly time for a change, and this text may be your first step in making that change a reality. In this text, Mr. Gierach skillfully walks us through the history of the international war on drugs, and he does so with personal anecdotes so that we may better appreciate the realities of the war on drugs and what it takes to fight against them. This text will make sense of the senseless and provide numerous pathways forward. The simple reality is that the World War on Drugs is over 60 years old, and it is far from over. Unless we can find and implement a silver bullet solution.

Brian A. Ford

Preface

My thesis underlying this book is that the so-called "War on Drugs," drug prohibition, is not only at the heart of the global drug problem but is also at the heart of myriad, collateral, drug-war driven and drug-war aggravated societal crises and problems. My assessment of the magnitude of the harm caused by the War on Drugs: it is inestimable, causing more harm to public health, safety and welfare, human rights, freedom, democracy and civilized society overall than any preceding public policy in the history of mankind. My motivation for writing this book is to help build public opinion in opposition to the War on Drugs in order to accelerate its inevitable end. My view is that by legalizing drugs, reducing drug prices, increasing drug tolerance and understanding, and by "taking the profit out of the drug business," many collateral prohibition harms can be ameliorated. In addition, legal, licensed and regulated drug outlets will better enable us to control product purity, potency and labeling, reducing the number of accidental overdose deaths caused by fentanyl and other contamination of recreationally consumed synthetic and organic substances. My vantage point is that of a nonsmoking prosecutor who is addicted to tobacco and who moderately uses alcohol, the two most dangerous drugs. My search for the key to ending the War on Drugs includes over thirty years of failed attempts and initiatives. My strategy in writing a book on this subject is to help build public opinion against the War on Drugs to such an extent that recalcitrant political leaders will no longer be politically viable.

Part One - The Project: End the War on Drugs

Chapter 1 - The Opening Epilogue

A little unusual, I suppose, but I'd like to start this manuscript with the Epilogue. It would be a shame to have a reader willing to pick up "The Silver Bullet Solution," start to read it, and set it down before getting to the very end. It's not uncommon for an author to make this part of his or her book the most concise, cogent, and convincing point "in conclusion" when some readers have already dropped off. The message of this book is too important to let that happen. Therefore, I say to the last words — in this book — "You shall be first."

Part One of this book analyzes the War on Drugs, its origins, essence and expansion; it tracks one man's search for the key to end it and takes direct aim at it.

The War on Drugs: The Worst Public Policy Known to Mankind

For over thirty years, I have searched for a means to bring about an end to America's War on Drugs. Initially, I was attracted to drug policy reform because of Chicago's horrific, unending, systemic violence, unavoidably caused by the prohibition of substances, an "Al Capone Era" reincarnation. Soon after engaging the drug war in battle, I concluded that drug prohibition, better known as "the War on Drugs," was not just the heart of America's violence problem; it was also the heart of a dozen other American crises as well.

What crises are those?

The list of crises is expansive but includes these topics: guns, gangs, addict crime, turf-war crime, unaffordable bullet-hole healthcare, the corruption of kids and police, trade imbalance, money laundering, immigration, abusive policing, shrinking personal freedoms, racism, mass incarceration, unfair sentencing and criminal injustice, police department militarization, growing intolerance of one another, our differences and weaknesses, and a lack of empathy, among others. Because this long string of crises is caused by or at least aggravated by the War on Drugs, I have reached a summary conclusion about it.

In my opinion, the War on Drugs is the most ill-conceived, counterproductive and comprehensively damaging public policy ever enacted into law in the history of mankind.

Is it really that bad? Yes.

It's A World War on Drugs

Not only that, but it is much more than America's drug war; it is a "World War on Drugs." No human being can escape its bite or adverse consequences. As with all wars, the drug war brings pain, heartache and unspeakable atrocities, tragedies and casualties. The irony is that the harm, pain and heartache sought to be prevented by declaring and waging the War on Drugs is the very thing accomplished by it. Instead of saving our loved ones from drugs, the synergistic combination of human greed, prohibition's entrepreneurial opportunity, and the economic laws of price, supply and demand increase drug invention, cultivation, production, potency, availability, use, addiction, disease, accidental overdose and death.

It's a Pax Romana Antithesis

Not only is the drug war more than just an American war, its duration is also often overlooked. Author and professor Steven B. Duke and coauthor Albert C. Gross correctly noted, as their book title asserted, the War on Drugs is America's longest war.[1] It was declared by President Richard Nixon fifty-two years ago and continues yet. In contrast, America's war in Afghanistan ended in July 2021 and lasted only twnety years. Mistakenly, the Afghanistan War has been called "America's longest war."[2] It is not. Fifty-two years is longer than twenty years.

Furthermore, if you calculate the duration of the *world's* longest war, a war to which America is a party combatant, from the date when national representatives to the United Nations ("the UN") "codified" it, it is really a sixty-year-old war. Started in 1961, the UN has been complicit in promulgating a global drug war for more than sixty years, "the World War on Drugs." Not only is the drug war the "Longest World War," it is fast approaching a Pax Romana Antithesis, a period of one hundred years

---

[1] Stephen B. Duke and Albert C. Gross, *America's Longest War: Rethinking Our Tragic Crusade Against Drugs* (New York: G. P. Putnam's Sons, 1993)

[2] Julian Borger, "Afghanistan: America's 'longest war' ends amid accusations of betrayal," *The Guardian*, July 4, 2021, https://www.theguardian.com/world/2021/jul/04/afghanistan-americas-longest-war-ends-amid-accusations-of-betrayal.

of global war instead of global peace.[3] If calculated from the year of enactment of the United States federal law regulating and taxing the production, importation and distribution of opiates and coca products, the 1914 Harrison Narcotics Tax Act,[4] the drug-prohibition "conflict" is already old enough to be an antique.[5]

The kickoff date for the modern World War on Drugs was 1961, the year when 186 nations began to join hands and one-by-one subscribed to the *1961 Single Convention on Narcotic Drugs*[6], a United Nations document that outlaws and criminalizes recreational drug use. (Hereinafter, the convention will be referred to simply as the "1961 Single Convention.") The term "recreational drug use" is used many times in this manuscript. It is an overly broad term seemingly insinuating fun, holiday, pleasure-seeking, or perhaps even a morally deprecating purpose. Correctly understood, as the term is used in this manuscript, it simply encompasses any change in mood, consciousness or mindset accomplished by substance ingestion. Even more precisely, as used herein, the term means drug-use for any purpose other than for a "scientific" or "medical" reason.

Unwisely, the 1961 Single Convention "takes a prohibitionist approach to the problem of drug addiction, attempting to stop all non-medical, non-scientific use of narcotic drugs. Article 4 requires nations to limit use and possession of drugs to medicinal and scientific purposes... and Article 36 requires Parties [nations] to adopt measures against cultivation, production, manufacture, extraction, preparation, possession, offering, offering for sale, distribution, purchase, sale, delivery..." [and provides that] "in the cases of [unspecified] serious offences that they shall be liable to adequate punishment particularly by imprisonment or other penalties of deprivation of liberty."[7] That drug-intolerant criminalization approach is implemented by the 1961 Single Convention mandate that all nations that are parties to the treaty must enact national laws enabling and mimicking UN drug schedules and prohibitions.

---

[3] "The Pax Romana," *US History*, https://www.ushistory.org/civ/6c.asp, accessed March 22, 2023.

[4] *Wikipedia*, s.v. "Harrison Narcotics Tax Act," https://en.wikipedia.org/ wiki/Harrison_Narcotics_Tax_Act, accessed March 22, 2023.

[5] Edward M. Brecher, *Licit and Illicit Drugs: Consumers Union Report* (Boston: Toronto, Little, Brown and Co., 1972), p. 49.

[6] *United Nations, UNODC,* https://www.unodc.org/pdf/convention_1961_ en.pdf.

[7] *Wikipedia*, s.v. "Single Convention on Narcotic Drugs," https://en.m.wikipedia.org/wiki/Single_ Convention_on_Narcotic_Drugs.

Nine years later in 1970, the United States enacted its national law pursuant to that treaty mandate, its Controlled Substances Act.[8] "The Controlled Substances Act (CSA) Title II of the Comprehensive Drug Abuse Prevention and Control Act of 1970 is the federal U.S. drug policy under which the manufacture, importation, possession, use and distribution of certain narcotics, stimulants, depressants, hallucinogens, anabolic steroids and other chemicals is regulated.... Within the CSA there are five controlled substance schedules at the federal level (Schedules I-V) that are used to classify drugs based upon their: abuse potential, accepted medical applications in the U.S., and safety and potential for addiction."[9] The following year, 1971, President Richard Nixon formally declared America's War on Drugs. Other nations also dutifully passed like-minded national laws implementing drug prohibition, basically, all nations sharing in the disastrous folly.

Searching for the Key to End the Cursed World War on Drugs?

As these pages will demonstrate, I have diligently searched for a means to end the World War on Drugs, because it is so harmful to so many people in such devious, creative and cursed fashion. It truly is so brilliant in its conception, intolerance and capacity to cause harm that I have often referred to the War on Drugs as "the Curse of Solomon." I hasten to add, apologies to King Solomon.[10] No one as bright as Solomon would have tolerated such war-filled intolerance for sixty years. The War on Drugs is the new eternal damnation, a merger of Life, Purgatory and Hell — an irreversible, permanent state of war, intolerance, innocent victims, bloodshed and misery for all people and civilization itself. The War on Drugs is the consummate repudiation of the universal laws of the Cosmos and the inalienable rights of human beings.

In December 1994, I wrote a 2,200-word essay, entitled "The Curse of Solomon" that sought to answer the question, "What Is the Key to Turning 'Off' the Cursed World War on Drugs?" The essay ended with this paragraph: "[The drug] prohibition scourge and all its horrors would eventually end.... Without a soldier or drug agent in sight, one American after another, and another, would simply rediscover old truths. It is easier to addict than cure; that tolerance is better than intolerance; that prioritizing

---

[8] "Title 21 United States Code (USC) Controlled Substances Act," https://www.deadiversion.usdoj.gov/21cfr/21usc/811.htm.

[9] Medically reviewed by Leigh Ann Anderson, PharmD., CSA Schedule, *Drugs.com*, https://www.drugs.com/csa-schedule.html, accessed August 21, 2021.

[10] *Wikipedia*, s.v. "Solomon," https://en.m.wikipedia.org/wiki/Solomon. Accessed March 16, 2023.

drug crimes tends to minimize serious violent crime; that self-discipline is more powerful than a book of laws however large; and that anti-drug strategies attune to universal economic laws are effective deterrents to drug use and abuse unlike man-made laws that challenge them. This is how the world's Drug Civil War would end. For with Solomon-like wisdom the same key that had engaged prohibition would be in the hands of the people to turn back and disengage the curse."

In my search for an effective means to end the war on drugs, I considered writing a book in the early 1990s. A few books have reportedly changed the world for the better.[11] There was *The Jungle* by Upton Sinclair and *Uncle Tom's Cabin* by Harriet Beecher Stowe. There are others, too. I considered writing a novel about drugs or drug-dealing, but television and movie houses are replete with shows and movies telling the stories of prohibition: drug-trade violence, double-crossing, cheating, corrupting, informing, incarcerating, overdosing, dying, disease, injustice and other horrors associated with drugs, dealing and drug war, so much so that these drug-war evils had become commonplace. Horrible drug-war consequences have become a civilization norm, something to be expected. Such a novel would be mundane, commonplace and likely, unmoving.

Once before in 1995, I tried to interest literary agents in a compilation of my anti-drug war creative writing. I titled it, "The Hub of the American Crisis: Drugs or Dopes."[12] Some of it found print in newspaper columns, articles and letters. But the book effort failed. I was told, one cannot get a compilation published unless you are a Mike Royko-type icon or celebrity. Well, twenty-eight years later, maybe it is time for my second turn at bat.

A Melancholy Task This Manuscript

Writing this manuscript, I feel a certain dread, a kind of futility, a trailing shadow of hopelessness that keeps trying to creep onto my iPad screen and into this manuscript. Just look at the long list of credible people, some very well known, who have fought for an end to the War on Drugs. There was Walter Cronkite, Abraham Lincoln, Milton Friedman, William F. Buckley, Jr. and many more. They, too, have failed to bring

---

[11] Rosamond Hutt, "9 novels that changed the world," *World Economic Forum*, March 3, 2016, https://www.weforum.org/agenda/2016/03/10-novels-that-changed-the-world/.

[12] *Gierach Tumblr*, https://jamesgierach.tumblr.com/post/ 673203316731346944.

peace to a world torn apart by bad drug policy. How can my efforts accomplish any more constructive drug policy change than these great souls?

Below I have selected a few names of the many great drug-policy reformers who have preceded this day, and their words of wisdom, collectively and effectively saying, it is time to end the War on Drugs. The fact that there are so many such great predecessor reformers magnifies my doubt that anything I might say here will matter. But more positively and constructively, in this "opening epilogue" I am trying to bundle the drug-peace words of many wise people into a great big snowball. Thinking — maybe, just maybe — this effort will be the straw that breaks the snowball loose, causing it to roll down the mountainside, picking up momentum and doubters, adding adherents to sensible drug policy, and finally crashing successfully over the worldwide drug-war battlefield, burying all its failure, futility and fear. Selecting these names enabled me to share their words and collective drug-policy wisdom. Some such quotations are set forth here, and others are sprinkled throughout this manuscript. Their words represent their valiant efforts to turn the world from drug war back to a state of drug peace.

Therefore, in a sense, this opening epilogue is really the "Collective Epilogue" of some great minds more than it is mine. Read and consider the power and wisdom of their thoughts, their ideas and their comments, all of which reveal the fault and futility of the drug war, its counterproductive impact, and the myriad collateral harms that accompany it.

"Some middle ground must be found that recognizes current realities and at the same time reduces the high risk of personal harm frequently created by existing tough [drug] law-enforcement practices."

– Professor and Author Arnold Trebach

"Less self-destruction by drug users just is not within the ability of law enforcement to bring about, unless we're willing to become a drug-free society at the cost of not being a free country."

– Commodities Trader Richard J. Dennis

"Attempts to stamp out illicit drug use tend to increase both drug use and drug damage."

– Author Edward M. Brecher

"Just about every American was shocked when Robert McNamara, one of the master architects of the Vietnam War, acknowledged that not only did he believe the war was 'wrong, terribly wrong,' but that he thought so at the very time he was helping to wage it. That's a mistake we must not make in this tenth year of America's all-out war on drugs."

– Broadcaster Walter Cronkite

"If you were to pass a law requiring people to go to church on Sunday, it wouldn't work....My position on drugs is that our drug laws aren't working, and that more net damage is being done by their continuation than would be done by withdrawing them from the books."

– Conservative William F. Buckley

"The war on drugs has had many effects, some good, more, in my opinion bad. I propose here to concentrate on a single effect, the cost of human lives.... In the mid-1960s, the homicide rate started to rise, and then soared after the war on drugs was launched by President Nixon and continued by his successors.... Many other things were going on during the decades from the 50s to the 80s. However, there seems little doubt that the war on drugs is the single most important factor that produced such drastic increases."

– Economist Milton Friedman

"Henry Smith Williams died still trying to end the drug war, his uncharacteristic book ['Drug Addicts Are Human Beings:...'] and his [Henry's] efforts at speaking out in favor of his brother's [Edward's drug policy reform] beliefs almost entirely suppressed and forgotten."

– Physician, Author, Attorney Henry Smith Williams

"Some twenty thousand doctors were charged with violating the Harrison [Narcotics] Act alongside Edward Williams, and 95 percent were convicted."

– Author Johann Hari

"Any positive change."

> – Harm Reductionist Dan Bigg

"Our future drug policy will have to be much... more respectful of human rights.... The threshold step will be redefining drugs as primarily a health and social issue rather than only a law enforcement battle."

> – Physician and Aussie Drug Policy Reformer Alex Wodak

"The US led the world into the war on drugs, and now America must help lead us out of it. The war on drugs does not and cannot reduce harm. It fuels negative and perhaps unintended consequences, and it is outdated in the face of new challenges and threats."

> – Political Leader and Chairwoman of Global Commission
> on Drug Policy Helen Clark

"It's a joke.... We're losing badly the war on drugs...You have to legalize drugs to win that war. You have to take the profit away from these drug czars."

> – Businessman Donald Trump

*"Removing the prohibitions from consensual activities will probably take place due to popular opinion within **both** political parties. When Prohibition was enacted in 1920, both parties strongly favored it. By 1924, the Republicans still strongly favored it, and the Democrats were vacillating. By 1928, the Democrats opposed it, but the Republicans still favored it. By the election of 1932, both parties opposed Prohibition. That's the politics of change."[13]*

> – Author Peter McWilliams

"You can get over an addiction, but you can never get over a conviction."

> – New Jersey State Trooper and Undercover Narc Jack A. Cole

---

[13] Peter McWilliams, *Ain't Nobody's Business If You Do*, (Los Angeles: Prelude Press, 1993), p. 765.

"Prohibition will work great injury to the cause of temperance. It is a species of intemperance within itself, for it goes beyond the bounds of reason in that it attempts to control a man's appetite by legislation, and makes a crime out of things that are not crimes. A Prohibition law strikes a blow at the very principles upon which our government was founded."

– Woodsman Abraham Lincoln

"I welcome Mr. Bush and Mr. Dukakis as lieutenants – but I am the general in this war to fight drugs."

– Presidential Candidate Reverend Jesse Jackson (1988)

"This [War on Drugs] *is a crime against humanity. [It's] a war on Black and Brown and must be challenged by the highest levels of our government in the war for justice."*

– Civil Rights Leader Reverend Jesse Jackson (2011)

*"Take a look at the children born addicted to drugs, talk about those who find themselves in the emergency wards, if you will doctor, with the illnesses attributed to this.... The **time is now not to find a "Silver Bullet" or one answer**, but to find a coordinated policy, where we can educate and attempt to prevent."*[14]

– Drug Warrior and Politician Charles Rangel

Despite the earnest efforts and words of wisdom spoken by these good and talented people, the War on Drugs continues to rage in 2023. It is not an uplifting thought. So, what can I write here that might change that? I would like to ask U.S. Rep. Charles Rangel, today — nearly thirty-three years after he spoke during the just noted *Firing Line* debate: "Is it time, now, to reach for the Silver Bullet, to reach for the one solution that is always 'off the table,' to reach for drug peace to replace drug war?"

---

[14] *Firing Line,* "A Firing Line Debate: Resolved: That Drug Prohibition Has Failed," March 15, 1991, The Board of Trustees of Leland Stanford Junior University, https://youtu.be/Mouh8gE2CMg.

Searching for the Key to End the War on Drugs

Searching for over thirty years for a means to change the drug-war world, I have tried many different keys on "the Drug War Gordian Lock"[15] and found many that did not work well. I tried politics and poetry, billboard messaging and bullhorn speaking, leafleting, community policing, resolution writing, politician and editorial board pleading, journalist prodding, parade float-building, church-preaching, demonstrating and demonizing. You can read about some of those efforts in these pages. I created a drug policy reform nonprofit organization, intentionally and offensively naming it, "The Drug Corner."[16] And I volunteered my services for a dozen years on behalf of an international, educational, nonprofit organization founded in 2002, called "Law Enforcement Against Prohibition" (LEAP), now known as "Law Enforcement Action Partnership." LEAP is an organization composed of currently serving and former soldiers in the war on drugs — police, prosecutors, judges, federal agents, undercover narcotics officers and other criminal justice professionals. After decades of service in the front lines of the War on Drugs, we LEAP law-enforcement "soldiers," individually and collectively as an organization, now oppose it. Before starting my search for the key to End the War on Drugs, I already had accumulated much life experience to draw upon.

I prosecuted drug cases and homicide cases in Cook County, Illinois; I defended drug offenders and one person accused of a double murder. I represented local liquor control commissioners (mayors) and defended liquor licensees in towns where I did not represent the local liquor commissioner, including "Gazanders," purportedly the largest purveyor of alcohol in Illinois at one time. I litigated domestic consequences of parental drug use relating to child custody and visitation issues. I served municipalities and various units of local government and library districts as attorney, churches as councilman, a not-for-profit women's domestic violence shelter as advocate, and a local Crusade of Mercy chapter in Oak Lawn as its president.

I experienced loss-of-life outcomes for drug-using clients, friends, and relatives. I helped write Illinois' 1970 Constitution as an elected delegate, and I worked for Chief Judge John Boyle in the Office of Research and Development, Circuit Court of Cook County, Illinois, then the largest unified court system in America. I washed dishes for

---

[15] Akin to the "Gordian Knot," *Wikipedia*, https://en.wikipedia.org/wiki/Gordian_Knot, accessed March 16, 2023.

[16] *The Drug Corner*, Statement of Purpose, https://jamesgierach.tumblr.com/post/667933174743154688 .

a restaurateur, worked as a bank teller, spent two summers as a dockman, several summers as a lifeguard and diving instructor, and one summer as assistant to Roy Berkenfield, the residential real estate loan "department" of Beverly Bank, located on Chicago's South Side.

Who Could Think Such "Drug Legalization" Thoughts?

Quickly synopsizing some of my views about drugs, I dislike what drugs can do to people, but I like what drugs can do for people. In my view, drugs are neither good nor bad; drugs are inanimate, physical substances, lacking any moral dimension. Drugs are amoral — neither "evil" nor "God-sent." At various times over thirty-plus years, I have advocated for drug decriminalization, drug medicalization, and drug legalization of some drugs, all drugs, and "legalized free drugs for addicts only." I've supported every drug policy reform that strikes a blow against drug prohibition and intolerance, aligned myself with every harm-reduction initiative great and small, and endorsed every decent human-rights resolution coming to my attention.

To enable the reader to better understand and judge the merit of my words and opinions, it may be helpful to disclose and share some of my life experiences and educational influences that have impacted my views concerning violence, drugs, punishment, and a host of related subjects.

Personally, I'm a husband, father, grandfather, son, uncle, nephew, Godparent and Godchild, neighbor, coworker, co-director, friend, adversary and a colleague. I was raised Lutheran. As a youth inexperienced in the world of finance and purchasing my first traveler's checks, when the bank teller asked "What denomination?" I answered "Lutheran," much to the amusement of bank employees within earshot. I was raised by two great parents, beside four sisters and no brothers, by the YMCA, and good people and teachers like those found everywhere. I am a seventy-eight-year-old, white, Madison Wisconsin-born, suburban Chicagoan raised after a short stint on "Avenue D" located on Chicago's East Side, a few blocks from Indiana and its steel mills. I believe in moderation in all things but enjoy living life, sometimes to excess, in sharp contradiction to that belief. I'm a reformed tobacco smoker.

I attended Oak Lawn Community High School located in southwest Cook County, Illinois, Michigan State University where I earned a Bachelor of Arts degree in 1966, and DePaul College of Law, where I earned a Juris Doctorate degree in 1969.

My Addiction History

Cigarettes are my only personal experience with addiction, though I have had relatives who were alcohol afflicted. Because this manuscript is about drugs, addiction, human weakness, greed, intolerance and such, my personal experience with addiction is relevant. Please bear with me as I share the story of my addiction. Tobacco consumption, like any mind-altering drug consumption, is not to be taken lightly. "The confirmed smoker acts under a compulsion which is quite comparable to that of heroin."[17] My addiction report will poke fun at my own weakness, expose my jovial survivor's take on the subject, and tell of my near-death experience.

It was long ago. I was a college student, but I can still hear the wonderful sound of a dozen Zippo lighters flicked open at the end of a lecture hall class at Michigan State University, and the sound of an abrasive wheel turning against a flint. I can still hear the inviting scratch of a sulfur-tipped match tip against a sandy surface, smell the burning sulfur, and see the flickering flame brought to the end of a neatly rolled cigarette. Ah, I loved it. Oh, to be young and tobacco-invincible again! I love my tobacco memories... blowing smoke rings, exhaling smoke out one facial orifice and simultaneously inhaling it through another, lighting a match in a matchbook using only one hand, and so on. It was mesmerizing like watching cream swirl and diffuse in a hot cup of coffee with the slightest touch of the tip of a spoon, like the unpredictable transformation of light seen through a kaleidoscope with the smallest adjustment. I still love tobacco.

I smoked two packs a day for about twenty years starting at the age of eighteen. As a youngster, I committed to memory every behavior, nuance, sequence, sight and smell associated with my father's filtered-cigarette smoking and "Mixture 79" pipe-smoking practices. I also studied the craftiness of my grandfather's Bull Durham tobacco cigarette rolling, licking, lighting, smoking, inhaling, exhaling, coughing and extinguishing practices. I bought my first cigarettes as a fourteen-year-old camper in Eagle River, Wisconsin.

I was too young to purchase tobacco, and I had no means to leave Camp Eagle Crest or get into town, St. Germain, Wisconsin, to buy cigarettes. But my camp counselor, a Chicago public school teacher named Tom Starnakey (phonetic) bought them for me. One pack of Chesterfields, as I recall. Terrible tasting, each one, really. No

---

[17] Edward M. Brecher, *Licit and Illicit Drugs: Consumers Union Report* (Boston: Little, Brown and Co., 1972), p. 533.

reflection on the brand. I used my upside-down tennis lid cover for an ashtray and was careful blowing smoke through the cabin window screen into the darkness of night, because of the nearby outside, overhead light, and I didn't want to get caught "being bad." Just experimenting really, rather like a Plymouth Pilgrim first meeting a smoking Indian.

Smoking-Assisted Homicide

Tom Starnakey was an avid reader, a Camp Eagle Crest waterfront director and instructor who taught me great lifesaving maneuvers, enabling me to earn my YMCA Senior Life Saving patch. He was a good young man, and a good camp counselor who delighted in throwing me or another misbehaving camper over his shoulder and affectionately giving us "the Starnakey Bounce." Lucky for Tom there were no tobacco-induced homicide statutes back then like there are drug-induced homicide statutes today.[18] If there had been, and if I had died of cigarette-induced tobacco smoke, say from cancer, I would not want Tom prosecuted. Tom didn't decide I'd try smoking. I decided.

Years later as a prosecutor, I relished the thought of one day prosecuting someone who had been forced by another person to involuntarily ingest a drug against their will. Not surprisingly that case never came along. Overwhelmingly, drug use is a voluntary behavior.

I say, prosecutors should leave the Indian-Pilgrim, Starnakey-Gierach transactions alone. Consensual behavior has its assumed risks and, generally, bad outcomes should not be considered a crime vis-à-vis substance providers and substance consenters.

After my youthful five-year smoking hiatus, I put 35 cents into a Theta Chi fraternity vending machine as a Michigan State University freshman, pulled the lever, and out dropped my first pack of Salem cigarettes, my second pack of smokes ever. Not coincidentally, my father smoked that mentholated brand.

---

[18] "An Overdose Death Is Not Murder: Why Drug-Induced Homicide Laws Are Counterproductive and Inhumane," *Drug Policy Foundation, 2017,* https://drugpolicy.org/sites/default/files/dpa_drug_induced_homicide_report_0.pdf, accessed August 26, 2021.

The Power of Addiction

I smoked with every human activity except during coital relations and showers, and closely before and after those activities, too. After a torturous Chicago O'Hare International-to-Heathrow Airport flight in the 1980s, I swore off intercontinental air travel forever. My thanks to compassionate flight attendants who seeing my anguished condition allowed me to smoke one blessed cigarette in the rear of the plane contrary to flying rules. I smoked everywhere — in court, in airports, beside "No Smoking" signs, at work, at home and play. Shamefully, tobacco smoking had turned me, a Christian-raised and God-fearing man into a lawbreaker, a criminal of sorts.

I was hooked. Every activity and routine of life was modified and shaped to accommodate smoking tobacco. The bad habit of smoking behavior would at times bring to mind the powerful, anti-smoking essay (yellowed teeth, smelly breath...) I had written about it in high school. Still, I was a health-conscious tobacco smoker, a shallow inhaler like Bill Clinton but not so much as he says he was. I had an expensive air purifier installed directly overhead in my individual law office, another one in our law library, and a third one in our law office conference room.

There were times when I would not smoke for maybe half a day. Then when I did light up, and first inhaled, wham! Right to the brain. I was walloped. In my limited experience, the fastest way to get a drug to the brain is through the lungs; "the lung bone's connected to the brain bone... " With the second and succeeding inhalations, everything was fine again, normal. Strangely, what is definitely not good for someone's health can be medicinal for an addict and enable him or her to feel — not high, not low, not buzzed — just "normal." The human body really is an amazingly durable machine. Think of how many generations, eons of mutations and natural selections it took to arrive at such an intelligent being as I. Lol!

My cough was terrible. One night on the way home, I'd stopped at a discount tobacco store and started coughing something awful as I was walking to the door of the store. I coughed so badly, so many times in continuous succession, I thought I might cough my lungs right out of my chest. It was a horrible thought, followed by the thought that if that did happen, I'd have no choice but to re-swallow them to get my lungs back into my chest. Then my mind said to me, "You dummy, you are coughing yourself to smithereens, and you're headed into a store to buy more of what's killing you at a discounted price, plus tax."

Then there was the really bad head cold that soon headed for my chest and lungs, typical of a smoker. It was so bad, regardless of my fealty sworn to Salem cigarettes, I just could not inhale the smoke. I was really sick. During the first few days of no smoking, I could have gone through walls, torn people to pieces. I was truly a chemically-deprived, dangerous human being. Fortunately, I had money and could buy what I needed to fix what was wrong with me. My financial health was like a buffer between me and the evil I was capable of inflicting on others deprived of my drug.

I was addicted to tobacco. I admit it! I loved cigarettes — the smell, the sight, the feel of it! I still do. I need a cigarette!

"Calm down, Jim."

> *"Treatment is not a prerequisite to controlling drug consumption, or even to abstinence. Most drug users who quit, including heroin addicts and tobacco addicts, do so without treatment."*
>
> — Steven B. Duke and Albert C. Gross

Cigarettes and Jolly Ranchers

Okay, I'm all right. I'm just trying to give the reader some perspective regarding my experience with addiction. I've heard it said that quitting smoking is more difficult than quitting heroin. Whether that's so, I can't say.

Back to my head-to-chest cold. That's just the way it goes for smokers with head colds. The cold travels from the head to the chest, horrible coughing, awful stuff coagulating, grabbing the little bronchioles, defying expulsion. My little alveoli were solidifying, turning into tiny burnt carbon cinders. The chest pain was so bad inhaling more smoke I just could not smoke. I told myself, "Jim, you're really sick. Give your lungs a break. Don't smoke for an entire day." Radical thought.

Well, I made it one day, two days, three days. I had to. Inhaling hurt. With the help of tennis, more jars of Jolly Ranchers hard candies than most stores stock, and saying "Just not today, maybe tomorrow," I was cured. I didn't smoke for three years. I felt great. Tennis three or four times a week, winning matches, chasing down put-away ground strokes, rushing the net, serve and volley tennis with never a tobacco thought.

As fate would have it, one evening I attended a political function that ended in a bar in Oak Lawn, Illinois. I was offered a cigarette by a friend at about 8 p.m. and accepted the offer. Mistake. Before I went to bed, I had smoked two packs of cigarettes.

I smoked so much I could have urinated menthol crystals and made peppermint Life savers of the evaporated remains. I was addicted to tobacco, nicotine really. It's a mind-altering substance, assuming I had a mind when it came to tobacco.

The Smoking "Lights" Gimmick

My experience gave me some understanding of addiction. I learned that "It's easy to quit smoking. I've done it a million times." I knew Dr. Knapp, a psychiatrist in the building where I practiced law who treated smokers looking to "modify their behavior." I knew about and experimented with "lights," cigarettes with filters dotted with little holes, enabling clean air to enter the cigarette filter and mix with the smoke and toxic gases. The filter diluted the burning tobacco smoke. But I soon realized that smoking lights necessitated that I smoke more cigarettes to overcome the dilution and bring my nicotine level into normal range, no less important than keeping blood sugar or creatinine levels within normal range. The cigarette lights idea was as brilliant a marketing and sales idea as the "New Coke" was not.[19]

As a smoking college student, I also knew what it was like studying late into the night, drinking a chocolate-coffee stimulant mix to stay awake until my fingers started to twitch all by themselves, lighting a cigarette and reaching for the ashtray to set it down and finding another nearly new cigarette already burning there — an experience raising the practical and philosophical question: which one shall I put out? I also experienced falling asleep with a cigarette burning between my two fingers and being awakened by burnt tender skin. Dangerous. And ouch! I also knew how awful it was to mistakenly light the wrong end of the cigarette, the shrinking butt fibers melting like heated plastic and oh, the putrid (poisonous?) smell. Yucky! Thank goodness, I never played with needles!

Smoking: Twenty Years On, Three Years Off, and Ten Years On

Well, soon my medical chart history read: twenty years smoking, three years not, and ten years smoking, again.

The next turn in the road of my smoking career came unexpectedly. It was Saturday morning, 1998 and I was driving to my law office approaching the intersection of Harlem Avenue and 127th Street, located in Palos Heights, Illinois. I was caught by a traffic light. As I sat and waited for the traffic light to change, I replayed in my head

---

19 *Wikipedia*, s.v. "New Coke," https://en.m.wikipedia.org/wiki/New_Coke, accessed March 16, 2023.

several, occasional symptoms I had recently experienced: a short blip, center-of-my-head pain with the inhalation of a puff of cigarette smoke, suspecting it might be caused by an immediate cardiovascular contracting response to the nicotine; and the mild discomfort of the weight of my wife's head on my chest the night before. I thought to myself, no pain in my chest, none down my arm. My law office was straight ahead from that traffic control light and Palos Hospital was to the left one mile away.

"Which way, Jim?" I turned left, pulled the car to the front door of the emergency room, engine still running, walked in and announced, "I think I'm about to have a heart attack."

"Please have a seat. We'll be right with you."

"You don't understand. I think I'm about to have a heart attack."

That clicked. Next thing I knew, things were hopping. They had me on a stretcher, vitals, EKG leads attached. It was like a scene from *Mash*, the television show. An hour or so later, all tests came back normal. A lone nurse came to my bedside and quietly said, "You know. They can't make you stay here."

A little later the ER doctor came in again. I said, "You know, I could go. Everything's normal."

"Sure, you can leave. We have people leave and collapse outside the door all the time."

"Listen, Doc, I didn't say I was leaving. I was just saying, I could leave if I wanted to."

"I think you should talk to a cardiologist."

I did. I related the quizzical story of my brief head pain, explained it had happened several times before, and shared my health history with her. No previous heart issues, healthy, active...

"No chest pain? Pressure on the chest? Tightness?"

"No."

"No pain down the arm?"

"No."

"I don't like the fleeting head pain. It's bizarre, atypical. I think you should stay overnight."

"Okay."

In the middle of the night another nurse checked on me and said, "We'll, you're throwing PVCs. (No, not polyvinyl chloride plastic piping, but rather premature ventricular contractions.) I don't know what you have but you're not going anywhere."

Most People Quit Smoking After a Serious Medical Event

Most people quit smoking after a serious health event. Or maybe not.[20]

During my open-heart bypass surgery at Advocate Christ Medical Center (ACMC) located in Oak Lawn, Illinois, Patroklos S. Pappas, M.D. held my heart between his two hands and whispered, "Don't smoke." I heard him. But it was not my heart he was talking to; it was my venous system.

After surgery and sidestepping a "98-percent occluded LAD," short for left-anterior-descending artery, nicknamed "the widow-maker," and one other cardio-artery in like condition, I promptly headed to a gas station and bought one pack of Winston cigarettes. Winston regulars had become my brand of choice over the years to avoid a menthol-crystal buildup in the lungs, and to decrease the number of cigarettes needed to counteract nicotine dilution caused by those little filter holes in cigarette lights. Why the trip to the gas station?

My thinking: If I decided I would smoke again, post-surgery (like my father did after his four blockages and bypass surgeries over the years), I did not want to have to run out to buy them. I wanted peace of mind, knowing I could have a cigarette whenever I wanted it. I put the single pack of Winstons in the top drawer of my dresser amongst my socks.

Addiction is a tricky business. Having learned myself just how difficult it was to quit smoking, I thought, *"I won't quit. I just won't smoke."*

Somehow it didn't sound so ominous, so permanent. "Quitting" sounded too much like making a New Year's Resolution and keeping it. That's the greatest risk of making resolutions: you might keep it. On the other hand, if you never make a resolution, you can't break it and disappoint yourself. And there is a subtle difference here between "quitting" and "just not smoking." Any psychiatrist worth their salt can pinpoint it.

---

[20] Edwin D. Boudreaux, Ph.D., Simon Moon, Ph.D., [...], and Douglas M. Ziedonis, M.D, M.P.H, "Intentions to Quit Smoking: Causal Attribution, Perceived Illness Severity, and Event-Related Fear During an Acute Health Event," *Ann Beh Med*, December 2010, https://www.ncbi.nlm.nih.gov/pmc/articles/PMC3532886/.

I just read a Narcotics Anonymous post about addiction that is so good, that says so much in so few words, I have to share it. "I got high because I wanted to. Then it became a habit. Then it became a necessity. I got clean out of necessity. Then it became a habit. Now I live clean because I want to."

"The Prohibition Gateway" to Drugs

Rounding out my addiction experience and completing my disclosure statement, I drink alcohol, but I have never used an illicit drug. No, not even marijuana. I reached legal age more or less "drug-free" (alcohol, cigarettes and chocolate excepted) and be-fore "the Prohibition Gateway" had a chance to get me. No D.A.R.E. classes — just health class, Sunday School, the YMCA, good parents, and my own good judgment.

So, that's my addiction story. Different in some respects from stories of other "addicts," but in some respects probably very similar.

Why Am I Doing This?

"Why are you doing this?" That was the first question that came out of the mouth of *Chicago Tribune* editorial board member, **R. Bruce Dolt**, in 1994 during my candidate interview, also attended by **Don Wycliffe**, as I campaigned for governor of Illinois. I was running for public office to reform drug policy to prevent crime and ameliorate a dozen drug-war driven and drug-war aggravated crises. My campaign literature prom-ised "Illinois' First Drug Policy Reform Governor," though, as Bruce's question im-plied, with no hope of succeeding. Who in their right mind would run for elective public office in America in the early 1990s, saying, more or less, let's legalize drugs?

Why this manuscript? Why this project? Same answer.

I am searching for a means to bring about an end to the World War on Drugs.

In that search, I feel the same sense of urgency that my co-panelist Sergio Ferragut felt as we sat on the speakers' stage in Mexico City in 2012 to discuss drugs, crime and drug policy before an auditorium filled with people anxious to stop prolific violence and lawlessness in Mexico. The event was organized and funded by **Mexico Unido Contra Delincuencia** (MUCD), a nonprofit organization. Sergio, an expert in the field of money-laundering prevention, wrote *A Silent Nightmare: The Bottom Line and Challenge of Illicit Drugs*. The MUCD organization and anxious attendees from across Mexico were desperately searching for a solution to an epidemic of unrelenting hom-icides and missing persons in Mexico. At that point in time, a 100,000 people had been killed. Six years later, the Mexican violence crisis ballooned to 250,000 people dead and 37,400 people missing.[21] Since December 2006, when the government launched a controversial military anti-drug operation, Mexico has recorded more than 340,000 murders, according to official figures.[22] So, I'm back to the book idea. But most books — unlike *Uncle Tom's Cabin, the Holy Bible* and so forth — are not game-changers.

Might a "Silver Bullet Solution" to Myriad Crises Catch the Public's Interest?

In 1993, authors Steven B. Duke and Albert G. Gross released their book, called *America's Longest War: Rethinking Our Tragic Crusade Against Drugs* (New York: G. P. Putnam, 1993). I thought the book was so thoughtful, powerful and persuasive that no more drug policy books would be needed. I also recalled that Steven Duke had been one of President Bill Clinton's law professors and, maybe, there was a relationship there that might advance the interests of drug peace over war.

However, sandwiched sometime between two of President Clinton's more famous pronouncements — "It's the economy, stupid" and "Let's hire a hundred thousand more police officers" — President Clinton said, "If drugs were legal, I don't think [my brother] would be alive today." Personally unable to take the words of Steven Duke and Albert Gross to heart, the Clinton Administration continued the futile, counterproductive war on drugs.[23]

Because the politically popular war on drugs continued to make trouble for America, three years after the publication of *America's Longest War,* accomplished and respected journalist Dan Baum authored *Smoke and Mirrors: The War on Drugs and The Politics of Failure.* Shortly after release of his book, I joined a panel of speakers that included **Peter B. Bensinger, Sr.**, the first administrator of the Drug Enforcement Agency, former Chicago Police Superintendent **LeRoy Martin**, and drug treatment advocate **Melody M. Heaps** of Treatment Alternatives to Street Crime (T.A.S.C.), now known as Treatment Alternatives to Safe Communities.

---

[21] José de Córdoba and Juan Montes, "'It's a Crisis of Civilization in Mexico.' 250,000 Dead. 37,400 Missing.," *The Wall Street Journal,* November 12, 2018. https://www.wsj.com/articles/its-a-crisis-of-civilization-in-mexico-250-000-dead-37-400-missing-1542213374.

[22] "Four handcuffed bodies found in burned-out wreckage helicopter in Mexico with hand-written 'criminal messages,'" *CBS NEWS,* July 4, 2022, https://apple.news/ACZxE3vysQ7SfNQOMoZDTZw.

[23] Francis Wilkinson, "A Separate Peace: the Clinton administration has abandoned the rhetoric of the war on drugs, but it hasn't stopped fighting the war," *Rolling Stone,* May 5, 1994, https://www.rollingstone.com/politics/politics-news/a-separate-peace-59273/.

We panelists were enjoying amicable conversation in an anteroom preliminary to our panel discussion regarding drugs, crime, punishment and treatment when Peter asked me what book I was holding. I told him it was a new book about drugs and drug policy. He asked if he could see it. I passed the book to him. He quickly examined it, front, back, Table of Contents and summarily pronounced his verdict, "5,000 copies at most," quickly dismissing the book, and sending it back around to me. I shared my experience with Dan Baum who replied, "Depressing." It was and it is. I don't know how many copies Dan Baum sold, but I do know the war on drugs continues to rage. My conclusion: It's time for another Earth-shaking book. Here it is!

The general public may not be particularly interested in a book about drugs, but the masses may very well be interested in a Silver Bullet Solution that could quickly and comprehensively ameliorate myriad, drug-war-driven prohibition crises. Drug legalization is that Silver Bullet Solution to many such crises.

For example, (1) minority communities need restoration of peace to their neighborhoods destroyed by drug- and turf-wars, retaliatory shootings and addict crime. (2) Policing needs mission recovery, police again working to prevent and solve violent crime rather than deploying legions to track consensual, adult drug behavior, forgoing the pattern and practice of policing for drug profits, grants and spoils. (3) Accidental drug overdose needs prevention by licensing drug dealers, requiring fixed hours and places of business, a limited number of outlets, and product labels that enable drug consumers to know what they are putting into their bodies. (4) Gangs need defunding largely by ending drug prohibition, thereby upsetting the gangbanger need to be armed with guns for business, protection and idle recreation. (5) Immigrants need resurrection of their home countries in Central and South America to become safe and productive places to live without threat of drug-prohibition violence, corruption and rule, necessarily driving drug-war refugees to the U.S. southern border with Mexico and thereby attempting to circumvent U.S. immigration rules. (6) Racism in America needs dismantling by destruction of its last best refuge — drug prohibition, drug criminalization, mass incarceration, stigmatization and disqualification. (7) Criminal justice needs systemic contraction and better statistical racial parity reflecting its racist recovery. (8) Healthcare, like criminal justice, needs to be made more affordable by reducing violent crime and thereby ending bullet-hole healthcare and mass incarceration, (9) all while restoring a little empathy for one another and resurrecting the virtue of tolerance.

From this suggested vantage point — the alleviation of crises — this manuscript is not a book about drugs, though the subject of drugs runs through its veins. More aptly, this book is about sunrise on a Silver Bullet Solution seen, appreciated and understood by the public at large as a new public policy regarding drugs with the power to lift civilization out of the ditch and place it back onto civilized rails.

What is a "Silver Bullet" anyway? A Silver Bullet is "something that provides an immediate and extremely effective solution to a given problem or difficulty, especially one that is normally very complex or hard to resolve. The phrase is almost always used in a statement that such a solution does not exist."[24]

Closing this "Opening Epilogue," I wonder aloud, "Why does there have to be an Epilogue, anyway?" When I get to the end of a book and arrive at an "Epilogue," I think, "All those words and pages and there is still an epilogue I have to read to finish this book. Couldn't the author just have said it before the Epilogue? Why wait?"

Hopefully the reader can see here in my "Opening Epilogue" the message of this book: we must end the war on ourselves and each other, the World War on Drugs. What follows explains why we should do that pronto.

> *"The US led the world into the war on drugs, and now America must help lead us out of it. The war on drugs does not and cannot reduce harm. It fuels negative and perhaps unintended consequences...."*
>
> — Former New Zealand PM Helen Clark

---

[24] *The Free Dictionary by Farley* s.v. *"Silver Bullet,"* https://idioms.thefreedictionary.com/silver+bullet, accessed March 16, 2023.

Chapter 2 - The Big Question:
Is It Time to End the War on Drugs?

Is it time to end the "World War on Drugs?"

The short answer is **Yes!**

The long answer is also **Yes!** But the long answer that follows is a long story.

U.S. Presidents, U.S. Senate Advice and Consent, and UN Drug Treaties

President John F. Kennedy appointed Harry Anslinger, Commissioner of the Federal Bureau of Narcotics to lead the United States' participation in the plenipotentiary 1961 Conference that would produce the 1961 Single Convention on Narcotic Drugs, the foundation of global drug-control policy.[25] That was America's first and perhaps biggest drug policy mistake. Harry Anslinger was an arch-drug prohibitionist, who as a youngster had a *Silence of the Lambs*-like Clarice experience, Clarice played by Jodie Foster,[26] from which he seemingly never recovered. As Harry himself said, "I never forgot those screams."

What screams? As a twelve-year-old boy visiting a neighbor's farmhouse, Harry heard the shrieking, howling and haunting screams of a woman. The woman's husband instructed Harry to take a horse and cart "as fast as [you can] go" into town to retrieve a package from the pharmacy. Soon Harry learned the package contained drugs desperately needed to quell her chemical craving.[27]

The UN Conference for the Adoption of a Single Convention on Narcotic Drugs met at UN Headquarters from January 24 to March 25 1961, and adopted "The Single Convention on Narcotic Drugs."[28] The UN Commission on Narcotic Drugs (CND) reported the Conference adoption of the Convention, noted the Convention was open for signature as of March 30, 1961, and invited expeditious review, signature

---

[25] *Drug Enforcement Agency Museum*, https://museum.dea.gov/exhibits/online-exhibits/anslinger/late-years, accessed March 16, 2023.

[26] *Wikipedia, s.v.* "The Silence of the Lambs," https://en.wikipedia.org/wiki/The_Silence_of_the_Lambs_(film), accessed March 16, 2023.

[27] Johann Hari, *Chasing the Scream* (New York: London, Bloomsbury, 2015), p. 8.

[28] "United Nations Conference for the Adoption of a Single Convention on Narcotic Drugs, 24 January - 25 March 1961, New York," *United Nations, Conferences, Drugs*, https://www.un.org/en/conferences/drug/newyork1961.

and ratification of, or accession to, the 1961 Convention by all United Nations member and nonmember States.[29] Article 41 of the 1961 Single Convention provided that it would become effective upon the ratification and accession of forty countries.

The United Nations' Backdoor World War on Drugs

The UN Single Convention on Narcotic Drugs did not declare a "World War on Drugs" per se.

Rather than declaring a war on drugs in terms of what drug use is *unlawful*, the 1961 Single Convention defined *the limits of lawful drug use* and from that definition unlawful drug use can be deduced. In doing so, the framers of the 1961 Single Convention were not condemning the act of drug use, sale, production and associated behaviors so much as they were condemning that behavior if based upon drug use for a "*bad purpose*," an "*evil*" purpose. Clauses two and three of the Preamble to the 1961 Single Convention equate addictive drug use with evil: "Recognizing that addiction to narcotic drugs constitutes a serious evil for the individual and is fraught with social and economic danger to mankind," (Clause three) and "Conscious of their duty to prevent and combat this evil,..." (Clause four).

In other words, drug prohibition was not expressed in clear and direct terms declaring "Recreational drug use and sale... is prohibited." Instead, plenary recreational drug prohibition was accomplished through the backdoor, the 1961 Single Convention declaring a limitation on the *purpose* for which drugs could legitimately be consumed. If the purpose was legitimate, then the use and sale was legitimate. And conversely, if the purpose was illegitimate, then the use and sale was illegitimate. To unequivocally identify a bad purpose drug use, some drugs were placed into Schedule IV of the 1961 Single Convention, the most restrictive category, if the World Health organization found that "The drug, which is already in Schedule I, is particularly liable to abuse and to produce ill effects, and such liability is *not offset by substantial therapeutic advantages.*"[30]

[29]https://documents-dds-ny.un.org/doc/RESOLUTION/GEN/NR0/323/23/IMG/NR032323.pdf?Open Element, accessed August 23, 2021.

[30] *Wikipedia*, s.v. "Single Convention on Narcotic Drugs," https://en.wikipedia.org/wiki/Single_Convention_on_Narcotic_Drugs, emphasis added, accessed March 16, 2023.

A little convoluted perhaps but the purpose-of-use conceptualization was an effective means to declare a "World War on Recreational Drug Use" without saying so expressly.

Article 4 of the 1961 Single Convention expressed and mandated recreational drug prohibition in these terms: "The parties shall take legislative and administrative measures as may be necessary: (c)... To limit to exclusively to *medical* and *scientific* purposes the production, manufacture, export, import, distribution of, trade in, use and possession of drugs." (Emphasis added.) And in Article 36, this United Nations foundational drug-war treaty, mandated punishment for transgression. Article 36 required that nations signing, ratifying or acquiescing to the terms of the 1961 Single Convention must adopt measures that will ensure deviation from the medical or scientific purpose limitation is a "punishable offense" with "serious offenses" subjecting offenders to "adequate punishment particularly by imprisonment or other penalties of deprivation of liberty." In addition to the criminalization of *recreational drug use and sale* (along with sixteen other action verbs) provided in subparagraph 36(a), subparagraph 36(b) provided as follows: "Notwithstanding the preceding subparagraph, when abusers of drugs have committed such offences, the Parties may provide, either as an alternative to conviction or punishment or in addition to conviction or punishment, that such abusers shall undergo measures of treatment, education, after-care, rehabilitation and social reintegration in conformity with paragraph one of article 38?[31]

On February 6, 1967, six years after the plenipotentiary 1961 Conference that produced the 1961 Single Convention on Narcotic Drugs, President Lyndon B. Johnson delivered a Special Message to the Congress on Crime in America regarding narcotics and the 1961 Single Convention. He said: "If we are to succeed in controlling narcotics and dangerous drugs, we must work in concert with other nations. Most illicit narcotics — particularly heroin — come from and through other nations to our shores. Drugs, like epidemic diseases, must be controlled effectively everywhere. I shall shortly submit to the Senate, for its advice and consent, the '1961 Single Convention on Narcotic Drugs.' Fifty-four nations have acceded to that Convention, and we believe that other nations may follow. With the coming establishment of the Interna-

---

[31] https://www.unodc.org/pdf/convention_1961_en.pdf, Article 36, accessed March 16, 2023.

tional Narcotics Control Board as the only supervisory international agency, our accession to the Convention will allow us to have a proper voice in securing fulfillment by other countries of their treaty obligations."[32]

A month later on March 8, 1967, the United States Senate received the 1961 Single Convention from President Lyndon B. Johnson, and the U.S. Senate approved a resolution of advice and consent regarding its ratification on May 8, 1967, by an 84-0 vote.[33] Technically, U.S. Senate approval of the resolution does not operate as ratification itself; the exchange of documents between nations is the act that ratifies a treaty which then becomes part of international law.[34]

On May 25, 1967, the United States signed and ratified the 1961 Single Convention,[35] and the Convention 1972 Protocol was signed on November 1, 1972.[36]

Joining the 1961 Single Convention on Narcotic Drugs was America's second, huge, drug policy mistake, a long-term mistake that continues to feed many national and international crises on a daily basis. For support of this contention, see "Exhibit A," the topics discussed in the following Chapters 4, 5 and 6: More drugs, more crime and more corruption.

---

[32] John Woolley and Gerhard Peters, "The American Presidency Project," Lyndon B. Johnson, "Special Message to the Congress on Crime in America," February 6, 1967,

https://www.presidency.ucsb.edu/documents/special-message-the-congress-crime-america) (Online by Gerhard Peters and John T. Woolley, *The American Presidency Project*, https://www.presidency.ucsb.edu/node/237922, emphasis added.

[33] "*Congress.gov*, "Single Convention on Narcotic Drugs, 1961," https://www.congress.gov/treaty-document/90th-congress/7, accessed March 16, 2023.

[34] "The Senate does not ratify treaties. Following consideration by the Committee on Foreign Relations, the Senate either approves or rejects a resolution of ratification. If the resolution passes, then ratification takes place when the instruments of ratification are formally exchanged between the United States and the foreign power(s)," "About Treaties," *United States Senate*, https://www.senate.gov/about/powers-procedures/treaties.htm?back=https%3A%2F%2Fwww.google.com%2Fsearch%3Fclient%3Dsafari%26as_qdr%3Dall%26as_occt%3Dany%26safe%3Dactive%26as_q%3Dwhich+comes+first+the+presidents+approval+of+a+treaty+or+congress+is%26channel%3Daplab%26source%3Da-app1%26hl%3Den, accessed August 28, 2021).

[35] "15. Single Convention on Narcotic Drugs, 1961 New York, 30 March 1961, https://treaties.un.org/pages/ViewDetails.aspx?src=TREATY&mtdsg_no=VI-15&chapter=6.

[36] "18. Single Convention on Narcotic Drugs, 1961, as amended by the Protocol amending the Single Convention on Narcotic Drugs, 1961 New York, 8 August 1975," https://treaties.un.org/Pages/ViewDetails.aspx?src=TREATY&mtdsg_no=VI-18&chapter=6&clang=_en, accessed August 23, 2022.

Nixon Signs the Controlled Substances Act of 1970

Three years later in 1970, and one year before he would declare America's bipartisan War on Drugs — President Richard Nixon jump-started that war by signing an Act of Congress, the Controlled Substances Act of 1970.[37] By signing that Act,[38] a law that categorized controlled drugs into schedules,[39] Nixon had the United States of America fulfilling its voluntarily-assumed, international obligation to "Go to war over drugs." That was America's third strike in the important, deadly game of drug policy. That drug policy decision ruined policing, protected racism in criminal justice, damaged public health and made drug policy the common denominator to a dozen American and global crises collateral to drugs. For support of this contention, see "Exhibit B" topics discussed in Chapters 8 and 9: more HIV, AIDS, drug overdose, trade imbalance, policing for profit, informant policing, militarization of police departments, drug-war migration, immigration fencing, and so on.

On October 27, 1970, President Richard Nixon made some remarks at the time of signing the Controlled Substances Act: "I will in a very few moments be signing this piece of legislation which deals with the problem that the Attorney General has described. Fifteen months ago, I sent an urgent request to the Congress for legislation in this field. I requested it because our survey of the problem of drugs indicated that it was a major cause of street crime in the United States. Those who have a drug habit find it necessary to steal, to commit crimes, in order to feed their habit. We found also, and all Americans are aware of this, that drugs are alarmingly on the increase in use among our young people. They are destroying the lives of hundreds of thousands of young people all over America, not just of college age or young people in their twenties, but the great tragedy: The uses start even in junior high school, or even in the late grades. Under these circumstances, this is a national problem. It requires an urgent action on the part of the Federal Government and that action now has been taken by the Congress and, after fifteen months, finally the bill will be signed."[40]

---

[37] History.com Editors, *A&E Television Networks*, "War on Drugs," May 31, 2017, updated December 17, 2019, https://www.history.com/topics/crime/the-war-on-drugs, accessed August 18, 2021.

[38] *Wikipedia*, s.v. "Controlled Substances Act," https://en.wikipedia.org/wiki/Controlled_Substances_Act, accessed August 18, 2021.

[39] "CSA Schedules," Medically reviewed by Leigh Ann Anderson, PharmD., *Drugs.com*, https://www.drugs.com/csa-schedule.html, accessed March 23, 2023.

[40] President Richard Nixon, "Remarks on Signing the Comprehensive Drug Abuse Prevention and Control Act of 1970," October 27, 1970, *The American Presidency Project*, https://www.presidency.ucsb.edu/documents/

Thus three presidents — two Democrats and one Republican (Kennedy, Johnson and Nixon) with overwhelming bipartisan political support, and most importantly with American *public opinion* support — enlisted all Americans in a war with each other, a war that took parents from their children by mass incarceration, enabled children to afford abandonment of family support by selling drugs, divided neighborhoods, inspired gang signs and symbols, bred intolerance, even zero tolerance for drug users, a war that cuffed the Bill of Rights, individual freedom and sanctioned draconian punishments, militarized policing and winked at enforcement brutality. These latter drug-war developments often made police the enemy of the public, and vice versa. The war these three presidents started, because of a national [drug] problem, soon was seen as an international problem, justifying a World War on Drugs. In case there was any doubt, U.S. Representative Charles Rangel (D-NY) would later warmly recall in his 2007 memoir his partnership with Nixon on drug-war issues, writing that "Nixon was tough on drugs," and "[We] worked closely together on what was the beginning of our international war on drugs."[41]

Interestingly, the reasons President Nixon cited for declaring America's War on Drugs — festering street crime and youthful drug use — are among the reasons that I oppose it. Had President Nixon had the foresight that the world now has in hindsight, he could have entitled his October 27, 1970 signing remarks: "Crime and Drug Problems? You Ain't Seen Nothin' Yet."

The 1961 Single Convention Not Self-Executing

The obligation imposed on nations by the terms of Article 4 of the 1961 Single Convention is a key culprit that breathes monstrous Frankenstein life[42] into international convention law. The convention is not self-executing. In other words, the UN did not have the power itself to pass *criminal laws* making drug sales and drug possession a crime and make those laws binding on American citizens walking the streets of Los Angeles, New York or Detroit, Michigan, or the citizens of any other city or nation of

---

remarks-signing-the-comprehensive-drug-abuse-prevention-and-control-act-1970, emphasis added, accessed March 16, 2023.

[41] Brian Mann, "Profile: Charles Rangel and the Drug Wars," *New York Public Radio, WNYC,* August 17, 2013, https://www.wnyc.org/story/313060-profile-charles-rangel-and-drug-wars/, accessed August 23, 2021.

[42] *Wikipedia,* s.v. "*Frankenstein,*" https://en.m.wikipedia.org/wiki/Frankenstein, accessed August 18, 2021.

the world. Such power would be "self-executing."[43] However, the UN 1961 Single Convention codified the prohibition of recreational drug use, and all signatory, ratifying and acceding nations *agreed*, by operation of that signature or accession, voluntarily, to go home and pass domestic criminal laws that basically said what Article 4 said. As of February 2018, the Single Convention had 186 state parties.[44]

275 Million People Thrown Under the Bus

According to the latest figures available as of this writing and as furnished by **Ghada Waly**, Executive Director of the United Nations Office on Drugs and Crime, the 1961 Single Convention criminalizes the behavior of 275 million people. The World Drug Report 2021 noted: "Despite the proven dangers, drug use persists and, in some contexts, proliferates. Over the past year, around 275 million people have used drugs, up by 22 percent from 2010."[45]

This number is up nearly tenfold from the thirty million drug users in the early 1990s, under the UN drug-prohibition regime and protocol.[46]

Drug-war policies throw these 275 million, drug-using people under the bus "to save our children," but many of those people thrown under the bus are youngsters, our children. Exemplifying efforts to undo drug-war harm to children is the work of a Filipino organization, Save the Children. "Save the Children is alarmed that the anti-illegal drugs campaign (commonly referred to as "**tokhang**"), intended to make our communities safe, has actually made our communities a more dangerous place for children." The same Filipino source, Save the Children, in its official statement regarding children and the anti-illegal drugs campaign in the Philippines, noted, "Save

---

[43] *Wikipedia*, s.v. "Self-executing right," https://en.m.wikipedia.org/wiki/Self-executing_right, accessed August 18, 2021.

[44] *Wikipedia*, s.v. "Single Convention on Narcotic Drugs, https://en.m.wikipedia.org/wiki/Single_Convention_on_Narcotic_Drugs, accessed August 18, 2021.

[45] *World Drug Report 2021*, United Nations publication, Sales No. E.21.XI.8, Booklet 1, "Executive Summary, Policy Implications," Preface by Ghada Waly, Executive Director United Nations Office on Drugs and Crime, par. 4, https://www.unodc.org/res/wdr2021/field/WDR21_Booklet_1.pdf.

[46] *Firing Line with William F. Buckley*, "A Firing Line Debate: Resolved: That Drug Prohibition Has Failed," recorded March 15, 1991, debaters, Ira Glasser, Kildare Clarke, Charles B. Rangel, Jerry Falwell, Lois Herrington and Harold M. Voth, *The Board of Trustees of Leland Stanford Junior University*, https://youtu.be/Mouh8gE2CMg, 53rd minute of second hour.

the Children condemns the death of any child in relation to the war against illegal drugs."[47]

It is hard to fathom that the War on Drugs has saved any child, given its longstanding history of the abuse of children under the pretense of saving them. "As some [essays note] and as Human Rights Watch's work in Cambodia, the United States, Russia, and Thailand has shown, children often experience a wide range of human rights violations linked to drug control efforts. These include torture and ill treatment by police; extrajudicial killings; arbitrary detention; and denial of essential medicines and basic health services."[48]

Recognition of the Need for Treaty Revision Ten Years Ago

In 2011 at the fifty-year landmark of the 1961 Single Convention, a scholarly article written by **David Bewley-Taylor** and **Martin Jelsma**, explained the penal-basis of the UN World War on Drugs and made the following persuasive points indicative of the need for convention review and reform.

"...While codifying many previous regulations into one instrument, the [1961 Single] Convention marked an appreciable shift from a system concerned predominantly with 'restrictive commodity agreements' to a stricter and wider ranging multilateral framework that, while continuing this function, became *more prohibitive in focus*; a process that included increased emphasis on the non-medical and non-scientific consumption of scheduled drugs. Specifically within this reformulation, it introduced widely accepted *penal obligations* for signatory states to criminalize, under their domestic law, unlicensed production and trade and extended the pre-existing control regime to the cultivation of opium poppy, coca and cannabis. In *this way, the Convention provided the international law basis for the 'war on drugs'* that developed later against drug-related crops and farmers." (p.16)

---

[47] *Save the Children*, https://www.savethechildren.org.ph/our-work/our-stories/story/save-the-children-condemns-the-death-of-any-child-in-relation-to-the-war-against-illegal-drugs/.

[48] Rebecca A. Schleifer, foreword, *Children of the Drug War: Perspectives on the Impact of Drug Polices on Young People*, Damon Barrett, editor (New York: International Debate Educational Association, 2011), https://www.academia.edu/3453794/Young_Soldiers_in_Brazil_s_Drug_War?email_work_card=view-paper.

"Fifty years on, it is time for a critical reflection on the validity of the Single Convention today: a reinterpretation of its historical significance and an assessment of its aims, its strengths and its weaknesses.... (p.1-2)

"...[T]he Convention also forced many so-called 'developing countries' to abolish all 'non-medical and scientific' uses of the three plants [the poppy, coca and cannabis plants, p. 19] that for many centuries had been embedded in social, cultural and religious traditions. This included medicinal practices not accepted by modern medical science...(p. 17)

"The Single Convention lacks a rational and evidence-based scale of harm for Schedule I and IV substances...

"The instrument ironically failed to serve one of its original purposes of becoming the 'Single' Convention when the control regime developed further with the 1971 and 1988 treaties; both of which have led again to many inconsistencies within the current global drug control treaty system. Consequently, after fifty-years of existence, and given both the nature of the compromises made in 1961 and the inconsistencies created by the subsequent conventions, it is now clear that some form of revision is required. (p. 17)[49]

The assessment of Jelsma and his coauthor was right-on twelve years ago. UN drug-control treaties desperately need revision.

$500 Billion Big Business: United Nations Drug Prohibition

The drug-control paradigm structured by the 1961 Single Convention, a drug-prohibition paradigm, has made the illicit drug business one of the bigger business sectors in the global economy. As Colin P. Clarke noted, some experts estimate the global illicit drug trade to be a $500 billion (US) a year business.[50] Although opinions can

---

[49] David Bewley-Taylor and Martin Jelsma, "Fifty Years of the 1961 Single Convention on Narcotic Drugs: A Reinterpretation," *Transnational Institute (TNI)*, March 2011, Conclusions, p. 16-17, Emphasis added, https://www.tni.org/files/download/dlr12.pdf.

[50] Colin P. Clarke, 2016, "Chapter 6, The Global Illicit Trade in Illegal Narcotics, page 181," in OECD, *Illicit Trade, Converging Criminal Markets, Organisation for Economic Cooperation and Development (OECD iLibrary)* https://read.oecd-ilibrary.org/governance/illicit-trade/the-global-illicit-trade-in-illegal-narcotics_978926425 1847-9-en, p. 181, accessed March 16, 2023.

vary greatly as to the accuracy of that estimate, there is no question that the global, illicit drug trade operating in accordance with the prohibition model is big business. The enormity of the illicit drug business evidences, again, the failed, unrealistic and counterproductive nature of drug-prohibition policy.

Worldometer (Drug Statistics) notes that estimating illicit drug sales is extremely difficult but cited a 1998 UN publication for these figures: "With estimates of $100 billion to $110 billion for heroin, $110 billion to $130 billion for cocaine, $75 billion for cannabis and $60 billion for synthetic drugs, the probable global figure for the total illicit drug industry would be approximately $360 billion. Given the conservative bias in some of the estimates for individual substances, a turnover of around **$400 billion per annum** is considered realistic."[51]

Sergio Ferragut, an expert in retail and banking money-laundering prevention, who, again, I paneled with in Mexico City in 2012, wrote: "It is broadly believed that the illicit-drug trade is a *$400 billion business*."[52] Buttressing his statement, he later observed that "In the 2005 World Drug Report, the United Nations, for the first time since it began publishing the report, presented a detailed estimate of the global illicit-drug market at the producer, wholesale and retail levels for 2003... The total retail value of $322 billion reported is in the same order of magnitude of the widely publicized $400 billion figure mentioned earlier."[53] Perhaps the most powerful observation regarding the magnitude of the global drug business is by Ferragut: "Though the retail value of the illicit-drug industry is less than 1% of global GDP, it is still very significant in terms of other indicators; its value is higher than the GDP of 88% of the countries for which the World Bank has GDP data — 163 out of 184 countries."[54]

Interestingly, the $500 billion estimate of the illicit global drug business cited by Clarke excludes the revenues derived from the sale of two of the most popular, dangerous and deadly, but legal, mind-altering substances commonly used by mankind — *tobacco and alcohol*. The scope of the 1961 Single Convention does not control or regulate either of these substances.

---

[51] "Spending on illegal drugs this year: [a continuously increasing dollar number]," *Worldometer*, https://www.worldometers.info/drugs/.

[52] Sergio Ferragut, *The Silent Nightmare: The Bottom Line and the Challenge of Illicit Drugs* (Lulu.com, 2007), p. 37.

[53] Ibid., Ferragut, *A Silent Nightmare: ...*, p. 40.

[54] Ibid., p. 174.

The Alcohol Business

For perspective purposes, it is helpful to know the magnitude of the alcohol trade. "In 2020, the global market size of alcoholic beverages amounted to over 1.49 trillion U.S. dollars. The yearly revenue decreased by around 200 billion dollars compared to 2019. While estimates assume that the market size will again increase in 2021, it will take at least until 2022 before the market recovers and surpass the 2019 pre-pandemic (COVID-19) revenue."[55]

The Tobacco Business

Again, for perspective purposes, it is helpful to appreciate the size of the other most deadly mind-altering substance, tobacco. "Sales for the legal global tobacco market (2019) were worth approximately US $818 billion, according to the most recent estimates. The largest global tobacco category remains combustible cigarettes. With over 5,200 billion cigarettes consumed annually, it is valued at US $705 billion."[56]

The Size of Illicit Drug Markets

Back to the estimated size of UN "controlled drugs" (all the potentially "bad drugs," except alcohol and tobacco) and Chapter 6 of *Illicit Trade*, written by **Colin P. Clarke,** then of Carnegie Mellon University, Center for International Relations and Politics, Mr. Clarke concluded that "Taking the low and the high end of that range suggests that the value of the global illicit trade in illegal narcotics could be anywhere between US $45 billion and US $500 billion, a range so broad as to provide little analytic value."[57]

[55] "Worldwide alcoholic beverage market revenue from 2012 to 2025," *Statista Research Department,* June 16, 2021, https://www.statista.com/forecasts/696641/market-value-alcoholic-beverages-worldwide, accessed August 24, 2021.

[56] "The global market: Trends affecting our industry," *A Better Tomorrow (BAT),* https://www.bat.com/group/sites/UK__9D9KCY.nsf/vwPagesWebLive/DO9DCKFM#. Date of access?

[57] Colin P. Clark, *Illicit Trade, Converging Criminal Networks,* a report that "assesses the magnitude, flows and drivers of illicit trade and the illegal economy including: narcotics, human trafficking, wildlife, sports betting, counterfeit medicines, alcohol and tobacco....," https://www.oecd-ilibrary.org/governance/illicit-trade/the-global-illicit-trade-in-illegal-narcotics_9789264251847-9-en;jsessionid=_Ej0SCTQdOTgx7P6R7kuriM6.ip-10-240-5-187.

The Illinois Marijuana Business

Marijuana is the most commonly used illicit drug, and everyone is entitled to their opinion as to the value of black-market drug sales. But the *legal* Illinois recreational marijuana business in its fledgling second year, 2021, is projected to reach $1.9 billion. And "Even as legal weed sales in Illinois continue to shatter records nearly 18 months after they kicked off, the illicit pot trade is still dominating a total statewide market some experts have valued at over $4 billion."[58]

Equally elucidating is a recent headline regarding comparative demand for marijuana and alcohol in Illinois. Illinois legal marijuana sales were projected to surpass Illinois liquor sales in 2021.[59] And with $1.4 billion in legal, Illinois marijuana sales in 2021,[60] doubling 2020 sales, they surely did.[61] Those sales produced $387.7 million in taxes collected and remitted to the comptroller for the prior calendar year.

Russian Defense Spending

For perspective purposes, last one, Russia annual defense spending is $61.7 billion.[62]

The point here is that the drug trade is big business, and the UN global drug prohibition paradigm makes the business exponentially larger, despite its espoused goal to reduce drug supply and drug demand. Many people take advantage of the business opportunities offered by drug prohibition. As a reformed drug dealer once told me: "There is no limit to how much money you can make in the drug business. It's just a

[58] Tom Schuba, "Billions in black-market weed still selling in Illinois 18 months after marijuana legalized," *Chicago Sun-Times,* June 14, 2021, https://chicago.suntimes.com/cannabis/2021/6/14/22534079/illinois-dispensaries-illegal-legal-marijuana-cannabis-pot-bud-sale, accessed August 24, 2021.

[59] Benjamin Fearnow, May 3, 2021, "Illinois to Record $1 Billion Marijuana Sales by Year's End, Surpassing Liquor," *Newsweek,* May 3, 2021, https://www.newsweek.com/illinois-record-1-billion-marijuana-sales-years-end-surpassing-liquor-1588354.

[60] Greg Bishop, "Illinois legal cannabis sales nearly $1.4 billion in 2021, double last year's total," *The Center Square,* January 3, 2022, https://www.thecentersquare.com/illinois/illinois-legal-cannabis-sales-nearly-1-4-billion-in-2021-double-last-years-total/article_dafe48f6-6cc3-11ec-a174-db1ea990d6c7.html.

[61] Greg Bishop, "Illinois legal cannabis sales nearly $1.4 billion in 2021, double last year's total:

State collects more than $387 million in cannabis taxes," *The Center Square,* January 3, 2022, https://www.thecentersquare.com/illinois/illinois-legal-cannabis-sales-nearly-1-4-billion-in-2021-double-last-years-total/article_dafe48f6-6cc3-11ec-a174-db1ea990d6c7.html.

[62] "Countries with the highest military spending worldwide in 2020," *Statista,* https://www.statista.com/statistics/262742/countries-with-the-highest-military-spending/, accessed August 21, 2021.

question of what risk you're willing to take to make it." He intended to write a book about his experience, which he intended to title, "*What Risk?*"

Johann Hari summarized the situation well: "A man like **Arnold Rothstein** would always have been able to ferret out some criminal opportunity, but Arnold was *handed two of the largest industries in America, tax-free*. He immediately spotted that the prohibition of booze and drugs was *the biggest lottery win for gangsters in history*. There will always be large numbers of people who want to get drunk or high, and if they can't do it legally, they will do it illegally."[63] A number of well-known criminals followed in Rothstein's prohibition-blessed footsteps.

> Author Edward "Prohibition of drugs, like prohibition of alcohol, is **not** the answer."
>
> — M. Brecher

Al Capone (1899-1947)

Chicago is renowned for many things but possibly none more than Al Capone, a prohibition public policy benefactor. As Alphonse Capone saw it, "I'm just a businessman giving the people what they want."[64] Of course, Prohibition was accompanied by gang violence, the St. Valentine's Day Massacre, lawlessness and more problems.[65] "The forbiddance of alcohol ushered in an iconic era of bootleggers, speakeasies and a wholesale disregard for an amendment that engendered far more problems than its supporters had so naively believed it would resolve."[66]

Pablo Escobar (1949-1993)

Another successful businessman following in the footsteps of Arnold Rothstein was Pablo Escobar whose estimated net worth in 1993 was US $30 billion, the equivalent of US $64 billion as of 2021. Escobar headed the Medellín Cartel. "During the height

---

[63] Johann Hari, *Chasing the Scream* (New York: London, Bloomsbury, 2015), p. 52, emphasis added.

[64] *AZQuotes*, https://www.azquotes.com/.

[65] History.com Editors, "St. Valentine's Day Massacre," *History*, Last Updated, February 4, 2021, accessed January 5, 2022, https://www.history.com/topics/crime/saint-valentines-day-massacre.

[66] Julian Hitner, "California and Prohibition: Collateral damage, *Decanter*, July 21, 2019, accessed August 28, 2021, https://www.decanter.com/learn/california-and-prohibition-419995/.

of its operations, the Medellín Cartel brought in more than US $70 million per day (~$149.5 million in 2021 money). This level of income is roughly $26 billion per annum ($55.5 billion in 2021 money). Smuggling 15 tons of cocaine per day (worth more than half a billion dollars) into the United States, the cartel spent over US$1,000 per week purchasing rubber bands to wrap the stacks of cash they received, storing most of it in their warehouses. Ten percent of the cash had to be written off per year because of 'spoilage' due to rats creeping in and nibbling on the bills they could reach."[67]

Interestingly, Pablo Escobar once thoughtfully remarked, "The purpose of war is peace."[68] Maybe Escobar was thinking that peace is the inevitable outcome of all wars and fighting any war long enough leads to that realization. One can hope so. But thus far, regarding the War on Drugs that realization has yet to awaken. What is clear — the violence of the Capone Prohibition Era is no different than that of the Escobar Prohibition Era. "Incidentally, the Colombian cartels' continuing struggles to maintain supremacy resulted in Colombia quickly becoming the world's murder capital, with 25,100 violent deaths in 1991 and 27,100 in 1992. This increased murder rate was fueled by Escobar giving money to his hitmen as a reward for killing police officers, over 600 of whom died as a result."[69]

Joaquín "El Chapo" Guzmán (1957-present)

Continued drug prohibition policy following Escobar's death brought us another leading prohibition superstar, Joaquín Guzmán, nicknamed "Shorty" or "El Chapo." In a Sean Penn/*Rolling Stone* interview of the Mexican drug chieftain, El Chapo Guzmán said "It is true that consumption, day after day, becomes bigger and bigger... so it sells and sells."[70] A reporter and art editor for *The Guardian* reported that Guzmán said, "I supply more heroin, methamphetamine, cocaine and marijuana than anybody else in the world.... I have a fleet of submarines, airplanes, trucks and boats."[71] "Even when

---

[67] "*Wikipedia*, s.v. "Pablo Escobar,", https://en.m.wikipedia.org/wiki/Pablo_Escobar.

[68] Kaustav Ghosh, *Brilliant Read*, https://www.brilliantread.com/18-best-pablo-escobar-quotes-advice-thoughts-and-his-net-worth-2019/, February 17, 2019, accessed January 16, 2022.

[69] *Wikipedia, s.v.* "Pablo Escobar," supra; and Crime Museum, Pablo Escobar, https://www.crimemuseum.org/crime-library/drugs/pablo-escobar/, accessed March 16, 2023.

[70] Rolling Stone, "Watch El Chapo's Exclusive Interview in Its 17-Minute Entirety," *Rolling Stone*, January 12, 2016, accessed August 21, 2021.

[71] Benjamin Lee and Scott Bixby, "Sean Penn on El Chapo interview: 'I have a terrible regret," *Guardian*, January 15, 2016, accessed August 21, 2021.

I'm gone it won't make any difference. The [drug] business just grows and grows."[72] Succinctly, El Chapo [correctly] concluded that the drug business "will never end."[73]

The only question needing answer to thwart future Guzmáns of the world is this: Will governments of the world (and UN drug-control agencies) continue to delegate the control, regulation and competition over the huge drug trade to criminal agencies, transnational criminal organizations (TCOs). Or instead, will governments license drug dealers, and control and regulate the mammoth illicit drug business by transitioning to legal drug markets?

Who Is Ismael "El Mayo" Zambada?

Ismael "El Mayo" Zambada is El Chapo's longtime partner, who said in 2010 in a rare interview with the Mexican news magazine *El Proceso* that the problem of narcos is not going away: "As soon as capos are locked up, killed or extradited, their replacements are already around."[74] The fact that most people would not recognize the name Zambada evidences the truth of his statement.

Yet, the "Zambada García organization, the Sinaloa Cartel, receives multi-ton quantities of cocaine, mostly by sea from Colombian sources. After receipt of the cocaine, the Sinaloa cartel uses a variety of methods, including airplanes, trucks, cars, boats, and tunnels to transport the cocaine to the United States. Members of the cartel smuggle the cocaine to distribution cells in Arizona, California, Illinois, and New York....Zambada operates primarily in the States of Sinaloa and Durango but exerts influence along a large portion of Mexico's Pacific coast, as well as in Cancun, Quintana Roo, Sonora, Monterrey and Nuevo Leon.... Ismael Zambada has been featured on *America's Most Wanted*, and the FBI is offering up to US$5 million for information leading to his capture."[75]

---

[72] Joshua Nevett, "El Chapo: How Mexico's drug kingpin fell victim to his own legend," *BBC News Service*, July 17, 2019, accessed August 24, 2021.

[73] Rolling Stone video, https://www.rollingstone.com/politics/politics-news/watch-el-chapos-exclusive-interview-in-its-17-minute-entirety-35543/, accessed August 21, 2021.

[74] Jessica Loudis, "El Chapo: what the rise and fall of the kingpin reveals about the war on drugs." *The Guardian*, June 7, 2019, https://www.theguardian.com/world/2019/jun/07/el-chapo-the-last-of-the-cartel-kingpins, accessed August 21,2021.

[75] *Wikipedia*, s.v. "Ismael 'El Mayo' Zambada," https://en.wikipedia.org/wiki/Ismael_%22El_Mayo%22_Zambada, accessed March 16, 2023.

On June 17, 1971, in a press conference, President Nixon formally declared "America's War on Drugs" using these words: "America's public enemy number one is drug abuse. In order to defeat this enemy it is necessary to wage a new, all-out offensive.... This will be a worldwide offensive.... It will be government wide."[76]

Promoting the idea of a "Worldwide War on Drugs," both before and after President Nixon's June 1971 war declaration, the UN through cooperative multinational action expanded the drug war by adopting two additional drug-prohibition treaties: the 1971 Convention on Psychotropic Substances and the 1988 United Nations Convention against Illicit Traffic in Narcotic Drugs and Psychotropic Substances.[77] The Commission on Narcotic Drugs is mandated to decide on the scope of control of substances under the three International Drug Control Conventions (1961, 1971 and 1988 Conventions).[78] The treaties have received near-universal acceptance with almost every State in the world being a party to at least one.[79]

The United Nations Players in Global Drug Policy

Because the drug war is indeed a World War on Drugs, the United Nations and its principal organs and agencies become important players in global drug policy. To understand the international powers at work deciding there will be a global war on drugs, some understanding of the UN and its principal organs and agencies is necessary. First of all, the players. The UN drug policy players are: the United Nations General Assembly (GA), the Economic and Social Council (ECOSOC), the UN Commission on Narcotic Drugs (CND), the International Narcotic Control Board (INCB) and the UN Office on Drugs and Crime (UNODC). Second of all, an overview.

The UN was founded in October 1945. The United Nations is an intergovernmental organization whose purpose is to maintain international peace and security, develop friendly relations among nations, achieve international cooperation, and be a

---

[76] Video, President Nixon Declares Drug Abuse "Public Enemy Number One," *Richard Nixon Foundation*, The Richard Nixon Presidential Library and Museum, June 17, 1971; *YouTube*, https://youtu.be/y8TGLLQlD9M.

[77] "The International Drug Control Conventions," https://www.unodc.org/documents/commissions/ CND/Int_Drug_Control_Conventions/Ebook/The_International_Drug_Control_Conventions_E.pdf.

[78] *United Nations Office on Drugs and Crime*, "International Drug Control Conventions," https://www.unodc.org/unodc/en/commissions/CND/Mandate_Functions/Mandate-and-Functions_Scheduling.html, accessed June 18, 2022.

[79] Brian A. Ford, "From Mountains to Molehills: A Comparative Analysis of Drug Policy," *Academia*, https://www.academia.edu/3546783/From_Mountains_to_Molehills_A_Comparative_Analysis_of_Drug_Poli cy?email_work_card=thumbnail, page 6.

center for harmonizing the actions of nations.[80] It was established after World War II with the aim of preventing future wars.[81] The UN has six principal organs: the General Assembly (GA); the Security Council; the Economic and Social Council (ECOSOC); the Trusteeship Council (inactive since 1994); the International Court of Justice; and the UN Secretariat.[82] The UN Secretary-General serves as its chief administrative officer. For our purposes of understanding the role of the UN in drug policy, simplified greatly, the UN General Assembly and ECOSOC are both UN principal organs of important stature having differing roles, each designated as principal organs by the UN Charter itself (Chapter III, Article 7).[83] Because Article 11 of Chapter 4 of the UN Charter entitles any UN member to bring any question "relating to the maintenance of international peace and security" to the GA for discussion,[84] drug policy is a proper matter for GA discussion. And exercising that power, periodically, the UN General Assembly has held special sessions (UNGASS) regarding the drug problem as it did most recently in 2016.

As the main deliberative assembly of the UN,[85] at UNGASS 2016 regarding the global drug problem, the GA could have discussed abandonment of the foundational, recreational-drug-use prohibition principle and directed CND and UNODC to consider and draft proposed amendments of UN drug-control conventions. This directive could have set the stage for a more contemporary and effective international drug-control paradigm. But it did not. According to the UN Charter, each member of the General Assembly gets one vote.[86] The UN General Assembly elects all members of ECOSOC. (Chapter 4, Article 18)

ECOSOC was established under the United Nations Charter as the principal organ to coordinate economic, social, and related work of the fourteen UN specialized agencies, functional commissions and five regional commissions.[87] ECOSOC is important to global drug policy because it has the power to elect nation states to serve on

---

[80] *Wikipedia*, s.v. "United Nations," https://en.wikipedia.org/wiki/United_Nations, accessed March 16, 2023.

[81] Ibid.

[82] Ibid.

[83] *United Nations*, UN Charter, https://www.un.org/en/about-us/un-charter/chapter-3.

[84] Ibid., https://www.un.org/en/about-us/un-charter/chapter-4.

[85] *Wikipedia*, s.v. "United Nations," https://en.wikipedia.org/wiki/United_Nations.

[86] Ibid.

[87] "Economic and Social Council Background Guide," *UMass Lowell*, https://www.uml.edu/fahss/model-un/background-guides/economic-and-social-council-background-guide.aspx, accessed February 8, 2022.

the Commission on Narcotic Drugs (CND), comprised of fifty-three nations,[88] one of the functional commissions of the UN.[89] And CND is the main policymaking body of the UN with prime responsibility for drug-related matters.[90] As such, CND has the power to make decisions and adopt resolutions that determine drug policy consistent with UN drug conventions.[91] For example, CND at its 52nd Session approved a 2009 Political Declaration and Call to Action that sought to make the world "free of drug abuse" and "drug-free" by 2019.[92]

The CND was established by the Economic and Social Council (ECOSOC) in 1946, to assist the ECOSOC in supervising the application of the international drug control treaties. In 1991, the United Nations General Assembly (GA) expanded the mandate of the CND to enable it to function as the governing body of the UNODC.[93]

UNODC is not mentioned in or created by the UN Charter. Established in 1997, UNODC has approximately 500 staff members worldwide. Its headquarters are in Vienna, and it operates twenty field offices covering over 150 countries, as well as liaison offices in New York and Brussels.[94] By working directly with governments and non-governmental organizations, UNODC field staff develop and implement drug control and crime prevention programs tailored to countries' particular needs.[95]

Oversimplified for sure, but basically, the people of the countries of the world through their respective national leaders are the "boss" of the United Nations through the UN General Assembly; and the UN General Assembly is the "boss" of ECOSOC;

---

[88] "The CND has 53 member States that are elected by ECOSOC and is chaired by a Bureau, including one member per Regional Group," *UNODC*, "Commission on Narcotic Drugs," https://www.unodc.org/unodc/en/commissions/CND/index.html.

[89] *Wikipedia*, s.v. "United Nations Social and Economic Council," https://en.wikipedia.org/wiki/United_Nations_Economic_and_Social_Council, accessed March 16, 2023.

[90] *United Nations Office on Drugs and Crime*, "Commission on Narcotic Drugs," https://www.unodc.org/unodc/en/commissions/CND/index.html, accessed June 18, 2022.

[91] Ibid.

[92] *UNODC*, "Political Declaration and Action Plan map out future of drug control," https://www.unodc.org/unodc/en/press/releases/2009/March/2009-12.03.html.

[93] Ibid.

[94] *United Nations Office at Vienna*, https://www.unov.org/unov/en/unodc.html, accessed March 16, 2023.

[95] Ibid.

and ECOSOC is the "boss" of CND; and CND is the "boss" of the UNODC. Collectively, with the help of the INCB, these are the many UN drug policy players who have brought the world to a perpetual state of drug war.

The INCB is the independent and quasi-judicial monitoring body for the implementation of the UN international drug control conventions. It was established in 1968 in accordance with the Single Convention on Narcotic Drugs, 1961.[96] The INCB is an independent treaty body, one of the four treaty-mandated bodies under international drug control law (alongside the Commission on Narcotic Drugs, UNODC on behalf of the Secretary-General, and the WHO). The INCB is responsible for monitoring the control of substances pursuant to the three UN drug control conventions and for assisting Member States in their efforts to implement those conventions. It plays an important role in monitoring the production and trade of narcotics and psychotropics, as well as their availability for medical and scientific purposes, and in deciding which precursors should be regulated.[97]

There are many hands spoiling the broth of global drug policy.

International Overdose Awareness Day

The three international drug control treaties are the backbone of the failed and futile World War on Drugs, I cringe to realize today on International Overdose Awareness Day, August 31st annually.[98] Collectively, smoking, alcohol and illicit drug use kills 11.8 million people each year. This is more than the number of deaths from all cancers.[99] Who are the persons responsible for these deaths, these policies, these failures?

National and World Leaders: Aiders, Abetters and Facilitators

National and global leaders adopted, implemented and executed the terms of three international drug-control conventions with absolute executive and legislative immunity from customary principles of criminal law such as the imposition of criminal liability on anyone "aiding or abetting"[100] another in the commission of a crime. "In

---

96 *INCB*, https://www.incb.org, accessed March 16, 2023; and *Wikipedia*, "International Narcotics Control Board," https://en.wikipedia.org/wiki/International_Narcotics_Control_Board, accessed March 16, 2023.

97 *Wikipedia*, "International Narcotics Control Board," https://en.wikipedia.org/wiki/International_Narcotics_Control_Board, accessed March 16, 2023.

98 *Pennington Institute*, https://www.overdoseday.com.

99 *Our World in Data*, "Drug Use," https://ourworldindata.org/drug-use.

100 *Wikipedia*, s.v. "Aiding and abetting," https://en.wikipedia.org/wiki/Aiding_and_abetting.

United States law, absolute immunity is a type of sovereign immunity for government officials [executive, legislative and judicial officials] that confers complete immunity from criminal prosecution and suits for damages, so long as officials are acting within the scope of their duties. The Supreme Court of the United States has consistently held that government officials deserve some type of immunity from lawsuits for damages, and that the common law recognized this immunity."[101]

Thus, even if this executive and legislative action (the adoption of national laws implementing the three international drug-control treaties) effectively aided and abetted transnational criminal organizations by delegating all control and regulation of narcotic drugs consumed for recreational purposes to criminal organizations, executives and legislators enjoy absolute immunity for their enactment.

Yet, because of this effective delegation of power and authority, drug cartels are enabled to decide what illicit drugs will be sold, by whom, where, drug strength and purity, and at what price. This delegation of control and regulation of the recreational drug business, of course, also facilitates every local drug dealer and drug gang, making similar marketing and supply decisions locally. Tragically, this short-sighted delegation of power has universal catastrophic consequences, since all nations that are party to, or acquiesce in, international drug-control treaties are acting — as UN drug agencies like to say, using Vienna jargon — in a "cooperative, single-voice, balanced, and evidenced-based" manner.

The 2021 World Drug Report

Continuing drug-prohibition policies with national execution of UN drug-control conventions *guarantees* future reports even worse than those reported by the UNODC in the *World Drug Report 2021*, capsulized and excerpted below: (Apologetically, it takes several pages here to comprehensively condense the bad news of the sixty-page report, but comprehensive condemnation of global drug policy harm is worth the time spent and pain suffered reading this condensation.)

Cannabis products have almost quadrupled in strength in the United States of America and have doubled in Europe in the last two decades. (p. 22)

Drug markets on the dark web... are now worth at least $315 million in annual sales. (p. 24)

---

[101] *Wikipedia, s.v.* "Absolute Immunity," https://en.wikipedia.org/wiki/Absolute_immunity, accessed March 16, 2023.

The number of drug users in Africa is projected to rise in the next decade by as much as 40 percent, simply because of demographic changes. (p. 26)

Globally, the number of people using drugs is projected to rise by 11 percent by 2030 because of demographic changes alone. Low-income countries account for the lion's share of this rise. (p. 26)

Drug markets were temporarily disrupted in most parts of the world during the first phase of the COVID-19 pandemic, but they have recovered quickly. Nevertheless, the pandemic has triggered or accelerated some pre-existing trafficking dynamics. These include larger shipment sizes and increased use of land and waterway routes, private planes, air cargo and postal parcels and contactless methods for delivering drugs to consumers, such as mail delivery. (p. 30)

Most countries have seen an increase in the use of cannabis and non-medical use of pharmaceutical drugs such as benzodiazepines during the pandemic. (p. 32)

North America has seen a spike in opioid overdose deaths since the onset of the pandemic. For example, opioid overdose deaths in Canada were 58 percent higher during the quarter April–June 2020 as compared with the same period in 2019. (p. 32)

Fragile communities in opium poppy and coca bush cultivation areas have become increasingly vulnerable as the pandemic has affected their livelihoods. (p.34)

Changes already observed in drug use patterns, including increases in the use of cannabis and the non-medical use of pharmaceutical sedatives, are likely to accelerate the expansion of the market for these substances. (p. 34)

This is all likely to be fueled by innovation in the retail distribution of drugs, with street dealing becoming less prevalent as contactless methods such as online purchasing and delivery by mail – and even drones – become more common. (p. 34)

The number of NPS [New Psychoactive Substances] emerging on the global market fell from 163 in 2013 to seventy-one in 2019. However, the NPS problem has now spread to poorer regions... For example, seizures of synthetic NPS in Africa rose from less than 1 kg in 2015 to 828 kg in 2019. There was a similar trend in Central and South America, with seizures rising from 60 kg to 641 kg over the same period. (p. 36)

The cocaine trafficking route between South America and Europe is the second biggest in the world, and it is evolving. Supply chains once dominated by a few organized crime groups are changing, with many more groups involved. (p. 38)

The increased competition and efficiency of supply mean that cocaine is becoming more available, and the quality is rising. The purity of cocaine available in Europe has increased by 40 percent in the past decade, meaning that high-quality cocaine has, in effect, become cheaper per pure unit. (p. 38)

Afghanistan reported a 37 percent increase in the amount of land used for illicit cultivation of opium poppy during 2020 compared with the previous year. It was the third highest figure ever recorded in the country and accounted for 85 percent of the global total of opium production in 2020. (p. 40)

The expansion of methamphetamine manufacture adds complexity to the illicit drug economy of Afghanistan and increases the threat to countries in the region and beyond. (p. 40)

While the amount of methamphetamine seized increased threefold between 2011 and 2019, seizures of its internationally controlled precursors declined by 99 percent over the same period.... This dynamic is attributable to the agility of traffickers in changing the chemicals they use, thereby enabling precursors to bypass interdiction. (p. 42)

In 2019, medical professionals in West and Central Africa had access to four standard doses of controlled pain medication every day per one million inhabitants. In North America, the figure was about 32,000 doses. Patients with acute or chronic pain from serious illnesses such as cancer endure unnecessary suffering on a large scale. (p. 46)

Roughly 275 million people globally have used drugs in the past year, up from 226 million in 2010. This 22 percent increase was partly due to a 10 percent rise in the global population. (p. 48)

The amounts of fentanyl and its analogues seized globally have risen rapidly in recent years, and by more than 60 percent in 2019 compared with a year earlier. Overall, these amounts have risen more than twenty-fold since 2015. (p. 50)

Global cocaine manufacture doubled in output between 2014 and 2019 to reach an estimated 1,784 tons in 2019, the highest level ever. (p. 52)

In the period 2015–2019, more than 90 percent of the methamphetamine seized globally was seized in South-East Asia and North America. In North America, seizures increased eightfold, to 153 tons, between 2009 and 2019. In the same period, there was an eleven-fold increase in seizures in South-East Asia, to 141 tons. (p. 54)

Almost 50,000 people died from overdose deaths attributed to opioids in the United States in 2019, more than double the 2010 figure.... The crisis is now driven mainly by overdose deaths attributed to synthetic opioids such as fentanyl and its analogues. (p. 56)

There were more than eleven million people who inject drugs globally in 2019, of whom 1.4 million are living with HIV and 5.6 million with hepatitis C. (p. 60)[102]

Reading the results of the *World Drug Report* 2021 and seeing the consequences of UN drug-prohibition policy is like making an obituary page a song's chorus. Upcoming Chapter 4 embellishes the simple truth that "Drug War Means More Drugs," use and death.

> *"Tolerance implies no lack of commitment to one's own beliefs. Rather it condemns the oppression or persecution of others."*
>
> — President John Fitzgerald Kennedy

Summarizing the failures of global drug prohibition treaties, laws and policies — this year, after sixty years — is stupefying. Simply put, those failures did the following harm: greatly expanded drug quantity, potency, variety and availability; increased drug use, addiction and disease; boosted the fortunes and success of transnational criminal organizations; triggered the shooting of gangsters, law enforcement officers, innocent bystanders and tens of thousands of people; provided cover to political leaders who wrongfully invoked extrajudicial "street justice," sweeps and death penalty punishment for druggies and dealers; invited runaway prohibition corruption; endangered minorities and the poor; inflamed intolerance; trampled human rights; encouraged mass incarceration; and facilitated "the bad guys."

These national and global leaders should consider themselves identified as *drug-war facilitators, aiders and abetters* in the killer World War on Drugs. Of course, these leaders will never be prosecuted for their cameo drug-war roles. But it would be redeeming if prospectively they would work to end further drug-war harm by authorizing experimentation with national and local drug decriminalization and drug legalization programs, disavowing drug prohibition once and for all

---

102 *United Nations Office on Drugs and Crime,* "World Drug Report 2021," https://www.unodc.org/res/wdr2021/field/WDR21_Booklet_1.pdf, accessed March 16, 2023.

Chapter 3 - Drug War Means Intolerance

Drug war means drug prohibition, and drug prohibition means drug war. The two terms can be used interchangeably. *The foundational principle undergirding prohibition is intolerance.* And prohibition taken to its outer limits is called "zero tolerance." Intolerance comes in many flavors and many strengths. It is "the gateway drug" to hate, conflict and war; it is the repudiation of love, patience and understanding. When drug intolerance infects law enforcement and policing, drug war transforms citizens and criminal suspects into "the enemy," and in natural response, the public often perceives the police as "the enemy." Conforming dress, tactics and equipment to its new role, law enforcement officers don gear fashioned after military-styled helmets and vests, plan for no-knock raids that look like military operations, and deploy weaponry and shock grenades befitting combat maneuvers. The citizenry notices this deleterious police transformation as intolerance weeps into juvenile justice, criminal justice and the work of our political leaders, often implicating racial discrimination.

Child Suffers Nightmares

Analyzing data regarding the use of force by police involving children under sixteen years of age in 3,000 cases over eleven years, the Associated Press noted that forceable instances, many involving harsh if not brutal force, involved Black children though they comprised only 15% of the U.S. children population. One such child was Royal Smart who "remembers every detail: the feeling of the handcuffs on his wrists. The panic as he was led outside into the cold [Chicago] March darkness, arms raised, to face a wall of police officers. He was eight years old. Neither he nor anyone at his family's home on the South Side was arrested on that night two years ago, and police wielding a warrant to look for illegal weapons found none. But even now, in nightmares and in waking moments, he is tormented by visions of officers bursting through houses and tearing rooms apart, ordering people to lie down on the floor." Royal says of the aftermath from the incident, "I can't go to sleep. I keep thinking about the police coming."[103] Royal was treated like the enemy.

---

[103] Helen Wieffering, Colleen Long and Camille Fassett, "I can't go to sleep. I keep thinking about the police coming," *Associated Press*, October 21, 2021, https://www.pressreader.com/usa/chicago-sun-times/20211021/281659668240668, emphasis added.

Home Not Safe

"[Anjanette] Young [a social worker] was in her Near West Side home in the evening hours of February 21, 2019, when several [Chicago Police Department] officers came in, announcing a raid. Young was undressed and getting ready for bed at the time, and she was forced to remain naked in front of the officers for 40 minutes as the ordeal unfolded."[104]

No weapons were found, the subject of the no-knock search warrant, but on many scores the Chicago police bedtime raid on Anjanette's home was a success. Loud, aggressive, shockingly surprising, and no officers or civilians were physically injured. A little property damaged, the place left an untidy mess, but no one was shot. Yet what happened to Anjanette Young during the police raid on the wrong house, her psyche, her door, her home, her self-esteem as she was handcuffed nude and uncovered for too long, was horrible, inexcusable, just plain wrong. The Chicago City Council settled her lawsuit for $2.9 million.[105]

And that begs the question — should police be conducting raids such as this on someone's home? Should no-knock police raids in the night be okay in order to get the drugs, guns or the likes of **Mark Clark** or **Fred Hampton**?[106] If police had seized the drugs, guns, or person targeted in the search warrant, and if the raid had not targeted the wrong address, was the Anjanette raid conducted by a dozen Chicago peace officers okay? Is this the policing we want to see in nice neighborhoods like Winnetka, Palos Park, Ravenswood, or Ashburn? Maybe this wasn't a drug raid on Anjanette's house. Maybe the search warrant targeted something else entirely. But it looked like a drug raid. It looked like a War on Drugs police operation.[107] Anjanette was treated like the enemy.

104 Sam Charles, "Alleging conspiracy and cover-up, Anjanette Young sues Chicago, 12 officers over police raid," *Chicago Sun-Times*, February 22, 2021, https://chicago.suntimes.com/city-hall/2021/2/22/22295532/anjanette-young-sues-chicago-police-officers-botched-raid.

105 "Victim of botched Chicago police raid says settlement money doesn't bring her peace: 'I lost a lot of my life that night,'" *CBS News*, January 21, 2022, https://www.cbsnews.com/news/anjanette-young-chicago-police-department-raid/.

106 History editors, "Police kill two members of the Black Panther Party," *A&E Television Networks*, https://www.history.com/this-day-in-history/police-kill-two-members-of-the-black-panther-party, November 13, 2009, updated December 1, 2021, accessed February 20, 2022.

107 Gierach, James E., "Botched Chicago Police Raid [Wrong House]," *Gierach Blogs, Tumblr*, https://jamesgierach.tumblr.com/post/645562024917680128.

"Your Son Can Go 'Cold Turkey' Like Everyone Else"

My client, Peter [Smith] (name changed to avoid attorney-client confidentiality issues) was a white, twenty-five-year-old, disabled military veteran, a heroin addict in remission who honorably completed his military service but became an injecting heroin addict in the process. The good-natured young man lived with his father and was "on the wagon" thanks to his treatment with an experimental synthetic opioid, **Suboxone**, generically called buprenorphine, a synthetic opioid that also contains an **opioid antagonist**, a substance that interferes with or inhibits the physiological action of another.

Unfortunately, Peter noticed a motorboat in his neighbor's garage. He thought he could easily steal the motor and make some money. So, one night about midnight, he and a friend entered the neighbor's garage and tried to remove the motor. During the attempted theft, the neighbor, who was watching TV in his front room, heard a noise coming from his garage and interrupted them. Realizing they had been discovered, the two young men made a run for it. As he ran, Peter grabbed a weedwhacker and two fishing poles. I asked Peter why he took the weedwhacker, and he explained that you could go 20 mph with a weedwhacker motor mounted on a skateboard. So much for the criminal mind.

Peter ran home, a few doors away, but was quickly caught.

On March 7, 2007, Peter was charged with burglary. Thanks to the Cook County drug school diversion program, Peter had little criminal history, despite purchasing drugs 300 to 400 times in Dolton, Illinois, a Chicago suburb, "sometimes making four trips a day" from Oak Lawn and "hundreds of times" from a source located on Chicago's South Side. Yet, he had only one drug arrest in all his years of drug use, tending to confirm the observation of Rep. Charles Rangel (D-N.Y.) fifteen years earlier — "You have to be really unlucky to get arrested for a drug violation."

On March 29, 2007, Peter was released on electronic home monitoring, but rearrested on April 3, 2007 for "tampering with his monitoring device." Thirteen days later, Peter's father posted $3,000, the required ten-percent bail D-bond deposit. While in custody at the Cook County Jail, medicine, because Suboxone was "experimental and too new." A Cook County sheriff deputy explained, "Your son can go cold turkey like everyone else." Peter was treated like the enemy.

The morning after posting bond Peter's father found his son dead, curled up on the bedroom floor, a needle still in his arm and drugs and a spoon still on the nightstand. Days later Peter's grandmother, who had loaned Peter use of her car, received notice of a red-light traffic violation that occurred the afternoon before Peter's death near 87th and State Street, one of his heroin haunts. Is a young man with a substance addiction the enemy? Should jail authorities have allowed Peter access to Suboxone? Again, Peter was treated like the enemy.

Intolerance of Minorities, Commonly "The Enemy"

The criminalization of drugs puts police officers and correctional officers on the front lines of a rough and tumble drug war. War combatants are supposed to be tough and aggressive toward the enemy. Making law-enforcement officers (sworn to "serve and protect" people) drug-war soldiers crosses wires, changing the relationship between peace officer and citizen. Not uncommonly those crossed wires have peace officers abusing the trust and power assigned to them, some police officers using excessive force, particularly and disproportionately killing Black people.[108]

"In an analysis of 4,653 fatal shootings for which information about both race and age were available, the researchers found: Among unarmed victims, Black people were killed at three times the rate (218 total killed), and Hispanics at 1.45 times the rate of white people (146 total killed)."[109]

DOJ Consent Decrees

The U.S. Department of Justice, Civil Rights Division reported undertaking twenty-three "pattern and practice" investigations of U.S. police departments, resulting in entry of consent decrees in over half of them with other investigations resulting in out-of-court agreements and ongoing investigations.[110]

Regarding one such investigation of the Chicago Police Department, a DOJ press release noted: "The department's findings further note that the impact of CPD's pattern or practice of unreasonable force falls heaviest on predominantly Black and Latino

[108] Cheryl W. Thompson, "Fatal Police Shootings Of Unarmed Black People Reveal Troubling Patterns," *NPR*, January 25, 2021, https://www.npr.org/2021/01/25/956177021/fatal-police-shootings-of-unarmed-black-people-reveal-troubling-patterns.

[109] Brita Belli, "Racial disparity in police shootings unchanged over 5 years," *Yale News*, October 27, 2020, https://news.yale.edu/2020/10/27/racial-disparity-police-shootings-unchanged-over-5-years.

[110] "Police Reform and Accountability Accomplishments," *Department of Justice*, https://www.justice.gov/opa/file/797666/download,naccessed, accessed August 30, 2021.

neighborhoods, such that restoring police-community trust will require remedies addressing both discriminatory conduct and the disproportionality of illegal and unconstitutional patterns of force on minority communities."[111] Drug war policing demonstrates an intolerance not only of drugs but of minorities.

President Obama's Task Force on 21st Century Policing

The same factual bases that underpinned police department consent decrees across America led to the creation of President Barack Obama's Task Force on 21st Century Policing that issued its Final Report in May 2015. Task Force Recommendation 4.6 was this: "Communities should adopt policies and programs that address the needs of children and youth most at risk for crime or violence and reduce aggressive law enforcement tactics that stigmatize youth and marginalize their participation in schools and communities."[112] Discussing that recommendation the Task Force wrote, "Much has also been learned about the pathways by which adolescents become delinquent, the effectiveness of prevention and treatment programs, and the long-term effects of transferring youths to the adult system and confining them in harsh conditions. These findings have raised doubts about a series of policies and practices of *zero tolerance* that have contributed to increasing the school-to-prison pipeline by criminalizing the behaviors of children as young as kindergarten age."[113]

When it comes to drugs, the deleterious term "zero tolerance" has an all too familiar ring to it. Where does this intolerance come from? It comes from political leaders like First Lady Nancy Reagan, who "championed recreational drug prevention causes when she founded the 'Just Say No' drug awareness campaign, which was considered her major initiative as First Lady."[114]

---

[111] "Justice Department Announces Findings of Investigation into Chicago Police Department," January 13, 2017, https://www.justice.gov/opa/pr/justice-department-announces-findings-investigation-chicago-police-department, emphasis added, accessed August 30, 2021.

[112] "Final Report of the President's Task Force on 21st Century Policing," May 2015, https://cops.usdoj.gov/pdf/taskforce/taskforce_finalreport.pdf, 47, accessed August 24, 2021.

[113] Ibid., emphasis added.

[114] *Wikipedia, s.v.* "Nancy Reagan," https://en.m.wikipedia.org/wiki/Nancy_Reagan, accessed August 24, 2021.

"We won't win until the average parent believes drug reform protects kids better than the war on drugs."

— Drug Policy Reform Activist Ethan Nadelmann

Nancy Reagan Drug Intolerance and "Just Say No"

"The First Lady launched the 'Just Say No' drug awareness campaign in 1982, which was her primary project and major initiative as first lady... In 1982, Reagan was asked by a schoolgirl what to do when offered drugs; Reagan responded: 'Just say no.'...The phrase proliferated in the popular culture of the 1980s, and was eventually adopted as the name of club organizations and school anti-drug programs. Reagan became actively involved by traveling more than 250,000 miles (400,000 km) throughout the United States and several nations, visiting drug abuse prevention programs and drug rehabilitation centers.... In 1985, Reagan expanded the campaign to an international level by inviting the First Ladies of various nations to the White House for a conference on drug abuse. On October 27, 1986, President [Ronald] Reagan signed a drug enforcement bill into law, which granted $1.7 billion in funding to fight the perceived crisis and ensured a mandatory minimum penalty for drug offenses."[115] Unfortunately, intolerant, anti-drug ads were strikingly popular.[116]

First Lady Reagan's contribution in furtherance of intolerance, well-intended as it surely was, helped shape negative, counterproductive public opinion regarding drugs. That intolerant public opinion served to take parents from their children en masse, destroyed families, their economic stability and child-rearing opportunities. In the process, kids were immeasurably harmed, as drug-war mass incarceration became a drug-prohibition collateral crisis.

---

[115] *Wikipedia*, s.v. "Just Say No," https://en.m.wikipedia.org/wiki/Just_Say_No, emphasis added.

[116] Raychelle C. Lohmann, "Top Five Most Popular Anti-Drug Ads of All Time," *American Addiction Centers*, updated November 4, 2019, https://rehabs.com/pro-talk/top-five-most-powerful-anti-drug-ads-of-all-time/, accessed September 13, 2021.

America's Drug War "Mass Incarceration" Superlative

Eventually, drug intolerance transformed America from "the Land of the Free" into "the Prison Capital of the World."[117] As a result of drug-prohibition bloom, the U.S. earned discredit for attaining the highest per capita prison rate in the world[118] and the largest aggregate prison population in the world, a population approaching 2.3 million people.[119]

The War on Drugs had a huge impact on the explosion in America's prison population. "The state and federal prison population grew from 218,466 in 1974 to 1,508,636 in 2014, which is a nearly 600 percent increase. For comparison, the overall United States population had increased just 51 percent since 1974. The state and federal prison population remained fairly stable through the early 1970s, *until the war on drugs began.* Since then, it has increased sharply every year, particularly when Reagan expanded the policy effort in the 1980s, until about 2010."[120]

Further quantifying runaway drug-war incarceration in America, **Fareed Zakaria** wrote that "This wide gap between the U.S. and the rest of the world is relatively recent. In 1980 the U.S.'s prison population was about 150 per 100,000 adults. It has more than quadrupled since then. So something has happened in the past 30 years to push millions of Americans into prison. That something, of course, is the war on drugs. Drug convictions went from 15 inmates per 100,000 adults in 1980 to 148 in 1996, an almost tenfold increase. More than half of America's federal inmates today are in prison on drug convictions. In 2009 alone, 1.66 million Americans were arrested

---

[117] Pamela Engel, "Watch How Quickly The War On Drugs Changed America's Prison Population," *Business Insider,* Apr 23, 2014, https://www.businessinsider.com/how-the-war-on-drugs-changed-americas-prison-population-2014-4.

[118] "Countries with the largest number of prisoners per 100,000 of the national population," *Statista,* June 2, 2021, accessed August 24, 2021, https://www.statista.com/statistics/262962/countries-with-the-most-prisoners-per-100-000-inhabitants/.

[119] Wendy Sawyer and Peter Wagner, "Mass Incarceration: The Whole Pie 2020," *Prison Policy Initiative,* March 24, 2020, https://www.prisonpolicy.org/reports/pie2020.html.

[120] Lauren Carroll, "How the war on drugs affected incarceration rates," *The Poynter Institute, Politifact,* July 10, 2016, emphasis added, https://www.politifact.com/factchecks/2016/jul/10/cory-booker/how-war-drugs-affected-incarceration-rates/, accessed August 24, 2021.

on drug charges, more than were arrested on assault or larceny charges. And 4 of 5 of those arrests were simply for possession."[121]

America's Discriminatory Mass Incarceration

Of course, America's mass incarceration came with a familiar racial bias that disproportionately punished Blacks, prompting a carefully researched academic indictment of the War on Drugs, written by Michelle Alexander, *The New Jim Crow: Mass Incarceration in the Age of Colorblindness.*[122] With the election of President Barack Obama, a Black man, Michelle Alexander held hope for "an extraordinary opportunity for those seeking to end the system of mass incarceration in America."[123] "But before we kick back, relax, and wait for racial justice to trickle down, consider this: Obama chose Joe Biden, one of the Senate's most strident drug warriors, as his vice president. The man he picked to serve as his chief of staff in the White House, **Rahm Emanuel**, was a major proponent of the expansion of the drug war.... And the man he tapped to lead the U.S. Department of Justice — the agency that launched and continues to oversee the federal war on drugs — [**Eric Holder**] is an African-American former U.S. Attorney for the District of Columbia who sought to ratchet up the drug war in Washington D.C...."[124]

How will President Biden Answer the Big Question?

Senator Joe Biden, of course, is now President Joe Biden, and the verdict is still out on whether he has recovered from his drug-war weakness and proclivity. How will he answer "The Big Question" posed by this book in Chapter 2? Prognostication is worrisome because he is still stuck on even the federal legalization of marijuana sixteenth months, as of this writing, into the Biden Administration. The boom in big city violent crime[125] — directly or indirectly aggravated, certainly, by America's interrelated drug and gun policies — necessitates that the president reverse course and lead us away from

121 Fareed Zakaria, "Incarceration Nation: The war on drugs has succeeded only in putting millions of Americans in jail," *Time*, April 2, 2012, http://content.time.com/time/magazine/article/0,9171,2109777,00.html, accessed August 24, 2021.

122 Michelle Alexander, *The New Jim Crow: Mass Incarceration in the Age of Colorblindness,* New York: (The New Press, 2010).

123 Ibid., at p. 238.

124 Ibid., at p. 239.

125 Emma Tucker and Peter Nickeas, "The US saw significant crime rise across major cities in 2020. And it's not letting up," *CNN*, April 3, 2021, https://www.cnn.com/2021/04/03/us/us-crime-rate-rise-2020/index.html.

America's War on Drugs, a war where "We are the warriors and we are the vanquished; we are the villain and the victim."[126]

Will President Biden take the easy way out by replicating ineffective strategies that "get tough on crime," like President Bill Clinton's hiring a 100,000 more police officers, talking more gun control and lining expressways with surveillance cameras and topping telephone poles with ShotSpotters,[127] or will President Biden face America's longest war head-on, as courageously as he did America's twenty-year-old Afghanistan War, and end it?

President Biden must discover that to "Stop the Killing," we *must* "End the Drug War."

Will President Biden realize we must resolve to remove the *reason* people are shooting one another; the *reason* they have lost their tolerance, patience, understanding, and empathy of and for one another; the *reason* individuals have lost their moral compass, bearings and self-discipline?

In 1991, as chairman of the Senate Judiciary Committee, Sen. Joseph Biden (D-Del.) "blamed 'the three Ds' — drugs, deadly weapons and demographics — [for the escalation in murder totals]."[128] For President Biden to rightly decide the big drug-war question — that I claim is essential to stop the violence — he must reverse field from his past support of drug-prohibition policies, put aside his intuitive feelings, his early presidential hesitancy to confront drug-war thinking, and challenge prevailing public opinion regarding all drugs.

---

[126] James E. Gierach, "U.S. drug civil war," *Chicago Defender*, May 7, 1994, https://jamesgierach.tumblr.com/post/683958123276484608.

[127] *Yahoo Finance*, ShotSpotters share price, https://finance.yahoo.com/quote/SSTI/,

accessed October 4, 2021, and "OIG Finds That ShotSpotter Alerts Rarely Lead Police to Evidence of a Gun-Related Crime and that Presence of Technology Changes Police Behavior," Press Release, *City of Chicago, Office of Inspector General*, August 24, 2021, https://igchicago.org/2021/08/24/oig-finds-that-shotspotter-alerts-rarely-lead-to-evidence-of-a-gun-related-crime-and-that-presence-of-the-technology-changes-police-behavior/.

[128] "New, deadly record," editorial, *Southtown Economist*, August 6, 1991. Gierach notebooks, p. 593, a personal collection 1,529 pages of drug war stories from 1989 to 1992.

Federal Legalization of Marijuana

President Biden need not lead public opinion regarding the legalization of marijuana, because public opinion has already reformed itself. A large majority of Americans already favor the outright legalization of marijuana.[129] President Biden should immediately bring federal marijuana law into tune with existing American public opinion. But for President Biden's drug-war track record and the large serving of drug-war humble pie he must eat, legalizing marijuana federally should be an easy task for him. He should start eating now, today. Get it done.

President Biden: Lead Public Opinion Against All Drug Prohibition Policies

President Joe Biden must become another *Profile in Courage*. Not so easy for President Biden when it comes to drug policy but critical to the success of his presidency, and critical to the dramatic and comprehensive improvement of American public health, safety and welfare. He must lead the reformation of public opinion regarding all other controlled substances, rejecting failed drug prohibition, one drug substance after another, and another, until not one commonly used "illicit drug" is prohibited. Please note — Being anti-drug prohibition is not the equivalent of being pro-drug use. Just the opposite is true. See the discussion of how drug prohibition accomplishes the exact opposite of what it was intended to do, Chapters 4, 5 and 6. And for the record, as a former drug prosecutor and naturalist, I adamantly oppose recreational drug use (except those I use, which by happenstance are currently legal). Last note — as this chapter points out and as President John F. Kennedy said: "Tolerance implies no lack of commitment to one's own beliefs. Rather it condemns the oppression or persecution of others."

American public opinion is not yet overwhelmingly against the War on Drugs. It needs to be. "[In a poll released June 9, 2021 by the Drug Policy Alliance (DPA) and the American Civil Liberties Union (ACLU)], 83 percent of respondents believe the

---

[129] Ted Van Green, "Americans overwhelmingly say marijuana should be legal for recreational or medical use," *Pew Research Center*, April 16, 2021, https://www.pewresearch.org/fact-tank/2021/04/16/americans-overwhelmingly-say-marijuana-should-be-legal-for-recreational-or-medical-use/.

drug war to be a massive failure."[130] One of President Biden's paramount responsibilities as president is to lead that solid, anti-drug war public opinion and nurture it into full bloom tolerance and drug legalization. Why? As this book weightily demonstrates, drug prohibition is the common denominator to many American crises — not only with drugs, crime and corruption, but also at least a dozen other American crises, many of them global crises, as argued in Chapters 4, 5, 6, 8, 9 and 10 below.

How did America get so far off track and become so radically anti-drug, pro-intolerance and punitive? First Lady Nancy Reagan did not accomplish that feat alone. She had help. Help came from respected sources like the Partnership for a Drug-Free America, D.A.R.E., the Ad Council, the prison industry, law enforcement and even the United Nations.

The Partnership for a Drug-Free America

The Partnership for a Drug-Free America (PDFA) greatly helped arouse anti-drug disdain. Founded in 1985–the well-intended, New York City-based non-profit organization was initially called "the Partnership for a Drug-Free America," then "Partnership to End Addiction,"[131] and now "The Partnership for Drug-Free Kids." The partnership is perhaps best known for its iconic, if now comical, TV-ad called, "This Is Your Brain on Drugs."[132] The ad enjoyed its heyday, but its audacity prompted an excellent rebuttal ad produced by the Drug Policy Alliance.[133]

The Partnership for a Drug-Free America was the brainchild of advertising executives. "In the mid-1980s, a small group of advertising professionals... formed the Media-Advertising Partnership for a Drug-Free America, a concept for a non-profit organization born from the American Association of Advertising Agencies (AAAA). The idea was to harness the power of the media to turn the tide on teen drug abuse. This goal was implemented by compelling research-based consumer advertising. At the time the Partnership was created, the nation was in the throes of the crack cocaine epidemic. The Partnership focused its efforts to help reduce demand for those drugs through

---

[130] Alex Norcia, "Poll Shows Huge Public Opposition to 'War on Drugs,' After 50 Years," *Filter*, June 9, 2021, https://filtermag.org/war-on-drugs-poll/.

[131] *Wikipedia*, s.v. "Partnership to End Addiction," https://en.m.wikipedia.org/wiki/Partnership_to_End_ Addiction. Accessed March 18, 2023.

[132] "Your brain on drugs," video, *YouTube*, https://youtu.be/GOnENVylxPI.

[133] Rebuttal, "Your brain on drugs," video, *Drug Policy Alliance*, https://twitter.com/drugpolicyorg/ status/1428540073528659974?s=21, August 19, 2021.

public service advertising (PSA) campaigns. The organization first entered the wider public consciousness in 1987, with its "This is Your Brain on Drugs" broadcast and print public service advertisements (PSAs), which used the analogy that if a person's brain is an egg, then using illegal drugs would be like frying it. This advertisement became a hallmark for the organization. The Partnership has won numerous advertising and efficacy awards for its PSA campaigns. Over the past two decades, the public service advertisements have grown to target more illegal drugs like heroin, methamphetamine, ecstasy, marijuana, and others."[134]

The Partnership, more appropriately named "the Partnership for Intolerance," made over 3,000 ads by 2011. Well-intended or not, the Partnership spread a drug sentiment that, judging from drug use results, cooked the goose of many youngsters as its anti-drug advertisements put "Just say no" words on their lips, drug preoccupation on their minds and, too often, harmful drug substances into their bodies.

The Partnership for a Drug-Free America had a second problem — the incongruity of being anti-drug use but silent on tobacco and alcohol use. "Ironically, the intended scope of the [PDFA anti-drug] campaign restricted its reach. Alcohol and tobacco were off limits. The networks would hardly have opened up commercial time for hard-hitting spots on booze, thereby risking ad dollars from beer and wine makers. Memory of the disastrous loss of revenue from cigarette companies in the early 1970s, the result of **John Banzhaf**'s adroit exploitation of the FCC's Fairness Doctrine, was still relatively fresh. And while tobacco ads were now off TV, they still appeared in magazines and newspapers that the PDFA was also asking to carry its advertising."[135]

"This Is Your Brain on Drugs" Short-Circuited

The sleeper advertising principle overlooked by anti-drug forces and the producers of Partnership public service announcements is that an anti-drug commercial is first and foremost a drug commercial. Endless anti-drug advertising brought "DRUGS" to the attention of kids incessantly. From that vantage point, an ad is a "drug ad" whether it aims to promote drug abstinence or drug use. Over the past thirty years, I have accumulated a set of drug policy axioms. One of those axioms pertains to PSAs such as

---

134 *Academic Dictionaries and Encyclopedias*, s.v. "Partnership for a Drug-Free America," https://en-academic.com/dic.nsf/enwiki/1125431, emphasis added, accessed March 16, 2023.

135 Joseph Moreau, "I Learned it by Watching YOU!" The Partnership for a Drug-Free America and the Attack on 'Responsible Use' Education in the 1980s," *Journal of Social History Advance Access*, February 23, 2016, https://academic.oup.com/jsh/article-abstract/49/3/710/2412940, accessed August 24, 2021.

those produced by the Partnership for a Drug-Free America, to wit: "An anti-drug ad is first and foremost a drug ad."[136] In my view, such an ad unproductively brings kids attention repetitively to drugs. And I question whether that is where we want to direct it, so often.

Peter Kozodoy, an advertising professional, wrote an article, entitled, "This Is Your Brain On Drugs,"[137] in which he commented on an article discussing the impact of reduced spending on the ad, "Your Brain on Drugs." The article Kozodoy was commenting on was called, "Whatever Happened to the Ad War on Drugs: After Peaking at a Rate of $1M in Media Time a Day in Late 80s, Anti-Drug Campaign Airtime Has Been on Steady Decline."[138] Kozodoy said: "Let's jump ahead for a moment to the conclusion: In 2003, an average 70% of high school students saw anti-drug ads while overall use was around 32%, according to The Future Study out of the University of Michigan. In 2013, an average 28% of high school students saw anti-drug ads, while about 32% of the population used marijuana.

"Conclusion: Ads don't work on drug use. Or do they?

"Well, it depends on whom you ask. Some independent studies show great declines in middle and high school usage during heavy ad spending, but the majority of studies are inconclusive. As advertisers, there are other factors we must consider when it comes to analyzing the effectiveness of advertising on drug use. One factor hinges on the advertising tenet of frequency: put something into the consumer's mind enough times, and that consumer will take interest.

"Today's marijuana debates are a perfect example – now that it's in the news and top-of-mind for consumers, we are seeing an uptick in consumption."

"Drugogenic" Anti-Drug Advertising

In my mind, the anti-drug advertising push has been "drugogenic;" it pushed and pulled kiddie drug use to new heights. Over the past four years, just under half of high-

---

[136] "Gierach Drug Policy Axioms," Axiom No. 7, https://jamesgierach.tumblr.com/post/ 6483569517350 91200/gierach-drug-policy-axioms. See Appendix hereto.

[137] Kozodoy, commenting on "Your brain on drugs," https://health.gem-advertising.com/blog/this-is-your-brain-on-drugs.

[138] E.J. Schultz, *Adage,* March 24, 2014, https://adage.com/article/news/happened-ad-war-drugs/292262, accessed August 24, 2021.

school seniors (46.6 to 48.9 percent) had used illicit drugs during their lifetime.[139] It was counterproductive, especially when delivered by a D.A.R.E police officer in uniform,[140] rather than by a school health teacher, who before the days of D.A.R.E. might have mentioned without much fanfare: "Don't use airplane glue in a small room or without plenty of ventilation, because it can cause brain damage and central nervous system problems; or since alcohol is dangerous and intoxicating, if you're going to try it, wait until you are of age; or cleaning agents under the cupboard are for cleaning." Or the teacher may have simply repeated the tried-and-true lesson taught mostly by parents, "Don't do it," or its recidivist corollary rule, "Don't ever do that again!"

Another anti-drug prevention strategy for kids of dubious value was Random Student Drug Testing (RSDT). Want to play football or volleyball? Urinate in this cup.[141] Another strategy to save our kids is a commercially available kit to test your child's hair clippings for drugs. It works the same in business and industry where human relations departments can search for distrustful, drug-using employees.[142]

Solutions Crafted In "The Drug-Prohibition Sandbox"

The problem with all these drug-prevention and drug-education initiatives and solutions are that they were all crafted in "the drug-prohibition sandbox." Leaders and virtue-o-sos started with drug prohibition as the model of good parenting, good teaching, and good preaching, and then moved on to design educational and prevention programs they hoped could undo the harm they saw, blindly and deafly, caused by loudly beating drug-prohibition drums.

Take glue-sniffing. It can unquestionably cause very serious, permanent neurological and central nervous system harm. Such a discovery was made and publicized in 1959 in the Sunday *Denver Post*, an isolated story about kids innocently exposed to airplane glue that prompted repetition and warnings across the country. Edward M.

[139] "Monitoring the Future Study: Trends in Prevalence of Various Drugs," *National Institute on Drug Abuse, Advancing Addiction Science,* https://www.drugabuse.gov/drug-topics/trends-statistics/monitoring-future/monitoring-future-study-trends-in-prevalence-various-drugs.

[140] Natalie Wolchover, "Was D.A.R.E. Effective?" *Future US, Inc., Life Science,* March 27, 2012, https://www.livescience.com/33795-effective.html.

[141] "Helpful or Harmful," *MST Services,* May 1, 2019, https://info.mstservices.com/blog/student-drug-testing-helpful-harmful.

[142] "Hair Testing," US Drug Test Centers, https://www.usdrugtestcenters.com/hair-follicle-drug-testing.html?gclid=CjwKCAiA55mPBhBOEiwANmzoQsqT2B1LsN8_e4G7hO-O6n0rczuEZ6sVC8U6NE1PbZky2qu-caAUURoC41UQAvD_BwE, accessed January 18, 2022.

Brecher wrote a chapter[143] called, "How to Launch a Nationwide Drug Menace." Soon promulgation of the story, publicized for the purpose of sharing a warning to protect kids, had created a new attractive nuisance for kids, another something to "Don't Do." But instead of preventing drug use, "These warnings [regarding the hazards associated with glue-sniffing]... seemed to be a highly effective lure."[144]

Or take hair-testing. No need to trust your child regarding suspected drug use. Just snip a lock of their hair for a sample to test. Preferably, do it while they are sleeping so they do not know you don't trust them. Drug test your kid's hair today, so you can sleep well tonight, knowing — "Did he, or didn't he, do drugs?" Test kits are widely available[145], but one big risk is a false positive and another is the loss of a trusting parent-child relationship.

The Ad Council Anti-Drug Ad

The Ad Council also took a stab at anti-drug advertising with its production of "Users Are Losers, 1987."[146] It was more pleasant to watch than seeing your brain fry in an egg pan — good music and children singing happily (mostly children too young to use drugs).

Who sides with the Ad Council, one might wonder? Only Who's Who in corporate America. And the power of the Ad Council is difficult to overestimate. "The Ad Council partners with advertising agencies which work pro bono to create the public service advertisements on behalf of their campaigns. The organization accepts requests from sponsor institutions for advertising campaigns that focus on particular social issues. To qualify, an issue must be non-partisan (though not necessarily unbiased) and have national relevance. The Ad Council distributes the advertisements to a network of 33,000 media outlets — including broadcast, print, outdoor (i.e., billboards, bus stops), and Internet — which run the ads in donated time and space. Media outlets

---

[143] Edward M. Brecher, *Licit and Illicit Drugs: Consumers Union Report* (Boston, Little, Brown and Co., 1972), chapter 44.

[144] Ibid., p. 327.

[145] American Screening Corporation, "Drug Test Hair," https://www.americanscreeningcorp.com/pc_combined_results.asp?pc_id=9756473BD01F4F01BFA64DBABFC7FF5D&gclid=CjwKCAjw4KyJBhAbE iwAaAQbE0yD6AXkZ76JPw5G0UUQsylCMrrtX6bEOTOzsho352ePiG0N2cDymBoCJA0QAvD_BwE, accessed January 18, 2022.

[146] "Crime Prevention, 1979-Present," including video, ANA Educational Foundation (AEF) https://aef.com/classroom-resources/social-responsibility/ad-council-campaigns-made-difference/crime-prevention/. Accessed March 18, 2023.

donate approximately $1.8 billion to Ad Council campaigns annually. If paid for, this amount would make the Ad Council one of the largest advertisers in the country."[147]

My hope is at some point the Ad Council, the Partnership for a Drug-Free World, along with all thinking people in the world, will acknowledge the unintended consequences of its well-intended drug PSAs and help repair public thinking concerning harmful drug prohibition.

Who else helped sell drug intolerance in America and around the world?

> *"The highest result of education is tolerance."*
>
> — Author Helen Keller

D.A.R.E. — "The School for Drugs"

Before the creation of D.A.R.E. in 1983, many kids never saw what heroin looked like, never saw a needle outside of a medical setting, never smelled the pungent odor of burning marijuana, and likely never heard the word "pungent" until their friendly D.A.R.E.-officer hit the school system, classroom by classroom, school year after school year. The mistake known as "Drug Abuse Resistance Education" (D.A.R.E.)" was made on day one of its founding and continues to this day. Like so many other anti-drug organizations powered by drug-intolerant insistence, D.A.R.E. goals sound good: "D.A.R.E. envisions a world in which students everywhere are empowered to respect others and choose to lead lives free from violence, substance use, and other dangerous behaviors."[148] Unfortunately, too often, the D.A.R.E.-outcome is an intolerant, drug-full, drug-using and violent society that is unsafe for kids and adults.

I have read about D.A.R.E. trying to understand the thinking behind it. Here is one description of its work written by two critical writers: "D.A.R.E. asks uniformed police officers to go into schools to warn students about the dangers of drug use and underscore the pluses of a drug-free way of life. In most cases, the officers do so once a week, typically for 45 to 60 minutes, for several months. D.A.R.E. is immensely popular; according to the program Web site, it has been put in place in 75 percent of

---

[147] *Wikipedia*, s.v. "Ad Council," https://en.m.wikipedia.org/wiki/Ad_Council, accessed March 17, 2023.

[148] D.A.R.E., https://dare.org/, accessed January 18, 2022.

U.S. school districts and 43 countries. D.A.R.E. bumper stickers, D.A.R.E. T-shirts, and police cars emblazoned with the word D.A.R.E. are familiar fixtures in many U.S. communities."[149]

As Lilienfeld and Arkowitz suggest, not only doesn't D.A.R.E. help kids regarding drug use, it may actually have a "boomerang effect" on kids regarding "milder drugs," the world's greatest killers, alcohol and tobacco. They reported: "In a 2002 review psychologist **Chudley Werch**, now president of PreventionPLUSWellness in Jacksonville, Fla., and health educator Deborah Owen of the University of North Florida reported a slight tendency for teens who went through D.A.R.E. to be more likely to drink and smoke than adolescents not exposed to the program. Small negative effects for D.A.R.E.-like programs on drinking and smoking were also reported in a 2009 study by public health professor **Zili Sloboda** of the University of Akron and her colleagues. The reasons for these potential boomerang effects are unclear. Yet by emphasizing the hazards of severe drug abuse, D.A.R.E. may inadvertently convey the impression that alcohol and tobacco are innocuous by comparison."[150]

In 2014, I drafted a comprehensive, proposed amendment of UN drug-control treaties for world leaders on behalf of myself and LEAP. My draft of the Gierach/LEAP "Proposed Amendment of United Nations Drug Treaties — 2014,"[151] recognized the potential harm that could be caused by these "milder drugs" — alcohol and tobacco — arguably the most harmful of mind-altering substances. This addition could enable the UN to better categorize and rank the most harmful drugs, hopefully, better regulating and controlling such substances without confusion or exclusion of the most dangerous and most harmful substances. Neither of these drugs is presently within the scope of drug substances controlled by UN treaty.

---

[149] Scott O. Lilienfeld and Hal Arkowitz, "Why 'Just Say No' Doesn't Work, originally published with the title "Just Say No?" in SA Mind 25, 1, 70-71 (January 2014), doi:10.1038/scientificamericanmind0114-70, and republished by *Scientific American Mind*, January 1, 2014, https://www.scientificamerican.com/article/why-just-say-no-doesnt-work/, accessed January 18, 2022.

[150] Ibid., emphasis added.

[151] Gierach/LEAP, "Proposed Amendment of United Nations Drug Treaties — 2014, https://www.unodc.org/documents/ungass2016/Contributions/Civil/Law_Enforcement_Against_Prohibition/ LEAP_UN_Treaty_Amendment_2.26.1421-1.pdf, English; https://www.unodc.org/documents/ungass2016// Contributions/Civil/Law_Enforcement_Against_Prohibition/FINAL-3-Spanish_LEAP-Treaty-Amendment_5.27.14-1.pdf, Spanish.

My draft of the Preamble to the Gierach/LEAP "Proposed Amendment of United Nations Drug Treaties — 2014," and the entire Proposed Amendment, was unanimously adopted by the LEAP Board of Directors. The Preamble recognized the harmful potential of alcohol and tobacco with these added preamble convention words:

"*Mindful* that no United Nations treaty regulates or controls *alcohol* or *tobacco* despite the commonality of use of these substances and the fact that 'Alcohol has recently been identified as one of the world's top ten health risks, accounting for about the same amount of global disease as tobacco.... [and] the fact that global alcohol consumption has increased in recent decades, with most or all of the increase occurring in developing countries,' and

"*Concerned* that 'Alcohol-related death and disability account for even greater costs to life and longevity than those caused by tobacco use, according to the global burden of disease study sponsored by the World Health Organization (WHO) and the World Bank,' and aware that 'net deaths from alcohol totaled more than three-quarters of a million in 1990,' and

"*Impressed* by the realistic approach, regulatory scope, dominant national assignment of responsibility, and spirit of international cooperation reflected in the WHO Framework Convention on Tobacco Control (FCTC), 2003, and Protocol to Eliminate Illicit Trade in Tobacco Products, 2013, and

"*Recognizing* that the WHO Framework Convention on Tobacco Control is a landmark for the future of global public health and has major implications for world health goals,..." [152]

D.A.R.E. did not champion inclusion of alcohol or tobacco in amended UN drug control conventions. Eventually, the D.A.R.E. program expanded from Los Angeles, across America, and into forty-three other countries.[153] Rather than helping with the problem of youthful drug use, in my opinion, D.AR.E. contributed to it. Since 1983, many D.A.R.E. students — excluding those who overdosed and died on drugs and those killed in street gun violence triggered by drug war — help make up a significant share of the estimated 269 million drug users around the world in 2018.[154]

---

[152] Ibid.

[153] Landmark recovery Staff, "Why the DARE program Failed," May 18, 2020, *Landmark Recovery*, https://landmarkrecovery.com/why-the-dare-program-failed/, accessed August 30, 2021.

[154] John Elflein, "Global drug use - Statistics & Facts," *Statista*, April 20, 2021, https://www.statista.com/topics/7786/global-drug-use/, accessed January 18, 2022.

United Nations Drug Intolerance:
2009 Delusions of A "Drug-Free" World

While D.A.R.E., the Ad Council, and the Partnership for a Drug-Free America spread drug intolerance across America, the UN spread drug intolerance globally. It did so in March 2009 in Vienna, Austria, during the High-Level Segment of the United Nations Commission on Narcotic Drugs (CND), promoting an intolerant society "free of drug abuse." The CND adopted a Political Declaration and Plan of Action on International Cooperation towards an Integrated and Balanced Strategy to Counter the World Drug Problem[155] (hereinafter "the 2009 Political Declaration & Plan of Action"). The Political Declaration portion of the document included the true statement that "Drug trafficking and abuse pose a major threat to the health, dignity and hopes of millions of people and their families and lead to the loss of human lives." But the text ignored the helping hand played by drug prohibition in drug-trafficking, as it expressed determination "to tackle the world drug problem and to actively promote a society free of drug abuse in order to ensure that all people can live in health, dignity and peace, with security and prosperity..."[156]

UN drug-free mythology and the CND 2009 Plan of Action continued to promote the idea of a drug-free world by use of a 1989 UN Drug Control Program poster that pictured a young girl alongside an unrealistic message: "A Drug-Free World — We Can Do It." The Plan of Action laid out in thirty-two pages how drug demand and drug supply were going to be harnessed.[157] The magnitude of this delusional wishing was manifested ten years later when substance production, availability, use and drug abuse was accounted for in the Shadow Report prepared by the International Drug Policy Consortium (IDPC) in 2019.[158] Part Two of that report evaluated "progress made in addressing the 'world drug problem' since the adoption of the 2009 Political Declaration and Plan of Action." (Pages 25-88) Suffice it to say, the world deserves an "F" grade for the results of its efforts. Opium poppy cultivation was up 125%, coca

---

[155] "Political Declaration and Plan of Action On International Cooperation Towards An Integrated and Balanced Strategy To Counter The World Drug Problem," UNODC, https://www.unodc.org/documents/ commissions/ CND/CND_Sessions/CND_52/Political-Declaration2009_V0984963_E.pdf.

[156] Ibid., p. 7, emphasis added.

[157] Ibid., pp. 27-49.

[158] "Taking stock: A decade of drug policy - A civil society shadow report," 2019 Ministerial Segment, https://idpc.net/publications/2018/10/taking-stock-a-decade-of-drug-policy-a-civil-society-shadow-report. Date accessed?

bush production was up 30%,[159] 803 new synthetic drug concoctions were invented,[160] deaths directly associated with drug use were up 60%,[161] less than 1% of the half of drug-trafficking revenues funneled into money laundering was seized (the whole of those revenues estimated to be $426-652 USD Billion),[162] and illicit demand for ecstasy, cannabis and opioids was up by 33%, 17% and 16%, respectively.[163]

The 2009 Declaration and Plan continued to march society down the wrong, well-worn road — the 1961 Single Convention International Highway.

The truth is that mind-altering substances are forever intertwined with the existence of mankind — past, present and future. Attempts to "actively promote a society free of drug abuse" and use is a delusional goal. Either drugs are regulated by law and license, or drugs are uncontrolled by lawlessness and licentiousness, exacerbating drug use and abuse. Delegating drug control to transnational criminal organizations is the result of unrealistic expectations of the power and ability of government to control the appetite of mankind regarding drugs. And the attempted control of the drug appetite of mankind is the goal of the CND, and UN drug-control treaties.

Compare and contrast these statements regarding the power of government to regulate drug supply and drug demand. Chicago commodities broker **Richard J. Dennis** wrote: "Less self-destruction by drug users just is not within the ability of law enforcement to bring about, unless we're willing to become a drug-free society at the cost of not being a free country."[164] In contrast, Dr. Lochan Naidoo, a South African physician and then-president of the International Narcotics Control Board (INCB) wrote: "One of the most fundamental principles underpinning the international drug control framework, enshrined in both the 1961 Convention and in the Convention on Psychotropic Substances of 1971, is the limitation of use of narcotic drugs and psychotropic substances to medical and scientific purposes. This legal obligation is absolute

---

[159] Ibid., p. 26.

[160] Ibid., p. 27.

[161] Ibid., p. 27.

[162] Ibid., p. 27.

[163] Ibid., p. 27.

[164] Richard J. Dennis, "The Ethics and Economics of Legalization," *New Frontiers in Drug Policy* (Washington D.C.: The Drug Policy Foundation, 1991), p. 392-93.

and leaves no room for interpretation."[165] And finally, U.S. President Abraham Lincoln explained: "Prohibition will work great injury to the cause of temperance. It is a species of intemperance within itself, for it goes beyond the bounds of reason in that it attempts to control a man's appetite by legislation, and makes a crime out of things that are not crimes. A Prohibition law strikes a blow at the very principles upon which our government was founded."[166]

While elimination of drug abuse is an admirable wish for society, embraced by the 2009 Political Declaration and Plan of Action, the reality of life was better recognized in the Foreword to that document, as expressed by **Antonio Maria Costa**, the UN Under-Secretary-General and UNODC Executive Director: "Every year world markets are still supplied with about *1,000 tons of heroin* (equivalent), another *1,000 tons of cocaine* and untold volumes of marijuana, cannabis resin and synthetic drugs. So there is still much more to be done."[167]

Like the intolerant, drug-free objective of the Partnership for a Drug-Free America, the Political Declaration & Plan Action of the Commission on Narcotic Drugs is more than unrealistic, it is delusional. For so long as Earth is occupied by people, Earth will be flush with drugs used for recreational purposes. Political declarations and plans of action instituted by international bodies had best accept that reality and, more realistically, make plans that better control and regulate drugs. Drug users and abusers are not the enemy, and intolerance that outlaws, criminalizes, marginalizes and punishes hundreds of millions of people for "Doin' what comes naturally"[168] is a big mistake.

As presently waged, the delusional World War on Drugs is plagued by The Three Pillars of Drug Prohibition: More Drugs, More Crime and More Corruption. In other words, the World War on Drugs is "drugogenic," criminogenic and "corruptogenic."

165 Lochan Naidoo, Foreword to Report of the International Narcotics Control Board for 2014, March 3, 2015, E/INCB/2014/1, https://www.incb.org/documents/Publications/AnnualReports/AR2014/English/AR_2014.pdf, p. iii, accessed August 22, 2021, emphasis added.

166 Schaffer Library of Drug Policy, https://www.druglibrary.org/schaffer/lincoln.htm

167 "Statement of Under-Secretary-General and UNODC Executive Director Antonio Maria Costa...," Commission on Narcotic Drugs, 52nd Session, 2009, p. 1, https://www.unodc.org/documents/commissions/CND/CND_Sessions/CND_52/Political-Declaration2009_V0984963_E.pdf.

168 Song from the musical, *Annie Get Your Gun*, https://youtu.be/Og_hAsXXDIA.

Part Two
The Counterproductive War on Drugs

Chapter 4 - Drug War Intolerance Means More Drugs

The War on Drugs is *drugogenic*, meaning drug prohibition policy puts more drugs uncontrolled and unregulated, everywhere. Ironically, the harder drug prohibition laws are pushed, the stronger, more plentiful and troublesome prohibited drugs become. (Gierach's Drug Policy Axioms Nos. 2 and 6, respectively)[169] Unrealistically, we seize drugs by the ton and prosecute drug offenses by the gram.

Irrationally, law enforcement and the public view news of big drug seizures as evidence of the success of drug-prohibition policy when more thoughtfully we must recognize that "Large drug seizures are evidence of drug-war failure, not success." The larger the drug seizure, the greater the evidence of drug policy failure.[170]

The intrinsic "drugogenic" nature of drug prohibition policies is best evidenced by the great number and variety of its failures, to wit: drug seizures by the ton, the crack-cocaine epidemic, the invention of 803 new psychoactive substances and analogues over the past decade, the popularity, potency and price of marijuana, the escalation of heroin purity, and the fentanyl-heroin-opioid overdose phenomenon.

Drug Seizures by The Ton

Illicit drug ubiquity has become a drug-war norm, and huge drug busts have become a law-enforcement expectancy. So much so, it takes a drug bust measured by the ton to make much news. Nonsensically, again, *we seize drugs by the ton and prosecute drug offenses by the gram.* Endless instances of drug seizures and busts by the ton are telling: "18 Biggest Drug Busts In U.S. History," included a report of the October 2020 seizure of 2,200 pounds of meth, a synthetic "heroin drug upper," and 900 pounds of

---

169 https://jamesgierach.tumblr.com/post/671961048125980672/gierach-drug-policy-axioms.

170 Gierach, James E., Trinity Christian College PowerPoint presentation, April 25, 2014, Slide No. 6, https://www.dropbox.com/s/nekmom3dpzqb2p5/Trinity%20Christian%20College_4.25.12.ppt?dl=0.

cocaine and 13 pounds of heroin.[171] The ton of meth seized in 2020 is reminiscent of the 15-ton meth seizure in Mexico in 2012 during my attendance at an anti-drug and anti-violence conference. I attended a conference in Mexico City as a speaker for Law Enforcement Against Prohibition (LEAP), the event sponsored by **México Unido Contra la Delincuencia** (MUCD). During the conference, Mexican authorities seized 15 tons of meth in a single bust in Guadalajara, amounting to thirteen million doses and valued at $14 billion.[172]

In a third huge meth seizure, this one in June 2020, law enforcement authorities seized 18 tons of meth in the northern hills of Myanmar on the Myanmar-China border, mostly in the form of tiny pink pills, nearly 200 million of them stuffed into bulging sacks. There was so much meth to display, authorities needed a pasture the size of a football field to display their catch. *The World*, a public radio program, broadcast the story, and author Patrick Winn rhetorically questioned, "How could such drug factories exist without discovery?" The answer: "Myanmar's government has known about the labs [in their country] for years. The same goes for the United States' Drug Enforcement Agency (DEA) and Chinese intelligence. Even *The World* knew it was there, writing in 2015 that the area contains 'a number of heroin and meth refineries.'"[173]

Repetitive gigantic drug busts reasonably suggest that the world is overrun with illicit drugs, a fact evidencing *the failure and futility* of the World War on Drugs. Individual drug-war busts, headlined from high-intensity drug spots around the world, tell the sad story of a world where "Drugs-R-Us." For example, a Jacksonville, Florida television station, *News4Jax,* reported an Associated Press story, June 8, 2021, dubbed "Operation Trojan Shield," where 800 people were arrested and 32 tons of drugs, including cocaine, cannabis, amphetamines and methamphetamines, were seized in a

---

[171] Ty Haqqi, *Insider Monkey*, October 17, 2020, https://www.yahoo.com/now/18-biggest-drug-busts-u-032831451.html, accessed September 2, 2021.

[172] Damien Cave, "Mexico Seizes Record Amount of Methamphetamine," *The New York Times*, February 9, 2012, https://www.nytimes.com/2012/02/10/world/americas/mexico-seizes-15-tons-of-methamphetamine.html?referringSource=articleShare, accessed September 2, 2021.

[173] Patrick Winn, "A massive Asian drug bust has stirred a fentanyl mystery," *The World*, June 10, 2020, https://www.pri.org/stories/2020-06-10/massive-asian-drug-bust-has-stirred-fentanyl-mystery, accessed September 2, 2021.

global sting operation.[174] *Newsweek* and news organizations around the world carried the ANON-Internet App, Operation Trojan Shield story.[175]

Reuters reported "12 Tons of Cocaine Seized in Biggest Drug Bust in Colombia's History," November 9, 2017, republished by *NBC News*[176], but Colombian coca farmers can always cultivate more as evidenced by another big, drug bust story in July 2021, "Costa Rica Seizes 4.3 Tons of Colombian cocaine, 2nd-biggest Bust in its History."[177]

Following another big drug bust in July 2019, it was hypothesized that "The vast quantity [of drugs seized, 39,500 pounds, or 17.9 metric tons of cocaine] may reflect a supply glut. Global cocaine manufacturing surged by a quarter in 2016 to 1,410 tons, according to the World Drug Report 2018. The production boom is centered in Colombia, where cultivation of the coca plant rose 17% to 171,000 hectares in 2017, according to the UN." Humorously, this drug-bust story weighed in at the equivalent of three African bull elephants, perhaps "the elephant(s) in the room," and interestingly the bust brought JPMorgan into the story.[178]

Huge, repetitive drug seizures over time convincingly demonstrate that "Drug War Means More Drugs Not Less."

Development of Crack Cocaine

In 1961, the first year of the UN World War on Drugs and the onset of the 1961 Single Convention folly, crack cocaine did not exist though the coca plant from which

[174] Erik Avanier, "More than 800 arrested, over 32 tons of drugs seized in global sting operation DEA among agencies involved in Operation Trojan Shield, which began by creating message service for crooks," *The Associated Press*, June 9, 2021, republished by News4Jax, https://www.news4jax.com/ news/2021/06/09/more-than-800-arrested-over-32-tons-of-drugs-seized-in-global-sting-operation/, accessed September 2, 2021.

[175] Lauren Giella, "32 Tons of Drugs Seized Across 16 Countries in FBI-Led Sting Operation Against Organized Crime," *Newsweek*, June 8, 2021, https://www.newsweek.com/32-tons-drugs-seized-across-16-countries-fbi-led-sting-operation-against-organized-crime-1598547, accessed September 2, 2021; *Wikipedia, s.v.* "ANON," *https://en.wikipedia.org/wiki/ANOM*, accessed January 19, 2022.

[176] "12 Tons of Cocaine Seized in Biggest Drug Bust in Colombia's History," *NBC News*, https://www.nbcnews.com/news/world/12-tons-cocaine-seized-biggest-drug-bust-colombia-s-history-n819246, accessed September 2, 2021.

[177] "Costa Rica seizes 4.3 tons of Colombian cocaine, 2nd-biggest bust in its history," *Reuters*, July 18, 2021, https://www.reuters.com/world/americas/costa-rica-seizes-43-tons-colombian-cocaine-2nd-biggest-bust-its-history-2021-07-19/, accessed September 2, 2021.

[178] Theron Mohamed, "4 surprising facts about the $1 billion worth of cocaine found on a ship owned by JPMorgan," *Business Insider*, July 11, 2019, https://markets.businessinsider.com/news/stocks/cocaine-ship-jpmorgan-boat-liberian-flag-1-billion-drugs-surprising-2019-7, accessed September 2, 2021.

it was derived preexisted for an eternity. According to an article promulgated by American Addiction Centers (AAC), a nationwide network of leading substance abuse and behavioral treatment facilities, "Crack first appeared in small batches in major cities in 1981. The police didn't recognize this new rock-like material, but chemical analysis showed it was basically cocaine as freebase (rather than as the hydrochloride salt). As the technique spread, though, it gained more adherents. The first large-scale use, and presumably mass production, was observed in 1984 in Los Angeles."[179]

Renowned economist Milton Friedman once observed, "Crack [cocaine] would never have existed if you had not had drug prohibition."[180]

The "freebasing cocaine technique" preceded crack cocaine. "What is commonly referred to as cocaine is actually cocaine hydrochloride. By adding a chemical compound that includes ammonia, it allows a reaction that draws out a more pure form, or base form, of cocaine. Essentially, by a chemical process, the cocaine becomes free from its sodium base. This is where the term 'freebase' comes from. The next step takes a form of ether to dissolve the cocaine. This form of ether is highly combustible and often results in explosions in the labs that create freebase cocaine."[181] The explosive nature of the freebasing process can be avoided by using sodium bicarbonate (baking soda) to remove hydrochloride from cocaine. The end result is crystal rocks that can be smoked in a pipe.[182] **Richard Pryor** would advise, don't try it.[183]

The development of crack cocaine evidenced the fact that drug-prohibition policy encourages drug invention, making new drugs available to consumers.

[179] Editorial staff, "A Complete History of Crack Cocaine," *American Addiction Centers,* updated July 19, 2021, https://rehabs.com/blog/a-complete-history-of-crack-cocaine/, accessed September 1, 2021; see also reviewed by Shirley Hutchinson, "History of Cocaine in America," accessed July 12, 2022, https://riveroaks treatment.com/cocaine-treatment/illegal-history-in-america/.

[180] Ben Duronio, "Crack Would Have Never Existed If You Had Not Had Drug Prohibition," *Insider,* July 31, 2012, https://www.businessinsider.com/milton-friedman-drugs-legal-2012-7, accessed August 22, 2021.

[181] "What Is Freebasing?" *Vertava Health,* https://vertavahealth.com/blog/what-is-freebasing/, accessed September 1, 2021.

[182] Adrienne Santos-Longhurst, "Everything You Need to Know About Freebasing," *Healthline,* February 20, 2020, https://www.healthline.com/health/freebasing.

[183] Dana Rose Falcone, "Richard Pryor's Widow Jennifer Lee Calls His 1980 Fire Incident a Suicide Attempt: 'He Warned Me,'" *People,* March 15, 2019, https://people.com/movies/richard-pryors-1980-fire-suicide-attempt/.

803 New Psychoactive Substances (NPS) Invented

My first in-person exposure to an annual session of the United Nations Commission on Narcotic Drugs (CND), Vienna, Austria, was in March 2012, followed by three successive years of attendance and participation. For me, those experiences reinforced the idea that drug prohibition policy encourages drug invention. That first year, attendees like myself were told that in the past year, *fifty new synthetic drugs* were invented. A year later at the end 2013 annual CND session, the International Narcotic Control Board advised that *100 new synthetic drugs* were invented the prior year. The following year, my fellow attendees were informed that more than *300 new synthetic drugs* were invented during the preceding year.

Finally and more comprehensively, "the Shadow Report," released by the **International Drug Policy Consortium (IDPC)** in 2018, discouragingly noted that during the preceding decade (2009-2018), *803 new psychoactive substances* were invented, laboratory-invented synthetic drugs and new substances had been recorded in over 111 countries and territories.[184]

The IDPC Shadow Report, entitled "Taking Stock: A Decade of Drug Policy, a Civil Society Shadow Report," was prepared in anticipation of a decennial review of UN drug policy and the upcoming High-Level Ministers meeting of the Commission on Narcotic Drugs 2019. The report powerfully presented evidence of the inventive-incentive nature of drug prohibition policy. An Executive Summary describes the scope of the work and report: "'Taking stock: A Decade of Drug Policy' evaluates the impacts of drug policies implemented across the world over the past decade using data from the United Nations, complemented with peer-reviewed academic research and grey literature reports from civil society."

One might wonder why nations and the UN cannot simply outlaw the invention of new synthetic drugs? Because human inquisitiveness and inventiveness cannot be successfully outlawed, any more than gravity, drugs or the future. Secondly, one might wonder what incentivizes the invention of new synthetic drugs when, forever, nature dependably provided organic drugs that work so well to accomplish much the same psychoactive effects? Here's one answer.

---

[184] Marie Nougier, *"A Taking Stock: a Decade of Drug Policy, a Civil Society Shadow Report,"* International Drug Policy Consortium, 2018, p. 27, http://fileserver.idpc.net/library/Shadow_Report_FINAL_ENGLISH.pdf, accessed September 1, 2021.

Rockefeller-Style Draconian Drug-Sentencing

Draconian drug punishments enacted by our elected political leaders necessitated inventiveness and drug-cartel flexibility. Mandatory minimum sentencing was largely the brainchild of New York Governor Nelson Rockefeller, who "launched his campaign to toughen New York's laws at a press conference in January 1973 — almost exactly 40 years ago. He called for something unheard of: mandatory prison sentences of 15 years to life for drug dealers and addicts — even those caught with small amounts of marijuana, cocaine or heroin.... Due in part to Rockefeller-style laws [commonly known as "The Rockefeller Drug Laws"], the nation's prison population exploded from 330,000 in 1973 to a peak of 2.3 million.... Studies put the price tag of America's vast prison system at between $63 billion and $75 billion a year.... Half a million Americans are serving long sentences for nonviolent drug offenses. Those inmates make up 48 percent of the inmate population in federal prisons."[185]

Commonplace, draconian, drug-crime sentencing gave drug entrepreneurs and their chemists good reason, *incentive*, to attempt to circumvent draconian drug penalties and punishments by inventing new drugs and taking advantage of *ex post facto* legal principles.

Newly invented drugs cannot be against the law, because, logically and often constitutionally, legislatures cannot outlaw what does not exist until it does exist. New drugs first must be discovered, scheduled and legislatively criminalized before people can be prosecuted for using or selling them. And that all takes time.

Ex Post Facto Laws and Constitutional Protections

In the United States, the criminalization of what may come by way of invention cannot be allowed because the U.S. Constitution prohibits enactment of *ex post facto laws*. "An *ex post facto* law is a law that retroactively changes the legal consequences (or status) of actions that were committed, or relationships that existed, before the enactment of the law. In criminal law, *ex post facto* laws criminalize actions that were legal when committed,...; it may change the punishment prescribed for a crime, as by adding new

---

[185] Brian Mann, "The Drug Laws That Changed How We Punish," *National Public Radio*, February 14, 2013, https://www.npr.org/2013/02/14/171822608/the-drug-laws-that-changed-how-we-punish, accessed September 1, 2021.

penalties or extending sentences..."[186] Amnesty laws are the converse, a form of *ex post facto* laws that decriminalize yesterday's unlawfulness or past penalties.[187]

"Ex post facto laws are expressly forbidden by the United States Constitution in Article 1, Section 9, Clause 3 with respect to federal laws and by Article 1, Section 10 with respect to state laws.... *Ex post facto* criminalization is also prohibited by Article 7 of the European Convention on Human Rights, and Article 15(1) of the International Covenant on Civil and Political Rights..."[188]

"The Yellow List" and the Drug Scheduling Quagmire

Even if tomorrow's new psychoactive substances could be outlawed today, such a solution would still be problematic, because there is institutional time lag built into the process of adding drugs to the "Yellow List"[189] of prohibited drugs.

It is not a simple matter. The recent effort to add ketamine to the list is a good example of the difficulties. "The current system for placing substances under international control, which is set out in the relevant treaties, and involves technical review by the WHO and a political vote at the UN Commission on Narcotic Drugs. We demonstrate that the process has both normative and democratic deficits. These deficits interfere with an appropriate consideration of the real-life benefits and unintended consequences of scheduling, with striking an appropriate balance between the interests of ensuring access to medicines and limiting the harms associated with their nonmedical use." [190]

"The issue at the heart of this debate [regarding adding the anesthetic ketamine to the Yellow List], however, remains very much alive. Various medicines are not currently scheduled as controlled substances even though they have psychoactive proper-

---

186 *Wikipedia*, s.v. "*Ex post facto* law," https://en.m.wikipedia.org/wiki/Ex_post_facto_law, accessed January 20, 2022.

187 Ibid.

188 Ibid.

189 "List of Narcotic Drugs Under International Control," Annex to Forms A, B and C 58th edition, August 2019, *International Narcotic Control Board*, https://www.incb.org/documents/Narcotic-Drugs/Yellow_List/58th_Edition/Yellow_List_-ENG.pdf, accessed January 20, 2022.

190 Diederik Lohman & Damon Barrett, "Scheduling medicines as controlled substances: addressing normative and democratic gaps through human rights-based analysis," April 21, 2020, *BMC Int Health Hum Rights 20, 10 (2020)*, https://doi.org/10.1186/s12914-020-00231-1, accessed September 1, 2021.

ties that can trigger the attention of the international drug control system. The non-medical use of some of these medicines is not uncommon.... This question is likely to keep rearing its head and generating controversy. These seemingly remote decisions in Vienna have very real consequences for medical practice and public health. While non-medical use is a serious problem, it is also clear that *national and international scheduling leads to reduced availability and accessibility of medicines...*, [and] may negatively affect perceptions of the medicine (creating a 'chilling effect' on prescribing)... and may drive up cost..."[191]

The conclusion to this discussion is plain enough. Drug prohibition, draconian penalties, *ex post facto* laws, constitutional principles, and the drug-scheduling process intersect, and that dynamic *incentivizes the prolific invention of new drugs*, adding to the world drug problem.

Marijuana Popularity, Price, Potency and Plenty

Marijuana is the most commonly used and plentifully produced illicit drug in the world. "Unlike other plant-based drugs, for which cultivation and production are concentrated in only a few countries, cannabis is produced in almost all countries worldwide."[192] Globally, the drug was used by 200 million people in 2019.[193]

Foolishly assigned the duty, police fly around in helicopters looking for marijuana grows.[194] It does not seem like it would be very difficult to find. Within two miles of my home located in suburban Cook County, home of Chicago, police found a 6,000-plant grow in the Sneed Woods,[195] and two years earlier, a 30,000-plant grow in the Crabtree Nature Center Forest Preserve near northwest suburban Barrington.[196] In another Chicago marijuana moment, authorities seized 11 tons of pot that traveled

---

[191] Ibid., Background, par. 2, 3.

[192] *World Drug Report 2021*, Booklet 3, p. 11, https://www.unodc.org/res/wdr2021/field/WDR21_Booklet_3.pdf.

[193] Ibid.

[194] James Filippello, Retired Police lieutenant & Book Author, answering the question, "How does law enforcement find where cannabis is growing using helicopters?" *Quora, Inc.*, https://www.quora.com/How-does-law-enforcement-find-where-cannabis-is-growing-using-helicopters, accessed March 17, 2023.

[195] Carmen Greco Jr., "Pot farm destroyed in Cook County Forest Preserve," *Chicago Tribune*, August 19, 2009, https://www.chicagotribune.com/news/ct-bn-xpm-2009-08-19-28503867-story.html.

[196] Jeff Long, "Cops bust, then burn pot farm in woods," *Chicago Tribune*, July 25, 2007, https://www.chicagotribune.com/news/ct-xpm-2007-07-25-0707241209-story.html, accessed September 4, 2021.

from Mexico to Chicago Heights in six railroad cars.[197] The prohibition of marijuana has served to increase marijuana production, its potency and availability to such an extent that its price has fallen. All these outcomes are unwanted and unintended.

The Production of Pot

Across the border in Mexico in 2008, Mexico was producing 21,500 metric tons of marijuana annually, according to the U.S. Department of Justice, National Drug Intelligence Center.[198] The seizure of a dozen tons of pot now and then becomes meaningless busy work given such data, a drop in the marijuana ocean. According to the report, the cost of that production was $75 per pound, and the sale price was $6,000 per pound.[199] The inundation of the world with marijuana is thus a simple matter of economics.

Drug prohibition dramatically increases the price of marijuana, just as drug legalization can dramatically reduce it. Only excessive state and local drug taxation can operate to neutralize the marijuana legalization weapon and protect extralegal marijuana sources. Conclusion: economics drives the marijuana business, just as it does all illicit drug businesses and every other type of business. As Professor Jonathan Caulkins and his coauthors explained,[200] marijuana prohibition has built-in costs, such as the extra costs of running a covert operation, and higher employee wages due to legal risk. But with the advent of marijuana legalization, prices plummet. Players in the legal drug market concur.[201] States now aggressively tax cannabis sales. Colorado has a 15 percent excise tax, but the cost of production and running a business is much lower.[202]

The Price of Pot

"As the U.S. legal marijuana market matures, pot is getting cheaper than ever. The price per pound has fallen at least 25 percent in Colorado since last year, according to

---

197 *ABC7Chicago* archives, December 16, 2010, https://abc7chicago.com/archive/7847380/.

198 "National Drug Threat Assessment 2011," *U.S. Department of Justice, National Drug Intelligence Center,* August 2011, p. 29.

199 Ibid., p. 30.

200 Beau Kilmer, Jonathan Caulkins and Mark Kleiman, *Marijuana Legalization: What Everyone Needs to Know* (Oxford: Oxford University Press, 2012).

201 "As Price Plummets to Historic Low, Marijuana Entrepreneurs Need to Adapt," *GeoShephard,* https://geoshepard.com/marijuana-price-plummets-entrepreneurs-need-adapt/, accessed September 2021.

202 Ibid.

data from Colorado's Department of Revenue. Sally Vander Veer, co-founder of Medicine Man, a marijuana cultivator and retailer, says that in 2010, her company would
have been able to sell a pound of marijuana for $5,000. That was during the early days
of the above-ground legal marijuana market. Today, a pound goes for as low as $1,000
to $1,200. According to Colorado's Department of Revenue, the wholesale price per
pound for marijuana reached a historic low of $1,471 per pound, a drastic 24.5 percent
drop since 2016. Vander Veer says her company's margins for flower dropped by 40
percent in one year."[203]

The Potency of Pot

Likewise, drug prohibition dramatically increased the potency of cannabis, commonly
called "marijuana."[204] Authoritatively, UN data confirms the steadily escalating potency of marijuana over the past twenty-five years from 4 percent to over 14 percent
THC content.[205] According to Patrick Lynch, "Regardless of the tales you hear, there
is no question that marijuana was less potent back then [in the 1960s and 1970s]. One
of the main reasons was the quality of weed available."[206] Continuing, Lynch points
out that "product degradation caused by improper or prolonged storage of marijuana
and development of more accurate liquid chromatographic testing rather than gas
chromatography complicate judging the degree of increased potency of marijuana over
the past 50 years. Nevertheless, 20 years ago THC percentage [the primary psychoactive ingredient in marijuana] averaged 4 percent and now "apparently the average
THC in Colorado weed is 18.7%!... [even] over 20%."[207]

"A study by ElSohly et al., published in *Biological Psychiatry* in April 2016, looked
at changes in cannabis potency from 1995 to 2014. In all, almost 39,000 samples were
analyzed. The team found that marijuana had an average potency of 4% THC in 1995.

203 Ibid.

204 *Wikipedia*, s.v. "Etymology of cannabis," https://en.wikipedia.org/wiki/Etymology_of_cannabis, and Anna
Wilcox, "The Origin of the Word 'Marijuana," *Leafly Holdings, Inc.*, March 6, 2014, https://www.leafly.com/
news/cannabis-101/where-did-the-word-marijuana-come-from-anyway-01fb, both accessed September 4, 2021.

205 "*World Drug Report 2021*," Booklet 3, p. 30, https://www.unodc.org/res/wdr2021/field/WDR21 _Booklet_
3.pdf.

206 Patrick Lynch, "Average THC Strength Over Time: A 50-Year Look at Marijuana Potency," *Way of Leaf*,
July 1, 2021, updated November 1, 2021, accessed January 20, 2022, https://wayofleaf.com/blog/average-thc-
content-over-the-years.

207 Ibid.

Once again, it is tough to take this figure at face value, but there is no question that weed was still weaker."[208]

The ElSohly study concludes, "Overall, the potency of illicit cannabis plant material has consistently increased over time since 1995 from ~4% in 1995 to ~12% in 2014."[209]

Rumpelstiltskin Prohibition Magic

Drug-prohibition policy is a form of **Rumpelstiltskin** magic that spins straw into gold and "grows money on trees" and plants (hydroponically) without dirt.[210] The magical pot-profit genie has also incentivized invention of synthetic concoctions and pot wannabes like dangerous K2 and Spice.[211] The magic worked so well in America that ditch-weed blossomed into a drug-consuming norm and its cultivation became a fine art.[212] "In previous years, upwards of 97 percent of all pot seized by law enforcement was categorized as 'ditchweed' — a term the DEA uses to define 'wild, scattered marijuana plants with no evidence of planting, fertilizer or tending.'"[213]

Over fifty years of marijuana prohibition the industry grew so dramatically that, despite UN disenchantment with cannabis use for any purpose as reflected in its drug-control treaties, its use became so commonplace that state after state in the United States of America began legalizing and regulating marijuana markets. As of this writing, recreational marijuana is legal in eighteen states in the USA and the District of

---

[208] Ibid.

[209] Mahmoud A. ElSohly, "Changes in Cannabis Potency Over the Last 2 Decades (1995–2014): Analysis of Current Data in the United States," *Biological Psychiatry*, January 19, 2016, https://www.biologicalpsychiatry journal.com/article/S0006-3223(16)00045-7/fulltext, accessed September 2, 2021.

[210] "Hydroponics: Growing Cannabis Without Soil," *Amsterdam Genetics*, February 5, 2021, https://www.amster damgenetics.com/hydroponics-growing-cannabis-without-soil/, accessed February 16, 2022.

[211] "Spice/ K2, Synthetic Marijuana," *US Department of Justice, Drug Enforcement Agency*, https://www.dea.gov/factsheets/spice-k2-synthetic-marijuana, accessed May 14, 2022.

[212] Brian Barth, "How to Grow Cannabis in Your Garden," *Modern Farmer*, August 23, 2018, https://modern farmer.com/2018/08/how-to-grow-cannabis-in-your-garden/.

[213] Paul Armentano, "So where did all the ditchweed go?" *NORML*, August 5, 2008, https://norml.org/blog/2008/08/05/so-where-did-all-the-ditchweed-go/.

Columbia, and medical marijuana is legal in 37 states.[214] Illinois is one such state. In its nascent first two years, Illinois marijuana is already a billion-dollar enterprise.[215]

In short, drug prohibition exploded marijuana price, potency, profits, production and use, all factors providing a powerful economic incentive to grow, tweak and sell marijuana.

The Fentanyl-Heroin Overdose Phenomenon

Perhaps the newest and most convincing evidence of the drugogenic nature and harmful consequences of drug-prohibition policy is the ever-increasing number of accidental deaths caused by the blind mix of illegal heroin and medically legal fentanyl. The deadly mixture of the two substances is now commonly found and sold on illicit drug markets, worldwide. Ironically, the government endeavors to protect public health by outlawing recreational opioid sales when taking that course of action prevents health and legal authorities from requiring accurate and honest drug labeling. Drug labeling could provide drug users with important information regarding drug content, dosage, potency and warnings. Such prohibition folly also prevents government inspection of drug cultivation, manufacture and final product. It also foils systematic oversight of drug-selling operations that could be accomplished through drug-dealer licensing and by limiting the number of licenses issued and requiring sales to be made from fixed places of business premises during regular designated hours, much as is accomplished by licensing liquor establishments.

From a user's perspective, drug prohibition makes drug use a much riskier business — often a deadly business. Drug prohibition makes drug use a "Guess What" drug policy choice. In that environment, drug users — even experienced, harm reduction experts like the great, late-Dan Bigg — cannot adequately and reliably protect themselves.[216]

---

[214] Jeremy Berke, Shayanne Gal, and Yeji Jesse Lee, "Marijuana legalization is sweeping the US. See every state where cannabis is legal," *Business Insider*, updated July 9, 2021, https://www.businessinsider.com/legal-marijuana-states-2018-1#new-mexico-13.

[215] Kyle Jaeger, "Illinois Continued Record-Breaking Marijuana Sales Streak In May, State Officials Report," *Marijuana Moment*, June 3, 2021, https://www.marijuanamoment.net/illinois-continued-record-breaking-marijuana-sales-streak-in-may-state-officials-report/.

[216] Maia Szalavitz, "Dan Bigg Is a Harm-Reduction Pioneer and His Overdose Doesn't Change That," October 24, 2018, https://www.vice.com/en/article/7x3yag/dan-bigg-overdose-harm-reduction, accessed September 2, 2021; on April 4, 2017, 18 months before his death, Dan Bigg appeared as my first guest on "Chicago's War on

Drug-prohibition means more drug overdose deaths, not fewer. It's a 21st century phenomenon. Maggie Fox reported on CDC's National Center for Health Statistics' (NCHS) data, noting that in 2020, 93,000 human beings (Americans) overdosed and died, a 29.4% increase from the 72,151 deaths projected for 2019. Fox quoted an NCHS statement, "Overdose deaths from synthetic opioids (primarily fentanyl) and psychostimulants such as methamphetamine also increased in 2020 compared to 2019. Cocaine deaths also increased in 2020, as did deaths from natural and semi-synthetic opioids (such as prescription pain medication)," Fox noting "As in recent years, inappropriate use of opioids was behind most of the deaths. The NCHS reported that overdose deaths from opioids rose from 50,963 in 2019 to 69,710 in 2020."[217]

"Drawing from the latest available death certificate data, the Centers for Disease Control and Prevention estimated that 100,300 Americans died of drug overdoses from May 2020 to April 2021. It's not an official count. It can take many months for death investigations involving drug fatalities to become final, so the agency made the estimate based on 98,000 reports it has received so far."[218]

Globally 115,000 People Died of Opioid Overdose in 2017

Globally, "according to [the World Health Organization] estimates, approximately 115,000 people died of opioid overdose in 2017. And opioid overdoses that do not lead to death are several times more common than fatal overdoses."[219] Founded in 1948, WHO is the United Nations agency that connects nations, partners and people to promote health, keep the world safe and serve the vulnerable. Heroin is an organic opioid, a poppy plant drug-product.

For historical perspective and understanding, heroin (diacetylmorphine) was trademarked, marketed and commercialized by Bayer[220] in 1898 as a cough suppressant and

---

Drugs," a CAN-TV series of 13 shows. Video, https://www.dropbox.com/s/33xt5tbexbd47wo/Chicago%20War%20on%20Drugs%20with%20Dan%20Bigg.mp4?dl=0.

217 Maggie Fox, "Drug overdose deaths in 2020 hit highest number ever recorded, CDC data shows," *CNN*, July 17, 2021, https://www.cnn.com/2021/07/14/health/drug-overdose-deaths-2020/index.html, accessed September 2, 2021.

218 Mike Stobbe, "US overdose deaths topped 100,000 in one year, officials say," *AP News*, November 17, 2021, https://apnews.com/article/overdodse-deaths-fentanayl-health-f34b022d75a1eb9776e27903ab40670f.

219 "Opioid overdose," *World Health Organization*, August 4, 2021, https://www.who.int/news-room/fact-sheets/detail/opioid-overdose, accessed September 2, 2021.

220 *Wikipedia, s.v.* "Bayer," https://en.m.wikipedia.org/wiki/Bayer, accessed March 17, 2023.

over-the-counter treatment for other common ailments.[221] After it's addictive properties were discovered, it was removed from medical inventories and pharmacy shelves. But illicit markets soon took over and brought drug users the world over organically produced heroin. Fifty years ago in the United States, heroin was commonly 2-percent pure but over the years, black-market competition and greed soon offered drug users increased heroin potency, often ninety-percent pure. The **National Institute on Drug Abuse** (NIDA) provides much information about heroin and health problems associated with heroin use.[222]

The "Undifference" Between Fentanyl and Heroin

American Addiction Centers explain some of the differences between two popularly used opioids in an article entitled, "Fentanyl vs. Heroin: An Opioid Comparison."[223]

"Heroin is derived from morphine, which is a natural substance that is removed from the seed of the opium poppy plant. Heroin is distributed as a white or brown powder, or as a black, tacky substance known as 'black tar' heroin. It is classified as an illegal drug with no accepted medicinal uses in the United States (Schedule I controlled substance) by the Drug Enforcement Administration (DEA). It is typically injected, smoked, or snorted when abused.

"Fentanyl is a synthetic (manmade) opioid that is similar to morphine; however, the National Institute on Drug Abuse (NIDA) warns that it is 50-100 times more potent than morphine. [Gierach interjection: unless diluted or 'cut' by a manufacturing process to a strength of one-fiftieth or one-hundredth, or other desired potency.] The chemical structure of fentanyl is slightly different from that of heroin. Fentanyl was originally synthesized as a powerful analgesic (pain reliever), and it is still used medically to treat severe pain following surgery or for chronic pain in people who are opioid-tolerant, which means that other painkillers aren't as effective. Unlike heroin, fentanyl does have some accepted medicinal uses, so it is classified as a Schedule II

---

[221] S Hosztafi, "The History of Heroin," *National Library of Medicine*, https://pubmed.ncbi.nlm.nih.gov/11862675/, accessed March 17, 2023. To

[222] "Heroin Drug Facts," *Institute on Drug Abuse*, https://www.drugabuse.gov/publications/drugfacts/heroin, accessed March 17, 2023.

[223] Marisa Crane, B.S., "Fentanyl vs. Heroin: An Opioid Comparison," *American Addiction Centers*, update January 7, 2022, accessed January 17, 2022, https://americanaddictioncenters.org/fentanyl-treatment/similarities.

controlled substance by the DEA. Schedule II drugs still have a very high potential for abuse and addiction despite their specific medical uses.

"Overdose fatalities involving heroin or fentanyl are rising. The Centers for Disease Control and Prevention (CDC) reports that close to 30,000 Americans died from an opioid overdose in 2014. Overdose deaths from synthetic opioids like fentanyl nearly doubled from 2013 to 2014, and heroin overdose fatalities quadrupled from 2002 to 2013, the CDC publishes.

"People may not even realize that the drug they are taking contains fentanyl, as it is often passed off as pure heroin. Fentanyl is more potent than heroin and can therefore cause a toxic buildup and lead to overdose faster and in lower doses. An opioid overdose becomes dangerous when breathing is slowed too much. Pulse also slows, body temperature drops, and individuals often become mentally confused, drowsy, and lethargic. Pinpoint pupils and potential loss of consciousness are further indicators of an opioid overdose."[224]

In the first half of 2021, 90 percent of all opioid deaths in Chicago involved fentanyl.[225] Yet public attitudes and political realities continue to resist harm-reduction remedies such as safe-injection sites, drug treatment centers, pharmaceutical-based addiction treatment, drug maintenance programs for persons addicted to drugs, widespread naloxone availability, clean needle distribution, drug-dealer licensing, and government inspection and regulation of legalized illicit drug products. Commenting on this sad reality regarding safe-injection sites, Illinois state Rep. **LaShawn K. Ford** commented on the political reality, noting that support for safe injection sites is "bad politics."[226]

Reflecting that same popular sentiment, and not in my backyard sentiment (NIMBY), the **Haymarket Center** recently filed a civil rights lawsuit in federal court regarding a village's denial of zoning relief to permit the conversion of a Holiday Inn into a disparately needed 240-bed, drug treatment facility in Itasca, Illinois, following

---

[224] The last two paragraphs no longer appear in this advertisement, noticed in update dated, January 7, 2022, last accessed January 21, 2022.

[225] David Struett, "Tackling Opioids' Alarming Toll: As overdose deaths hit record, pressure grows for safe places to inject drugs in Chicago," *Chicago Sun-Times*, January 17, 2022, https://chicago.suntimes.com /news/2022/1/ 17/22865346/opioid-overdose-safe-injection-sites-heroin-fentanyl.

[226] Ibid.

two years of pleading, petitioning and thirty-five public hearings.[227] Treatment centers, safe injection sites and legalized and labeled drugs could change the course of the deadly fentanyl overdose phenomenon, but lifesaving, healthy drug policy is counterintuitive and frightening to the current, vocal "silent majority."[228] But necessity is the mother of invention, and thus New York City, recognizing the necessity to meaningfully address the overdose crisis, courageously authorized the opening of the first two safe-injection sites in the US in the neighborhoods of East Harlem and Washington Heights in November 2021. This course of action followed "signs of other intelligent life" in European and Canadian cities that have had success with such programs.[229]

Physicians Not Principally to Blame for Opioid Overdose

Some people believe that the opioid overdose epidemic in recent years was caused by physicians overprescribing pain medicine such as hydrocodone and oxycodone. Lawsuits against drug companies based on that notion have just been settled (July 2021). However, as columnist Jacob Z. Sullum noted, "Per capita opioid prescriptions in the United States, which began rising in 2006, fell steadily after 2012, reflecting the impact of government efforts to restrict and discourage medical use of these drugs. Yet in 2019, when the dispensing rate was lower than it had been in 2005, the U.S. saw more opioid-related deaths than ever before."[230]

"Last... Opioid-related deaths jumped by 40%. As opioid prescriptions fell, the upward trend in fatalities (which typically involve more than one drug) not only continued but accelerated. That perverse effect was entirely predictable. The crackdown on pain pills drove non-medical users toward black-market substitutes, replacing legally manufactured, reliably dosed products with drugs of unknown provenance and composition. While that was happening, illicit fentanyl became increasingly common

---

[227] Katlyn Smith, "Haymarket sues Itasca over village's rejection of addiction rehab center," *Daily Herald*, updated January 11, 2022, https://www.dailyherald.com/news/20220111/haymarket-sues-itasca-over-villages-rejection-of-addiction-rehab-center.

[228] *Wikipedia*, s.v. "Silent majority," https://en.wikipedia.org/wiki/Silent_majority, accessed March 17, 2023.

[229] Jeffery C. Mays and Andy Newman, "Nation's First Supervised Drug-Injection Sites Open in New York," *New York Times*, November 30, 2021, https://www.nytimes.com/2021/11/30/nyregion/supervised-injection-sites-nyc.html?referringSource=articleShare.

[230] Jacob Z. Sullum, "Drug warriors made opioid epidemic worse," *Chicago Sun-Times*, 7/28/21, https://chicago.suntimes.com/columnists/2021/7/28/22597967/opioid-epidemic-pain-management-war-drugs-jacob-sullum, accessed September 2, 2021.

as a heroin booster or replacement, making potency even more variable. In 2020, according to the CDC's projections, 'synthetic opioids other than methadone,' the category that includes fentanyl and its analogs, were involved in 83% of opioid-related deaths, up from 14% in 2010," Sullum writes.[231]

A "Guess What" Drug Policy

As we can plainly see, drugogenic drug-prohibition policy has its drawbacks. "The Russian Roulette," "Guess What," "Just Say No," UN recreational drug prohibition policy is the overdose killer, the stalking Grim Reaper. We should all be fed up with it by now, scrap drug prohibition, and cut our heartbreaking losses.

Before leaving the subject of the present fentanyl-overdose phenomenon, it is constructive to remember the 2004 heroin overdose phenomenon when Chicago ranked No. 2 in heroin overdose deaths. The lesson to be learned from these deaths is that they are as much a reflection of the drug policies chosen to control mind-altering substances as they are a reflection of the nature of the substances sought to be controlled. The Prohibition policy end of the prohibition-legalization continuum, ironically, obstructs drug control while the Legalization policy continuum end facilitates it. Strange but true. Good drug policy is counterintuitive. In the drug policy world, what sounds like good policy is often bad policy; and what sounds like bad policy may very well be good policy. From this history derives Gierach Drug Policy Axiom No. 6: "The harder we try to suppress drugs, the more they flourish."[232]

In my experience as a Cook County prosecutor, drug prohibition policy transformed two-percent Chicago heroin into ninety-percent pure heroin that led to the headline, "Chicago Is No. 2 In Heroin Deaths," *Chicago Sun-Times*, March 29, 2004—memorialized, again, in my Trinity Christian PowerPoint presentation slide.

Recreational Drugs Shipped by Plane, Train and Submarine

By January 1995, I had read and observed that recreational drug exports of every major category were being delivered around the world by every means of transportation imaginable and creatively, too. Drugs were shipped inside cadavers, bottles of purported baby formula, cement fence posts, absorbed into blue-jeans fabric later to be removed

---

[231] Ibid.

[232] Gierach, James E., "Gierach Drug Policy Reform Axioms," https://jamesgierach.tumblr.com/ post/65713188 0316043264/gierach-drug-policy-axioms.

by centrifuge, bodily cavities, snakes and vehicles of every sort. Boeing 727s and French-made Caravelle jets were being used to transport six tons of cocaine into Mexico and America in a single flight; radar-guided mini-subs were used to transport three tons of narcotics out to sea from Colombia; and 40,000 doses of LSD were transported in a magazine carried by a passenger on a train in Paris.[233] Every destination in the world was a recreational drug port-of-call with mind-altering substances shipped by plane, train and submarine.

Frustrated with drug-prohibition consequences, I penned a satirical article from *The Drug Corner*, called "Drug Exporters Prefer to Ship by Train," January 10, 1995 (unpublished). Tongue-in-cheek, the article explained some of the drawbacks of alternate modes of drug delivery other than by train. "U.S. mail is too slow and Tijuana drug tunnels are too immobile. Iraq is working on mobile scud drug-launchers but hitting the intended target remains a problem.... Flights laden with drug produce over water present unique risks. For good reason, pilots of cocaine-laden flights invariably fly with their headlights turned off making it difficult to see the runway and land the plane.... And when a Medellín drug plane crashes into the Gulf of Mexico, Pacific or Atlantic Oceans six tons of cocaine mix with salty water forming cocaine-calcium chloride, a compound (or is it a mixture) that is difficult to separate, and even more difficult to retrieve. Equally exasperating to drug barons, flying fish eat the cocaine, and fishermen complain the fish are flying so 'high' they just won't bite.... And the trouble with transporting drugs by submarine is that once submerged a sea captain can't see where he is going. A sea captain charting a course, say for Lake Michigan, might mistakenly surface in Tokyo Bay. And drug laws and punishments vary greatly between different ports-of-call."

Unfortunately, satire did not carry my drug-policy-reform message any further or more successfully than my no-nonsense political campaigning a few years earlier. Regardless, the indisputable fact remained — "Drug War Intolerance Means More Drugs."

---

[233] Gierach, James E. satire, "Drug Exporters Prefer to Ship by Train," Jan. 10, 1995, prompted by news, https://jamesgierach.tumblr.com/post/673186576444030976/gierach-satire-drug-exporters-prefer-to-ship-by.

IDPC and Its "Shadow Report"

The **International Drug Policy Consortium (IDPC)** is a single, nongovernmental organization and a collective of 194 [234] drug policy reform, harm reduction and human rights organizations working to untie the world from its drugogenic prohibition curse (my characterization not IDPC's). The curse is cast like a spell by intolerant and punitive UN drug conventions and implemented by national drug laws. IDPC is a civil society organization led by Executive Director, **Ann Fordham**.

In a United Nations setting, "A civil society organization (CSO) or non-governmental organization (NGO) is any non-profit, voluntary citizens' group which is organized on a local, national or international level."[235] And NGOs can apply for "special consultative status" with the **United Nations Economic and Social Council (ECOSOC)**, one of the six principal organs of the UN, and special consultative status with the Economic and Social Council provides non-governmental organizations (NGOs) with access to ECOSOC.

Extensively utilizing the work and reports of United Nations agencies, IDPC prepared a 138-page document that "evaluates the impacts of drug policies implemented across the world between 2009 and 2018, complemented with peer-reviewed academic research and grey literature reports from civil society." Sadly, during the most recent decade examined (2009-2018), global drug cultivation, production, invention, and use of every sort has increased significantly.[236]

"This *Shadow Report* was drafted by **Marie Nougier**, IDPC's Head of Research and Communications. The following members of the IDPC team have extensively contributed to, and reviewed, the Shadow Report: Ann Fordham, Christopher Hallam, Coletta Youngers, Gloria Lai, Heather Haase and Jamie Bridge." With 685 endnotes and acknowledgement of some fifty contributors and reviewers, the document is a superb work and signpost clearly warning and informing world leaders, global drug policy is headed the "WRONG WAY!"

The Rt Hon. Helen Clark, former Prime Minister of New Zealand (1999-2008), member of the **Global Commission on Drug Policy**, and former Administrator of the United Nations Development Programme (2009-2017), wrote the Forward to the

---

[234] IDPC Members Directory, https://idpc.net/, accessed March 17, 2023.

[235] "The UN and Civil Society," *United Nations,* https://www.un.org/en/get-involved/un-and-civil-society.

[236] "The Shadow Report," http://fileserver.idpc.net/library/Shadow_Report_FINAL_ENGLISH.pdf, pp. 8, 11, 27.

138-page Shadow Report, noting that "current drug policies are a serious obstacle to other social and economic objectives: progress on combating the HIV epidemic had been significant in the last 20 years, but is now stalled among people who inject drugs; prison overcrowding has worsened, with a fifth of the world's inmates being arrested for drug-related offences and mostly for drug use alone; and the 'war on drugs' has resulted in millions of people murdered, disappeared, or internally displaced."[237]

This work of civil society, and IDPC in particular, is so good, so thorough, and so convincing that right-minded people the world over must agree that the World War on Drugs is an abysmal failure, and one of the basic premises of this book chapter: "Drug War Means More Drugs." And that being the indisputable fact, we must all look in the mirror and ask ourselves — "Of what benefit is the UN-shepherded 'World War on Drugs?'"

None. Absolutely, none. Proof of this truth is beyond all reasonable doubt and debate: *Drug War Intolerance Means More Drugs Not Less.*

---

[237] The Shadow Report, Forward, http://fileserver.idpc.net/library/Shadow_Report_FINAL_ENGLISH.pdf.

Chapter 5 - Drug War Intolerance Means More Crime

The War on Drugs is also *criminogenic*. Drug prohibition policy makes violent crime the inseparable shadow of drugs, needlessly. Does anyone need to be convinced that drug prohibition causes violence? Without drug legalization, there can be no peace from drug-gang violence from Chicago[238] to Durban, South Africa;[239] Sydney[240] to Rio de Janeiro;[241] London[242] to Beijing;[243] Juarez[244] to Manila;[245] or from anywhere to somewhere else.

The examples that might be cited individually, collectively, locally, nationally, and internationally... are endless and everywhere. Print media, radio, television, and the Internet are replete with violence stories driven by drug-prohibition policy. Reporting this news is like trying to report on the horrors of any war. Stories of atrocity and tragedy are simply ubiquitous, one more disquieting than the next. New examples of horrific drug-war violence are happening this very moment, this morning, this afternoon, tonight — piling on top of those from the day and night before.

The bad news of the day should have us all thinking and realizing: *we need, the world needs, a new drug policy strategy.* Wherever one might live in America or the

---

[238] "Bodies stacked at Cook Co. morgue buried," *WLS-TV*, April 25, 2012, https://abc7chicago.com/archive/8635656/.

[239] Lee Rondganger, "Bodies pile up as Cape Town's Hard Livings gang goes to war in Durban," *Independent Online*, December 7, 2021, https://www.iol.co.za/news/bodies-pile-up-as-cape-towns-hard-livings-gang-goes-to-war-in-durban-a97c039f-f0a8-4e60-8364-f266baa0c74e.

[240] Tita Smith, "Cops slam Sydney's 'obsession with cocaine' for fueling deadly gang crime plaguing the city's streets – including kidnappings, deaths and shootings," *Daily Mail Austria*, November 28, 2020, https://www.dailymail.co.uk/news/article-8997147/Sydneys-obsession-cocaine-fuelling-deadly-gang-crime-plaguing-citys-streets.html.

[241] Rodrigo Viga Gaier, "Violent 24 hours in Rio de Janeiro, as shootouts plague city," *Reuters*, August 27, 2020, https://www.reuters.com/article/us-brazil-violence/violent-24-hours-in-rio-de-janeiro-as-shootouts-plague-city-idUSKBN25O00J.

[242] Mark Townsend, "London killings: 'It's like a war zone. How did it come to this?'" *The Observer* Gangs, republished, *The Guardian*, May 1, 2021, https://www.theguardian.com/society/2021/may/01/london-killings-its-like-a-war-zone-how-did-it-come-to-this.

[243] Hollie McKay, "Behind the Deadly Rise of the China-Mexican Cartel Alliance That Is Killing Americans," *Coffee or Die Magazine*, April 9, 2021, https://coffeeordie.com/china-mexican-cartel-alliance/.

[244] Julian Resendiz, "Body count from drug cartel wars earns Mexican cities label of 'most violent in the world'" *FOX59*, April 21, 2021, https://fox59.com/news/national-world/body-count-from-drug-cartel-wars-earns-mexican-cities-label-of-most-violent-in-the-world/.

[245] Daniel Berehulak, "They Are Slaughtering Us Like Animals," *The New York Times*, December 7, 2016, https://www.nytimes.com/interactive/2016/12/07/world/asia/rodrigo-duterte-philippines-drugs-killings.html.

world, just look and listen to see and hear about deadly drug-gang violence,[246] escalating expressway shootings,[247] stabbings[248], and increasing numbers of mass shootings.[249] Monday is day 185 of the year [2022], and the country has already experienced at least 309 mass shootings so far. At least 309 in just over twenty-six weeks. This averages out to more than eleven a week.[250] We must connect the violence dots; and we must separate the prohibition concept from the drug policy of tomorrow to stop inevitable drug-prohibition violence.

The subject of this chapter — drug war-invited crime and violence, more than any other harm or unintended drug-war consequence — progressively distracted me from my chosen career as a lawyer thirty years ago, twenty years into my forty-five-year legal career. It motivated me to advocate a very unpopular political idea — End to the Drug War to Restore Peace. It relentlessly drove me then, and still drives me now, down my sidetracked life path of drug policy reform. Just thinking about the subject of this chapter, the relationship between drug prohibition policy and violent crime, makes me feel like the elephant in the room has been set on my dinner plate. "Where to begin? Where to end? What can be said?"

Connecting the dots of this challenging topic into a single chapter, I will discuss addict crime, turf-war crime, and the classification of homicides for the purpose of prevention. I will allude to violence in Chicago, American big cities, global homicide rates, and compare recent violence to that of the Capone Era, a previously failed substance prohibition experiment. In this chapter I will also broach the mix of bad firearms policy, bad drug policy and male testosterone that makes drugs the lifeblood of gangs, and gangs the bloodbath of communities, noting the contagious, retaliatory,

---

[246] Zusha Elinson, "Gang Violence Drives Rise in Murder Rates in Some U.S. Cities," *The Wall Street Journal*, August 20, 2021, https://www.wsj.com/articles/gang-violence-drives-rise-in-murder-rates-in-some-u-s-cities-11629486712.

[247] Danielle Wallace, "Chicago expressway shootings continue to surge despite $12.5M grant, federal intervention," *FOX News*, July 26, 2021, https://www.foxnews.com/us/chicago-expressway-shootings-surge.

[248] Mark Townsend, "London killings... ," supra.

[249] Daniel Victor and Derrick Bryson Taylor, "A Partial List of Mass Shootings in the United States in 2021," *New York Times*, June 29, 2021, https://www.nytimes.com/article/mass-shootings-2021.html?referringSource= articleShare; and Elizabeth Wolfe and 11 contributors, "2 house parties, an Easter fete and a mall were among the sites of at least 10 weekend US mass shootings," *CNN*, April 18, 2022, https://www.cnn.com/2022/04/18/us/us-shootings-easter-weekend/index.html.

[250] Saeed Ahmed, "Halfway through year, America has already seen at least 309 mass shootings," *NPR*, May 15, 2022, https://apple.news/AjpYJJjeWQXKMmpcwxBs7pQ.

ping-pong nature of such bloody violence. Also in this chapter, I will review two opportunities, both missed, to extricate American society from its violent drug-war morass, one statewide in Illinois and one nationwide in America, leaders ducking the central issue. Finally, I will discuss a UN Sustainable Development Goal aimed to reduce violence and the role of UN drug treaties obstructing accomplishment of that goal.

A Violence Misperception

Initially, some people mistakenly think that drug users become intoxicated and in, and because of, their intoxicated state — they commit violent crime. That certainly is neither the usual case, nor my experience. The heroin addict, for example, generally injects his dope, experiences a utopian "high" and promptly crashes. As my ENT, the late Dr. Elias Karas explained, a heroin addict ingests heroin and "harmlessly curls up like a dog on a rug and falls asleep." It is when a person addicted to drugs wakes up, wants (or needs) more dope, and discovers that he or she has no drugs, and no money to buy more, that public safety is at high risk. That's also when personal property of others is likely to disappear. I call stealing, robbing and burglarizing to obtain money to buy drugs "Addict Crime" to distinguish it from gangs fighting over drug turf that I call "Turf-War Crime."

Addict Crime

On September 30, 1991, I announced my candidacy for Cook County state's attorney, the public office responsible for prosecuting crime in Chicago and its suburbs. Cook County is comprised of fifty city wards and thirty suburban "towns," legally known as townships. I delivered a fiery kickoff speech with atypical content to a sleeping public and inattentive media. I declared: "We are losing the War on DRUGS. CRIME is out of control. And TAXES are breaking the back of taxpayers.... Despite vigorous law enforcement, and the fact that Illinois has the fastest-growing prison population in the country,[251] we are experiencing a record [high] homicide rate and a robbery every twelve minutes.

"We know that DRUGS are the root of the problem. Drug dealers care more about profiting from the drug trade than whether our children become hooked on drugs. Like you, I loathe drugs, and I despise drug dealers.

---

[251] Wes Smith, "State's prisons test the limits," *Chicago Tribune*, March 31, 1991, "Illinois spent $536 million in the last 14 years to build 15 medium and minimum security prisons to try to house a prison population that is growing faster than any other state's in the nation." Gierach Notebooks, p. 472.

"Today, I announce my candidacy… and a war on drug dealers and the illicit drug profits they reap at our expense. Confiscation of the assets of drug dealers who have already made a fortune in the drug business and imposition of harsher jail sentences [upon them] is not weapon enough. I want to wage a war on drug dealers which 'takes the profit out of drugs,' a war that sews the pockets of drug dealers shut before they make a sale. I want to hurt drug dealers in their pocketbooks….

"Contrary to popular political rhetoric, I do not believe we can build enough jails, impose enough mandatory-minimum sentences, or hire enough police, judges, prosecutors, and other court personnel to effectively address the problem of drugs and crime."

It was a challenging campaign kickoff speech, contradicting popular drug-war rhetoric, well-exemplified by President George H.W. Bush's 1989 "get tough on drugs" speech, where he promised to build more prisons to house 24,000 more prisoners, increase drug-war spending by billions of dollars, and impose tougher sentencing while pushing the first National Drug Control Strategy.[252]

The night of my candidacy announcement, I listened to radio broadcasts hoping to hear some word of my candidacy announcement. Discouragingly not one word. But I did hear a story about a drug-motivated crime broadcast that same night on either WBBM, the CBS Chicago all-news radio affiliate, or WMAQ, the NBC Chicago all-news radio affiliate.[253] The broadcast reported a woman on Chicago's West Side or South Side (I forget which) who entered an apartment vestibule after dark and rang one doorbell after another until finally an old man answered. Reportedly she asked for a drink of water and the old man buzzed her in to help her. Upon gaining entry, the woman proceeded to beat the man to death with a two-by-four (a piece of wood). She was caught and arrested while searching the man's apartment looking for money to buy drugs. I called the radio station, explained what I had said about "Addict Crime" at my candidacy announcement and suggested the radio station link the candidacy story and the drug story, or run them back-to-back. It did not. Unfortunately,

[252] President George HW Bush Speech on Drugs, 1989, video, https://youtu.be/mtlkyBk6rcc, and Dan Check, "The Successes and Failures of George Bush's War on Drugs, *DrugSense.org*, http://tfy.drugsense.org/bushwar.htm.

[253] *Wikipedia*, s.v. WBBM, https://en.m.wikipedia.org/wiki/WBBM_(AM) and WMAQ, https://en.m.wikipedia.org/wiki/WSCR, respectively, accessed March 17, 2023. .

the lady with the two-by-four made a better standalone news story than my campaign message linking drug addiction and addict crime.

In contrast to Addict Crime, Turf-War Crime is distinctly different. Another story from the 1990s era still haunts me and exemplifies the mate to Addict Crime, "Turf-War Crime."

Turf-War Crime and a Jeep Cherokee

A young lad named La'Mayne Brasswell Bland, age seventeen, was a good boy who sang in the church choir and worked two jobs, one at McDonald's and one at White Castle. But early he sensed his life would not get any better than this. When La'Mayne quit school, he told his stepfather, John Bland, "I'm going to end up dead, anyway."[254] La'Mayne dreamed of one day owning a Jeep Cherokee, and he decided to sell drugs just long enough to raise enough money to buy one, he told his girlfriend. He ended up shot dead, killed by rivals, his body dumped in his family's front yard. R.R. Rayner III, owner of a funeral home on Chicago's South Side, said of the boy, "[He] wasn't really a member of any gang. But I guess he had some friends.... One young boy after another. Five through here in just the last week. We've got another one right now, 19 years old, just down the hall." Coming home from the funeral late that night, John Bland put the key to his house in the lock just as a youngster frantically ran by, out of breath, chased by other youngsters. "He headed down an alley followed by the others. Soon thereafter, gunshots. 'Pow! Pow! Pow! Pow!' It never stops. It never stops at all," John said.

I was so moved by the story that I headed to the Bland home and met Ramona Bland, La'Mayne's mother. As I crossed the front yard where this lad's body was unceremoniously dumped by his competitors, I observed it was a nice home situated amongst well-kept buildings and shielded by a wrought iron fence. I conveyed my condolences to Ramona and explained my efforts to change this norm by running for state's attorney seeking to end drug prohibition. She signed a letter authorizing me to tell her son's tragic story in my efforts. Capping what happened to La'Mayne, John Bland commented: "I don't know how you can get raised out here and not become a part of what goes on. You had Prohibition, with the Italians and the Irish and liquor

---

[254] Zay N. Smith, "Victims of violence laid to rest, 'Sometimes even an embalmer cries at what he sees,'" *Chicago Sun-Times*, September 11, 1991. Gierach notebooks, p. 696.

and guns. Now it's Blacks and Hispanics and drugs and guns. You tell me the difference. And you tell me how to escape it."[255]

The Endless World War on Drugs

Sadly, the drug war is designed to have no end. No one predicts or foresees its end, because it is more an intolerant state of mind or state of being than a battle plan. It's foolish. The UN World War on Drugs declared a war on Mother Nature's plants and on an inexhaustible supply of man-made, laboratory-produced variants. Betting against either man or Mother Nature is foolish. Waging a war against both is self-defeating.

And regardless of which drug-producing, drug-consuming or drug-transiting country in the world you might live in — just read, watch or listen to learn of unacceptable levels of violence nearby and far away. For example, take today's news from Mexico: "The bodies of ten people were found in the central Mexican state of Zacatecas on Thursday, nine of them hanging from a bridge, in apparent gang-related killings, according to local officials."[256]

Violence has become a Western Hemisphere dietary staple, a man-eating main course.

One hundred years ago, Prohibition — alcohol prohibition — brought world-renowned, gangster-style violence to America. Why would the prohibition of other mind-altering substances used for recreational enjoyment — just like alcohol — not cause the same prolifically violent consequences? Why?

> *"In retrospect, a drug-free America had no more chance of success than an alcohol-free America."*
>
> — Author Mike Gray

---

[255] Ibid.

[256] Reuters Staff, "Bodies found hanging from bridge in Mexico; gang violence blamed," *Reuters*, November 18, 2021, https://apple.news/Akl7mhEFHSvaHEUFmQ_dhWw.

"Caponeville" or "Chi-Raq"

For some years now, Chicago has been called, "Chiraq," because more people were dying from gun violence in Chicago than in Iraq, a country at real war. "[However computed], the number of Americans murdered in Chicago still tops U.S. deaths during the wars in Iraq & Afghanistan over the same time period [2001-2016]."[257] Six years ago, in 2015, **Spike Lee** produced, directed and co-wrote with Kevin Willmott, an American musical crime comedy called, *Chi-Raq*,[258] underscoring the same point. Chiraq fits, but "**Caponeville**," home of Al Capone and Prohibition, fits just as well.[259]

The War on Drugs has turned the clock back to the days of Chicago's Capone gangsterism, a culture of belonging to organized violent gangs. This past weekend (July 26, 2021) in Chicago seventy-three people were shot and twelve died, as of Tuesday, in "the shooting gallery."[260]

"As violent crime continues to skyrocket in Chicago and other cities, Illinois Gov. J.B. Pritzker... signed an executive order declaring gun violence a public health crisis in Illinois and pledged to provide more resources to community organizations that focus on combating the problem. The additional resources promised by Pritzker will draw from federal and state funding, including $50 million in the current budget. But the $100 million in appropriations in each of the next two years laid out by Pritzker is far from a sure thing, with the governor only saying his administration would work with state legislators to secure the funding.... Like other major cities across the U.S. in 2021, Chicago has experienced some of its worst violence in years as the country continues to navigate the twists and turns of the COVID-19 pandemic."[261]

---

[257] Andrew Holt, "Chicago vs. Iraq & Afghanistan," January 3, 2017, blog post, https://apholt.com/2017/01/03/chicago-vs-iraq-afghanistan/.

[258] *Wikipedia, s.v.* "Chi-Raq," https://en.m.wikipedia.org/wiki/Chi-Raq, accessed March 17, 2023.?

[259] Law Enforcement Against Prohibition, video, *YouTube*, https://youtu.be/rGUe6LvNOfk; Javier Sicilia's, "Caravan for Peace and Justice," Julián Aguilar, "Caravan From Mexico to Fault U.S. Drug Policy During Visit to Texas," *The Texas Tribune*, August 15, 2012, https://www.texastribune.org/2012/08/15/caravan-mexico-seeks-condemn-us-drug-policy/.

[260] Katherine Rosenberg-Douglas and Naya Gupta, "12 fatalities among 73 people shot during the weekend in Chicago," *Chicago Tribune*, July 26, 2021, https://www.chicagotribune.com/news/breaking/ct-chicago-shootings-violence-weekend-roundup-20210726-yt26zmfj3rbztl6sdokumfs75q-story.html.

[261] Jeremy Gorner and Dan Perella, "Pritzker pledges to fight violence," *Chicago Tribune*, November 2, 2021, https://digitaledition.chicagotribune.com/html5/mobile/production/default.aspx?edid=8e0e6d4d-4bd5-4f8a-a81f-59a948971e13, emphasis added.

> *"Crime, as it happens, is a problem that can be solved in quick and pragmatic fashion, by legalizing the sale of drugs to adults, while retaining laws protecting children."*
>
> — Commodities Trader Richard J. Dennis

500 Shootings Over Independence Day 2021

In 2021 just over the Independence Day weekend celebration, "At least 233 people were killed and 618 people were injured by gun violence in more than 500 shootings across the [United States]..., a 26% drop from last year's holiday weekend, according to the latest data compiled by the Gun Violence Archive."[262] In a story about another recent violence-filled weekend in the Land of the Brave, seven people were killed, and more than forty people were injured in ten mass shootings across the USA. These "mass shootings," defined as having four or more victims, were perpetrated in Atlantic, City New Jersey; Richmond, Virginia; Dallas, Texas; Oakland, California; Anchorage; Alaska, Baton Rouge, Louisiana; Minneapolis, Minnesota; a Denver Colorado suburb, and near South Bend, Indiana.[263] In 2022, through November 25th, the USA experienced 611 mass shootings.[264]

Have Americans lost their minds? Do we Americans suffer from a Second Amendment disease or defect of the brain? Are "We, the People," drug-war possessed and gun crazy?

Certainly, there are many reasons for so many shootings. And just as certainly, bad gun policy and bad drug policy in America rank high on the blame scale. These two

---

[262] Emma Tucker, Omar Jimenez and Kristina Sgueglia, "More than 230 people fatally shot in shootings over the Fourth of July weekend," *CNN*, July 7, 2021, https://www.cnn.com/2021/07/05/us/us-shootings-july-fourth-weekend/index.html.

[263] Hollie Silverman and Amir Vera, "7 killed, more than 40 injured in 10 mass shootings across the US over the weekend," *CNN*, June 21, 2021, https://www.cnn.com/2021/06/21/us/gun-violence-weekend-roundup/index.html.

[264] Brian Bushard, "611 Mass Shootings Recorded So Far In 2022 — Second-Worst Year For Gun Violence In Almost A Decade," *Forbes*, November 25, 2022, https://www.forbes.com/sites/brianbushard/2022/11/25/611-mass-shootings-recorded-so-far-in-2022-second-worst-year-for-gun-violence-in-almost-a-decade/?sh=e6a6a2c152ce.

dynamics have joined together to kill some of us and break the hearts of the rest of us with death by violence.

Contagious "Ping-Pong" Violence

Violence is catching. Here's how it works. If you shoot my loved one, I'm gonna shoot your loved one. If you shoot into a crowd of my friends or fellow gang members, I'm gonna shoot into a crowd of your friends and neighbors. Simple as that. If I report your misconduct to the police, my doorstep, my family and my friends become nearly indefensible against your threats, intimidation and retaliatory violence. I know that. But if I help myself to retaliation, if I don't "rat" on you to the police, maybe I'll get even, maybe even anonymously, and you won't know for sure who to go after in the relentless, play of "ping-pong" violence. That's the mindset. Rather than "Turn the other cheek," street justice says, "Fire another round."

Epidemiologist **Gary Slutkin, M.D.** became known for advocating that violence is a disease and creating **Cure Violence**, an NGO. Employing violence interrupters through CeaseFire,[265] inter alia, his advocacy showed some success. I debated Dr. Slutkin on a Chicago-area cable-TV sponsored by the League of Women Voters in the early 1990s. I agreed with his advocacy but faulted his disease model understanding of violence because, beginning until now, it said not one word about the effect of drug prohibition on violence, a big oversight. Thus, Cure Violence is just another mainstream violence solution taken with the drug-prohibition poison pill. (See Chapter 10)

Comparing Capone Prohibition Days to Guzmán Prohibition Days

Maggie Sivit, digital and engagement producer for WBEZ Chicago, a radio station and investigative reporting source, set out to answer a question posed by Hyde Park resident Molly Herron, "How does Chicago's gang violence today compare to gang warfare under Al Capone?" Maggie compared and reported on the differences between the Capone Prohibition Era and the current Drug Prohibition Era, particularly regarding violence, relying in part on the work and reports of the **Illinois Crime Commission**, a nonprofit organization, and the **University of Chicago Crime Laboratory**,

---

265 Gary Slutkin, "CeaseFire," *Philanthropy News Digest*, March 17, 2009, https://en.m.wikipedia.org/wiki/Cure_Violence.

which analyzes violence statistics, demographics, and economic, social and psycholog-ical factors, rather than test-tube contents and fingerprints; it is more a think tank than a conventional crime laboratory.[266]

Maggie observed, "It's a good question, because the answer challenges what we think we know about violence and murder in both Capone's time and ours. Yes, there are crime stats that compare violence in the two eras, but those numbers actually ob-scure the most interesting points of comparison that stretch almost a century, like how people have been killed, who was targeted, and why."[267]

Perhaps surprising to some, "With a national murder rate of 4.96 per 100,000, the United States murder rate is well below the 6.9 global murder rate average in 2010."[268]

Likely also surprising to some, Maggie Sivit reported that "The average homicide rate during Capone's reign was about 12 murders per 100,000 residents, according to numbers collected from bulletins of the **Chicago Crime Commission** and the Illinois Crime Survey of 1929.... Bottom line: The homicide rate was probably lower during the Capone era than in 2016. But it wasn't much lower than rates seen in the past dozen years or so. It's also important to point out that murder rates in the Capone era and last year are both lower than rates seen during the '70s, '80s, and '90s."[269] Of course, I interject and note that those three decades were the first decades to follow adoption of the 1970 Controlled Substances Act, the Act by which the United States implemented the 1961 Single Convention drug-prohibition policy, a political decision that rolled out the red carpet for violent criminogenic behavior.

Thoughtfully, Maggie reiterated an observation made by the Illinois Crime Survey 1929: "As the authors of the Illinois Crime Survey saw it, the most insidious effect of Chicago gang violence of the 1920s was not the dissolution of society into 'lawless-ness': It was that the gangster supplanted the legal system of law and order with a system of his own. [The gangster] used force to accomplish and guarantee trade regu-lations, to free himself from competition, to resolve conflicts and settle disagreements,

---

266 "Urban Labs, Crime Lab," *University Chicago*, https://urbanlabs.uchicago.edu/labs/crime, accessed March 17, 2023.

267 Maggie Sivit, "History of Violence: Chicago During The Capone Era and Today," *WBEZ Chicago*, June 4, 2017,   https://www.wbez.org/stories/history-of-violence-chicago-during-the-capone-era-and-today/6bff3ad9-097a-42e8-ac23-bc90d83d5bdb.

268 Gierach, James E., "Gun Violence Follows Drug Prohibition Gold Vein," August 4, 2020, https://jamesgierach.tumblr.com/post/656591147931680768.

269 Sivit, supra, emphasis added.

to reward his friends and punish his enemies. And other people saw him do it. And simultaneously they saw corruption among judges, abuses by police, and the selfishness of politicians."[270] Sounds familiar.

Painful Violence

The early decades of this millennium are replaying Prohibition's tune. Drug prohibition has brought us full circle a hundred years after the last American substance prohibition. Will we ever learn? So many Americans are hurting from prohibition-related, prohibition-influenced and prohibition-driven violence that there is a shortage of grief counselors and social workers. One parent who lost a child to gun violence soon thereafter expressed her grief so powerfully, explaining, "I didn't want to die. But I didn't want to live either."[271] During the "Shooting 90s," Chicago gang violence was so incessant and painful that cartoonist **Jack Higgins** often movingly depicted it in riveting cartoons, like one picturing youngsters down, shot and bleeding in the street as a passerby asks, "Whose colors are Baby Blue and Pink?"[272]

Governor Jim Edgar's 1993 Task Force on Crime and Corrections

During the early 1990s, violence was so bad and prisons were so overcrowded that Illinois' Governor Jim Edgar appointed a Task Force on Crime and Corrections, chaired by **Anton R. Valukas**. The Task Force held hearings regarding these problems, eventually concluding its work and declaring Illinois could not build its way out of its crime and corrections crisis. But it then went on to recommend building more prisons without any mention or suggestion of revamping drug-prohibition policy.[273] Yet, the final report of the Task Force mentioned the subject of drugs *124 times in 103 pages,*

---

[270] Sivit, supra, emphasis added.

[271] Claudia Lauer, "A Lot of People are Hurting, Grief Counselors in Short Supply stretched to the limit with gun violence across the country," *Associated Press,* republished, *Chicago Sun-Times,* July 25, 2021, https://paper.suntimes.com/html5/reader/production/default.aspx?pubname=&edid=9b70b360-bcc4-4833-abb4-5e1c90628896&pnum=34.

[272] Jack Higgins, E.g., "Who's colors are Baby Blue and Pink?" *Chicago Sun-Times,* April 12, 1996, https://www.google.com/search?q=chicago+suntimes+Higgins+drawings+gangs&tbm=isch&ved=2ahUKEwj49 5CJy43yAhWyoK0KHQuyCgoQ2-cCegQIABAC&oq=chicago+suntimes+Higgins+drawings+gangs&gs_ lcp=ChJtb2JpbGUtZ3dzLXdpei1pbWcQAzoECB4QCjoFCCEQqwJQ148BWPmvAWDUtQFoAHAAeACA AZgCiAGkCZIBBjEwLjAuMZgBAKABAcABAQ&client=mobile-gws-wiz-img&ei=JWcFYbjRH7LBtg WL5KpQ&bih=1057&biw=820&rlz=1C9BKJA_enUS936US939&hl=en-US#imgrc=JDbr7oXCyNaDzM.

[273] Final Report, "Gov. Edgar's Crime and Corrections Task Force," March 1993, https://www.ojp.gov /pdffiles1/Digitization/142786NCJRS.pdf.

as my critique of its work pointed out.[274] Its recommendations numbered 4 and 4A did recommend drug treatment for inmates, but nothing about prohibition policy itself.

I attended one of the Task Force hearings held in Chicago in the summer of 1993, asking to testify as a former Cook County prosecutor regarding the critical need for drug policy reform to prevent some violent crime. My request was denied by Chairman Valukas who ruled that drug policy was beyond the scope of the governor's charge to the Task Force.

The "What Risk" Witness Silenced

During a Task Force hearing day recess, I met a handsome, white, middle-aged man. He looked a little like Paul Newman and told me he was a restaurateur from a western Chicago suburb. I asked him why he was attending. He explained he was a former drug dealer who sold drugs to professional athletes in Florida and on the East Coast, but who was eventually caught and served time in a Colorado penitentiary. He claimed to have been the biggest supplier of drugs in the Colorado prison where he was incarcerated but they never could catch him. He explained he also hoped to testify at the Edgar Task Force hearing, because of his experience and knowledge as an accomplished former drug dealer. He said, "There is no limit to how much money a drug dealer can make selling drugs. It's just a question of what risk one is willing to take to make it." He said he intended to write a book about his experience, in which he would disclose how he successfully smuggled drugs into prison, and he would title it, *What Risk?*

His message and mine went unheard by the Task Force. Instead, it heard from witness after witness, each of whom had a politician's, law-enforcer's, or judge's hand in creating the crisis they were tasked to fix. During the same hearing break when I met the "What Risk" restauranteur, I noticed the front page of the *Chicago Defender*, a Chicago-based, African-American newspaper founded in 1905 by Robert S. Abbott, once considered the most important newspaper of its kind. That day's issue of the *Chicago Defender*, front page, portrayed a drawing of a young black child lying in the street, shot and bleeding to death. The headline impertinently asked, "Where Are Our Leaders?"

---

[274] Gierach, James E., "Task force shuns ideas to break drug-crime-jail-tax cycle," *Illinois Issues*, May 1993, https://www.lib.niu.edu/1993/ii930510.html.

"Where Are Our Leaders?"

I grimaced and thought to myself. "They are here." State senators and representatives, county sheriffs, judges, law enforcement brass, powerful attorneys, the head and former heads of the Illinois Department of Corrections, and even the first administrator of the U.S. Drug Enforcement Agency. The very people who gave us this disastrous, criminogenic drug-war policy — they are here. The witness list roster,[275] like the Task Force membership itself,[276] largely consisted of leaders who helped make the rules that helped make the crime and corrections policy mess.

Epitomizing the misdirection of the Task Force's work and product, one Task Force member was none other than an America's twentieth century drug-prohibition icon, **Peter Bensinger**. Mr. Bensinger was perfectly credentialed for maintaining the drug-war status quo. He was a former director of the Illinois Department of Corrections, the current director of the Illinois Criminal Justice Information Authority, and former and first head of the Drug Enforcement Agency (DEA). In later life after retiring from government work, Mr. Bensinger capitalized on American's prohibition-magnified drug problem by operating a private business called Bensinger DuPont & Associates, Inc. (BDA), a business providing employee assistance programs. Its services included work-life services, training and education, compulsive gambling services, research, drug testing management and background checks. BDA provides services to businesses and government agencies.[277]

Geriatric Prisons Costly and Unwise

Judge Thomas R. Fitzgerald, a Task Force member and Chief of the Criminal Division of the Circuit Court of Cook County, who later would become Chief Justice of the Illinois Supreme Court (who I debated regarding drug policy at the **Union League Club of Chicago**, moderated by **Ron Magers**), sarcastically quipped at one point during the Task Force hearings: Illinois criminal penalties were so severe and sentences so

---

[275] Final Report, "Gov. Edgar's Crime and Corrections Task Force," March 1993, https://www.ojp.gov/pdffiles1/Digitization/142786NCJRS.pdf,

Witness List, page 116-124. Task Force Member List, p. 2. My written submittal to the Task Force was innocuously mentioned in the Final Report without mention of its drug policy reform content in Appendix B, p. 115.

[276] Ibid.

[277] Bensinger DuPont & Associates, Inc., https://www.bloomberg.com/profile/company/0538345D:US; and Insomis Corp., https://completemarkets.com/company/bensingerdupont, both accessed March 17, 2023.

long that one day Illinois would be running "a geriatric prison system." Insightful, humorous, but not very funny. The cost of housing old people and providing medical care to them is very expensive. Not part of the Task Force story I'm telling, but a federal law-enforcement officer once cautioned me — "Never seize anything that eats." Whether speaking of horses, cows, dogs or people, maintaining captive beings is labor intensive and expensive. Equally true is that as men grow older, testosterone levels plummet (see Chapter 11, Reason 4), and the impetuosity and aggressiveness of youth is naturally drained from their loins, brains and bodies. Authority? Morgan Freeman, *The Shawshank Redemption.*[278]

Chapter 3 of the Task Force Final Report outlined major crime and corrections issues and described the criminal progression: first came the drug-prohibition offenders, then came the drug-prohibition violent offenders. The report expressed it this way: "The accelerated growth in the inmate population is driven in large part by increased admissions of serious offenders and parole violators with new sentences. In the late 1980s, many new felony admissions to the Department of Corrections emanated from drug-related offenses, primarily Class 2, 3, and 4 felony offenses. In FY92, however, this trend reversed itself, as the growth in admissions for serious offenses - Murder and Class X and Class 1 felonies - far outstripped those for lower class offenses. In addition, the number of violent offender admissions surpassed the number of drug offender admissions for the first time in years."

Despite recognition of these facts, the Task Force chairman ruled drug policy was beyond the scope of the Task Force work, preventing drug policy reformers from testifying. I say, if drug-policy reform was beyond the scope of Governor Edgar's Task Force work, then a solution to Illinois' crime and corrections crisis in 1993 was beyond the reach of his Task Force.

Illinois Kicked the "Drug Policy Reform Can" Down the Road in 1993

Governor Edgar's Task Force on Crime and Corrections of 1993 kicked the can down the road, as the Final Report itself recognized on page twelve of its Final Report under the heading, "Conclusion: Address the Underlying Causes of Prison Crowding." The report said: "Finally, the Illinois Task Force on Crime and Corrections urges the Governor and the General Assembly to look specifically at ways to address the underlying causes of the growth of crime in Illinois. *Unfortunately, the ultimate answers to the*

---

[278] *The Shawshank Redemption, YouTube,* video clip, https://youtu.be/cGo5rXUAH2o.

problems of crime and violence (and the prison crowding that comes with them) are outside the practical scope of this Task Force's charge. They are subsumed in the answers to the overarching problems confronting our society, including poverty, unemployment, lack of education, the decreased stability of the family unit and decline of moral values, street gangs, the ready availability of handguns and assault rifles, *and drugs.* While the Task Force believes that its recommendations will alleviate the current crowding crisis, the ultimate solutions to crime and prison crowding must focus not on the current prison population, but on the current preschool population and their families."[279]

President Obama's Task Force on 21st Century Policing Kicked the Can in 2015

Sadly, President Obama's Task Force on 21st Century Policing of 2015 also kicked the drug-policy-reform can down the road in the same fashion as Governor Edgar's Task Force. Lamenting the limited breadth of its assignment, the Obama Policing Task Force wrote in its final report: *"The President should support and provide funding for the creation of a National Crime and Justice Task Force to review and evaluate all components of the criminal justice system for the purpose of making recommendations to the country on comprehensive criminal justice reform."* (Seven years later now, no president has created or funded such a task force.) "Several witnesses at the task force's listening sessions pointed to the fact that police represent the 'face' of the criminal justice system to the public. Yet police are obviously not responsible for the laws or incarceration policies that many citizens find unfair. This misassociation leads us to call for a broader examination of such issues as drug policy, sentencing and incarceration, which are beyond the scope of a review of police practices."[280]

Optimistically, having known Obama Task Force co-chair Charles Ramsey for years and having addressed his graduate school law-enforcement students at Lewis University in Romeoville, Illinois,[281] I requested the opportunity to testify before the Obama Task Force regarding drug-legalization policy as it impacted policing. But my

---

[279] Final Report, Gov. Edgar's Crime and Corrections Task Force, supra, https://www.ojp.gov/pdffiles1/Digitization/142786NCJRS.pdf, p. 12, emphasis added, accessed March 17, 2023. .

[280] Final Report, "The President's Task Force on 21st Century Policing," May 2015, https://cops.usdoj.gov/pdf/taskforce/taskforce_finalreport.pdf, p. 7, emphasis added.

[281] Gierach, James E., Lewis University guest speaker announcement, Nov. 9, 1993, https://jamesgierach.tumblr.com/post/673185525519302656/gierach-guest-speaker-lewis-university-nov-9.

offer was declined. Live testimony was by invitation only, and the Obama Task Force determined that drug policy was not within the scope of President Obama's charge.

Denied the opportunity to testify, I submitted my thoughts in writing to the Obama Task Force, just as I did with the Edgar Task Force. My written statement was made on behalf of Law Enforcement Against Prohibition (LEAP) and called on the Task Force to recommend to President Obama an End to the War on Drugs. Fruitlessly, my complete statement (available here)[282] was filed and made a part of the archives of the Obama Task Force report of proceedings.

Police Don't Make the Rules

During a 2012 police show-and-tell press conference, former Chicago Police Superintendent **Garry McCarthy** (May 11, 2011 to Dec. 1, 2015) matter-of-factly made the same observation as the Obama Task Force: Police don't make the rules. The superintendent stood in front of two tables loaded with guns seized over the weekend in raids in several high-crime police districts, targeting drug sales.[283] I was seated front row center before him wearing my black LEAP T-shirt that said in big, bold, red letters, "Cops Say Legalize Drugs," and the back said, "Ask me why?"

As McCarthy wound down his remarks, I was the first "reporter" to bullet to my feet with hand raised. But as soon as I did, the superintendent launched back into further discussion. That little scenario replayed several times. Each time as his remarks seemed to be concluding I was first on my feet with my hand in the air. To his everlasting credit, Superintendent McCarthy recognized me first for a question though he knew what was coming, a barrage of drug-prohibition questions.

"Mr. Superintendent, isn't this just Prohibition all over again? Al Capone Prohibition? Aren't we just going to have two more tables of guns next weekend? And aren't drug dealers going to continue selling drugs without interruption? Isn't that the reason for all the guns and violence?"

---

[282] Gierach/LEAP Statement, Pres. Obama's Task Force on 21st Century Policing, supra, https://jamesgierach.tumblr.com/post/643840011552391168/pres-obama-task-force-21st-century-policing.

[283] "Chicago Police Arrest 300, Nab 100 Weapons In 3-Day Drug Crackdown," *CBS Chicago*, August 26, 2012, https://chicago.cbslocal.com/2012/08/26/chicago-police-arrest-300-nab-100-weapons-in-3-day-drug-crackdown/.

Respectfully with dignified composure and truth on his side, Superintendent McCarthy simply proclaimed, "I don't make the laws. It's my job to enforce them." He was right. No further questions.

Agreed, maybe the superintendent's 2012 press conference was not the best forum for my questions. But I remain puzzled to this day that with all the TV cameras, photographers and print reporters in the room, not one journalist had the savvy, insight or inclination to record, photograph or report on the exchange between the superintendent and me. It was the meaningful essence of what happened during that police press conference that day. Seizing guns, busting some drug dealers, and announcing a crackdown on drugs was about as newsworthy and useful to stopping crime as the day's traffic report. Chicago regularly seized 5,000 to 7,000 guns a year, and from January 2017 to May 2020 the area around the Monticello Avenue drug market had 2,424 drug arrests and 19,241 narcotics-related calls.[284] And drug busts with twenty-two drug dealers arrested in one fell swoop in neighborhoods like Chicago's Humboldt Park were routine.[285]

Maybe Governor Edgar's and President Obama's Task Forces were not appropriate forums for consideration of major drug policy reform, any more than was Superintendent McCarthy's press conference. But what forum is the appropriate one? I continued searching for that forum — a forum where ending drug prohibition policy is within the scope of a task force charge given by a president or a governor.

> "In the mid-1960s, the homicide rate started to rise, and then soared after the war on drugs was launched by President Nixon and continued by his successors.... Many other things were going on during the decades from the 50s to the 80s. However, there seems little doubt that the war on drugs is the single most important factor that produced such drastic increases."
>
> — Economist Milton Friedman

[284] Chuck Goudie, "City on pace for record year in gun seizures," *ABC7, Chicago*, November 17, 2016, https://abc7chicago.com/news/city-on-pace-for-record-year-in-gun-seizures/1612941/.

[285] Claire Hao, "22 charged in West Side drug bust after yearlong federal investigation," *Chicago Tribune*, July 21, 2020, https://www.chicagotribune.com/news/breaking/ct-heroin-drug-bust-humboldt-park-20200721-ajiacen22jfxnbzshbs7xwzr5m-story.html.

Why Are People Shooting One Another?

The prohibition of recreational substances is a common reason why people are shooting one another. It was so in 1920s and it is so again today, alcohol back then, assorted drugs now. Today, as we ask "why" a homicide occurred, classifying the motivation of the actor may help prevent some of them, because some homicides are more preventable than others. Mental illness, domestic relationships and hate-driven homicides are less preventable than drug-business homicides.

In my experience — that included a stint prosecuting in the Homicide Unit of the Cook County Grand Jury and the Homicide/Sex preliminary hearing court in Chicago (Branch 66) — homicides can be broadly categorized by three motivating factors: (a) hate homicides, (b) homicides committed by "crazy" people, and (c) homicides perpetrated for financial gain.

Hate Homicides

Homicides motivated by hate are difficult to predict and, therefore, very difficult to prevent. Homicides commonly falling into the "hate classification" are those committed by "haters," a broad spectrum of persons who hate others, often strangers, simply because of the other person's identification with a particular race, creed, color, religion, sexual orientation, political affiliation, nationality, immigration status (the "foreigners and aliens"), or gang affiliation. Hate motivates many killings. The targeted Jewish synagogue massacre of 2018 exemplifies a hate-motivated killing spree.[286] The racist targeting of Blacks and slaughter of ten people grocery shopping at Tops — a Buffalo, New York supermarket — on a Saturday, May 14 2022, allegedly committed by an eighteen-year-old white man exhibits like venomous hate.[287]

Also falling into the "hate category" of killings are homicides committed by estranged domestic partners, feuding family members and in-laws. Love turned to hate is fertile homicide turf. I recall the ex-husband-and-wife family reunion a block from my home in Oak Lawn, Illinois, fifty some years ago. Both ex-partners happened to be practicing physicians who had two children together. Though divorced years earlier, the family reunited for dinner in the old family home. The reunion ended with the

[286] Campbell Robertson, Christopher Mele and Sabrina Tavernise, "11 Killed in Synagogue Massacre; Suspect Charged With 29 Counts," *The New York Times*, October 27, 2018, https://www.nytimes.com/2018/10/27/us/active-shooter-pittsburgh-synagogue-shooting.html?referringSource=articleShare.

[265] Susanne Rust and Richard Winston, "Gunman kills 10 at Buffalo supermarket in attack called a racially motivated hate crime," *Los Angeles Times*, May 14, 2022, https://apple.news/AGpubtzkmTdy2ox5VkKABsg.

father using a shotgun to kill his ex-wife and fleeing son, my high-school classmate. Hate, like love, knows no bounds.

Homicides Committed by "Crazies"

Homicides committed by persons "out of their minds" are also very difficult to predict and, therefore, again, difficult to prevent. As we often hear following such unexpected homicides, "Who would have thought...?" Lucidity can come and go for some, and the question is: how "out-of-touch" is Tom, Dick or Sally? It is not always easy to identify "who's nuts" and "who's not," or who "would never do such a thing," and who would.

Persons suffering from delusions, paranoia, schizophrenia, or other mental disease or defect possess a condition that is inherently fertile and irrational ground for homicide, a disease or defect that constitutes a condition endangering the lives of others and themselves. But even a relatively normal, healthy, human brain can be taxed by environment, chemistry, relationships, predicament, pressure, stress, hate, physiology and many other factors, making it difficult to diagnose mental illness, or predict future behavior. Such was the case of a Chase Bank teller stabbed to death by a crazy man in September 2021 in Chicago.[288] Mental illness-triggered homicides, just like hate-motivated homicides, are difficult to predict and, therefore, again, difficult to prevent.

Homicides Committed for Profit

But drug trafficking and retaliatory killings are the big drivers of homicide.[289] The Bureau of Justice Statistics (BJS) manages a data center and clearinghouse to support drug control policy research. Its Fact-Sheet data supported the following conclusion: "Drug trafficking generates violent crime. Trafficking in illicit drugs tends to be associated with the commission of violent crimes. Reasons for the relationship of drug trafficking to violence include: competition for drug markets and customers, disputes and rip-offs among individuals involved in the illegal drug market, individuals who participate in drug trafficking are prone to use violence and locations where street drug

---

288 Liz Nagy and Maher Kawash, "Stabbing at Chase Bank: Man charged in employee's murder at River North branch, victim ID'd," *ABC 7 Chicago*, September 3, 2021, https://abc7chicago.com/chase-bank-stabbing-chicago-600-n-dearborn-jessica-vilaythong/10996024/.

289 Amy Craddock, Ph.D., James J. Collins, Ph.D., and Anita Timrots at the Office of National Drug Control Policy (ONDCP) Drugs & Crime Clearinghouse, "Fact Sheet: Drug-Related Crime," *U.S. Department of Justice*, Bureau of Justice Statistics (September 1994, NCJ–149286), https://bjs.ojp.gov/content/pub/pdf/DRRC.PDF, accessed September 6, 2021.

markets proliferate tend to be disadvantaged economically and socially; legal and social controls against violence in such areas tend to be ineffective. The proliferation of lethal weapons in recent years has also likely made drug violence more deadly." [Gierach interjecting — firearms are essential tools of the drug-trafficking trade.]

"BJS examined homicides in the 75 most populous counties in the United States in 1988. Many of the homicides involved drugs or drug trafficking, including the following: drug manufacture, dispute over drugs, theft of drugs or drug money, a drug scam, a bad drug deal, punishment for drug theft, or illegal use of drugs. One of these circumstances was involved for 18% of defendants and 16% of victims."[290]

In 2021 and earlier Chicago Police Superintendent David Brown said, much like his many predecessors, that Chicago violence is driven by drug-gangs and easy access to guns. Chicago police superintendents seem to recognize that gangs gravitate to drug crimes. It is less certain how many of them believe that gangs are encouraged and enabled by governmental laws and societal endorsement of drug prohibition.

Drugs: The Lifeblood of Gangs and the Death Knell to Many

Charles H. Ramsey, co-chair of President Barack Obama's 21st Century Policing Task Force, said in 1991 when he was Chicago's narcotics unit police commander, "In 1988, the year of the city's first crack cocaine arrest, only two of the 25 police districts reported arrests for the drug. This year, only one district seems free of it."[291] That same year, F. Thomas Braglia, director of the Northeastern Metropolitan Enforcement Group, said "Drug sales are the 'lifeblood' of gangs. If we can cut off their profits from drug sales, we may prevent their further growth into other criminal enterprises."[292]

Charles Kyle, assistant professor of sociology at De Paul University, would likely agree with that assessment. In 1990, he said, "Drugs are the economy of gangs," adding "the increase in gang violence also can be linked to the loss of manual-labor jobs in the metropolitan area, leaving young people with far fewer employment opportunities."[293] And a Chicago police commander of the Deering district said in 1990, "Basically, the

---

[290] Ibid.

[291] Phillip J. O'Connor, "Crack Coke invades 24 of 25 City cop districts," *Chicago Sun-Times*, November 21, 1991, Gierach notebooks, p. 899.

[292] Ibid., emphasis added.

[293] William Recktenwald and Robert Blau, "Youth homicides up 22% in city, Gangs and drugs blamed for rise in murder rate," *Chicago Tribune*, January 28, 1990, Gierach notebooks, p. 102.

vast majority of violence is over territory for the drug business. It's an unfortunate waste of human life. I've seen it for years and years."[294]

Drug-gang violence is about the money. "A kilogram of cocaine (2.2 pounds) of cocaine sells for about $80,000 in Japan, $35,000 in France and $22,000 in Los Angeles."[295] The same price erraticism and "*Monopoly* money" reality drive violent crime. "The same kilogram of cocaine that brings $8,000 in Miami or $17,000 in Chicago may command $30,000 in Peoria [a downstate Illinois city] because of the relative scarcity there."[296] Meanwhile, "In Peoria, as drug-related crimes more than tripled last year [1988], to 418 from 126, the police department joined the FBI, the federal drug agency and sheriffs in three counties to conduct a major crackdown on thriving cocaine and methamphetamine rings."[297]

1991 Mayor Richard M. Daley: Police Raids Fail to Stem Violence

Chicago mayors cannot seem to stop the violence. "An exasperated Mayor Richard Daley conceded Wednesday that high-profile police raids are doing little to stem the tide of violent crime and that the city is in a desperate, failing holding action against the drug trade. Pounding his rostrum and waving his arms... the mayor reprised his criticism of the federal government for not doing enough to stop the flow of drugs into the country, and characterized the courts as corrupt and too lenient on drug dealers."[298]

2021 Mayor Lori Lightfoot: Intractable Drug Prohibition Violence

In 2021, thirty years after Mayor Daley's turn, Chicago Mayor Lori Lightfoot stood at the podium and criticized the feds for not doing enough to stop the guns [that follow the drugs, Gierach notes] and characterizes the courts as too lenient on the gun dealers. "We've got to redouble our efforts to call upon the federal government to help

[294] Ibid., emphasis added.

[295] Gary Marx, "Drug trade spreads in S. America," *Chicago Tribune*, August 18, 1991, Gierach notebooks, p. 633.

[296] Paul Weingarten and James Coates, "Drugs find home in heartland: Crime, addictions destroying small-town way of life," *Chicago Tribune*, September 10, 1989, Gierach notebooks, p. 51.

[297] Ibid.

[298] John Kass, "Frustrated Daley sees little hope in drug war," *Chicago Tribune*, August 15, 1991, Gierach notebooks, p. 627A.

us stop the flow of illegal guns into our city," Lightfoot said in June 2021.[299] A month later she announced the creation of a $1 million fund for illegal gun tips.[300] Two years earlier, she blamed the judges for gun violence. [301] Following a violent Labor Day weekend, 2021, she said, "Gangs in this city are a huge problem, and we need to continue our focus on them and hold them accountable…. There are people with guns who have absolutely no regard for the sanctity of life. Our children are becoming victims."[302]

And releasing her 2022 city budget proposal, Mayor Lightfoot said, "Over $400 million is allocated to priority investment areas identified by Chicago's violence reduction and community safety plan, named "Our City, Our Safety," in addition to ongoing investments and efforts by the City of Chicago and its partners. Since 2019, the city has tripled violence prevention and intervention investments. This represents a $35 million increase over two years from $15 million to $50 million — putting Chicago's anti-violence investment on par with New York City and L.A., proportionate to our population."[303] Then, too, Mayor Lightfoot just succeeded in getting her gang asset forfeiture ordinance through a City Council committee, a dubious attempt to use civil lawsuits to seize illegal proceeds, that she calls "blood money," from Chicago's most violent street gangs.[304]

Unfortunately, Mayor Lightfoot is putting nearly all her eggs in the "gun, root cause and anti-violence" basket and none in the "end drug prohibition" basket. Like

---

[299] Tahman Bradley, "Lightfoot condemns illegal guns, calls on federal aid to combat Chicago crime," WGN9, June 15, 2021, https://wgntv.com/news/chicago-news/lightfoot-condemns-illegal-guns-calls-on-federal-aid-to-combat-chicago-crime/.

[300] Craig Wall, "Mayor Lori Lightfoot announces $1M fund for illegal gun tips," ABC7, July 15, 2021, https://abc7chicago.com/chicago-shootings-mayor-lori-lightfoot-illegal-guns-reward-fund/10889429/;

[301] Alex Nitkin, "Lightfoot blasts lenient judges after deadly weekend: 'This doesn't make any sense to me,'" The Daily Line, August 7, 2019, https://www.thedailyline.com/lightfoot-blasts-lenient-judges-after-deadly-weekend_this-doesn_t-make-any-sense-to-me.

[302] CBS staff, "At Least 6 Killed, 59 Wounded In Chicago Labor Day Weekend Gun Violence," CBS Chicago, September 7, 2021, https://chicago.cbslocal.com/2021/09/07/chicago-labor-day-weekend-gun-violence-2021/.

[303] Office of the Mayor, Chicago, "Mayor Lightfoot Releases 2022 Budget Proposal," Press Release, September 20,   2021, https://www.chicago.gov/city/en/depts/mayor/press_room/press_releases/2021/september/2022BudgetProposal.html.

[304] Fran Spielman, "Lightfoot's gang asset forfeiture ordinance clears committee hurdle," Chicago Sun-Times, February 18, 2022, https://chicago.suntimes.com/city-hall/2022/2/17/22939848/lightfoots-gang-asset-forfeiture-ordinance-public-safety-committee-vote-crime-chicago-violence.

Daley lamented and said years ago, and Lightfoot surely feels now: There is little hope in the drug war, making a stop to violence a hopeless cause.[305]

International Homicide Patterns

The UNODC has recently studied the homicide problem globally, and concluded that because the global population is growing, the rate of global homicides is decreasing. However, there are "hotspots" of violence in the Americas and Africa where the number of homicides is increasing. Because the number of homicides and violence is increasing in these areas, the UN sustainable development goal of reducing violence may not be accomplished. The United Nations, aiming to make a better world by 2030, adopted 17 Sustainable Development Goals in 2015 following decades of work.[306]

Sustainable Development Goal 16, labeled "Peace, Justice and Strong Institutions," aims to "Promote peaceful and inclusive societies for sustainable development, provide access to justice for all and build effective, accountable and inclusive institutions at all levels." The SDG 16 has 12 targets. Target 16.1 provides "Significantly reduce all forms of violence and related death rates everywhere."[307]

Regarding SDG 16 and Target 16.1, the 2019 UN report regarding global homicides makes the following discouraging points:

"Progress on target 16.1 of the Sustainable Development Goals ("significantly reduce all forms of violence") is not on track; it is necessary to scale up crime and violence prevention programmes in order to achieve that target by 2030, in particular by devoting more attention to combating organized crime.

"Since the adoption of the Sustainable Development Goals in September 2015, the number of homicide victims has been increasing. If this trend is not reversed, the target of significantly reducing all forms of violence (target 16.1 under Goal 16) will not be achieved by 2030. To achieve this target, it is necessary to scale up efforts to prevent homicidal violence at all levels: subnational, national, regional and international.

---

[305] Kass, "Frustrated Daley sees little hope in drug war," supra.

[306] United Nations, Department of Economic and Social Affairs, Sustainable Development, https://sdgs.un. org/goals.

[307] Sustainable Development Goal 16, Target 16.1, Targets and Indicators, https://sdgs.un.org/goals/goal16, accessed September 10, 2021.

"Since the start of the twenty-first century, organized crime has resulted in roughly the same number of killings as all armed conflicts across the world combined. Moreover, just like armed conflicts, organized crime destabilizes countries, undermines socioeconomic development and erodes the rule of law.

"High levels of violence are strongly associated with young males, both as perpetrators and victims, so violence prevention programmes should focus on providing support to young men to prevent them from being lured into a subculture of violence (e.g., gangs, drug dealing, criminal lifestyle)."[308]

It is difficult for me to read these words — calls for scaling up efforts to prevent homicidal violence and suggesting violence prevention programs for young males — knowing that the UN drug-prohibition paradigm is the greatest single boon to such homicidal misbehavior.

United Nations Drug Treaties Inimical to SDG 16

United Nation recreational drug prohibition treaties and policies compete to defeat Sustainable Development Goal 16 and Target 16.1; they are mutually exclusive in operation. If the world is saddled with recreational drug prohibition championed by United Nations agencies and compromised by its funding of conforming programs, it cannot have Peace, Justice and Strong Institutions. UN drug conventions are "the Instruction Book" on how to accomplish "Global Violent Crime, Homicide and Corruption." Capone, Escobar, Guzmán, Rothstein and many others proved the point. These men from America, Colombia and Mexico were enabled by "the prohibition of booze and drugs... the biggest lottery win for gangsters in history," author Johann Hari commented.[309]

---

[308] "UNODC, Global Study on Homicide 2019," Vienna, 2019, UNODC Research, Booklet One, Executive Summary, p. 35-36, https://www.unodc.org/documents/data-and-analysis/gsh/Booklet1.pdf.

[309] Johann Hari, *Chasing the Scream* (New York: Bloomsbury 2015), p. 52.

Typifying this truism, Chicago police superintendents, one after another, state that most Chicago homicides are caused by gang members fighting over drug turf, the drug trade, and gang retaliatory killings. On July 22, 2020, fifteen people were shot outside of a Chicago funeral home. At a press conference regarding the incident, Chicago Police Superintendent David Brown said the shooting was likely gang related. "Someone gets shot, which prompts someone else to pick up a gun — this cycle repeats itself over, and over, and over again. This cycle is fueled by street gangs, guns, and drugs. In the case of the funeral shooting, rival factions repeated this cycle."[310]

> *"That drug abuse is more common among the impoverished, the unemployed; among the homeless and the mentally ill is not mere coincidence. Those who are deprived of the essentials of a decent life are in pain. People in pain look for relief wherever they can get it.... People without jobs, skills, intact families and money, or with untreated mental illness are much less likely to succeed in treatment programs...These are the root causes of the most intractable drug abuse in this nation. Unless these causes are ameliorated, many of our neediest people will remain enslaved by drugs."*
>
> — Steven B. Duke and Albert E. Gross

Always Other Contributing Factors and "Root Causes"

Recently, a number of other factors are being blamed for the spike in U.S. violence, including easy access to guns and straw purchasers;[311] interstate and transnational gun-trafficking,[312], the COVID-19 pandemic,[313] civil unrest following the George Floyd

---

[310] Lakeidra Chavis, "An Outdated Understanding of Chicago Gangs Could Be Hampering Gun Violence Prevention," *The Trace, Investigating Gun Violence in America*, July 31, 2020, https://www.thetrace.org/2020/07/chicago-gang-gun-violence-law-enforcement/.

[311] Joseph Choi, "Chicago police announce new anti-gun violence initiative," *The Hill*, July 19, 2021, https://thehill.com/homenews/state-watch/563787-chicago-police-announce-new-anti-gun-violence-initiative, accessed September 9, 2021.

[312] Steve Scherer and Anna Mehler Paperny, "In fighting gun crime, Canada has an American problem," *Reuters*, July 27, 2022, https://www.ctvnews.ca/canada/in-fighting-gun-crime-canada-has-an-american-problem-1.6004198.

[313] "Crime Rates During COVID-19: Pandemic Impact on Violence," *Vision of Humanity*, accessed July 29, 2022, https://www.visionofhumanity.org/the-covid-19-pandemic-and-the-impact-on-violence/.

police murder;[314] and bail reform.[315] Other root causes and social conditions related to unequal economic status, education, housing, healthcare and access to social services are also commonly blamed, as far back as 1991.[316]

The magnitude of Chicago civil disorder in May 2021 following the police murder of George Floyd in Minneapolis is not to be underestimated either. "The protests began in legitimate anger over the Minneapolis police killing of Floyd, but soon became an excuse for thousands to cross the line. Organized street gangs took advantage, but not only the gangs. Others did too — neighbors grabbing what they could through smashed windows," Chicago Tribune columnist John Kass wrote. "In just a few days last May, there were 15 homicides and 53 shooting victims linked to the protesting and violence; more than 2,100 businesses damaged or looted; 71 buildings set on fire; 57 weapons seized; and more than 700,000 prescription pills stolen from looted drugstores."[317]

Since 2020, Chicago has had a comprehensive plan to stop the violence, called "Our City, Our Safety."[318] What's missing from the plan? What's always missing from the plan? Drug policy reform. As with Mayors Richard M. Daley and Rahm Emanuel, both serving before Mayor Lightfoot, every imaginable scheme to stop the violence is on the table. Well,... except drug legalization.[319] But the mayor of Chicago cannot

---

[314] Jeremy Gorner and Paige Fry, *Chicago Tribune*, "Slain Chicago police Officer Ella French was part of community safety team, often worked by newer cops in city's toughest neighborhoods," August 14, 2021, updated September 19, 2021, https://qctimes.com/news/state-and-regional/crime-and-courts/slain-chicago-police-officer-ella-french-was-part-of-community-safety-team-often-worked-by/article_f240877f-db29-5015-ad1c-3eee95379c7e.html?mode=comments.

[315] CBS2 Chicago Staff, "Behind Police Leaders Claims That Bail Reform Is Responsible For Surge In Violence," *CBS Chicago*, August 13, 2021, https://chicago.cbslocal.com/2021/08/13/police-claims-bail-reform-increase-violent-crime-gun-violence/.

[316] Tom McNamee, "Murder on our streets: a disease with no easy cure," *Chicago Sun-Times*, September 11, 1991, Gierach notebooks, p. 694.

[317] John Kass, "Column: That thin line between order and chaos in Chicago and other towns," *Chicago Tribune*, June 5, 2021, https://www.chicagotribune.com/columns/john-kass/ct-chicago-looting-chaos-john-kass-2021 0605-fbg4f2akr5ed3amm4lbqldaw2y-story.html.

[318] City of Chicago, "Our City, Our Safety, a comprehensive plan to reduce violence in Chicago," (2020), https://www.chicago.gov/content/dam/city/sites/public-safety-and-violenc-reduction/pdfs/OurCityOurSafety.pdf.

[319] Gierach, "Cul-de-sacs Are Dead End As Effective Crime curbs," *Chicago Sun-Times*, January 30, 1993, https://jamesgierach.tumblr.com/post/674370431139053568.

have safe communities and drug prohibition, despite Lightfoot's 103-page "Our City, Our Safety," a comprehensive violence reduction plan.

Since Richard Nixon declared the War on Drugs in 1971, U.S. mayors, governors and presidents have tried every imaginable policy and initiative to stop violent crime without significant success, initiatives embracing treatment, prevention, punishment, education, military, border and law-enforcement options. (See Cockamamie drug prevention ideas, Chapter 10, "Anything but Drug Legalization.") But no longer president, governor or mayor has tried drug legalization.

"The Silver Bullet" to Stop the Killing

Shockingly, a simple answer to stopping the most preventable homicides — the gang-related and drug-related homicides — is there for the taking. Call it "The Silver Bullet Solution." Years ago, drug-warrior Representative Charlie Rangel said the silver bullet does not exist.[320] But it does.

Take the exorbitant profit out of drug-dealing by legalizing drug markets, drug sales, drug production and drug possession. Shift failed drug war policies out of gear and put the drug-war cart in reverse to save our kids, save our neighborhoods (especially neighborhoods comprised of poor, downtrodden and disadvantaged people of minority races), and restore hope. Stop making well-intended, well-reasoned comprehensive plans for stopping violence but always leaving out an essential ingredient to peace — legalized, controlled and regulated recreational drug markets. National representatives to the UN Commission on Narcotic Drugs, can you hear me?

Without including the Silver Bullet — drug legalization — in the solution mix, preventable killings cannot measurably be curtailed. Specifically, recreational drug legalization must be added to the mix of other important solution ingredients. That means government and twenty-first century society must repeal or comprehensively amend national legislative enactments adopted to implement the 1961 Single Convention. Of course, that convention and its progeny must also be repealed or comprehensively amended, eliminating recreational drug prohibition and substance criminalization as it now exists.

---

[320] Video, A Firing Line Debate: "Resolved: That Drug Prohibition Has Failed," March 3, 1990, *YouTube*, https://youtu.be/Mouh8gE2CMg, Minute 13, *Hoover Institute*.

Rewrite the Second Amendment

Guns are the most efficacious and commonly used instruments to commit homicides. Regardless of homicide motivation, guns are the weapon of choice for all categories of homicides — greed, hate and insanity. Therefore, it should be obvious to everyone that the U.S. Congress should enact laws that better control guns, an objective that inevitably collides with America's trust and confidence in guns and the Second Amendment. The U.S. Congress must — by constitutional amendment and/or by general law — revisit Americans' preoccupation with, and faith in, guns to attain peace and personal safety. Notably, none of the suggestions proposed in this manuscript are easy; certainly, the drug-legalization idea is not intuitive or easy, and Americans love of their guns is a challenge. Nevertheless, these ideas must be put into action to stop a big chunk of violent crime and avoid a host of collateral drug war-aggravated crises. (See Chapters 8 and 9) The time for that action is now.

Essential Cultural Change Needed: Just Say "Yes" to Drugs Politically but Say "No" to Drugs Personally

My idea for stopping much of America's gun violence is to remove the *reason* kids in gangs are shooting one another. My idea requires a change in the *economics of drug policy* that now supports gangs — the **Larry Hoover** Gangster Disciples-type gangs, the Al Capone-type gangs and the international drug cartels, too. My idea requires an essential cultural change — a new way of thinking about drugs, gangs and guns.

What kind of change? Changed founded on a simple reality: Drugs and drug use are forever and ever. Amen.

Is there one among us who thinks we can have a "drug-free" world as the United Nation's policymakers fantasized in 1989 posters and rhetoric fourteen years ago in the 2009 Political Declaration and Plan of Action? Does anyone believe there has been a moment in time, ever, when the world was drug-free? Or when some "bad fruit" was not identified and prohibited, even in the Garden of Eden? The new world drug order must accept the reality that drugs and drug use are forever. It must recognize that "Freedom and self-discipline regarding substances is more powerful than any prohibition law, and all the King's horses and all the King's men," Gierach Drug Policy Axiom No. 15.[321] It must embrace the practical wisdom that it's better for individuals to just say "Yes" to drugs politically but preferably say "No" to drugs personally.

---

[321] https://jamesgierach.tumblr.com/post/671961048125980672/gierach-drug-policy-axioms.

And these realities and rules accepted — What course should the new world drug order take?

Let's control and regulate drugs and guns. Let's largely cut gangs out of the half a trillion dollar (USD) uncontrolled global drug markets, annually.

We must learn that tolerating drug use by others is not the condonation of drug abuse by others. (See JFK's quotation, p. 59)

Zero Tolerance Not a Virtue

Zero tolerance is not a virtue. Chapter 3 discussed zero tolerance, a repository for hate and — left festering long enough — war, as in Drug War. The new world drug order must understand that the more nearly public policy and law approach zero tolerance — particularly regarding adult consensual behavior — the narrower life's bridge to liberty and happiness. As a hat worn by a traveler in the Seattle-Tacoma International Airport recently challenged, "Legalize Freedom." In contrast to the fault of zero tolerance — tolerance and understanding are virtues.

Concretely, my idea of how to stop violence is to take the profit out of drug-dealing, as we did with alcohol nearly a century ago in America. Legalize, control and regulate mind-altering substances. License drug outlets, limit the number of licenses, regulate content labels and warnings, control the manufacture, cultivation and distribution of drugs. Require government inspection of drug products. Take a third to half the money out of the illegal drug trade by making drugs legal. As also discussed earlier, some experts estimate the illegal drug trade is a US $500 billion a year worldwide business. Let's control and regulate it, and not delegate it to irresponsible drug entrepreneurs. By making drug sales and possession lawful, hugely inflated drug prices and profits are negated, and economic incentive is harnessed.

Legalizing drugs will not make drugs, guns or gangs disappear. Nothing will. But illegal drug-market revenues will no longer rival the sales of Walgreens drugstores, as the Gangster Disciples' revenues once purportedly did. The South Side Black Disciples', a rival gang to the Larry Hoover's Gangster Disciples, "distribution network for heroin and crack cocaine brought in as much as $300,000 a day."[322] Neither will legalizing drugs make guns disappear, but it may dissuade youngsters like La'Mayne

---

[322] Susan Chandler, "Gangs built on corporate mentality," *Chicago Tribune*, June 13, 2004, https://www.chicago tribune.com/news/ct-xpm-2004-06-13-0406130224-story.html, accessed September 9, 2021.

Bland from wanting to sell drugs just long enough to enable him to buy a Jeep Cherokee.

"31 Bullets" Miss Their Target

In 2018, the *Chicago Sun-Times* invited public comment and ideas aimed to curb Chicago gun violence with a project called, "31 bullets."[323] The project name was derived by dividing the billions of bullets manufactured in the United States annually by the U.S. population. The calculation determined that there were thirty-one bullets manufactured for each man, woman and child in the U.S., annually. I had hoped that just one of the thirty-one bullets in the series of articles and ideas to stop the violence would take aim at drug prohibition policy. None did. Not one of those thirty-one bullets, journalistically fired in 2018 under the editorial board leadership of **Tom McNamee**, chambered the essential "Silver-bullet" solution. Not even a mention.

Osiel Cárdenas Guillén

Osiel Cárdenas Guillén, a one-time policeman and leader of the Gulf Cartel, mentioned in Chapter 4, deserves further mention here, because of the violence implicit with drug-prohibition law enforcement. "In 2007, Osiel Cárdenas was extradited to the United States along with 15 other dealers and charged with the involvement of conspiracies to traffic large amounts of marijuana and cocaine. In exchange for a twenty-five-year sentence, he agreed to collaborate with U.S. agents in intelligence information, and US $30 million of his assets were extracted from underground bunkers and dispersed throughout various Texas Law Enforcement branches. When the Zetas discovered that he had been providing intelligence to the U.S., they declared war against the Gulf Cartel over the betrayal.

"'The Zetas split is really the first of a series of schisms and fractures in the major cartels' organizations that leads to the *incredibly prolific violence* that we see from 2008 to 2011,'" said David Shirk, principal investigator at the University of San Diego's Justice in Mexico Project. "It's really the beginning of the cartel wars. ... The last decade has been Mexico's Vietnam, only it's happening at home, right down the street, rather than televised from across an ocean.'"[324]

---

[323] Chicago Sun-Times Editorial Board, "31 bullets: A Chicago Sun-Times campaign to end gun violence," April 30, 2018, https://chicago.suntimes.com/2018/4/30/18621567/31-bullets-a-chicago-sun-times-campaign-to-end-gun-violence.

[324] Alec Banks, "5 Notorious Drug Lords You Should Know More About," *Highsnobiety*,

Nations Greatly Profiting Off the UN Drug-Prohibition Paradigm

Because drugs and drug-trafficking are so predictive of violent crime in our drug-prohibition world, it's important to identify the nations greatly profiting off the UN-led drug-prohibition paradigm. Renowned drug-producing countries that quickly come to mind might include Colombia, Peru, Mexico, Afghanistan, Myanmar, Laos, Thailand and others. Years ago, I kept track of nations not cooperating with U.S. prosecution of its War on Drugs, resulting in those countries not being certified by the U.S. as cooperating.[325] There were fewer then and I remembered them by mnemonics, "the ABCs of SIN," meaning Afghanistan, Bolivia, Colombia, Syria, Iran and Nigeria. More recently the list of nations with recalcitrant, major illicit drug involvement has grown.

"In September 2020, President Donald J. Trump identified 22 countries on the 'majors list' [of Drug-Producing and Trafficking Nations] for FY2021: Afghanistan, Costa Rica, Honduras, Pakistan, The Bahamas, Dominican Republic, India, Panama, Belize, Ecuador, Jamaica, Peru, Bolivia, El Salvador, Laos, Venezuela, Burma [now named Myanmar], Guatemala, Mexico, Colombia, Haiti, and Nicaragua."[326] But whether on the list of majors or not, illicit drugs and drug-gang violence are ubiquitous.

China

Interestingly, China — a major U.S. trading partner — evaded the Trump list of drug majors. Yet, "China has been a major source of U.S.-bound fentanyl and, more recently, precursors and production equipment (Figure 1). In January 2020, the DEA assessed that although China remained the 'primary source' of all fentanyl-related substances trafficked into the United States, other sources of fentanyl were emerging."[327] Continuing the Congressional Research Service wrote, "In recent years, *fentanyl* and its analogues have emerged as a major international drug control problem. Overdose deaths from their abuse have continued to rise, and a growing number of fentanyl

---

https://www.highsnobiety.com/p/famous-drug-dealers/, emphasis added, accessed September 9, 2021.

[325] "Narcotics Certification of Drug Producing and Trafficking Nations: Questions and Answers, March 27, 2000, 98-159, https://www.everycrsreport.com/reports/98-159.html.

[326] "The U.S. 'Majors List' of Illicit Drug-Producing and Drug-Transit Countries," *Congressional Research Service*, February 25, 2021, https://www.everycrsreport.com/reports/R46695.html.

[327] "Illicit Fentanyl and China's Role," *Congressional Research Service*, January 29, 2021, https://sgp.fas.org/crs/row/IF10890.pdf.

analogues appear marketed for nonmedical, often unregulated use. In September 2020, the International Narcotics Control Board reported the existence of 144 fentanyl-related substances with no currently known legitimate uses. The U.N. Office on Drugs and Crime estimates that *laboratories could potentially synthesize thousands of other fentanyl analogues.* As of December 2020, fentanyl and 26 fentanyl analogues are scheduled for international control pursuant to the U.N. Single Convention on Narcotic Drugs."[328]

The Chinese economy profits greatly by its natives manufacturing and distributing fentanyl to global consumers, aided by the UN drug-prohibition paradigm, even regarding medically and legally recognized fentanyl. Because fentanyl deaths were increasing in number (5,000 deaths in North America since 2013) — in 2017 U.S. Assistant Secretary of State for international narcotics and law enforcement William Brownfield was excited that the UN would make a better effort to control fentanyl precursor drugs, disrupting the global supply chain.[329] However, Brownfield's optimism that a prohibition tentacle could derail fentanyl supply to the U.S. was misplaced. "The U.S. set another record for drug overdose deaths last year with more than 107,000 fatalities, the Centers for Disease Control and Prevention estimated Wednesday. The provisional 2021 total represents a 15% jump from the previous record in 2020 and means there is roughly one overdose death in the country every 5 minutes. While drugs like opioid painkillers, other opioids and heroin cause many deaths, fentanyl is the leading killer, causing 71,000 deaths last year, which was a 23% jump from the year before."[330]

Interestingly, two months ago I was legally administered fentanyl during an operative procedure in a U.S. hospital without fear or a worry, because it was legal, controlled and regulated, the antidote to prohibition overdose. There's a lesson here that could save over 100,000 lives annually.

Myanmar

Meanwhile, Myanmar is on President Trump's list of "majors," and "Myanmar is fast becoming the world's biggest producer of methamphetamine and synthetic drugs —

---

[328] Ibid., emphasis added.

[329] Glen Hess, "U.S. hails UN move to restrict fentanyl precursors," *C&EN Global Enterprise,* March 27, 2022, https://pubs.acs.org/doi/10.1021/cen-09513-notw14.

[330] "US Records More Than 107,000 Drug Overdose Deaths for 2021," *VOA News,* May 11, 2022, https://www.voanews.com/a/us-records-more-than-107-000-drug-overdose-deaths-for-2021/6567089.html.

making the industry the most lucrative business in Southeast Asia," according to a *Byline* interview.[331] "Drug lords entwined with rebel groups in Myanmar's ungovernable border zone with Laos, Thailand and China — the notorious Golden Triangle — have been pumping record amounts of methamphetamine across Southeast Asia."[332] The value of regional precursor drugs and crystal meth is $70 billion a year, and the fastest way to make money is in the drug trade, money needed by the controlling military junta that seized government power and opposition armed ethnic rebel groups and pro-democracy elements opposed to the military junta.[333] Myanmar security forces have killed at least 512 civilians since the February 1, 2021 coup, according to the Assistance Association for Political Prisoners.[334] In 2012, Myanmar had a murder rate of 15.2 per 100,000 population. There were a total of 8,044 murders in Burma in 2012. Factors influencing Myanmar's high murder rate include communal violence and armed conflict, and the nation is perceived as one of the most corrupt.[335]

Are all twenty-two of these drug-producing, drug-consuming and drug-transit countries — identified as majors by former President Trump in 2012 — sites of serious drug-gang violence? For any reader in doubt, try any Internet search engine, search for "drug-gang violence" and add a country name. Testing my suggestion myself, I tried one country on the Trump list of majors and another not on his list, Equador (because I visited there in 2015) and South Africa (because it is home to former INCB president, Dr. Lochan Naidoo), respectively.

Ecuador

President Donald Trump, drug legalizer turned politician prohibitionist, included South American Ecuador in his list of majors. If drug violence is a measure, the ex-

331 "In Myanmar, Methamphetamine, Synthetic Drug Production Soars," *National Public Radio* and *WBEZ,* July 4, 2019, https://www.npr.org/2019/07/04/738791500/in-myanmar-methamphetamine-synthetic-drug-production-soars.

332 Vijitra Duangdee, "Myanmar's Descent into Chaos to Further Fuel Mekong Drug Trade: UN," *Voice of America*, March 31, 2021, https://www.voanews.com/a/east-asia-pacific_myanmars-descent-chaos-further-fuel-mekong-drug-trade-un/6203970.html.

333 Ibid.

334 "US Orders Non-Essential Personnel Out of Myanmar as Military Escalates Protest Crackdown," *Voice of America*, March 30, 2021, updated March 31, 2021, https://www.voanews.com/a/usa_us-orders-non-essential-personnel-out-myanmar-military-escalates-protest-crackdown/6203961.html.

335 *Wikipedia, s.v.* "Crime in Myanmar," https://en.wikipedia.org/wiki/Crime_in_Myanmar, accessed March 17, 2023.

president got that call right. Drug-gang violence afflicts free society and endangers those behind bars equally, as the Ecuador experience dramatically demonstrates. "Following [the] February 23, 2021 riots that left 80 inmates dead, [Ecuador's] President Lenín Moreno called the [Ecuadorian prison] violence a consequence of drug trafficking money infiltrating the country. Interior Minister Patricio Pazmino, who has since resigned, linked the riots to organized crime, citing the 22 tons of cocaine seized in the country in just the first two months of 2021. Pazmino told legislators that 'this wasn't a simple fight, but a confrontation between *criminal groups that want to control illicit markets*,' Primicias reported."[336]

Sold More Drugs in Prison than on Chicago Streets

Late last century or early this century, an Illinois inmate called me at my law office upon his release from behind bars. He said he read an article I wrote, just published in the *Chicago Defender*. He said he didn't think anybody on "the outside" understood. He told me he sold more drugs in prison than he sold as a free man on the streets of Chicago, the reason he was in prison. He said, on his arrival at **Stateville Correctional Center** the Gangster Disciples (GDs) street gang provided him, and each new inmate a Welcome Wagon homecoming gift — a pair of shower slippers, a prophylactic and a package of drugs. At that time the Illinois prison system was largely controlled (influenced?) by gang leaders[337] like **Larry Hoover** of the **Gangster Disciples**, and the Latin Kings. The former was a powerful Chicago-based street gang with 50,000 to 90,000 members. My caller explained he sold drugs in Stateville without permission from the GDs. He stopped for a time but started selling again which led to his being attacked and stabbed six times. He survived, served his time and called me. I asked him, "Now that you're out, what are you going to do?"

"What can I do? I'm a convicted felon, a Black man and poor. What can I do but sell drugs?" I offered free advice — maybe worth its price. I said of the few released inmates who avoid recidivism, some go to work for nonprofit organizations as counselors, violence interrupters or mentors, teaching life lessons best learned experiencing life on the wrong side of the law. I provided him with telephone numbers of several nonprofit organizations and wished him well.

---

[336] Shane Sullivan, "The Fuel Not the Fuse: Drug Trafficking and Ecuador's Prison Violence," *Insight Crime*, March 22, 2021, https://insightcrime.org/news/drug-trafficking-ecuador-prison-violence/.

[337] Gary Marx and Tribune Staff Writer, "Power Struggle Behind Bars," *Chicago Tribune*, November 10, 1996, https://www.chicagotribune.com/news/ct-xpm-1996-11-10-9611110209-story.html.

"I thought you were a brother when I read your article," he said.

"I am a brother," I replied. Wish I knew how his life progressed henceforth.

South Africa

Choosing just one more country that was not included on President Trump's list of major Drug-Producing and Trafficking Nations, like China, I searched for drug-gang violence in South Africa. Again, my search confirmed the presence of horrific drug-gang violence there,[338] well-explained in this interview report.

"I grew up in Sydenham Heights and even though there were gangsters and drugs back then we could play outside for hours and not worry about anything. Now there are just shootings and we are too scared to let our children play outside. They rather stay inside and play video games," she said. Another resident agreed. "Not just for the children but us adults as well. We all feel like prisoners in our homes because we are afraid to go out as we may get hit by a stray bullet. So many people are even scared to go to work," he said.

Wherever one might live in the world, we the people must just look and listen to see and hear about deadly, prolific and unrelenting drug-gang violence everywhere. We must connect the violence dots and point our collective finger at the World War on Drugs and reach the unavoidable conclusion that rings true beyond reasonable doubt: *Drug War Means More Crime Not Less.*

---

[338] Lee Rondganger, "Bodies pile up as Cape Town's Hard Livings gang goes to war in Durban," *Independent Online*, December 7, 2021, https://www.iol.co.za/news/bodies-pile-up-as-cape-towns-hard-livings-gang-goes-to-war-in-durban-a97c039f-f0a8-4e60-8364-f266baa0c74e.

Chapter 6 - Drug War Intolerance
Means More Corruption

The War on Drugs is "*corruptogenic*"; it causes corruption. Commonly, drug prohibition policies strip individuals of their sense of right and wrong, knock kids off the straight and narrow, subvert the law enforcement mission "to serve and protect," and destroy individual respect for the law, authority and one another.

Again, like writing about the unending criminogenic and "drugogenic" consequences of drug prohibition, the consequences of drug-prohibition policy serve up pervasive corruption in everyday life and the criminal justice systems of the world. In the 1990s, like every decade of the ongoing drug war, stories of law enforcement corruption at every level were so plentiful, I regularly downloaded those news stories to floppy disks under the umbrella, "Corruption." Late in 1997, I selected some of those stories to write an opinion piece on the debasing effect of drug prohibition on many law enforcement officers, correctional officers and government officials which was published under the caption, "Anti-Drug War Corrupts Too Many."[339] Rather than reinvent the wheel here, I set forth that newspaper article published in the *Chicago Tribune* here.

Anti-Drug War Corrupts Too Many

OAK LAWN — Again, in 1997, drug-war corruption took its toll on law enforcement in Chicago and around the world.

Recently, three Chicago police officers were convicted of robbing suspected drug dealers and stealing drug-dealer cash ($23,000) in a sting operation. The Gresham District officers will be sentenced March 23, the first day of another police officer's drug-trafficking trial — involving officers from the Austin District.

From a hemispheric perspective, the defilement of those charged with waging the drug war is commonplace — an often-hidden inevitable cost of drug war. The past year has witnessed arrests, charges and convictions for every sort of drug-war debauchery, snaring men in uniform.

Antonio Grace Mota, alias "the Cocaine King" and boss of the Brazilian leg of the Cali-cartel drug route to Europe, bribed his way out of São Paulo's Carandiru jail in

---

[339] Gierach, James E., "Anti-Drug War Corrupts Too Many," *Chicago Tribune*, Op-Ed, January 5, 1998, https://www.chicagotribune.com/news/ct-xpm-1998-01-05-9801050059-story.html.

Brazil. In New York State, 11 guards from the Metropolitan Detention Center were arrested for smuggling drugs into the jail in exchange for bribes ranging from $100 to $1,000 a week.

Mexico's former attorney general, Javier Coello Trejo, and Judicial Police Commander G. Gonzalez Calderone were accused of protecting cocaine shipments through Mexico. In February, after an American drug czar briefing, Mexico's drug czar Jesus Gutierrez Rebollo was arrested for taking bribes and allegedly tipping off drug chieftain Amado Carillon Fuentes to an impending raid at Carrillo's sister's wedding.

In Mexico City in May, federal prosecutors, federal police and a military officer were accused of stealing half a ton of cocaine seized from drug dealers. In Haiti, three policemen were arrested for stealing $700,000 from a woman's home during a police unit investigation of a drug drop, and more officers were arrested there for burglarizing a police station to extricate confiscated drugs.

This year also saw a Los Angeles city councilman arrested for cocaine possession, a Dominican Republic ambassador accused of accepting $1 million in bribes from drug traffickers while lobbying for the release of Colombian drug entrepreneurs, the arrest of the mayor of Cali for taking $200,000 in campaign contributions from cartel kingpins, and Detroit police officers indicted for illegal raids and traffic stops allegedly concocted to steal drugs, firearms and money.

Other 1997 drug-war abominations included reports that Mexican military officials copied computer files about anti-drug operations for drug dealers, the arrest of a dozen federal agents from the U.S. Customs and Immigration and Naturalization Service (one agent allegedly accepted a $1 million bribe to allow a truck loaded with a ton of cocaine past his border checkpoint), the kidnapping and torture of a member of the Tijuana drug cartel by Mexico's former head of anti-drug intelligence to extract information for a rival drug gang, the arrest of two Argentine police officers for drug possession while in Chile to extradite car thieves, and the arrest of two Mexican drug enforcement agency agents for failing to report their seizure of a 1.6-ton shipment of marijuana in April.

The corruption of a steady stream of public officers and officials is too high a price to pay for continuing a failed drug war that breeds disrespect for the law and its servants. [End]

Chicago's Sergeant Ronald Watts and Officer Joseph Miedzianowski

There is no end to the corruption stories attendant to drug-prohibition policing. Chicago Police Sergeant Ronald Watts and his team of corrupt officers provide a more recent example.

"CHICAGO – Disgraced former Chicago Police Sergeant Ronald Watts and his team of corrupt officers are responsible for hundreds of false drug convictions. To date, more than 100 such convictions have been thrown out in the largest mass exoneration in Chicago history. Those victims, later adjudicated innocent, were sentenced to over 274 years in prison.

"On Tuesday, July 20, 2021, 88 additional victims of Watts and his team will file a joint petition in the Circuit Court of Cook County seeking to vacate their wrongful drug convictions caused by Watts and his team. The petition asks the Court to overturn 100 convictions total for the 88 Black men and women in one of the most staggering cases of police corruption in Chicago history."[340] Watts was not a rare case.

Chicago Police Officer Joseph Miedzianowski, Chicago's "most corrupt cop," is another perfect example of a talented, decorated and brave police officer turned to rubbish by drug-war cancer. "During his 22-year police career, he received 59 citations for valor and arrests and was publicly praised for his high number of drug and illegal weapon busts. During this time he was also secretly revealing the identity of undercover police officers to gang members, protecting drug organizations, distributing crack cocaine, and supplying gang members with ammunition."[341]

---

[340] Press Conference: Court Petition for 88 victims of Disgraced Chicago Police Sergeant Ronald Watts," *The Exoneration Project*, July 19, 2021,

https://www.exonerationproject.org/blog/press-conference-announcing-court-petition-for-88-victims-of-disgraced-former-chicago-police-sergeant-ronald-watts/, accessed September 5, 2021.

[341] *Wikipedia*, s.v. "Joseph Miedzianowski," https://en.m.wikipedia.org/wiki/Joseph_Miedzianowski, accessed September 5, 2021.

Drug Prohibition Corruption Pervasive and Inexhaustible

Drug-war degradation of purpose is not limited to law enforcement. It reaches into every occupation and societal department from school bus driver[342] to car manufacturer,[343] and from school principal[344] to commodities' broker.[345]

In 1991, a U.S. District Judge Robert F. Collins was sentenced to six years and ten months in prison for scheming... to split a $100,000 bribe in return for a lighter drug sentence for a drug smuggler.[346] And the same year, Illinois Associate Judge W. Mark Dalton resigned after pleading guilty to marijuana possession, nineteen years after conviction for the same offense.[347] Drug war inconsistencies, corruption and hypocrisy reach everywhere.

"In Gutenberg, Iowa, June Osterhaus, the local Chamber of Commerce president, pleaded guilty last year to taking part in a three-state cocaine and marijuana ring masterminded by a 34-year-old corn farmer in nearby Maquoketa, Iowa. At its peak, the ring peddled two pounds of cocaine and 80 pounds of marijuana a month in Iowa, Wisconsin and Colorado. Osterhaus, 44, was running for a seat in the Iowa state legislature when she was arrested."[348]

Drug-war corruption is widespread, complicated and ingrained. If one remark can capture what drug prohibition does to society and policing, it might be the comment of Chicago police Sergeant Joe Kosala of the Twentieth District gang squad regarding drug stop, frisk and search, "They lie, so we lie."[349] Drug-war dishonesty infects law-

---

[342] Philip Franchine and Phillip J. O'Connor, "School bus drivers tied to drug sales, 16 indicted; some left kids during deals," *Chicago Sun-Times*, November 29, 1989, Gierach notebooks, p. 78.

[343] Judith Cummings, "Delorean Is Freed of Cocaine Charge by a Federal Jury," *The New York Times*, August 17, 1984, https://www.nytimes.com/1984/08/17/us/delorean-is-freed-of-cocaine-charge-by-a-federal-jury.html.

[344] Joseph P. Fried, "Principal Charged With Selling Cocaine," *The New York Times*, April 10, 1999, https://www.nytimes.com/1999/04/10/nyregion/principal-charged-with-selling-cocaine.html, accessed September 6, 2021.

[345] Commodities Broker Is Held As the Head of a Drug Ring," *UPI,* republished *New York Times,* September 22, 1983, https://www.nytimes.com/1983/09/22/nyregion/commodities-broker-is-held-as-the-head-of-a-drug-ring.html.

[346] "Judge Sentenced," *Chicago Sun-Times*, September 7, 1991. Gierach notebooks, p. 655.

[347] Christopher Wills, "Judge acing marijuana charges had earlier conviction," *Chicago Law Bulletin*, August 21, 1991. Gierach notebooks, p. 640.

[348] Paul Weingarten and James Coates, "Drugs find home in heartland," *Chicago Tribune*, September 10, 1989, https://www.latimes.com/lifestyle/story/2021-12-20/top-cannabis-stories-of-2021.

[349] Mike Gray, *Drug Crazy* (New York: Random House, Inc., 1998), p. 37.

enforcement society as a whole and jumps geographic boundaries far beyond Chicago and the Western Hemisphere.

"This Week's Corrupt Cops Stories"

David Borden is president and director of DRCNet Foundation and president and director of the Drug Reform Coordination Network, twin nonprofit advocacy organizations. The latter organization owns StoptheDrugWar.org. and has published contemporary drug-news stories on a regular continuing basis since 1997. The publication includes a section called, "This Week's Corrupt Cops Stories."

As an example of corrupt cops stories, Issue #1138, dated July 23, 2021 of the *StoptheDrugWar Chronicle* includes four law-enforcement corruption news stories, one regarding a Texas border agent, another an Ohio county jail guard, a third a Kentucky jail guard, and a f former Florida county sheriff's deputy. The last of the four stories reported this snippet: "In Marianna, Florida, a former Jackson County sheriff's deputy was sentenced Tuesday to 12 ½ years in prison for fabricating evidence and arresting innocent people. Zachary Webster was found guilty of 19 charges in cases where he planted drugs on people. He was convicted of racketeering, three counts of official misconduct, three counts of perjury, three counts of fabricating evidence, four counts of possession of a controlled substance, three counts of possession of drug paraphernalia, and two counts of false imprisonment."[350]

Corruption in law enforcement eats away at the very soul of the law, the foundation of civilized society, and the heart of democratic institutions. Nothing can more effectively undermine the public's trust and confidence in the law, police or society than the misdeeds of a corrupt law-enforcement officer. The damage to that trust and confidence caused by such an officer's repudiation of his or her honest duty is inestimable. For without respect, trust and confidence in the law and its servants, there is disrespect of the law, increased reliance on street justice, and hotspots of roving, mob misbehavior that resembles anarchy in the streets. The civil unrest following the George Floyd

---

[350] *Drug War Chronicle*, Issue 1138, July 23, 2021, https://stopthedrugwar.org/chronicle/2021/jul/14/weeks_corrupt_cops_stories, accessed September 5, 2021.

police murder is a good illustration,[351] and looked like the January 6, 2021 insurrectionist mob assault on the U.S. Capitol in Washington D.C.[352]

The reciprocating corruption-injustice relationship and the disrespect of law-anarchy interplay are lessons summarized succinctly in the commonly heard refrain: "No justice, no peace." And if there is corruption in law enforcement or the criminal justice system, there can be no respect for the law, and without respect for the law anarchy can be quick to follow.

Sadly, drug war means big, dirty money regularly passes by the nose of law enforcement and other governmental authorities, tempting misbehavior with no countervailing benefit to law, order or a drug-free society. Big money corrupts big time, again showing a fatal flaw to drug prohibition policy. Drug prohibition is unavoidably *corruptogenic*, an attribute that eats at the heart and soul of defendants, witnesses, informants, and law enforcement officers. Viewed macroscopically, the War on Drugs eats at the foundation of civilized society, justice, democracy and freedom.

---

[351] Kellie Carter Jackson, "The Double Standard of the American Riot," *The Atlantic*, June 1, 2020, https://www.theatlantic.com/culture/archive/2020/06/riots-are-american-way-george-floyd-protests/612466/.

[352] Intelligencer Staff, "Photos: A Day of Anarchy at the Capitol," *Intelligencer*, January 6, 2021, https://nymag.com/intelligencer/2021/01/photos-a-day-of-anarchy-at-the-capitol.html.

Part Three - The Dynamics of Drug War Failure

Chapter 7 - Why the "War on Drugs" Doesn't Work and Never Will

The War on Drugs does not work and never will because it ignores the realities of human nature, contradicts universal economic laws, and superimposes an ill-conceived and unworkable "Estimates System" on the nations of the world.

Human Nature: Greed and Entrepreneurial Spirit

Why all the drugs?

The War on Drugs incentivizes drug cultivation, drug production, drug invention and drug trade. Organic drugs are grown, and synthetic drugs are invented and manufactured. The War on Drugs is the fertilizer that works well on both. The magical "**Jack-and-the Beanstalk**" chemical that makes the fertilizer work so well is called "prohibition." This fertilizer is so powerful that it works everywhere regardless of climate, natural resources, national political structure, or the shape of the local playing field. Drug prohibition grows the illicit drug business and feeds drug dealers, gangbangers, and transnational drug cartels. National laws enacted by governments around the world breathe life into international drug-war policies that reward individual entrepreneurial ability, organizational smarts, discarded morality, and a willingness to resort to violence and corruption of "shorties."

No, not that "Shorty,"[353] not Guzmán — the "shorties," the kids. A trial court judge decision regarding a South Minneapolis drug gang known as the "The Rolling 30's" explained how drug gangs used juveniles to advance their business. The judge

---

[353] David Graham, "Captured drug lord 'Shorty' Guzman a cunning, brutal businessman," *Reuters*, February 22, 2014, https://www.reuters.com/article/us-usa-mexico-kingpin-guzman/captured-drug-lord-shorty-guzman-a-cunning-brutal-businessman-idUSBREA1L0WH20140222.

noted that "Shorties are at the bottom of the gang structure and sometimes serve as look-outs while other members are selling drugs."[354]

Such misbehavior and moral turpitude is tempted by unlimited profit potential offered by drug wars, as many *Frontline* reports document: e.g. "Inside the $400 Billion Global Business," identifying global drug prohibition winners, like the Arellano-Felix Organization from Mexico, and the Medellin and Cali cartels from Colombia.[355]

Successful Drug War Entrepreneurs

While not every drug dealer becomes a Guzmán, Escobar, Osiel Cárdenas Guillén, Frank Lucas, Griselda Blanco, alias "the Godmother of Cocaine," Leroy "Nicky" Barnes,[356] Amado Carillo Fuentes, alias "Lord of the Skies,"[357] Al Capone, Larry Hoover, or Tse Chi Lop[358] — the illicit drug business is an entrepreneur's dream. Millionaires and billionaires all, these businesspersons and their gangs and cartels thrived in the drug war made for them by prohibition laws.

"The Medellín Cartel was an empire of stunning sweep and unimaginable violence. At its height, it earned as much as $4 billion a year — most of it cash — for its members and controlled 80 percent of the cocaine supply in the United States, leaving tens of thousands of corpses in its wake."[359]

But let us look at the bottom of the drug prohibition food chain. What is the average annual income of a low-level, street drug-dealer? It is really difficult to say, since drug-dealing is an "under the table" operation, even if sales are often made in "open-air" drug markets. Income from drug dealing is largely unreported, untaxed and

---

[354] *United States of America v. Joe Darrell Edwards, Jr.*, CASE 0:07-cr-00297-DWF-JSM Doc. 406 Filed 09/05/08 Page 1 of 34, United States District Court, D. Minnesota, https://www.govinfo.gov/content/pkg/USCOURTS-mnd-0_07-cr-00297/pdf/USCOURTS-mnd-0_07-cr-00297-6.pdf, pp. 2 and 5.

[355] "Drug wars," *Frontline*, https://www.pbs.org/wgbh/pages/frontline/shows/drugs/business/, accessed March 17, 2023.

[356] Joe McGasko, "The 5 Most Notorious Drug Kingpins," *Biography*, updated February 7, 2020, https://www.biography.com/news/famous-drug-lords.

[357] Alec Banks, "5 Notorious Drug Lords You Should Know About," *Highsnobiety*, https://www.highsnobiety.com/p/famous-drug-dealers/, accessed March 17, 2023.

[358] Jeremy Douglas, "The man accused of running Asia's biggest drug trafficking syndicate...," *CNN*, October 24, 2019, https://www.cnn.com/2019/10/23/opinions/tse-chi-lop-revealed-opinion-intl-hnk/index.html.

[359] Peter Green, "The Syndicate: *How Cocaine Traffickers from Medellín Transformed the Multibillion Dollar Global Drug Trade,*" *Wall Street Journal*, https://www.wsj.com/ad/cocainenomics.

laundered with less than one-percent of laundered drug money discovered.[360] "DEA drug money interceptions amount to less than one billion dollar[s] — less than 1% of the U.S. drug business and less than 4% of the drug money estimated to travel to and through Mexico for laundering."[361] And competition is so fierce in open-air drug markets like those in Chicago's West Garfield Park neighborhood that violence harms other legitimate businesses in the area.[362]

Recognizing the difficulty estimating drug dealer income for this reason, nevertheless, in 1990, it was reported that the average American drug dealer earned $24,000 a year, quite a lot if one is otherwise unemployed, or having difficulty finding work as a convicted felon, parolee, probationer, or as a Black high-school student dropout.[363]

The "Windy City Weedfest" Waitress and The Sex-Abused Commodities Broker

More personally, I was more convinced of the economic incentive to deal prohibition drugs listening to my restaurant waitress over coffee and a roll. I arrived early to speak at Chicago's "Windy City Weedfest," an annual event in the early 90s, scheduled to be held in a park along Chicago's lakefront. Sharing the purpose of my upcoming talk with my waitress, an African American woman, she said she knew a ten-year-old who was selling crack cocaine and making $200 an hour. She asked me, how could that child be convinced to get an education and pursue a different career?

Another personal experience taught me the complexity of drug-war economics, temptation, and human nature. I had a minor client who had been sexually abused repeatedly during his years of participation in a youth organization for boys by a youth group leader. That abuse resulted in a substantial monetary settlement, followed by a rough road to adulthood. Regardless of his newfound personal wealth and suburban, religious, responsible, two-parent, close family, ethnically white rearing, the abused youth became a drug dealer. Of course, this evolution caused terrible family heartache,

360 Sergio Ferragut, *A Silent Nightmare: The Bottom Line and the Challenge of Illicit Drugs* (Lulu, 2007), p. 178.

361 Ibid.

362 Pascal Sabino, "Garfield Park Businesses Forced To Close As Open Air Drug Market, Crime Scares Off Customers — With No Help In Sight, Owners Say," *Block Club Chicago*, October 16, 2020, accessed September 11, 2020, https://blockclubchicago.org/2020/10/16/garfield-park-businesses-forced-to-close-as-open-air-drug-market-crime-scares-off-customers-with-no-help-in-sight-owners-say/.

363 Knight-Ridder Newspapers, "Average Drug Dealer Income: $24,000 A Year," *Chicago Tribune*, July 11, 1990, https://www.chicagotribune.com/news/ct-xpm-1990-07-11-9002260581-story.html, Gierach notebooks, p. 219.

disputes, disrespect of parents, and troubled, wild living that included the motorcycle death of his friend. This young man was making money and described the drug-business lifestyle as exciting, receiving calls for an "8-ball" (a quantity of drugs, an eighth of an ounce, 3.5 grams, most commonly referring to coke, i.e., crack-cocaine) at all hours of the day and night.

Fortunately for this youngster, the same prosecutor who prosecuted his sex abuser had become a prosecuting supervisor, who, in an understanding act of compassion, approved a complete dismissal of my client's felony drug case. (There's another story here about prosecutorial discretion, mandatory-minimum sentencing, federal sentencing guidelines, and racial fairness in the criminal justice system, but that is apparent.) The last I heard of this lad's life story, he had turned over a new leaf and became a successful commodities broker. The drug chapter in his life passed, his family healed, and he lived happily ever after.

About the same timeframe as the commodities broker story, **Janet Kidd Stewart**, a reporter who understood the economics of drug prohibition, thankfully, shared her understanding in an insightful four-page spread, headlined "$7 Billion Addiction, the Drug Trade In The City and Suburbs," *Chicago Sun-Times*, December 20, 1992. Her work and insight regarding the economics of drug prohibition was decades ahead of her time.

Journalist Janet Kidd Stewart — 1992 Drug Policy Insight

The *Chicago Sun-Times* published the four-page assemblage of drug stories, all written by staff reporter Janet Kidd Stewart. The stories were presented side-by-side, page-after-page, under the headings: "Drug Business Still Booming," "Dantrell's Legacy: What Will Stop the Killing," "The Illicit Economy of Drugs: Raw Materials, Importation by Cali and Medellin Cartels," "Prices On Streets of Chicago," "The Cost of Drugs: Wholesale to Retail," "'War on Drugs'? It's Uphill Battle," "Drug Bucks: The Profit Motive, [and] The Other Side of the Balance Sheet," "Market is Lucrative For Moonlighters," "Going After Tools of the Trade," and "Laundering Is an Arm of the Corporation." The assemblage should have won Stewart a Pulitzer Prize.

Thus, way back then, the "drugogenic" power of drug prohibition should have been understood by all. But it wasn't.

Human Nature: People Want to Use Drugs

People want to use drugs recreationally. They have always done so; and they will continue to do so, forever and ever. Amen. If it wasn't so, demand reduction would be like shooting ducks in a barrel. Do you use any drugs? Any mood or mind-altering substance? We all do. Different substances for different folks, but sure, we all use substances with the same general goal in mind, the chemical alteration of mind, mood or consciousness. To relax, to unwind, to heighten alertness, or to change pace or dimension.

Dr. Arnold S. Trebach has passed[364] but not before writing eight books regarding drug policy urging reform as far back as the 1987 publication of *The Great Drug War: And Radical Proposals That Could Make America Safe Again.*[365] His earliest published book, *The Rationing of Justice: Constitutional Rights and the Criminal Process,*[366] was written twenty-two years before enactment of the Anti-Drug Abuse Act of 1986 and the rise of constitutional abuses that followed it. Collectively, those abuses have aptly been called, "Drug War Exceptions to the Bill of Rights."[367] Four years before that enactment, Dr. Trebach wrote *The Heroin Solution.* In the latter book, he astutely observed and wrote "... that drugs are not the devil and that drug-law enforcement is not a crusade."[368] Maybe he should have written that "drug-law enforcement *should not be* a crusade." The able lawyer, American University professor and anti-Prohibitionist "radical" is credited with making opposition to the war on drugs respectable.

Arnold Trebach and the Reason People Use Drugs

Among the astute observations made by "radical" Dr. Trebach was this one: "My belief is that *the reason people use drugs 'recreationally' is that they like what the substances do to*

---

[364] Marco Perduca, "Goodbye Arnold Trebach, radical anti-prohibitionist in the USA," *Science for Democracy*, July 29, 2020, https://sciencefordemocracy.org/goodbye-arnold-trebach-radical-anti-prohibitionist-in-the-usa/.

[365] Arnold S. Trebach, *The Great Drug War: And Radical Proposals That Could Make America Safe Again*, First Edition, (New York: Macmillan Publishing Company, 1987).

[366] Arnold S. Trebach, *The Rationing of Justice: Constitutional rights and the criminal* process (New Jersey: Rutgers University Press, 1964)

[367] Gierach, James E., "War Becomes Hell: Freedom Is Victim on Drug Battleground," *Chicago Sun-Times*, July 1, 1995; "Super-Max or super tax?" *The Reporter*, April 29, 1993; "Protecting your privacy in a drug-war strip search," *Illinois State Bar News*, circa January 9, 1999. *See* these articles in full, https://jamesgierach.tumblr.com/post/674470773508931584. *Also see*, Gierach, "Inhumane Conditions in prison," *Chicago Tribune*, May 22, 2009, https://jamesgierach.tumblr.com/post/674481377945747456.

[368] Arnold S. Trebach, *The Heroin Solution* (New Haven: Yale University Press, 1993), p. 287.

their minds, their moods, and their bodies.[369] Apparently, they do. According to UN estimates, hundreds of millions of people annually use prohibited drugs. Millions more use licit mind-altering substances for the same unlawful recreational purpose. Marijuana is the most commonly used of the illicit drugs. Oops! Now, in many places cannabis is a licit substance. Historically, the classification of drugs as lawful or unlawful has been made on unscientific and nonsensical bases that prove fickle over time. Marijuana, for example has been classified as legal and used for medicinal purposes for centuries if not millennia, and at other times classified as unlawful and having no medicinal value. In recent time, the UN drug-control conventions require nations to criminalize the recreational use of marijuana, yet some nations nevertheless are legalizing it for medical and recreational use. Tobacco is another substance often irrationally categorized. During the 17th Century Ottoman Empire, tobacco use was classified as a crime warranting imposition of the death penalty while modern day law makes tobacco use legal, although it is known to cause cancer and serious health problems.

People use drugs for varied and understandable reasons. Some people suffer from physical pain, others recoil from the pressures of life. Some choose to numb themselves from the bite of addiction, poverty, mental illness, sex abuse, physical abuse, and war-made neurosis or psychosis. Others live "the life of Riley" and simply choose to use mind-altering substances other than beer, tobacco, caffeine, wine, vodka or chocolate, or in addition to those substances. The Rileys among us perhaps just step back from their day's work or play, put up their feet, and relax in the pursuit of happiness and enjoyment of individual, drug-choice freedom.

Understanding this reality and tolerating each other's circumstances, choices and weaknesses is essential, if we are to ever regain "Drug Peace" and exit "Drug War."

A wonderful book written by Andrew Weil, M.D. and Winifred Rosen, entitled *From Chocolate to Morphine: Everything You Need to Know About Mind-Altering Drugs,*[370] tells the story of the great variety of drugs to choose from and provides a great deal of factual information about the nature and effects of each. To pick and choose which of these substances to prohibit, demonize and build a prison fence around is, again, a fickle undertaking that defies human nature and universal laws of the Cosmos.

---

[369] Ibid., p. 289.

[370] Weil and Rosen, *From Chocolate to Morphine: Everything you need to know about mind-altering drugs* (New York: Houghton Mifflin Company, 2nd Ed. 1993)

Huh? What was that last one? "Defying universal laws of the Cosmos?" Never mind. Just a word of caution for time-travelers: do not smoke tobacco about c. 1650 in Bavaria, Saxony, and Zürich, because Sultan Murad IV of the Ottoman Empire decreed it a death-penalty offense.[371]

Universal Economic Laws

In this author's opinion, an end to the 1961 Single Convention "War on Drugs" is an inevitable societal advancement compelled by economic principles, universal laws of nature and scientifically deduced human rights, as discussed by Michael T. Takac.[372]

Economically, the War on Drugs causes, aggravates and aggregates so many societal crises adversely impacting public health, international relations, human rights and individual freedom, as later discussed in Chapters 8 and 9, that global and national economies simply cannot raise enough taxes to afford to pay the resulting bills. Bad drug policy guarantees myriad crises, deficit-spending and a deficit crisis. Economic laws, like gravity, cannot long be ignored. And as a part of the set of universal laws of nature, life and scientifically deduced human rights, long term, such economic and social harmony laws must be obeyed, or we perish. Takac discusses these concepts: "Natural law is the thread running through the tapestry of civil society, as the physical laws of nature guide [...] its flow."[373] "Knowing that life's unalienable rights are part of the laws of nature and all social entities have unalienable rights... the roadmap becomes clearer in the direction of social flow, a flow embracing social harmony by man's liberty in the moral pursuit of his own heaven [happiness]."[374] Hey man, far out.

Paraphrasing and attempting to articulate my understanding of Takac's work, it seems to me he is saying: When the laws of society become so conflicted and adversarial to universal laws of nature and scientific "contractual rights," either those societal laws must reform, and conform, or human life itself will be extinguished. I agree.

---

[371] Thomas Szasz, *Ceremonial Chemistry* (Holmes Beach, Florida: Learning Publications, Inc., 1985), Appendix, "A Synoptic History of the Promotion and Prohibition of Drugs," p. 186.

[372] Michael T. Takac, *Scientific Proof of Our Unalienable Rights: A Road to Utopia* (Fremont, California: Robertson Publishing, 5th Edition, 2019).

[373] Ibid., p. 15.

[374] Ibid., p. 133.

The United Nations "Estimates System"

Preceding the adoption of the 1961 Single Convention, global drug policy relied upon a system of estimating the narcotic needs of each nation in a vain effort to control them. The system was described thusly: "The principal foundations of the previous treaties remained in place in the [1961] Single Convention. Parties [to the 1961 Single Convention, meaning nations] were still required to submit estimates of their drug requirements and statistical returns on the production, manufacture, use, consumption, import, export, and stock build-up of drugs. The import certification system created by the 1925 Geneva Convention continued, and Parties were required to license all manufacturers, traders and distributors – all transactions involving drugs had to be documented. The Single Convention built on the trend of requiring Parties to develop increasingly punitive domestic criminal legislation. Subject to their constitutional limitations, Parties were to adopt distinct criminal offenses, punishable preferably by imprisonment, for each of the following drug-related activities in contravention of the Convention: cultivation, production, manufacture, extraction, preparation, possession, offering, offering for sale, distribution, purchase, sale, delivery on any terms whatsoever, brokerage, dispatch, dispatch in transit, transport, importation and exportation. Furthermore, the granting of extradition was considered 'desirable.'"[375]

Continuing that historical precedent, great reliance is placed on an estimated needs calculation each nation is required to make regarding the number of controlled substances it needs, annually. The estimated calculation is required of each nation that is a party to, or has acceded to, the terms of the UN 1961 Single Convention. Many articles of the 1961 Single Convention deal with the estimates system. As I write about this antiquated and poorly conceived foundational system, I'm munching on Oreo cookies,[376] and my mind is drawing a parallel to controlled substances. Oreos, like controlled substances, can both be consumed for conventionally acceptable reasons. Oreos are consumed for food nourishment, and drugs are consumed for medical or

375 Jay Sinha, "The History and Development of the Leading International Drug Control Convention," *Library of Parliament*, February 21, 2001, Prepared For The Senate Special Committee On Illegal Drugs, https://sencanada.ca/content/sen/committee/371/ille/library/history-e.htm?back=https%3A%2F%2Fwww.google.com%2Fsearch%3Fclient%3Dsafari%26as_qdr%3Dall%26as_occt%3Dany%26safe%3Dactive%26as_q%3Dwho+was+president+when+the+1961+single+convention+on+narcotic+drugs+was+adopted%26channel%3Daplab%26source%3Da-app1%26hl%3Den, accessed August 28, 3021.

376 Oreo is an American chocolate cookie advertised as "America's favorite cookie;" Jennifer Rosenberg, "A History of the Oreo Cookie," *ThoughtCo.*, September 13, 2019, https://www.thoughtco.com/history-of-the-oreo-cookie-1779206, accessed September 5, 2021.

scientific purposes — both consumptions accomplished for conventionally acceptable reasons. However, consumption of both can be for other purposes.

I like chocolate that sustains me and my mood. At the moment, it is enabling me to defer getting breakfast so I can write. For some others, controlled substances do much the same for them, stirring creative juices within them.[377] These are not nutritional, medical or scientific reasons for consumption. And I wonder what usefulness would be served, or reliability assured, if someone else decided, approved or monitored how many Oreos I needed. Or wanted. Or would eat. "Cookie need" is a matter best estimated in the eye of the beholder, the mouth of the muncher, and no governmental agency, international body, or third-party estimates system can do a better job determining my Oreo needs than me. Rumor has it that, like me, Oprah Winfield likes nothing more than eating an entire sleeve of Oreos in one sitting.[378]

The International Oreo Control Board

If I was compelled by UN treaty mandate to estimate my "Oreo Cookie Needs," and required to answer a lot of questions about my Oreo intake, and how many Oreos I had left over from last year, how many I'm going to buy, and how many I was going to give away to others, I probably wouldn't answer either, just like many nations don't answer their estimates questionnaire regarding controlled substances. And if I did answer, my answers would be incomplete, crummy, and not worth digesting. That reality is going to undermine the validity of the UN's estimate of my Oreo cookie needs. Not only that but if the UN and its agencies tried to cut back the number of Oreos I needed or wanted, I'd look for another way to get them.

And, of course, I'm not a factory or an Oreo-producing country. I'm just an Oreo-eating consumer. But if I was an Oreo-producing country, my estimates of world Oreo-needs would likely differ greatly from those of the International Oreo Control Board's (IOCB), modeled after the International Narcotic Control Board (INCB).[379]

---

[377] Amanda Patterson, "58 Famous Writers and Their Addictions," *Writers Write*, September 3, 2013, https://www.writerswrite.co.za/58-famous-writers-and-their-addictions/.

[378] Janaki Jitchotvisut, "Oprah Used To Eat An Entire Sleeve Of Oreos After Getting High," *First We Feast*, May 18, 2015, https://firstwefeast.com/eat/2015/05/oprah-munchies-david-letterman-oreos.

[379] It is the responsibility of national managers to determine and support their respective country's estimated needs for narcotic drugs sufficiently to international authorities. It is the responsibility of the International Narcotics Control Board (INCB) to review those estimates and make determinations that affect Import and Export Authorizations, inter alia, and ultimately national analgesic drug availability. The involved process can be studied here. "WHO Guidelines for the Pharmacological and Radiotherapeutic Management of Cancer Pain in

The importance of the estimates system, as the International Narcotics Control Board sees it, is expressed in the Foreword to the Report of the International Narcotics Control Board for 2020 by its President **Cornelis P. de Joncheere**. "The international drug control system is an example of multilateralism in action: Member States, which have committed to ensuring the availability of controlled medicines for patients in need, exchange information with each other, through *import and export authorizations* for controlled substances, and with the INCB, through reporting on licit requirements for and statistics on narcotic drugs, psychotropic substances and precursor chemicals. *This practical international cooperation is key* to ensuring that important medicines reach health professionals and patients and that precursor chemicals can be traded internationally for licit purposes while preventing diversion to illicit channels."[380] Sounds good enough, but it does not work that way. Most of the people of the world are deprived of reasonable access to pain medicine because of the estimates system, and the estimates system is unable to constrict or control drugs or precursor chemicals in the hands of illicit drug producers.

Proposal to Eliminate the UN 1961 Single Convention "Estimates System"

My draft of a proposed comprehensive amendment of United Nations drug conventions,[381] Article 7, entitled "Functions of the International Drug Control Board," (a newly conceptualized Board) *eliminated "the estimates system" entirely* for good reason. One very good reason was that this system unavoidably caused a chronic bottleneck that, year after year, prevented many patients in many parts of the world from accessing narcotic medicines needed during and following surgery and painful, end-of-life ordeals.[382]

Adults and Adolescents," ANNEX 5, Opioid Analgesics and International Conventions, the World Health Organization, https://www.ncbi.nlm.nih.gov/books/NBK537494/, accessed January 26, 2022.

380 Cornelis P. de Joncheere, Foreword, "International Narcotic Control Board Annual Report 2020," https://www.incb.org/documents/Publications/AnnualReports/AR2020/Annual_Report_Chapters/01_AR_2020_Foreword_by_the_INCB_President.pdf, emphasis added.

381 Gierach/Law Enforcement Against Prohibition, "Proposed Amendment of United Nations Drug Control Treaties – 2014," in English, https://www.unodc.org/documents/ungass2016//Contributions/Civil/Law_Enforcement_Against_Prohibition/LEAP_UN_Treaty_Amendment_2.26.1421-1.pdf, and in Spanish, https://www.unodc.org/documents/ungass2016//Contributions/Civil/Law_Enforcement_Against_Prohibition/FINAL-3-Spanish_LEAP-Treaty-Amendment_5.27.14-1.pdf.

382 Diederik Lohman & Naomi Burke-Shyne, "The Impact of International Drug Policy on Access to Controlled Medicines," Open Society Foundations, 2016, https://www.opensocietyfoundations.org/uploads/d61b7003-

Secondly, the system is inherently unreliable because of incomplete national reporting of estimated needs, a quarter of nations not reporting at all, and because of the other practical reality of dynamic drug-diversion and drug-invention. Poor data quality and low response rates from Member States have long persisted with the Annual Report Questionnaire (ARQ).[383]

The International National Narcotics Control Board has long recognized the first of these two serious shortcomings as seen in the opening paragraph of the Preface to its 2016 publication, entitled "Availability of Internationally Controlled Drugs: Ensuring Adequate Access for Medical and Scientific Purposes, Indispensable, adequately available are not unduly restricted." The INCB published its report noting: "Several decades ago, the international community made a solemn commitment with the Single Convention on Narcotic Drugs of 1961 as amended by the 1972 Protocol and the Convention on Psychotropic Substances of 1971: to make adequate provision to ensure, and not to unduly restrict, the availability of drugs that were considered indispensable for medical and scientific purposes. In recent decades, that promise has not been completely fulfilled. *Too many people still suffer or die in pain or do not have access to the medications they need.* Unnecessary suffering resulting from a lack of appropriate medication due to inaction and excessive administrative requirements is a situation that shames us all."[384]

The Estimates Bottleneck Must Go

The Preface of the 2018 INCB Report on the same subject, written by **Viroj Sumyai**, President International Narcotics Control Board, noted that adequate access to internationally controlled substances for medical and scientific purposes remained a serious problem, writing "... the goal of ensuring the availability of and access to narcotic drugs and psychotropic substances for medical and scientific purposes is still far from being universally met. *People are still suffering;* such people range from those who have to *undergo surgery without anaesthesia* to those without access to the medication they need

76d5-410c-8e2e-205cd6c8bf7c/impact-international-drug-policy-access-controlled-medicines-en-20160315.pdf.

[383] David R. Bewley-Taylor and Marie Nougier, "Measuring the 'World Drug Problem': 2019 and Beyond," *Collapse of the Global Order on Drugs* (United Kingdom: Emerald Publishing, 2018), Ch. 3.

[384] "Availability of Internationally Controlled Drugs: Ensuring Adequate Access for Medical and Scientific Purposes," INCB, 2015, https://www.unodc.org/documents/drug-prevention-and-treatment/INCB_ Access_Supplement-AR15_availability_English.pdf, emphasis added, accessed March 17, 2023.

and those who are *dying in unnecessary pain*. The imbalance in the availability of and access to opioid analgesics is particularly troublesome: the Board wishes to raise the alarm and a call to action, as data show that many of the conditions requiring pain management, including cancer, are prevalent, and that their prevalence is increasing in low- and middle-income countries, while the medicines and knowledge to alleviate the situation exist and are affordable."[385]

An excess in availability for consumption exists in the countries whose size is expanded (for example Australia, Canada and the United States of America) and the extremely low level of the need for opioid analgesics being met in areas of Africa, Asia, Central and South America, the Caribbean and Eastern Europe is shown by the shrunken size of those regions."[386]

People undergoing surgery and dying without adequate analgesics is barbaric. Such barbarity is unbecoming of twenty-first century medicine and the United Nations, especially after sixty years within which to get the 1961 Single Convention up and running properly. Time's up! The estimates system is the obvious obstruction to patients being treated humanely.

Gierach/LEAP Proposed Amendment — Article 7

For that good reason, again, the Gierach/LEAP Article 7 of the proposed amendment of UN drug treaties eliminated the unworkable estimates system entirely, and provided as follows:

"Article 7. Functions of the [Proposed, New] International Drug Control Board

[The former Article 19 required the Parties to annually submit estimates to the Board of the quantity of drugs required for medical and scientific purposes, the Convention prohibiting any recreational, religious or nonmedical/nonscientific research use of narcotic drugs as repeatedly noted in multiple articles of the Convention; Article 33 forbade, generally, a Party from permitting its nationals to even possess drugs; Article 20 required the Parties to furnish the Board with statistical returns regarding drug production, consumption, imports and exports, seizures of drugs, stocks of drugs, *inter alia*; Articles 21, 21 bis and 24 limited drug manufacture and importation, limited

---

[385] "Progress in ensuring adequate access to internationally controlled substances for medical and scientific purposes," *INCB*, International Narcotic Control Board Annual Report, 2018, https://www.incb.org/documents/Publications/AnnualReports/AR2018/Supplement/Supplement_E_ebook.pdf, p. 5, emphasis added, accessed March 17, 2023.

[386] Ibid., p. 5.

opium production and opium trade, and Article 25 imposed restrictions on opium straw; Articles 26 and 27 aimed to control coca leaves and coca bush, and Article 28 cannabis; Articles 19 and 31 imposed import and export restrictions, and Articles 23, 30 and 34 imposed licensing, labelling and record-keeping restrictions. Unfortunately, these drug control efforts produced adverse results as recited in the Preface to this Amendment — more drugs, more trafficking and more drug use. *Therefore, the foregoing articles concerning drug estimates and reporting systems, drug needs, plants and hectare-planting land areas, plant seizure and destruction, licensing schemes and import and export certificates are repealed by this proposed Amendment.* Also repealed are Articles 12-15, 17- 21, 21 bis, 23-31 and 34, as are the failed enforcement mechanisms found in Articles 14, 14 bis, 22, the mandate to create national opium agencies in Article 23, the First-Aid Kits drug exception for ships and aircraft found in Article 32, the sweeping possession prohibition found in Article 33, the mandates that Parties 'shall' take action found in Article 35 and 38, the penalties and 'deprivation of liberty' provisions found in Article 36, the enhanced penalties invited by Article 39, and the seizure and confiscation of drugs and equipment found in Article 37.]"[387]

The United Nations' estimates system needs to be scrapped, because a quarter of nations recognize the practical impossibility of the estimates task and do not even bother to complete the mandatory task, or do it incompletely, impugning its validity.

"As of 1 November 2020, the Board had received *annual statistical reports* from 158 States (both parties and non-parties) and territories on the production, manufacture, consumption, stocks and seizures of narcotic drugs covering the calendar year 2019 (form C), or *about 74 percent of those requested.* That number represents a decline compared with previous years (173 reports covering the calendar year 2018 were received in 2019 and 172 reports covering the calendar year 2017 were received in 2018)... [As of that date,] 56 Governments (26 per cent) – that is, 49 countries and seven territories – had not submitted their annual statistics for 2019.... Most countries and territories that have not submitted their reports are in Africa, the Caribbean, Asia and Oceania and some are in conflict and post-conflict situations, which, in addition

---

[387] Gierach/LEAP, "Proposed Amendment of United Nations Drug Treaties — 2014," https://www.unodc.org/documents/ungass2016//Contributions/Civil/Law_Enforcement_Against_Prohibition/LEAP_UN_Treaty_Amendment_2.26.1421-1.pdf, emphasis added.

to a general lack of human and financial resources arising from such situations, presents additional obstacles to drug control efforts."[388]

Like the unworkable estimated limits placed on Oreo cookie consumption by my hypothesized International Oreo Control Board, the UN estimated needs system regarding narcotic consumption must go, along with drug prohibition itself for the estimated needs, economic and human nature reasons cited.

---

[388] *INCB* Annual Report 2020, https://www.incb.org/documents/Publications/AnnualReports/ AR2020/ Annual_Report_Chapters/05_AR_2020_Chapter_II.pdf, p. 15, par. 82, emphasis added, accessed March 17, 2023.

Chapter 8 – Drug War: Common Denominator to Many Healthcare Crises

There are two sides to the Drug War Coin. Flip the coin. If the coin lands "Heads," drug dealers win; and if the coin lands "Tails," respectable people lose.

Part Two of this book discussed how the drug war brings us *more drugs, more crime and more corruption*. If that were not reason enough to end the War on Drugs, there is another side to the Drug War Coin that is equally as harmful, "Unintended Collateral Consequences." Part Three of this book explained in Chapter 7 why the War on Drugs doesn't work, and never will. But there's more. Unrelenting failure forecasts its own doom. But in the meantime, society suffers mercilessly, as also explained in Part Three, because *the War on Drugs makes societal problems, many of them crises, worse instead of better*. Pick nearly any American crisis and drug-prohibition policy worsens its punch. The same can be said for the problems and crises in many other countries.

Seventh Circuit Court of Appeals Bar Association Conference 1993

By May 24, 1993, almost thirty years ago, I had concluded that drug prohibition was the common denominator underscoring many crises in America. On that date respected Chief Judge **William J. Bauer** of the United States Court of Appeals, Seventh Circuit, moderated a panel discussion of judges and attorneys regarding sentencing guidelines and the war on drugs at a Seventh Circuit Bar Association Conference being held in Chicago. Generally, the panel was critical of the federal government's efforts to curb the drug trade, except for **Peter B. Bensinger**, the first Administer of the U.S. Drug Enforcement Agency. Bensinger argued that any softening of drug laws would increase drug availability, and another panelist, a Miami prosecutor, argued that any attempt to try and regulate drug use and sales might lead to civil lawsuits brought against the government.

Seventh Circuit Judge **Richard A. Posner** said the drug war was a failure, and those who endorse law enforcement as a cure for the drug trade "don't realize the limitations of government." U.S. District Court Judge **Suzanne B. Conlon** commented that federal sentencing guidelines were geared toward getting the "linchpin" in the drug-trafficking business, but often failed to do so, because higher ranking drug dealers had more information to provide prosecutors justifying deviation from the guidelines and secondly, because racial bias still worked to the advantage of white males.[389]

As a panelist, I said I favored allowing doctors to dispense drugs to addicts, much like Dr. John Marks prescribed them to his patients at the Merseyside Clinic in Liverpool, England from 1982-1995. "In an article in the medical journal *The Lancet*, published not long after his arrival in Liverpool, [Dr. Marks] argued that given that heroin users would continue using anyway if they were not yet ready to stop, providing a stable and clean supply of opiates was a humane and practical approach. It would protect the individual's health and also benefit society by undercutting the illicit drug trade and its associated 'gangsterism.'"[390]

I came to the Seventh Circuit Bar Association panel discussion armed with a graphic that displayed a number of named crises like numbers on a clock. The clock arm was a pointer that said, "A Drug-War Crisis," and could pivot and point to any of the named-crises. The crises named included: Addict-Crime, Turf-War Crime, Prisons, Gangs, Guns, Healthcare, AIDS, Corruption, Clogged Courts, Trade Imbalance, School Dropouts and Deficits, among others. In big, bold, red letters, the graphic was entitled, "National Crisis Wheel" and in matching bold, red letters written below the named crises were the words, "Al Capone and Pablo Escobar Support Prohibition."

A National Crisis Wheel

Unfortunately, Chief Judge Bauer disallowed my use of the 3-foot by 5-foot "National Crisis Wheel" graphic. His ruling foreshadowed thirty years of resistance from the powers that be regarding this author's central mission in life, the promotion of drug policy reform to stop violence and regain control of a dozen twentieth century societal problems, problems and baggage now dragged by continued drug prohibition policy into the twenty-first century, too. On that conference day, Judge Bauer hampered my ability to graphically project the central idea I sought to advance, then, and still today. The idea is simple enough. Regressed, antiquated, prohibition drug policy was, and is, the common denominator underscoring many American and global crises.

---

[389] "Panelists criticize 'war on drugs,' *Chicago Daily Law Bulletin*, May 25, 1993.

[390] Toby Sedden, "Prescribing heroin: John Marks, the Merseyside clinics, and lessons from history," *International Journal of Drug Policy*, 78 (2020) 102730, https://www.academia.edu/43669723/ Prescribing_heroin_John_Marks_the_Merseyside_clinics_and_lessons_from_history.

Regressed American and global drug policy impacts different countries differently, but universally the choice of drug prohibition as the "common and shared responsibility"[391] of all nations adversely impacts public health, international relations, human rights and individual freedom. A national list of crises is not necessarily the same for every country, say, as depicted by my 1993 United States "National Crisis Wheel," and the list of crises is expansive. Let's start with drug-war aggravated healthcare crises.

Adverse Public Health Consequences

The nature and scope of adverse public health consequences of UN drug prohibition policy seems to be inexhaustible. Those adverse public health consequences include accidental drug overdose caused by a lack of UN support for the regulation of legal, licensed, recreational drug outlets, the inspection of legal, recreational, psychoactive drug products, and notification to the public of drug content, purity and strength of recreational, psychoactive drug products (including appropriate warnings) by drug-labeling dictates.

Adverse public health consequences of UN drug policies also include the sharing and use of dirty, contaminated needles by injecting drug users that spread HIV, AIDS and hepatitis C. "Hepatitis C is a liver infection caused by the hepatitis C virus (HCV). Hepatitis C is spread through contact with blood from an infected person. Today, most people become infected with the hepatitis C virus by sharing needles or other equipment used to prepare and inject drugs."[392] The UN, and its anti-drug agencies, adamantly oppose these consequences but with equal fervor support prohibition policies that effectively send drug users to the black market where they find and share dirty needles used to inject unregulated drugs.

These adverse public health consequences of the drug war prompted and necessitated the growth of a large branch of the drug-policy-reform tree, called "Harm Reduction." *Undoing Drugs: The Untold Story of Harm Reduction and the Future of Addiction* written by Maia Szalavitz, excellently covers this subject. The UNODC also

---

[391] Portugal President Jorge Fernando Branco De Sampaio used the term "shared responsibility" in address to UN General Assembly Special Session, *UN General Assembly*, "Secretary-General Calls on All Nations to Say 'Yes' to Challenge of Working Towards Drug-Free World," June 8, 1988, Press Release, https://press.un.org/en/1998/19980608.ga9411.html.

[392] "Hepatitis C," *Centers for Disease Control and Prevention*, https://www.cdc.gov/hepatitis/hcv/index.htm, accessed September 23, 2021.

provided an excellent description of harm reduction — what it is, and the goals of harm reduction strategies.

Harm Reduction

"Harm reduction can be viewed as the prevention of adverse consequences of illicit drug use without necessarily reducing their consumption. [cite] The goal of harm reduction strategies and approaches is to reduce the negative consequences of drug abuse, not to eliminate the use of licit or illicit drugs [cite]. Harm reduction is a practical approach that employs a range of different strategies with the goal of minimizing the risk of the client contracting infectious diseases, overdosing, or suffering other consequences related to the use of substances. Strategies may include changing the way people consume drugs or ensuring that the environment in which they use minimizes the risks of negative consequences to their health (infections, overdose) or quality of life (legal problems, social and familial issues, etc.). Strategies can vary depending on the drug, the type of harm related to its consumption, and the individual who consumes the drugs [cite]."[393]

Harm reduction measures include clean needle and syringe exchanges, naloxone take-home programs, drug consumption rooms and heroin-assisted treatment. A table reporting the availability of these selected harm reduction responses in thirty European countries can be seen here.[394] Attorney Brian A. Ford categorized harm reduction, alternative but related drug policy choices that included a Portugal-style "public health model" that featured drug decriminalization and clean needles, a Netherlands-style "citizens' rights model" advanced by drug users and that domestically categorized drugs by a risk scale from acceptable (cannabis, certain tranquilizers and barbiturates) to unacceptable (opiates, cocaine, amphetamines and LSD), and a "global justice approach." The global justice approach "expands the dialogue of harms-reduction in 'consumer nations' to harms-reduction in 'producing' nations."[395]

---

[393] "Reducing the harm of drug use and dependence," *Treat[globe]net, International Network of Drug Dependence Treatment and Rehabilitation Resource Centres.* https://www.unodc.org/ddt-training/treatment/VOLUME %20D/Topic%204/1.VolD_Topic4_Harm_Reduction.pdf.

[394] "Czech Republic Country Drug Report 2017," *European Monitoring Centre for Drugs and Drug Addiction (EMCDDA),* p. 11, https://www.emcdda.europa.eu/system/files/publications/4511/TD0416912ENN.pdf, accessed March 17, 2023.

[395] Brian A. Ford, "From Mountains to Molehills: A Comparative Analysis of Drug Policy," p. 19-26, https://www.academia.edu/3546783/From_Mountains_to_Molehills_A_Comparative_Analysis_of_Drug_Poli cy?email_work_card=thumbnail, accessed March 17, 2023.

Harm Reduction Good — Harm Elimination Better

Harm reduction is good. It is better than harm oblivion. If there must be endless drug war, then harm reduction is a good fallback position to address adverse drug-war harms. But *harm elimination is better than harm reduction*, and an absence of drug war is the best drug policy to reduce most drug-war harms.

In 2007, **António Maria Costa** postulated that "Harm reduction is often made an unnecessary controversial issue as if there was a contradiction between prevention and treatment on one hand and reducing the adverse health and social consequences of drug use on the other. This is a false dichotomy. They are complementary." Mr. Costa's quotation appears in "Treatnet–International Network of Drug Dependence Treatment and Rehabilitation Resource Centres" which was created by the UNODC in 2005.[396] As Mr. Costa says, prevention, treatment and harm reduction are complementary. Agreed. But I hasten to add, drug prohibition is the enemy of all three — prevention, treatment and harm reduction — because drug prohibition causes harm and increases the demand placed on treatment and prevention services. Russia and the state of Indiana provide two good case studies, one national and the other more local, revealing that the "false dichotomy" is not prevention and treatment versus harm reduction; rather, it is drug prohibition versus prevention, treatment and harm reduction.

Russian and Indiana HIV/AIDS

In 2010, Russia had more heroin users than any other country, approximately two to three million users, and a serious AIDS problem. The AIDS problem compromised the lives of many Russians, officially 637,000 cases to unofficially one million cases, yet Russia banned methadone, an orally consumed, heroin-substitution product used to avoid inherent, disease-promoting injecting risks. Russian drug prohibition policy supported its methadone ban with criminalization tactics and exposure to a twenty-year prison sentence for would-be methadone suppliers.[397] Although the UN supported Russia with funds to combat HIV, Russia resisted harm-reduction strategies to

[396] Juana Tomás-Rosselló, "Treatnet–International Network of Drug Dependence Treatment and Rehabilitation Resource Centres," National Institute on Drug Abuse, 2007, https://www.drugabuse.gov/ international/. abstracts/treatnet-international-network-drug-dependence-treatment-rehabilitation-resource-centres, March 17, 2023.

[397] Amie Ferris-Rotman, "Insight: Russia says no to West's way with HIV," *Reuters*, December 21, 2011, https://www.reuters.com/article/us-russia-hiv-idINTRE7BK12X20111221.

address its one million to 1.5 million persons now estimated to be living with HIV in Russia.[398] Russia also received help from an international financing and partnership organization, the Global Fund to Fight AIDS, Tuberculosis and Malaria, an NGO, "the world's largest financier of AIDS, TB, and malaria prevention, treatment, and care programs."[399] Nevertheless, Russia has a problem.

"Critics say Russia's reluctance to adopt tried and tested means of reducing new HIV infections is a result of the ultra-conservative government policies that have been promoted by the powerful Russian Orthodox Church since Putin returned to the presidency for a third term in 2012."[400] Yet Russia's need for better thinking is dire as evidenced by the fact that "The Andrey Rylkov Foundation, which has around 25 members, is the sole source of free, clean needles and condoms for addicts in Moscow, a city of more than 12 million people."[401]

According to Vadim Pokrovsky, head of the Federal Research Center for AIDS Prevention and Control in Moscow, what does work to retard the spread of the virus is what Russia does not have, and Germany does have, namely, "compulsory sex education in schools, legal prostitution, as well as state-run clean needles programs and opioid substitution therapy."[402]

The Russian, conservative, traditionalist and "moral" approach to drugs and HIV is more akin to that of Indiana, where former U.S. Vice President Mike Pence resisted clean needles despite an AIDS epidemic in southern Indiana when he was governor there. Like Putin, Pence promoted anti-drug thinking, thereby propagating harm.[403]

---

[398] Marc Bennetts, "The epidemic Russia doesn't want to talk about," *Politico*, May 11,2020, https://www.politico.eu/article/everything-you-wanted-to-know-about-aids-in-russia-but-putin-was-afraid-to-ask/.

[399] *Wikipedia, s.v.* "The Global Fund to Fight AIDS, Tuberculosis and Malaria," https://en.m.wikipedia.org/wiki/The_Global_Fund_to_Fight_AIDS,_Tuberculosis_and_Malaria, accessed March 17, 2023.

[400] Ibid.

[401] Ibid.

[402] Ibid.

[403] Associated Press, "Pence's handling of 2015 HIV outbreak gets new scrutiny: The then-Indiana governor worried about distributing clean needles to drug users," *Associated Press*, February 28, 2020, updated same date, and republished by *NBC News*, https://www.nbcnews.com/politics/white-house/pence-s-handling-2015-hiv-outbreak-gets-new-scrutiny-n1144786.

Recreational Drug Prohibition: The Nemesis of Harm Reduction

The United Nations' hesitant and fallback position lending mixed support to harm reduction strategies regarding clean needles and heroin-substitute treatment, *inter alia*, is better than obliviousness. But its insistence on recreational drug prohibition spearheads harm-causing, global drug policy and remains the nemesis of effective harm reduction. Recreational drug prohibition is ground zero for drug-war harm, despite the UN's constructive adoption of ambitious Sustainable Development Goals related to HIV and AIDS.

The UN adopted Sustainable Development Goal No. 3 regarding "Good Health and Well-Being," but it overlooked the relationship between its adherence to drug prohibition policy to the facts it recited: "By the end of 2017, there were 21.7 million people living with HIV receiving antiretroviral treatment but 15 million more people were not."[404] The Target Goal for SDG No. 3 provides: "By 2030, end the epidemics of AIDS, tuberculosis, malaria and neglected tropical diseases and combat hepatitis, water-borne diseases and other communicable diseases."[405] The likelihood of attaining that laudable Target Goal is reduced because recreational drug users inject drugs, and a prohibitive drug environment drives injecting drug users into the black market where high prices and dirty needle-sharing practices abound, consequences inapposite to the SDG No. 3.

Accidental Drug Overdose No Accident

As mentioned earlier regarding fentanyl ("The Fentanyl-Heroin Overdose Phenomenon" in Chapter 4), people are dying of accidental drug overdose, largely as a consequence of the drug users not dependably knowing what substance and potency he or she is imbibing, and its contamination prospects. This is another direct and unacceptable cost of drug-prohibition policy measured in terms of unnecessary deaths of human beings. "Over 166,000 die from drug overdoses per year – more than half are younger than 50 years," according to *Our World In Data*.[406]

---

[404] United Nations, "Sustainable Development Goal No. 3, Good Health and Well-Being, Target Goal," https://www.undp.org/sustainable-development-goals#good-health.

[405] Ibid.

[406] Hannah Ritchie and Max Roser, "Opioids, cocaine, cannabis and illicit drugs," *Our World in Data*, last revised 2019, https://ourworldindata.org/illicit-drug-use, accessed October 10, 2021.

The death of 166,000 people is no accident when nations enacted drug laws mandated by UN drug-control conventions that obstruct the ability of 275 million users of illicit drugs: (a) to know the content, purity and potency of the substance in their hand by simply reading an accurate and appropriate product label, (b) to recognize immediately whether a drug product has been government-inspected, and (c) to purchase that substance in a legal and regulated drug market. Those deaths are simply an unacceptable cost of well-intended, drug-war life and love.

National leaders and UN authorities, officials and agencies who refuse to "Say Uncle"[407] and "throw in the towel"[408] regarding the World War on Drugs are not helping mankind when it comes time to choose between life and death, tolerance and intolerance, or drug peace and drug war.

The War on Drugs is a bloody fight to the death in the healthcare arena and on turf-war battlefields. Bloody fighting to the death should not be tolerated between dogs or fowl[409] competing for sport, betting or entertainment, and it should not be tolerated in drug wars between people in furtherance of pretentious sobriety, righteousness, or self-satisfaction. This man-eating, drug-war machine overseen by the Commission on Narcotic Drugs, the International Narcotics Control Board, and the United Nations Office on Drugs and Crime is designed to never run out of gas, never shut off, and that is an unforgivable error in public policy, just as surely as the lives taken by that public policy are forever unrecoverable.

National leaders, who put their heads in the drug-war sand while sending their representatives to Vienna annually in March to tend and attend the Commission on Narcotics Drugs, share that badge of irresponsible complacency and guilt. The casualty cost of this war is too great and too certain to let another year, another day, pass without excoriating intolerant, unworkable and failed United Nation drug policy dogma. That dogma equates with needless suffering, death and destruction served off an à la carte, "Yellow List" bill of fare prepared by the International Narcotics Board in cooperation with the World Health Organization.[410]

---

[407] *The Free Dictionary,* s.v. "say uncle," https://idioms.thefreedictionary.com/say+uncle.

[408] *Merriam-Webster,* s.v. "throw in the towel," https://www.merriam-webster.com/thesaurus/ throw%20 in%20the%20towel

[409] *Wikipedia* s.v. "Cockfight," https://en.wikipedia.org/wiki/Cockfight.

[410] "Access to Medicines and Health Products," *World Health Organization,* https://www.who.int/our-work/access-to-medicines-and-health-products/controlled-substances, accessed March 17, 2023; and Note 190, *supra.*

The United Nations' Estimates System Obstructs Patient Access to Meds

Speaking of the adverse public health consequences of drug prohibition policy, again. the bottleneck created by the United Nations' estimates system regarding narcotic medicines must be removed. As discussed in Chapter 7, this inevitable and torturous harm is facilitated by the U.N. estimates system. Viroj Sumyai, president of International Narcotics Control Board wrote (my emphasis added): "*People are still suffering;* such people range from those who have to *undergo surgery without anaesthesia* to those without access to the medication they need and those who are *dying in unnecessary pain.*" Helen Clark, president of the **Global Commission on Drug Policy**, and multiple other speakers point out on video that "Pain is a pandemic," regarding inadequate access to essential, controlled medicines five years after UNGASS 2016.[411] UNGASS 2016 was a United Nations General Assembly Special Session regarding the world drug problem held in New York City in April 2016. (See Chapters 18 and 19, infra.) The prevalent lack of access to these pain medicines in many parts of the world is another unnecessary, critical and chronic harm caused by bad UN drug prohibition policy. As time has shown, this harm cannot be repaired despite the work of UNGASS 2016 and civil society without treaty amendment.

Turf-War Cost in Terms of Violent Loss of Human Life

One of the bloodiest consequences of the drug-war mistake is unavoidable violence, violence associated with gangs fighting over disputed drug territory and black-market, drug-business disputes. Drug war is "gunogenic." If you're in the illicit drug business, the essential tool of the trade is a gun — a prerequisite really. The drug war puts more guns everywhere, just as it puts more drugs everywhere. More guns mean more shootings, and more shootings means more people shot.

As a result, gun violence is epidemic in the United States, Mexico, Brazil, Colombia, Central America countries and elsewhere. "Gun violence is a daily tragedy affecting the lives of individuals around the world. More than *500 people die every day* because of violence committed with firearms."[412] Regardless of the motivational particulars, drug-war gunplay causes bullet holes, and bullet-hole injuries escalate the cost of

---

[411] "Access to Essential Controlled Medicines: Five Years After UNGASS 2016," *YouTube*, https://youtu.be/ CFknvrQIWlI.

[412] "Gun Violence — Key Facts," *Amnesty International,*

healthcare dramatically. And sadly, the United States is ripe with gun history — the "Gatling Gun,"[413] the "Tommy Gun,"[414] the "Saturday Night Special,"[415] and the "Assault Weapon."[416]

Assault Weapons: Drug Dealers' Weapon of Choice

In the highly competitive prohibition drug business, drug dealers seek bigger and more deadly guns and, reactively, law enforcement gets bigger and more deadly guns.[417] Assault weapons tear human tissue to smithereens.[418] Extreme damage caused by an assault weapon like the AK-47 or AR-15 make assault weapons the drug dealers' weapon of choice.[419] "The leading manufacturers of semi-automatic rifles used to perpetrate the deadliest mass shootings in the United States have collected more than $1.7 billion in revenue from AR-15 style weapons over the past decade as gun violence across the country has surged, according to a House investigation presented on Capitol Hill..."[420]

Systemic Violence: An Inherent Feature of Recreational Drug Prohibition

Systemic violence is an inherent feature of recreational drug prohibition policy. "Zimring attributes the high levels of lethal violence in [the United States] to three factors that are often interrelated: '... a highly violent illegal drug trade, large numbers of

---

https://www.amnesty.org/en/what-we-do/arms-control/gun-violence/, emphasis added, accessed March 17, 2023.

[413] *Wikipedia,* s.v. "Gatling gun," https://en.wikipedia.org/wiki/Gatling_gun.

[414] *Wikipedia,* s.v. "Thompson machine gun," https://en.wikipedia.org/wiki/Thompson_submachine_gun.

[415] *Wikipedia, s.v. "Saturday night special,"* https://en.wikipedia.org/wiki/Saturday_night_special.

[416] *Wikipedia,* s.v. "Assault weapons," https://en.wikipedia.org/wiki/Assault_weapon.

[417] Chip Goines, "To 'Demilitarize' Police, First Ban Assault Weapons," *GBH,* July 20, 2020, https://www.wgbh.org/news/commentary/2020/07/20/to-demilitarize-police-first-ban-assault-weapons.

[418] Editor Board, USA TODAY, editorial, "The AR-15 rifle butchers the human body; so why is it legal, exactly?" *USATODAY,* November 9, 2017. https://www.usatoday.com/story/opinion/2017/11/09/ar-15-rifle-butchers-human-body-so-why-legal-exactly-our-view-debates-editorial/847868001/.

[419] Doug Struck, "AK-47 Called Weapon of Choice for Gangs, Drug Dealers," *Tulsa World,* Mar 26, 1989 Updated Feb 25, 2019, https://tulsaworld.com/archive/ak-47-called-weapon-of-choice-for-gangs-drug-dealers/article_74d244ba-0c00-5aec-9883-451a24e9bddd.html.

[420] Annie Karni, "Panel slams AR-15 style firearm ads," *New York Times,* July 28, 2022, https://digitaledition.chicagotribune.com/html5/mobile/production/default.aspx?edid=207ad4bf-2ba6-4448-8467-94b503845282.

handguns, and a tradition of male honor that includes 'a willingness to use extreme violence' to settle problems" (cite). If one can make the argument that the willingness to use extreme violence to settle problems is often dramatically epitomized in the rules of conduct used by street gangs (e.g., in retributive drive-by shootings or to enforce territorial boundaries) then one can extend Zimring and Hawkin's position further to argue that a good portion of lethal violence in America is attributable to guns, drug sales, and gangs."[421] "Additional studies have similarly implicated drug sales as leading to an increased likelihood of owning and carrying a firearm and to the commission of violent crimes (cites)."[422] "High rates of gun carrying, drug use, and violence among drug sellers are indicative of what Goldstein (1985) calls *the systemic violence inherent in the drug trade.*"[423] Surprisingly to some people — "Excepting possibly amphetamines and barbiturates, *there does not appear to be a direct psychophysiological relationship between violence and the use of other drugs such as marijuana, cocaine and heroin.* In fact, the use of these substances, especially heroin and marijuana, correlates with a reduced likelihood of violence (cite)."[424] It's the prohibition drug trade that puts guns into the hands of millions of people.

Violent Foundations: The Second Amendment and the 1961 Single Convention

Of course, because "the British are coming," United States history is steeped in a proud reverence for guns, evidenced by its foundational Second Amendment.[425] With this history, Americans know the cost of lost human life owing in part to the Guns "R" Us Second Amendment. Any doubt and the May 24, 2022 massacre of nineteen elementary school children in Uvalde, Texas,[426] or hundreds of other recent mass shootings

---

[421] James A. Swartz, "A Study of the Drug Use Forecasting Gun Addendum for Chicago Adult Male Arrestees," *Illinois Criminal Justice Information Authority*, June 1998, p. 2, https://www.ojp.gov/pdffiles1/Digitization/172255NCJRS.pdf.

[422] Ibid., p. 4.

[423] Ibid., p. 6, emphasis added.

[424] Ibid., p. 5, footnote 1, excerpt, emphasis added.

[425] *Wikipedia, s.v.* "Second Amendment to the United States Constitution," https://en.wikipedia.org/wiki/Second_Amendment_to_the_United_States_Constitution, accessed March 17, 2023

[426] Jake, Bleiberg, Jim Vertuno and Elliot Spagat, "Onlookers urged police to charge into Texas school," *Associated* Press, May 26, 2022, https://apnews.com/article/uvalde-texas-school-shooting-44a7cfb990feaa6ffe482483df6e4683.

in America this year,[427] serve as stark reminders. Add the lust of Americans for their guns to the love of drug traffickers for their guns used in a transnational, prohibitionist drug trade — and the world is a very dangerous place. The synergistic power of this unintended partnership between guns and drugs — between the Second Amendment and the 1961 Single Convention — is deadly. There can be no doubt.

41,500 Americans Killed by Gunshot in 2020

"As the nation mourns the more than 300,000 people killed by COVID-19 [by May 2022 one million casualties], Americans are also remembering the more than 41,000 people who died in gun violence this year. Many of the same Black and Latino neighborhoods in cities across the nation have been disproportionately affected by both epidemics... More than 41,500 people died by gun violence this year nationwide, which is a record, according to the independent data collection and research group Gun Violence Archive. That included more than 23,000 people who died by suicide."[428]

Turf-War Cost in Terms of Bullet-Hole Healthcare Dollars

The loss of human life is not the only collateral harm and cost of the drug-war norm. The concomitant financial cost of bullet-hole healthcare is daunting: the cost is US $154,000 per gunshot survivor. "Dead-on-arrival" gunshot healthcare costs are minimal, but roughly two-thirds of gunshot victims survive — implicating ambulance care, emergency room and trauma care, hospital care, intensive care, rehabilitation care, surgical intervention and disability support. "Every day, on average, 316 people in America are shot in murders, assaults, suicides and suicide attempts, unintentional shootings, and police intervention" and of those people, 106 die and 210 survive.[429]

---

427 Saeed Ahmed, "It's 21 weeks into the year and America has already seen 213 mass shootings," *NPR*, updated May 25, 2022, accessed May 26, 2022, https://www.npr.org/2022/05/15/1099008586/mass-shootings-us-2022-tally-number.

428 Grace Hauck, "They're not 'forgotten': America's other epidemic killed 41,000 people this year," *USA TODAY*, December 18, 2020, https://www.usatoday.com/story/news/nation/2020/12/18/gun-violence-deaths-americans-2020/3906428001/.

429 "Gun Violence Statistics," *Brady United Against Gun Violence*, accessed September 18, 2021, https://www.teamenough.org/gun-violence-statistics.

In Chicago alone in recent years, cumulatively, 3,000 to over 4,000 people are shot yearly.[430] In 2021, 4,300 people were shot in Chicago.[431]

US $154,000 : The Average Cost per Gunshot Survivor

"In 1992, gunshots killed 37,776 Americans.... Another 134,000 gunshot survivors... received medical treatment. *Annually, gunshot wounds cost an estimated U.S. $126 billion...* The gunshot... totals include U.S. $40 billion... in medical, public services, and work-loss costs. Across medically treated cases, costs average U.S. $154,000 per gunshot survivor..."[432]

Two years later, another news organization asserted the same average cost per gunshot victim. "Overall, the cost average per gunshot survivor is about $154,000 in the U.S."[433] More recently, looking at a wide range of direct and indirect costs from all gun violence in America, fatal as well as gun injuries, Sarah Bure-Sharps, research director at the gun control advocacy group says, "This epidemic is costing our nation $557 billion annually."[434]

Assimilating the healthcare costs of gunshot patients and the magnitude of that burden as a percent on the overall healthcare industry is a difficult task. It is a complex undertaking, because, as Heather Vallier, MD of the MetroHealth Medical Center in Cleveland, noted: "Unfortunately, a lot of people get shot more than once and in very tenuous places such as around their chest and abdomen. Many need surgical care because of bleeding and broken bones that need to be stabilized. All of those things are very expensive."[435]

---

[430] "Tracking Chicago shooting victims: 2,021 so far this year, 164 more than in 2020," *Chicago Tribune*, July 7, 2021, midyear, https://www.chicagotribune.com/data/ct-shooting-victims-map-charts-htmlstory.html.

[431] Gregory Pratt and Annie Sweeney, "Lightfoot, police leaders look to hit reset button," *Chicago Tribune*, January 5, 2022, https://www.scribd.com/article/551086209/After-Violent-2021-Mayor-Lori-Lightfoot-And-Police-Leaders-Look-To-Hit-The-Reset-Button-Again.

[432] T R Miller and M A Cohen, "Costs of gunshot and cut/stab wounds in the United States, with some Canadian comparisons," *National Library of Medicine*, May 1997, https://pubmed.ncbi.nlm.nih.gov/9183471/, emphasis added.

[433] Donovan Myrie, "What it costs to be shot: The financial impact of gunshot wounds," *Graham Media Group*, February 11, 2019, updated December 16, 2019, https://www.clickorlando.com/news/2019/02/11/what-it-costs-to-be-shot-the-financial-impact-of-gunshot-wounds/, accessed January 27, 2022.

[434] Eric Westervelt, "American gun violence has immense costs beyond the death toll, new studies find," *NPR*, July 21, 2022, https://apple.news/AfN21FUQuRhisgROGPUCByQ.

[435] Randy Dotinga, "Gunshot Victims Cost One Hospital $672,000 a Month, and It's Only Going Up," *MedPage Today*, September 1, 2021, https://www.medpagetoday.com/meetingcoverage/aaos/94317.

Trauma Unit Care: A Burden on the Hospital System

"[Trauma unit healthcare] is a huge economic burden to the hospital system."[436] "A single urban trauma center [MetroHealth Medical Center in Cleveland] that treated nearly 1,000 gunshot victims over a more-than 2-year period spent an average of nearly $675,000 a month on their care, a new report finds [,]" $18.1 million, over a 27-month period. [And "One-third of the patients were *uninsured* and 55% were *on Medicaid*.][437] "The researchers analyzed data on 941 gunshot victims who were treated at the level-one trauma center.... Of the wounds, 37% were to the extremities (average cost $19,294), 23% were to the skin/subcutaneous tissue ($4,331), 7% to the abdomen ($58,749), 7% to the chest ($3,424), 6% to the head or neck ($68,528), and 20% to two or more body regions (average costs of $22,202 for two regions and $23,056 for three).... 'Not too much is a mystery about hospital costs,' Thomas Weiser, MD, MPH, an associate professor of surgery at Stanford University School of Medicine in California, told *MedPage Today*. 'What we do not know is costs outside the hospital — rehab, home care, ongoing medication needs, etc. We really do not know much about long-term medical costs at all.'"[438]

The added financial burden on the healthcare system caused by persons shot in the drug war must be carefully assessed, because healthcare is such a big percent of US gross domestic product (GDP). In addition, that assessment is important because such a large portion of those patients are uninsured or covered only by Medicaid.

Healthcare One-Sixth of U.S. GDP

The healthcare system accounts for about one-sixth of U.S. GDP. "Healthcare spending in the United States increased 4.2 percent between 2016 and 2017 to $3.5 trillion, or $10,739 per person, and accounted for 17.9 percent of the Gross Domestic Product. Constituting nearly one-third of all healthcare expenditures, hospital spending rose 4.7 percent to $1.1 trillion during the same time period."[439]

---

[436] Ibid.

[437] Ibid., emphasis added.

[438] Ibid.

[439] Lan Liang, Ph.D., Brian Moore, Ph.D., and Anita Soni, Ph.D., "National Inpatient Hospital Costs: The Most Expensive Conditions by Payer, 2017," *Agency for Healthcare Research and Quality, H-CUP*, July 14, 2020, https://www.hcup-us.ahrq.gov/reports/statbriefs/sb261-Most-Expensive-Hospital-Conditions-2017.jsp.

Trauma Care Ten Percent of Total Medical Expenditures

Emergency and trauma care are expensive. "Trauma care in the United States contributes significantly to healthcare costs, costing nearly $163 billion per year, which equals nearly 10% of total medical expenditures in the United States. Moreover, healthcare spending in the United States accounts for about 18% of the gross domestic product, the highest of any industrialized nation."[440]

Obamacare, Trumpcare, Bidencare and "Single Payer"

Healthcare necessitated by bullet holes is largely unnecessary healthcare, because bullet holes caused by drug-war prohibition policy are unnecessary. No people are being shot fighting over control of liquor sales since Prohibition ended in America in 1933. Instead, the alcohol business is controlled and regulated by state law and local municipal licensing. "In the United States, liquor licenses are issued under different laws in each state.... Typically, each state may have regulations specific to that state, and some municipalities may also have their own local laws, as well. A licensing process makes it possible for governments to enforce laws regarding the service of alcohol that would otherwise be difficult to police. For example, many jurisdictions have limits on the numbers of drinks an establishment may serve a customer, zero discounts on drinks, and rules that require unfinished bottles of wine to remain in the restaurant or bar in which it was served. It would be difficult to stay on top of such rules if the government was solely responsible for policing these practices, but *if bars and restaurants are afraid of losing a liquor license it makes it possible to enlist the establishments' cooperation.* [And to] further reinforce this sense of value, liquor licenses are usually *limited in number* and often have very *high fees* associated with their acquisition."[441]

---

[440] Michael Scott, MD, MPH, Waleed Abouelela, MBS, David N. Blitzer, MD, Timothy Murphy, MSN, RN, Gregory Peck, DO, Matthew Lissauer, MD, "Trauma Service Utilization Increases Cost But Does Not Add Value for Minimally Injured Patients," *Elsevier Inc.*, May 3, 2020, https://www.valueinhealth journal.com/article/S1098-3015(20)30148-0/fulltext#relatedArticles.

[441] "What is a Liquor License and Why is it Such a Big Deal?" *HG.org*, legal information site, https://www.hg.org/legal-articles/what-is-a-liquor-license-and-why-is-it-such-a-big-deal-31444, accessed October 11, 2021, emphasis added.

> *"There is a strong correlation between the violent crime rate and drug law enforcement: when drug prohibition increases so does the homicide rate. Similarly, countries with greater enforcement of their drug laws have more violent crime. Eliminating drug prohibition would likely cut the homicide rate in the United States by 25–75 percent."*
>
> — Economist Jeffrey A. Miron

There is no reason to expect a less favorable impact on gun violence when drug prohibition ends than when alcohol Prohibition ended. "The homicide rate in the US reached its highest figure in the final year of Prohibition, with 9.7 homicides per 100,000 people in 1933, before falling to roughly half of this rate over the next ten years..."[442] Granted, however, the liquor business outlets were frequently speakeasies that served many people at a time, whereas drug sales often involve one-on-one sales. This feature of drug prohibition puts more guns in more hands that may, based on the violence accompanying marijuana legalization, cause transitional violence as drug dealers learn that prohibition is over and that other criminal choices aren't such easy pickings.

Despite any transitional spike in crime, drug legalization can stop the killing, reduce the number of bullet-hole survivors, and give affordable healthcare a chance. Without legalizing recreational drug use and establishing legal, regulated drug markets, neither Obamacare nor Trumpcare, nor anyone else's care, can afford to pay these survivor bullet-hole bills, any more than individuals. "Two-thirds of people who file for bankruptcy [in the United States] cite medical issues as a key contributor to their financial downfall.... An estimated 530,000 families turn to bankruptcy each year because of medical issues and bills."[443] Similarly, a change in the economic structure of healthcare fashioned by coverage design (e.g., universal coverage) or by payment scheme (e.g., single payer) cannot relieve the excessive drug-war burden placed on the healthcare system.

---

[442] "Suicide and homicide rate changes during Prohibition (1920-1933) in the United States from 1900 to 1950 (rate per 100,000 people)," *Statista*, https://www.statista.com/statistics/1088644/homicide-suicide-rate-during-prohibition/, accessed October 11, 2021.

[443] Lorie Konish, "This is the real reason most Americans file for bankruptcy," *CNBC*, February 11, 2019, https://www.cnbc.com/2019/02/11/this-is-the-real-reason-most-americans-file-for-bankruptcy.html.

Apparent from this discussion, many drug-war harms fall inside the healthcare arena. Drug use is a healthcare problem, and only remotely and incidentally should it become a law-enforcement problem. Making drugs a Drug Enforcement Agency (DEA) assignment, or a state or local law enforcement matter, transforms policing into "morality policing." That's a fundamental "no-no" for policing, according to **Peter Christ**, a co-founder and former fellow director of Law Enforcement Against Prohibition (LEAP). In a YouTube video, seen by nearly 1.5 million people, Peter explains how the drug war destroys the mission and usefulness of policing, destroys police-community relations, respect for law and police, and invites untold police abuses discussed in the next chapter.[444]

Drug War: A Harm-Making Machine that Never Sleeps

Many other equally grievous, multifarious and unnecessary drug-war harms fall outside the realm of the healthcare arena. The drug war is a harm-producing machine that never rests and never sleeps, reminiscent of *The Terminator*, a role played by Arnold Schwarzenegger.[445] Drug prohibition is the common denominator underscoring many crises in America and around the world, but we can fix that abomination by ending the elective World War on Drugs. Drug war was a societal choice; and drug peace can be the same.

---

[444] "Retired Police Captain Demolishes the War on Drugs," *WGRZ*-TV, October 25, 2012, https://youtu.be/W8yYJ_oV6xk.

[445] *YouTube*, https://youtu.be/7Ntksk9SpPs.

Chapter 9 – Drug War: Common Denominator to Many Societal Problems

Beyond the public health arena, the War on Drugs undermines some of the most basic underpinnings of civilized society. Any civilized society requires law and order, and the policing function is the means by which the executive branch of government, or the executive function of government, is carried out. Traditionally, police are hired to "serve and protect" the community. "In 1829, Sir Robert Peel established the London Metropolitan Police Force. He became known as the 'Father of Modern Policing,' and his commissioners established a list of policing principles that remain as crucial and urgent today as they were two centuries ago. They contain three core ideas and nine principles."[446] Synopsizing those three core ideas: The primary goal of policing is preventing crime, not catching criminals. The key to preventing crime is earning public support. And police earn public support by... hard work... enforcing laws impartially, hiring officers who represent and understand the community, and using force only as a last resort. Good policing builds community trust and support that in turn enlists the help of the community in the overall goal of preventing crime.

Morality Policing Subverts the Policing Mission

Police are supposed to catch criminals and prevent crime and violence. Police are supposed to be helpers of the citizenry, not their harassers. However, police, in the name of the "War on Drugs," instead, often, ravage communities with brute force, discriminatory enforcement, "stop and frisk" practices, and "no knock" police raids. One day the police are arresting a family member for a nonviolent "drug crime" and the next day are looking for community cooperation with an investigation to solve a homicide case. One day the police are enforcing laws regarding real crime (nonconsensual, damage to person or property) and the next day enforcing laws regarding crimes that are not crimes. Legislators by passage of criminal statutes can transform common, adult, consensual behavior into criminal behavior, thereby empowering and inviting police to cross the line with abuse and transgression. Abraham Lincoln commented on prohibition which dramatically impacts policing. Lincoln said, "Prohibition... is a species

---

446 "Sir Robert Peel's Policing Principles," *Law Enforcement Action Partnership* (LEAP), formerly "Law Enforcement Against Prohibition" (LEAP). https://lawenforcementactionpartnership.org/peel-policing-principles/, accessed October 15, 2021.

of intemperance within itself, for it goes beyond the bounds of reason in that it attempts to control a man's appetite by legislation, *and makes a crime out of things that are not crimes.*" (My emphasis.)

Ignoring the wisdom of Lincoln and pursuing a prohibitionist War on Drugs, legislators, and police pursuant to legislatively granted authority, have subverted the policing mission in America and around the world. Instead of preventing crime and catching criminals, the War on Drugs has criminalized drug behavior between consenting adults and normalized *morality policing*. The UN, its drug agencies, and many countries have degraded policing by joining in the foolishness — doing their part to degrade policing by prohibiting recreational drug use and sale. Remember — joining in this "common and shared responsibility" has exposed 275 million people to criminal arrest and prosecution, "throwing 275 million people under the bus."

"Policing for Profit" and "Informant Policing"

The prohibition transformation of policing reallocated countless hours of policing time to stakeouts, surveillance, overtime, snooping for drug crimes, grooming and paying confidential informants, and normalized making deals with criminals. A deal might enable a culprit to simply avoid arrest, receive a grant of formal immunity, a reduced sentence in another unrelated criminal matter, or go on the law-enforcement informant payroll and be paid cash. The use of these "Get out of jail free" cards are used to enlist the cooperation of one bad guy to facilitate the set up or apprehension of another. And what drug arrestee has not heard the informant-inviting question — "Where did you get the drugs?"

These policing techniques constitute *informant policing*, techniques not uncommon or unneeded in the policing and prosecuting world. I have made such deals in murder cases, for example, granting a codefendant armed-robbery time rather than murder time in trade for, hopefully, truthful testimony against a codefendant who pulled the trigger. Making such deals is dirty business, but necessary when other evidence is insufficient to satisfy the "beyond a reasonable doubt" criminal standard of proof. But informant policing should never become the norm in "consensual crime" cases, as it has, in the typical hand-to-hand, low-level drug deal between willing buyers and sellers of drugs. Victims of real crime do not consent to rape, armed robbery, carjacking or battery. Willing buyers and sellers of drugs do. Willing participants in a routine drug transaction are in *pari delicto*, both whistling a happy tune. This transformation of Sir Robert Peel policing to normalized informant policing destroys trust in police and irreparably undermines good police-community relations.

Drug-war policing has a second major fault — it enables police to financially gain based on the outcome of their work. That should never be the structure of a criminal justice system. Drug-war policing engages law enforcement services that enable officers to earn and collect overtime pay, court time, engage in drug raids and service of "no-knock" warrants, and the seizure of the plunder and profits of drug dealers — in short, *policing for profit*. In our drug-war world, law enforcement agencies immediately acquire a pecuniary interest in the proceeds of criminal activity, a share of the plunder, through lawful seizure, confiscation, civil and criminal forfeiture of the property of citizens, and police grants. "From 1985 to 1993, [U.S.] authorities confiscated $3 billion of cash and other property based on the federal Asset Forfeiture Program, which included both civil and criminal forfeitures."[447]

"Asset forfeiture is one of the worst strategies of the failed world war on drugs. It sweeps suspected and actual drug-war assets from the lap of drug dealers and pours them into the lap of law enforcement like pirates. Though the drug war is lost and over, and everyone knows it, its gravy train riders support it because of their personal economic interests."[448]

Basically, civil and criminal forfeiture laws and drug-war grants have worked a novation of the parties (though a legal novation requires the consent of all parties), enabling cops to interject themselves into the position of the drug criminals and enjoy the trappings and winnings of drug-dealing criminals. Policing for profit was resoundingly criticized by authors Eric Blumenson and Eva Nilsen, twenty-five years ago, who wrote: "The Nixon Administration officially declared the 'War on Drugs' twenty-five years ago. It has continued, at escalating levels, ever since. Today we annually spend $15 billion in federal funds and $33 billion in state and local funds annually to finance this war. Recent FBI crime statistics report that in one year there were almost 1.5 million drug arrests, of which 500,000 were arrests for marijuana possession. Sixty

---

447 *Wikipedia*, s.v. "Civil forfeiture in the United States," https://en.wikipedia.org/ wiki/Civil_forfeiture_in_the_United_States

448 Gierach, James E., "Asset forfeiture is worst strategy of failed war on drugs," *Chicago Sun-Times*, letter to editor, April 25, 2016, https://chicago.suntimes.com/2016/4/25/18346862/asset-forfeiture-is-worst-strategy-of-failed-war-on-drugs.

percent of [U.S.] federal prisoners are incarcerated for drug offenses. This massive out-pouring of money and effort has brought us record numbers of drug seizures, asset forfeitures, and prosecutions. But by more meaningful measures the drug war has been an extraordinary failure. Drugs are more available, at higher purity and lower prices, than they were at the start of the decade. Drug dependence in the inner city and among teenagers has increased substantially. And our drug problem continues to produce massive amounts of crime, $20 billion in annual medical costs, a third of all new HIV infections, prisons filled with non-violent offenders, and the attendant decimation of inner-city communities. By all accounts, we have thus far been unable to spend and jail our way out of this problem."[449] So true.

However, federal funds spent on the U.S. drug war in FY 2021 is now $40.4 billion, not the $15 billion spent annually twenty-five years ago,[450] and the cost of waging its drug war now exceeds $1 trillion.[451]

The War on Drugs: A License to Pirate

The War on Drugs is not unlike a license to pirate, the license enabling the good guys to pirate the property and goods of the bad guys. After all this is war and "All is fair in love and drug war." And I should note, the illicit drug business is a cash business, tempting some drug police officers and correctional officers to go beyond a legal share of the bounty. (*See* Chapter 6, "Drug War Intolerance Means More Corruption.") In short, drug-war policing undermines community trust in the police, the viability of law and order, and the community's willingness to help prevent and solve crime. Chicago's unsuccessful rate of solving murder cases is exemplary. "Among the nation's largest cities, Chicago stands out for both its high murder rate and for the number of its murders that go unsolved. In recent years the police have been solving about 4 of every 10 murders in the city, but police data show the rate is even worse when the

---

[449] Eric Blumenson and Eva Nilsen, "Policing for Profit: The Drug War's Hidden Agenda," *University of Chicago Law Review*, January 14, 1997 Revision, http://www.fear.org/chicago.html.

[450] "Total federal drug control spending in the United States from FY 2012 to FY 2022," *Statista*, https://www.statista.com/statistics/618857/total-federal-drug-control-spending-in-us/, accessed March 17, 2023.

[451] Nathaniel Lee, "America has spent over a trillion dollars fighting the war on drugs. 50 years later, drug use in the U.S. is climbing again," *CNBC*, June 17, 2021, https://www.cnbc.com/2021/06/17/the-us-has-spent-over-a-trillion-dollars-fighting-war-on-drugs.html.

Tombstone replica made by show host Jim Gierach
for guest Greg Zanis on CAN-TV series, "Chicago's War on Drugs" 2017,
noting deaths by overdose (OD) and gunshot wounds (G.S.W.)

Fox32Chicago, Chicago police superintendent Garry McCarthy takes the podium,
August 24, 2011, reporting how two police dogs sniffed out a stash of six tons
of marijuana on Chicago's West Side. Courtesy WFLD-TV

Jim Gierach political campaign for Cook County state's attorney 1992.
The "Cook County Jail" float carried a drug policy reform message in the
Columbus Day Parade in Chicago

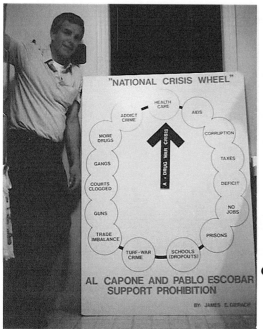

Gierach "Drug-War National
Crisis Wheel,"1993, Palos Heights,
Illinois, prepared for use
at a U.S. Seventh Circuit
Bar Association event

Gierach-designed and -constructed float for Chicago's
Bud Billiken Day Parade, August 2001, Palos Park, Illinois

"Ministers Against the Drug War," Chicago's
Bud Billiken Day Parade, August 2001

1997

Village of Worth, Cook County, Illinois, billboard dedication by
The Drug Corner, an Illinois not-for-profit organization

Louisiana State Penitentiary Angola, La., Aug. 18, 2011.
The guard rides atop a horse that was broken in and trained by incarcerated
people (Image: AP Photo/Gerald Herbert)

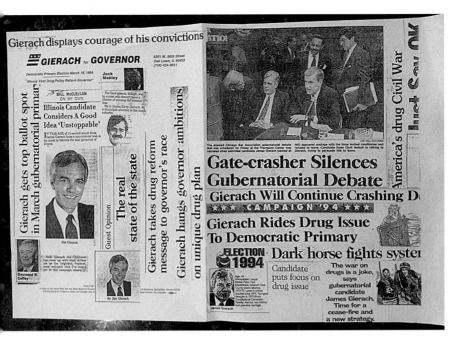

Gierach's Short-lived Political Life (1992-1994)

Gierach banner created for Chicago's Bud Billiken Parade
in 2001, here displayed before the White House
by members of Law Enforcement Against Prohibition (LEAP), concluding
Mexican poet Javier Sicilia's Caravan for Peace across America, 2012

Mexico City, drug policy conference, pictured left to right,
James E. Gierach, Sergio Farragut and United Nations
representative Antonio L. Mazzitelli. Not pictured to the left,
panel moderator California Judge James P. Gray
from Law Enforcement Against Prohibition (LEAP)

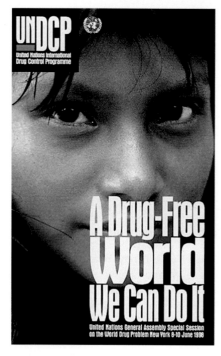

1989 UN General Assembly
Special Drug Control Program Poster

Annie Machon and Jim Gierach of Law Enforcement Against Prohibition
taking a drug-policy-reform message to the UN Commission on Narcotic Drugs,
Vienna, March 2012

Gierach/LEAP "Proposed Amendment of United Nations Drug Treaties—2014,"
English and Spanish

Jelsma-Gierach Meeting at CND 2013, discussing the need for comprehensive UN drug treaty amendment. Other meeting attendees included Czech drug czar Jindřich Vobořil and LEAP and ENCOD representatives

CAN-TV, June 6, 2017, "Chicago's War on Drugs," series show host Jim Gierach with guest Cook County Board Pres. Toni Preckwinkle

victim is African American. [The solve rate was 22 percent when the victim was African American, 33 percent for Hispanics, and 47 percent for Whites.]"[452]

"Consensual Crime" Not "Real Crime"

It is important to see the drug-war-policing transformation for the perversion it is, and to recognize the distortion it causes to a civilized society. *Real crimes against persons or property are not consensual.* People do not consent or voluntarily submit to rape, pillage, robbery, theft, carjacking or murder. But law-abiding people do consensually buy, sell and use mind-altering drugs. This observation begs the question: Is consensual, adult, drug behavior really a crime?

Is consensual adult drug behavior *malum in se* crime (unlawful because of its very nature in all times and all societies with or without statutory law), or is it merely *mala prohibita* crime (unlawful only because lawmakers decided to make it a crime)?

Point a finger at a policing problem and the finger points most directly at drug prohibition, drug intolerance and *morality policing*. Morality policing is a favorite term of Peter Christ, a retired police captain of the Tonawanda Police Department, New York. Captain Christ was one of five police officers who founded Law Enforcement Against Prohibition (LEAP), an international, educational, nonprofit organization founded in 2002, now known as Law Enforcement Action Partnership. Author Peter McWilliams was right condemning consensual crime (like drug crime) and morality policing, as the title of one of his bestselling books proclaimed, *Ain't Nobody's Business If You Do.*[453]

---

[452] Chip Mitchell, "Chicago's Dismal Murder Solve Rate Even Worse When Victims Are Black," *WBEZ an NPR Station*, October 9, 2019, https://www.npr.org/local/309/2019/10/09/768552458/chicago-s-dismal-murder-solve-rate-even-worse-when-victims-are-black.

[453] Peter McWilliams, *Ain't Nobody's Business If You Do* (Los Angeles: Prelude Press, 1993).

Much of the talk intended to improve policing concerns these important topics: police accountability, transparency, civil police review boards, cameras on police, modifying police qualified immunity, stopping the proclivity of White police officers for shooting Black civilians, the Black Lives Matter movement, and so on. While these topics are certainly important, they are not the core problem. The core policing problem today is the subversion of the policing mission, morality policing, and the ongoing policing crime against humanity — a crime called, the "War on Drugs." The commonly discussed policing topics must not detract from the core policing problem.

> *"This is a crime against humanity. The war on drugs is a war on Black and Brown and must be challenged by the highest levels of our government in the war for justice."*
>
> — Civil Rights Leader Rev. Jesse Jackson, Sr.

Racism: The War on Drugs, Its Last Best Refuge

Police officers are necessarily invested with great discretion in the performance of their duties. That discretion enables and necessitates that police officers think, fashion impromptu solutions, deescalate trouble, and use their best judgment keeping the peace in fair and reasonable application of the law to all people regardless of race, creed, color, ethnicity, sexual preference, and many other artificial differences between people. The fair and thoughtful exercise of discretion necessarily invested in police officers enables us to say, confidently — "There's nothing better than a good police officer." And contrarily when good discretion, restraint and smart thinking are lacking, we must recognize — "There's nothing worse than a bad cop." A bad cop is one who abuses the power and discretion entrusted to them by their office.

Recognizing that simple truth, few legislative mistakes hold greater potential for damage to societal well-being, law and order, and police-community relations than the criminalization of drugs. Handing police officers a weapon carrying such potential for abuse invites discriminatory abuse of minorities, the disadvantaged and the innocent at the whimsical, carte blanche discretion of the police. For that reason, back in 2015 at least one former prosecutor called for an end to the war on drugs to improve police-community relations.[454] Historically, we must remember that the declaration of America's War on Drugs purposely aimed to abuse and persecute minorities and liberal "lefties," despite all the "save the kids" facade and fanfare. This truth is indisputable since we know that President Nixon invoked a War on Drugs for the specific purpose of wreaking havoc on Blacks and lefties, as Nixon's henchman John Ehrlichman openly acknowledged. "We knew we couldn't make it illegal to be either against the [Vietnam] war or black, but by getting the public to associate the hippies with marijuana and blacks with heroin, and then criminalizing both heavily, we could disrupt those communities. We could arrest their leaders, raid their homes, break up their meetings, and vilify them night after night on the evening news. Did we know we were lying about the drugs? Of course we did."[455]

The despicable racial aspects of America's War on Drugs provided the raw meat and inspiration for Michelle Alexander's book, *The New Jim Crow: Mass Incarceration in the Age of Colorblindness.*[456] Those aspects also inspired an article simply entitled, "Racism" by award-winning journalist Hoag Levins. Levins wrote, quoting panel discussion moderator Eugenia South, "When we think about what fueled mass incarceration, what laws and policies were created that led to both the ballooning of the prison population and the racial disproportionality of who is there, the War on Drugs is really front and center."[457]

Black Lives Matter

Police stops for "driving while Black," White police officers killing Black men disparately, and drug-war policing with disproportionate arrest, conviction and incarceration disparities along racial lines destroy respect for police, law and order, and one another. "Sadly, the trend of fatal police shootings in the United States seems to only be increasing, with a total 654 civilians having been shot, 111 of whom were Black, as of September 2021. In 2020, there were 1,021 fatal police shootings, and in 2019 there

---

[454] Gierach, James E., "To Improve Police-Community Relations, End the War on Drugs," *HuffPost*, September 1, 2021, https://www.huffpost.com/entry/war-on-drugs-policing_b_8071632?1441122732=.

[455] Dan Baum, "Legalize It All," interview and quotation of Pres. Richard Nixon's domestic-policy adviser John Ehrlichman, *Harper's Magazine*, April 2016, https://harpers.org/archive/2016/04/legalize-it-all/.

[456] Michelle Alexander, *The New Jim Crow...* (New York: The New Press, 2010).

[457] Hoag Levins, "Racism," discussing, inter alia, structural racism and racial disparities in Buprenorphine treatment, *University Pennsylvanian LDI*, June 7, 2021, https://ldi.upenn.edu/our-work/research-updates/the-war-on-drugs-as-structural-racism/.

were 999 fatal shootings. Additionally, the rate of fatal police shootings among Black Americans was much higher than that for any other ethnicity, standing at 37 fatal shootings per million of the population as of September 2021."[458]

"The Black Lives Matter Movement, formed in 2013, has been a vocal part of the movement against police brutality in the U.S. by organizing 'die-ins,' marches, and demonstrations in response to the killings of black men and women by police. While Black Lives Matter has become a controversial movement within the U.S., it has brought more attention to the number and frequency of police shootings of civilians."[459]

The War on Drugs Put Blacks in a Bad Place

An article written by **Aaron L. Morrison**, an award-winning multimedia journalist based in New York City, where he is a national race and ethnicity writer for The Associated Press, is so powerful and indicting of drug-war policies and consequential racial harm, policies incidentally supported by American presidents and American Black Caucus leadership, excerpts are set out here without need for amplification.

"The racial disparities reveal the war's uneven toll. Following the passage of stiffer penalties for crack cocaine and other drugs, the Black incarceration rate in America exploded from about 600 per 100,000 people in 1970 to 1,808 in 2000. In the same timespan, the rate for the Latino population grew from 208 per 100,000 people to 615, while the white incarceration rate grew from 103 per 100,000 people to 242.

"Although Nixon declared the war on drugs on June 17, 1971, the U.S. already had lots of practice imposing drug prohibitions that had racially skewed impacts. The arrival of Chinese migrants in the 1800s saw the rise of criminalizing opium that migrants brought with them. Cannabis went from being called 'reefer' to 'marijuana,' as a way to associate the plant with Mexican migrants arriving in the U.S. in the 1930s.

"The domestic anti-drug policies were widely accepted, mostly because the use of illicit drugs, including crack cocaine in the late 1980s, was accompanied by an alarming spike in homicides and other violent crimes nationwide. Those policies had the backing of Black clergy and the Congressional Black Caucus, the group of African

[458] Research Department, "Number of people shot to death by the police in the United States from 2017 to 2021, by race," *Statista*, accessed October 16, 2021, https://www.statista.com/statistics/585152/people-shot-to-death-by-us-police-by-race/.
[459] Ibid.

American lawmakers whose constituents demanded solutions and resources to stem the violent heroin and crack scourges.

"The deleterious impacts of the drug war have, for years, drawn calls for reform and abolition from mostly left-leaning elected officials and social justice advocates. Many of them say that in order to begin to unwind or undo the war on drugs, all narcotics must be decriminalized or legalized, with science-based regulation.

"Experts say Nixon's successors, Ronald Reagan, George H.W. Bush and Bill Clinton, leveraged drug war policies in the following decades to their own political advantage, cementing the drug war's legacy. The explosion of the U.S. incarceration rate, the expansion of public and private prison systems and the militarization of local police forces are all outgrowths of the drug war."[460]

Nothing much more needs to be said to repair racial injustice, except "End the drug war!"

The Coming "President Biden National Crime and Justice Task Force" — Maybe?

Criminal justice unfairness in the United States had become so obvious and ubiquitous that President Obama appointed a Task Force on 21st Century Policing (2015).[461] The Task Force soon recognized that the criminal justice problem was bigger than just policing abuses and too many deaths of Blacks at the hands of the police, prompting the Task Force to articulate an important overarching Task Force recommendation, to wit: "The President should support and provide funding for *the creation of a National Crime and Justice Task Force to review and evaluate all components of the criminal justice system* for the purpose of making recommendations to the country on comprehensive criminal justice reform. Several witnesses at the task force's listening sessions pointed to the fact that police represent the 'face' of the criminal justice system to the public. Yet police are obviously not responsible for laws or incarceration policies

---

[460] Aaron Morrison, "50-Year War on Drugs Imprisoned Millions of Black American's," *AP News*, July 23, 2021, https://apnews.com/article/war-on-drugs-75e61c224de3a394235df80de7d70b70.

[461] *Wikipedia*, s.v. "President's Task Force on 21st Century Policing," https://en.wikipedia.org/wiki/President%27s_Task_Force_on_21st_Century_Policing, accessed October 16, 2021.

that many citizens find unfair. *This misassociation leads us to call for a broader examination of such issues as drug policy, sentencing and incarceration, which are beyond the scope of a review of police practices.*"[462]

Task Force cochair **Charles H. Ramsey** served as Deputy Police Superintendent of the Chicago Police Department before he assumed the role of Chief of the Metropolitan Police Department in the District of Columbia and later, in January 2008, the role of Commissioner of Police in Philadelphia. I knew Chief Ramsey since the 1990s because as an adjunct professor at Lewis University, Romeoville, Illinois, he invited me to speak to his law-enforcement graduate class regarding drug legalization. I sought the opportunity to testify before the Task Force on behalf of LEAP, as its Board executive vice-chair at the time. My request was denied, the Task Force determining that my call to improve policing by ending the War on Drugs was beyond the scope of its charge.

Nevertheless, I filed my written statement on behalf of Law Enforcement Against Prohibition (LEAP) calling for the Task Force to recommend to the president that he end the War on Drugs. My statement (set out here in full)[463] was received and referenced in its Final Report as a part of the Task Force proceedings but without its content.[464] Constructively, the Task Force called upon the president to create a new Task Force, the National Crime and Justice Task Force, where review of the War on Drugs would be within the scope of its charge. President Obama failed to create such a Task Force during his remaining twenty months in office, perhaps his greatest presidential failing. Now the responsibility to fix America's broken criminal justice system and harness the disastrous U.S. War on Drugs falls on President Biden. Unfortunately, that likelihood is doubtful given President Joe Biden's reticence to take up even the relatively noncontroversial issue of federal legalization of marijuana, and his historic support for a bigger and more expensive drug war than that of President George H.W. Bush.[465]

---

462 "The President Task Force on 21st Century Policing, Final Report, May 15, 2015, p. 7, https://cops.usdoj.gov/pdf/taskforce/taskforce_finalreport.pdf, emphasis added.

463 Gierach, James E., "Pres. Obama Task Force 21st Century Policing Recommendation: End the War on Drugs," https://jamesgierach.tumblr.com/post/643840011552391168/pres-obama-task-force-21st-century-policing.

464 Final Report, supra, p. 76.

465 *See* Sen. Joe Biden rebuttal address regarding Pres. HW Bush 1989 Drug War Speech, https://youtu.be/mtlkyBk6rcc.

Disrespect for Law and Law Enforcers

In the meantime, large American cities are confronted with growing lawlessness, perhaps supplying illustration of the familiar refrain of the oppressed — "No justice, No peace." However, while cognizant of the lawlessness, the right wing of the political spectrum sees the criminal justice problem differently: "Some of the policies being pushed right now, such as the George Floyd Justice in Policing Act, give rise to concerns of people in cities across the country experiencing the 'Ferguson Effect' on steroids. Understandably, police are retiring and resigning in large numbers. This is aggravated by continuous calls to defund the police and knee-jerk reactions to blame police officers whenever a police-civilian interaction goes awry without first getting the facts about what actually happened."[466]

Lawlessness is the nature of a society that embraces laws unworthy of respect, and police officers charged with the duty to enforce them and in the process adversely impacting community trust and safety. In 2021, violent crime continued to heighten in Chicago — shootings, robberies, carjackings and expressway shootings. "In Chicago, from 2019 to 2020, homicides jumped by more than 50%, according to the [Federal Bureau of Investigations]. Chicago Police Superintendent David Brown talked about those numbers Monday and what's causing it. The city's top cop spoke at the City Club, putting much of the blame for Chicago's gun violence on the illicit drug trade. 'Gangs fighting over turf are destroying lives and communities, killing innocent children, young people and adults,' Brown said."[467]

Lawlessness and Disrespect Increasing Police Fatalities

Lawlessness bred by citizen disrespect of the law also puts law enforcement officers in added danger. Police officers are being shot on routine traffic stops,[468] on Chicago

---

[466] Laura Ries and Zach Smith, "The Death of Law and Order Is Destroying America," *The Heritage Foundation*, April 19, 2021, https://www.heritage.org/crime-and-justice/commentary/the-death-law-and-order-destroying-america.

[467] Craig Wall "Chicago gun violence, illicit drug trade blamed for increase in homicides, superintendent says - FBI data shows Chicago homicides are up 56% in 2020," *ABC 7 Chicago*, September 27, 2021, https://abc7chicago.com/chicago-crime-fbi-police-homicide/11054083/, emphasis added.

[468] Alta Spells and Claudia Dominguez, "A Chicago police officer is dead and another is fighting for his life following a shooting during a traffic stop," *CNN*, updated August 10, 2021, https://www.cnn.com/2021/08/07/us/chicago-police-officers-shot/index.html.

expressways,[469] and on always dangerous domestic calls.[470] Nationwide, police officers are dying in a muddle of unrelenting violence on duty.[471]

By early August 2021, forty-seven U.S. police office were killed, including the ambush, stabbing and shooting of Officer Gonzalez. "Pentagon Protection Force Agency Officer George Gonzalez... was allegedly killed by a 27-year-old suspect who ambushed him while he was patrolling the Pentagon bus station last week, first stabbing him and then shooting him with his own weapon, according to law enforcement sources. Gonzalez's ambush and the fatal shooting of Chicago Police Officer Ella French is part of the 47 police officer killings so far in 2021, according to the FBI's Law Enforcement Officers Killed and Assaulted Program (LEOKA)."[472] According to the National Law Enforcement Officers Memorial Fund, Preliminary Fallen Officer Fatalities in 2021 (January 1 through October 20, 2021) are up 39 percent over 2020 (January 1 through October 20, 2020).[473]

The Difficult Choice: Drug Prohibition or Safe Communities

What more needs to be said? Reiterating my comments to President Obama's 21st Century Policing Task Force: "As American street gangs prove daily, *we cannot have safe communities and drug prohibition.* It's one or the other, but not both. With drug prohibition not only do we want for safe communities but there is also little respect for the rule of law, law enforcement, and its mission. For example, when 7.4 percent of the U.S. population violate an unpopular marijuana prohibition law monthly, no

---

[469] Rosemary Sobol, "Ill. state trooper dies after shooting on Chicago highway," *Chicago Tribune,* October 1, 2021, https://www.police1.com/traffic-patrol/articles/ill-state-trooper-dies-after-shooting-on-chicago-highway-qm5kUNX3WLu8CdJz/; David Struett, "Dan Ryan Shooting Upstages Gov's News Conference on Making Expressways Safer," *Chicago Sun-Times,* February 7, 2022, https://chicago.suntimes.com/crime/2022/2/7/22921725/pritzker-kelly-illinois-state-police-expressway-shooting.

[470] "Chicago police shooting: Man yelled 'you will die' after CPD officer shot in face, prosecutors say," *Sun-Times Media Wire,* October 20,2021, https://abc7chicago.com/chicago-police-shooting-officer-shot-cpd-lincoln-park/11146867/).

[471] Luke Barr, "Law enforcement reacts as January sees 24 police officers shot, including 4 killed," *ABC NEWS,* January 28, 2022, accessed January 29, 2022, https://abcnews.go.com/Politics/law-enforcement-reacts-january-sees-24-police-officers/story?id=82533167.

[472] Luke Barr, "'Alarming' increase in law enforcement officers killed this year," *ABC News,* August 12, 2021, https://abcnews.go.com/US/alarming-increase-law-enforcement-officers-killed-year/story?id=79401302.

[473] "Preliminary Fallen Officer Fatalities Comparison," National Law Enforcement Officers Memorial Fund, https://nleomf.org/memorial/facts-figures/officer-fatalities-by-state/preliminary-fatalities/, accessed October 21, 2021.

amount of improved community policing, better training, or racially representative hiring can fix the problem. When competing drug gangs fight over lucrative drug turf and battle police trying to stop their business operations, violence escalates, guns get bigger and deadlier, and *people become 'the enemy'* and are treated as such, engendering disrespect. The militarization of local police and the use of ever-more force (battering rams, tanks, smoke and concussion grenades, assault weapons, etc.) make police the enemy to people on the battlefield and their families, friends, neighbors and relatives, and police militarization is the inevitable consequence of drug-war policing, again breeding disrespect and animosity. Likewise, in a drug-prohibition environment, corruption in the criminal justice system becomes more prevalent, and corruption is again anathema to respect for law-enforcement officers, their mission and the law...."

The ink of this manuscript cannot dry overnight without more wet blood spilled onto its pages accentuating the urgency of righting lawlessness, policing and drug-prohibition madness. Not all violent instances are necessarily the direct result of drug prohibition, but prohibition serves to arm the most vulnerable among us often turning an argument or carjacking into a shooting. "CHICAGO — Two people were killed in a shooting and carjacking in the city's Logan Square neighborhood. A 25-year-old man was sitting at a bus stop in the 3900 block of West Fullerton Avenue when he was approached by another man who opened fire after an argument. The man was shot in the chest and pronounced [dead] at the scene. [And in a separate incident this morning] 1 killed, 2 shot across 3 incidents Wednesday in Logan Square. The gunman then ran to the 2300 block of North Keystone Avenue where he shot a 41-year-old man and stole his vehicle. The 41-year-old was taken to Illinois Masonic Medical Center where he was pronounced dead. No one has been taken into custody and police are investigating."[474]

Getting Death-Penalty Tough on Drugs

The general public is opposed to drugs, especially drugs they don't use. Bad drugs are the drugs other people use and abuse. The log in the other guy's eye is always bigger than the log in my eye. The disdain for those bad drugs gave birth to an intolerance difficult to match in history, an animosity so ferocious that it devolved into Zero Tol-

---

474 Erik Runge, "2 dead in Logan Square shooting, carjacking," *WGN 9*, October 21, 2021 / 04:42 AM CDT / Updated: October 21, 2021 / 04:50 AM CDT, https://wgntv.com/news/chicagocrime/2-dead-in-logan-square-shooting-carjacking/.

erance. Historically, tolerance was seen as a virtue, but drug-war thinking makes in-tolerance a virtue as discussed in Chapter 3. Determining which mind-altering sub-stances are the "bad drugs" is a fickle proposition, a moving target. For example, dur-ing the Ottoman Empire in the 16th Century, smoking tobacco was a death-penalty offense.[475]

A 2015 article by The Economist says thirty-two countries have the death penalty for drug-smuggling, though only six countries are known to routinely execute drug offenders — China, Iran, Saudi Arabia, Vietnam, Malaysia, and Singapore.[476] Brazil should probably be added to the list because of recent de facto extrajudicial cleansing of the streets of suspected drug traffickers, though Brazil's 1988 Constitution abol-ished capital punishment for all non-military offenses. "The death of Rodrigo dos San-tos added to a record number of killings by the police in Rio last year — 1,814 — a surge of hundreds in a state with a long history of police brutality and a political lead-ership that has vowed to 'dig graves' to stop crime."[477] Rodrigo, a sixteen-year-old, was speeding downhill on a motorcycle in Rio de Janeiro, a knapsack packed with mariju-ana, cocaine and pellets of crack on his back when two police officers raised their rifles and eliminated him.

America's Immigration Problem Aggravated by Central American Drug-Pro-hibition Violence

As this chapter noted at its outset, the World War on Drugs creates and aggravates many societal problems — more than can be fully discussed in one book. But one such crisis warrants inclusion and discussion here and now. Drug prohibition breeds law-lessness, violence and corruption so badly that many people in Central America are forced to flee their homes in Honduras, Guatemala and El Salvador, traversing Mex-ico, and finding themselves at the inhospitable southern United States border. It is a crisis for fleeing migrants, drug-war refugees really, and it is a crisis for an already unsatisfactory American immigration system. In 2000, the United Nations General

---

[475] Szasz, Thomas, *Ceremonial Chemistry* (Holmes Beach, Florida: Learning Publications, Inc., 1985), Appendix, p. 186)

[476] T.W., "Which countries have the death penalty for drug smuggling?" *The Economist*, April 29, 2015, https://www.economist.com/the-economist-explains/2015/04/28/which-countries-have-the-death-penalty-for-drug-smuggling.

[477] Manuela Andreoni and Ernesto Londoño, "'License to Kill': Inside Rio's Record Year of Police Killings," *The New York Times*, May 18, 2020, https://www.nytimes.com/2020/05/18/world/americas/brazil-rio-police-violence.html?referringSource=articleShare.

Assembly adopted the United Nations Convention against Transnational Organized Crime and the Protocols Thereto.[478] The three protocols relate to trafficking in persons, migrants and firearms, but the adoption has done little to prevent transnational organized crime. In contradictory fashion, the good intentions of this treaty are overwhelmed by the economic support guaranteed to transnational criminal organizations by UN drug-control conventions.

UNICEF observed: "In communities characterized by extreme violence, gang attacks and criminal activities, young men, women and teenagers in northern Central America are particularly vulnerable. Violence, especially death threats associated with recruitment, directly affect children and adolescents. Children described facing several push factors, including different types of violence and the lack of opportunities and services in their countries. Adults described receiving threats by gangs aimed at their entire family, which led many to leave their community with all their children in order not to leave them at risk."[479]

800,000 Drug-War Refugees Seek Asylum

Such widespread violence and lawlessness motivated hundreds of thousands to leave home. "By the end of 2019, over 800,000 people from El Salvador, Guatemala and Honduras had sought protection either within their countries or had crossed international borders seeking asylum to escape interrelated threats, including escalating levels of gang violence and persecution, among other push factors. While some young women and girls are victims of sexual and gender-based violence perpetuated by gang members, young men are exploited for criminal ends, including drug-running, or are fully recruited into criminal groups."[480]

Because this flood of migrants adversely impacts the U.S. immigration system so visibly, it remains a hot political issue in America. President Donald Trump hoped he could fence migrants out and temper their desire to immigrate to the United States by

---

[478] United Nations Convention against Transnational Organized Crime and the Protocols Thereto," *UNODC*, https://www.unodc.org/unodc/en/organized-crime/intro/UNTOC.html, accessed March 17, 2023.

[479] "Death threats and gang violence forcing more families to flee northern Central America – UNHCR and UNICEF survey," *UNICEF*, December 17, 2020, https://www.unicef.org/press-releases/death-threats-and-gang-violence-forcing-more-families-flee-northern-central-america.

[480] Ibid.

separating migrant children from their parents, a plan that generated universal outrage.[481] The driving force behind the migratory flight — drug prohibition — remains for President Biden to address, but will he?

"On Wednesday, President Joe Biden tapped his second-in-command, Vice President Kamala Harris, to head the effort to curb the migration of families and unaccompanied children fleeing Mexico and Central America for the lifeline just across America's border.... Biden officials said Harris will have two goals: Working to slow the flow of 'irregular migrants' by addressing 'the root causes' that prompt them to leave their home countries, *Politico* reports, 'as well as strengthening relationships' with Mexico, El Salvador, Guatemala and Honduras, where most of the migrants come from... Biden visited Central America several times and tried to work with officials to stem the burgeoning tide of migrants heading our way. Given that thousands of children and families have continued to flood our borders, Biden clearly failed. But Harris' biggest hurdle won't be headquartered in Central America. It's right here at home, where legions of Republican elected officials and activists are chomping at the bit. They aim to demolish all Biden administration initiatives, and especially one that seeks a humane policy for handling desperate migrants who seek harbor."[482]

The words of Emma Lazarus's famous 1883 sonnet "The New Colossus" — "Give me your tired, your poor/ Your huddled masses yearning to breathe free" — did not exclude drug-war refugees, nor should it.

U.S. Insistence on Drug War Policy for Central America Attracts Immigrants

The simple truth is that a dominant root cause prompting migrant flight from their own country are the threats, intimidation, corruption and violence[483] inherent in the prevailing drug prohibition policies at work in Central America. Counterproductively, the United States insists on drug prohibition steadfastness from Central American

---

[481] Maggie Jo Buchanan, Philip E. Wolgin and Claudia Flores, "The Trump Administration's Family Separation Policy Is Over," *The Center for American Progress*, April 12, 2021, https://www.americanprogress.org/article/trump-administrations-family-separation-policy/.

[482] Laura Washington, "Republicans don't want Kamala Harris to succeed on immigration. That's why she must," *Chicago Sun-Times*, column, March 28, 2021, https://chicago.suntimes.com/columnists/2021/3/28/22352957/republicans-dont-want-vice-president-kamala-harris-to-succeed-on-immigration-laura-washington.

[483] "Central American Migration: Root Causes and U.S. Policy," *Congressional Research Center*, updated October 27, 2021, https://sgp.fas.org/crs/row/IF11151.pdf.

countries — the dominant, overriding issue that instigates the need for many people to flee home. Bad American and UN drug policy drives the flight and stacks immigrants at the Mexican American border. Avoiding the drug prohibition heart of the problem thus far, President Biden plans to increase the number of hearing officers and facilities to expedite immigration hearings and better accommodate the hordes of immigrants. His nominee for U.S. Customs and Border Protection Commissioner, Chris Mangus, said as much: "...Congress could do more to address the surge by giving CBP more resources and increasing the number of immigration judges."[484]

But that does nothing to relieve the pressure on the immigration pipeline, pressurized by drug-war policies that catalyze exodus. Not smart. "Raul Delgado, who heads the development studies unit at the University of Zacatecas, sees a 'vicious, pervasive cycle' in tougher U.S. border restrictions. They make immigrant smugglers more necessary, which in turn empowers criminal gangs, who in turn prey on local people, who have to leave their home communities because of the violence."[485]

This Biden immigration course is analogous to hiring 100,000 police officers, erecting a border fence, or building more prisons to fight crime caused by drug prohibition rather than fixing bad drug policy. "Vice President Kamala Harris can only fix America's immigration problem if that reform includes an end to the World War on Drugs."[486] And it is not at all clear at this juncture that the Biden Administration has figured that out.

President Trump, "The Drug Legalizer," Knew Better; Does President Biden?

In 1990 businessman Donald Trump knew the War on Drugs was a foolish, unworkable drug policy. He said then, "It's a joke.... We're losing badly the war on drugs...

---

[484] Daniel Wiessner, "Republicans grill Biden nominee for Border Protection chief," *Reuters*, October 19, 2021, https://www.reuters.com/legal/government/republicans-grill-biden-nominee-border-protection-chief-2021-10-19/.

[485] Mark Stevenson, "Cash to Mexico Booms," *Associated Press*, January 25, 2022, https://siouxcity journal.com/lifestyles/health-med-fit/mexicos-remittances-pass-50-billion-surge-during-pandemic/article_0b32bb2f-a293-5223-9461-6c1437180c58.html.

[486] Gierach, James E., "Immigration Reform Depends on Drug Policy Reform," *Gierach Blogs, Tumblr*, March 29, 2021, https://jamesgierach.tumblr.com/post/647200873050718208/immigration-reform-depends-on-drug-policy-reform.

You have to legalize drugs to win that war. You have to take the profit away from these drug czars."[487]

But transitioning to the political world and very able to understand mob intuitive-thinking as well as lead public opinion — President Trump apparently lost his understanding of why the drug-war business thrives. On September 24, 2018, just before a UN high-level meeting, President Trump invited national leaders to New York City for an event for the purpose of reconfirming global support for UN drug conventions, the heart and foundation of the War on Drugs. The event was called a "High-Level Event on the Global Call to Action on the World Drug Problem,"[488] and as a condition of invitation, nations were asked to sign a compact to that effect. The United States orchestrated the event, and President Trump sat beside U.S. Ambassador to the United Nations, **Nikki Haley**, as she delivered her drug-war remarks.[489] What friendly leader of the United States could refuse the heavy-handed invitation whether a particular friendly nation agreed or not with the drug war. For example, **António Guterres**, Secretary-General of the United Nations, and former Prime Minister of Portugal who during his second term in 2001 saw Parliament decriminalize all drugs for personal consumption, was uncomfortably in attendance.

President Trump knew better what to do with drug prohibition in 1990 as a businessman than he did in 2018 as a politician. He understood then what we all need to understand now. The War on Drugs is the common denominator not only to innumerable, global and American healthcare crises but also to assorted other crises like broken law and order, bad policing, racism, police fatalities, death penalty punishment, money laundering, immigration, and more.

---

[487] Knight-Ridder Newspapers, "Trump Backs Legalizing Drugs," *Chicago Tribune, April 15, 1990*, https://www.chicagotribune.com/news/ct-xpm-1990-04-15-9001310473-story.html, accessed August 22, 2021.

[488] State of Ambassador Nikki Haley Remarks, September 24, 2018, https://usun.usmission.gov/remarks-at-a-high-level-event-on-the-global-call-to-action-on-the-world-drug-problem/.

[489] Ibid., video of the "High-Level Event," "Global Call to Action on the World Drug Problem," *YouTube*, https://youtu.be/XSz5DePsGd8, September 24, 2018, accessed March 17, 2023.

Chapter 10 - The Silver Bullet Solution: Anything but Drug Legalization

People living in high crime neighborhoods ravaged by gang violence, shootings and lawlessness demand that their political leaders *"Do Something!"* In frustration, people march, demonstrate, and close expressways led by their religious and community leaders, trying to express their grief over lost loved ones and demanding relief from relentless violence that never comes.[490] But the violence keeps happening.

In numerous other metropolitan Chicago neighborhoods, most people experience little violence. They harbor little or no fear nestled in their comfortable and safe nesting places. And though those lucky, safe people may empathize with Chicagoans who live in crime-infested neighborhoods, and residents of other big cities with like dangerous neighborhoods, the violence seems remote, removed, almost hypothetical. Just reading newspaper accounts of violence emanating from "America's murder capital,"[491] a title passed from city to city from year to year, doesn't fully carry the distinctive smell of burnt gunpowder, the shocking sound of gunfire, or the sight of human blood on the sidewalk.

Chicago: A Tale of Two Cities

Comparing and contrasting these life circumstances enlightens awareness like seeing day and night side by side. "It's a classic tale of two Chicagos, one of them safe and prosperous, the other one dangerous and poor — and both of them growing more so."[492] There exists a Continental Divide between majority and minority communities across big-city U.S.A., a divide between rich and poor, between White and Black and Brown neighborhoods, between courtroom defense and prosecutor tables,[493] and between gang-free America and gang-full America.

---

[490] Matt Masterson, "Dan Ryan March: Pfleger, Activists Shut Down Expressway for Anti-Violence Protest," *WTTW News*, July 7, 2018, https://news.wttw.com/2018/07/07/dan-ryan-march-pfleger-activists-shut-down-expressway-anti-violence-protest.

[491] "Neighborhood Scout's Murder Capitals of America – 2022," The Neighborhood Scout Team, January 3, 2022, https://www.neighborhoodscout.com/blog/highest-murder-rate-cities.

[492] "Tale of Two Chicagos: Violence Plagues City's South, West Sides," *NBCNews*, April 21, 2014, https://www.nbcnews.com/news/us-news/tale-two-chicagos-violence-plagues-citys-south-west-sides-n86166.

[493] Gierach, James E., "Two World's Colliding on the 19th Floor," *Illinois Police and Sheriff News*, May 17, 1997, https://jamesgierach.tumblr.com/post/672663834211876864/illinois-police-and-sheriffs-news-published-by.

Crime-Ravaged and Safe Neighborhoods in the Same Boat

In 1992 as a candidate running for Cook County state's attorney (Cook County includes Chicago and a matching population of suburbanites), I ran on the idea that *drug policy reform was essential to stop the violence.* I endeavored to sell the idea that all Cook County residents, regardless of address, were just in different ends of the same boat regarding violent crime. Although it was primarily Black and Brown kids getting shot in faraway Chicago neighborhoods (maybe five or ten miles away from my safe suburban home), Cook County Hospital medical bills and Cook County Jail incarceration costs (a 10,000-inmate sprawl) linked our diverse neighborhoods and lifestyles in the form of real estate tax bills. In 1997, Cook County faced over $1 billion in uncollectible debt for health care services accumulated over seventeen years.[494]

In 1992, the Cook County Jail Average Daily Population was about 7,000 inmates and that number steadily increased until it peaked at a little over 10,000 inmates in 2003.[495] In 2011, demographically the male population was 66.7 percent Black, 20.7 percent Hispanic, and 12.7 percent White. For better perspective and appreciation of who was under the criminal justice hammer, the racial composition of Cook County in 2010 was White 55.4 percent, Black 24.8 percent, Hispanic 24 percent, and Asian 6.2 percent.[496] In 2011, Admissions by Current Offense Type reflected these top four categories of crime: Violence 20,567, Drugs 19,238, Property 12,790 and DUI/Traffic 11,022.[497]

Nationally, in 1992 U.S.A., jails were full. "At midyear 1992 local jails held an estimated 444,584 persons. A majority of jail inmates were black or Hispanic. White non-Hispanic inmates made up 40% of the jail population; black non-Hispanics,

---

[494] Robert Becker, "$1 Billion Debt Write-Off Sought," *Chicago Tribune*, May 12, 1997, https://www.chicago tribune.com/news/ct-xpm-1997-05-12-9705120145-story.html.

[495] David E. Olson, "Population Dynamics and the Characteristics of Inmates in the Cook County Jail," *Loyola University Chicago, eCommons*, 2012, https://ecommons.luc.edu/cgi/viewcontent.cgi?article=1000&context= criminaljustice_facpubs.

[496] *Wikipedia* s.v. "Cook County, Illinois," https://en.wikipedia.org/wiki/Cook_County,_Illinois, accessed March 17, 2023.

[497] Olsen, supra.

44%; Hispanics, 15%; and non-Hispanic inmates of other races, 1%. And the U.S. local Jail population increased from 209,582 in 1982 to 444,584 in 1992."[498]

"Take the Profit Out of Drugs..."

My 1992 campaign slogan was "Take the Profit out of *Drugs*; to Take *Crime* off our Streets; and *Taxes* off Our Backs." Catchy and insightful I thought but it just didn't sell. Talking soft on drugs, soft on crime and opposing more prison construction advertised my political death wish. Even a preacher who for years led weekly Chicago anti-violence marches and marshaled his congregates to close the Dan Ryan Interstate 94 Expressway used his parish newsletter to advise his parishioners not to vote for Gierach for state's attorney.

Joycelyn Elders and Jim Gierach Bite the Dust

Just saying the words *"drug legalization"* to voters can cause a contagion of brain cramps and burn out the brightest bulbs. Ask Joycelyn Elders what the mention of those words did for her as U. S. Surgeon General, as a Black physician, who gently but bravely "suggested that legalizing drugs might help reduce crime and that the idea should be studied."[499] President Bill Clinton could have supported her, but instead he said, "If drugs had been legal my brother would be dead."[500]

My 1992 drug policy reform campaign in a Democratic Primary Election had me up against two power forces — the Cook County Democratic Party machine and intuitive voter thinking. Regardless, in a four-way race, *I received 103,581 vote*s — not enough. Whereas my opponents received the following vote totals: Patrick J. O'Connor 390,449; Patrick T. Murphy, 152,976; and Kenneth A. Malatesta, 96,593.[501] The victor, Pat O'Connor, then a Chicago alderman, asked me privately at a Cook County Democratic Party slate-making session months before, "What do you want?" to get out of the primary. He expected, I think, a reply asking for something for me like a

---

[498] Allen J. Beck, Thomas P. Bonczar and Darrell K. Gilliard, "Jail Inmates 1992," *U.S. Department of Justice, Bureau of Statistics*, https://bjs.ojp.gov/content/pub/pdf/ji92.pdf.

[499] *Wikipedia* s.v. "Joycelyn Elders," https://en.wikipedia.org/wiki/Joycelyn_Elders, accessed March 17, 2023.

[500] John Morgan, "UFC exec asks for softer stance against marijuana users," *USA TODAY, March 21, 2013*, https://www.usatoday.com/story/sports/ufc/2013/03/21/ufc-marijuana-stance-nevada-state-athletic-commission/2007669/.

[501] *Wikipedia* s.v. ""1992 Cook County, Illinois elections," https://en.wikipedia.org/wiki/1992_Cook_County,_Illinois_elections, accessed March 17, 2023.

coveted judgeship. If so, he was mistaken. I wanted drug policy changed and violent crime again prioritized. You just can't talk sense to a true believer like me. Murphy was the Cook County Public Guardian, and Malatesta was the Chief of the Criminal Division of the Cook County State's Attorney's Office under Richard M. Daley. My election was not meant to be.

Congressman Bobby Rush: "All Options Are on the Table"

In 2000, eight years after my political message was defeated with me, Chicago violence continued to rage. Violence was so systematic, unrelenting and deadly that at *all options were on the table*, according to U.S. Representative Bobby Rush (D-Chicago) when in 2000 he called an "Emergency African American Leadership Summit to address the violence that plagues predominantly African-American communities."[502] But were they? Eighteen years later, Mary Mitchell wrote a column about Rush's 2000 crime summit, noting "Missing from the present-day conversation on gun violence is the role drug trafficking plays in corrupting the moral fabric of low-income communities. Policymakers are more concerned about opioid overdoses than about the drug trafficking turning neighborhoods into war zones. The drug dealing contributes to the distribution and use of illegal weapons on the street; lures children into criminal behavior; and hooks users who then turn to crime to support their addictions. It also makes poor neighborhoods where drugs are sold ground zero for aggressive policing. And while there are people who shoot other people for reasons other than territorial disputes, too many of the shootings are gang- and drug-related." Indeed, there were and are.

Drug Prohibition Causes the Violence, Not Drugs

Mary Mitchell further wrote, "James E. Gierach, a former prosecutor and longtime advocate of drug policy reform, has waged a crusade across the country to end the War on Drugs that he says has led to violence in neighborhoods. 'It is not the drugs that cause the violence, it is drug prohibition that is causing it,' Gierach says. In an interview in 2000, he pointed out that these 'anti-violence summits' go back as far as 1992, when pols held a 'Stop the Killing' conference in the wake of the murder of 7-year-old

---

502 Mary Mitchell, "The role drugs play in Chicago carnage," *Chicago Sun-Times*, August 8, 2018, https://www.pressreader.com/usa/chicago-sun-times/20180809/281487867175454.

Dantrell Davis.[503] Davis was shot and killed as he walked to school with his mother in the CHA's Cabrini Green public housing development.

'We are just going to continue burying the bodies if we don't get rid of this drug war,' Gierach told me back then. And that's exactly what we've been doing — burying black and brown bodies. [Congressman] Rush acknowledged at the 2000 summit that *politicians should at least have a discussion about how to take the profit out of drug use, though the subject didn't end up on the agenda.* He agrees that past summits and conferences haven't gotten much traction. 'We can't get any traction because it is being viewed from a *political expediency prism which translates into an election-year focus* — is it going to help or hurt my election or re-election agenda?' he told me in a telephone interview. 'The kind of approach needed right now is a spiritual revival,' said Rush, who is also a pastor."[504]

No "Stop the Violence" Idea Too Cockamamie

Politicians made an endless number of desperate attempts to answer the call of voters to "do something" about the violence. Those efforts included and embraced every solution imaginable regardless of how cockamamie. In 1989, there was proposal to sell "Drug War Bonds" that 259 House members from both sides of the aisle cosponsored, including then-Representative Richard J. Durbin [D-IL-20], now Senator Dick Durbin (D-Illinois) and Majority Whip.[505]

Other cockamamie violence prevention ideas in Illinois included the construction of cul-de-sacs,[506] creation of statewide grand jury authority,[507] building a Tamms Super Max prison,[508] and more recently a million dollar City of Chicago fund to pay for

---

[503] *Wikipedia*, s.v. "Dantrell Davis," https://en.wikipedia.org/wiki/Dantrell_Davis, accessed March 17, 2023.

[504] Ibid., Mary Mitchell.

[505] The "Drug War Bonds' bill, "H.R.2972 - Drug War Bond Act of 1989," https://www.congress.gov/bill/101st-congress/house-bill/2972/cosponsors?r=5&s=1&q=%7B%22cosponsor-state%22%3A%22Nebraska%22%7D.

[506] Gierach, James E., "Cul-de-sacs Are Dead End as Effective Crime Curbs," *Chicago Sun-Times*, January 30, 1993, https://jamesgierach.tumblr.com/post/674370431139053568.

[507] "Statewide Grand Jury Act," https://www.ilga.gov/legislation/ilcs/ilcs3.asp?ActID=1992&ChapterID=54, accessed March 17, 2023.

[508] Laurie Jo Reynolds and Stephen F. Eisenman, "Tamms Is Torture: The Campaign to Close an Illinois Supermax Prison," *Creative Time Reports*, May 6, 2013, https://creativetimereports.org/2013/05/06/tamms-is-torture-campaign-close-illinois-supermax-prison-solitary-confinement/.

tips regarding illegal guns.[509] "[Chicago Mayor Lori Lightfoot] noted that Chicago police have already confiscated more than 6,300 guns this year, and are on pace for more than 12,000–which would be a record number of guns seized in a year."[510] Actually 12,000 may not be a record. According to columnist Phil Kadner, "Chicago seized 19,675 firearms in 1990, including 16,211 handguns."[511]

Multi-million Dollar "Root Cause" and "Stop-the-Violence" Programs

Some solutions are multi-million dollar "root cause," or violence prevention, or violence interruption, or "weed and seed" programs. "On [December 29, 2020] Chicago CRED, CP4P and the anti-violence group READI Chicago acknowledged 'big setbacks' last year after the city's murder total hit 769, one of the highest in decades, and proclaimed: '2020 must be an aberration, not a trend.' The groups noted that they and others are expected to get nearly $60 million in public funding this year in addition to the $30 million they're getting from private sources.... Chicago's murder rate should be on par with other big cities,' according to Arne Duncan, CRED's founder and a former U.S. education secretary and Chicago schools CEO. 'Right now, we're not even close. We have to think and act very differently.'"[512]

As of September 2021, Chicago Mayor Lori Lightfoot increased the anti-violence budgeting to $400 million. "Over $400 million is allocated to priority investment areas identified by Chicago's violence reduction and community safety plan, "Our City, Our Safety," in addition to ongoing investments and efforts by the City of Chicago and its partners."[513]

---

[509] Craig Wall, "Mayor Lori Lightfoot announces $1M fund for illegal gun tips," *ABC 7 Chicago,* July 15, 2021, https://abc7chicago.com/chicago-shootings-mayor-lori-lightfoot-illegal-guns-reward-fund/10889429/.

[510] Ibid.

[511] Phil Kadner, "Waging a war on street gangs without help," *Southtown Economist,* April 11, 1991. Gierach notebooks, p. 490.

[512] Frank Main, "Chicago's not-so-random gang violence: Just 6% of gang 'factions' tied to most shootings studied," *Chicago Sun-Times,* January 8, 2021, https://chicago.suntimes.com/2021/1/8/22216223/chicago-gang-violence-factions-shootings-andrew-papachristos.

[513] "Mayor Lightfoot Releases 2022 Budget Proposal," *Office of the Mayor,* September 20, 2021, press release, https://www.chicago.gov/city/en/depts/mayor/press_room/press_releases/2021/september/2022BudgetProposal.html.

Endless "Stop the Violence" Initiatives Include Gun Control

Chicago and Illinois have tried every anti-violence initiative imaginable. Recently, hope is being placed on a new federal effort to prevent straw purchasers of guns from profiting by the resale these guns. "Earlier this summer [2021], Attorney General Merrick Garland announced the Justice Department was creating strike forces in five cities — including Chicago — to target gun trafficking."[514] These initiatives are not new or groundbreaking.[515]

The Push for More Gun Control

More gun control is always near the top of the list of solutions to the violence crisis flaring endlessly in poor and disadvantaged communities across America. Indeed, two years ago the U.S. Congress had 110 such bills aimed at better controlling guns to stop mass killings and shootings.[516]

More recently, "The House approved a pair of bills on Thursday aimed at expanding and strengthening background checks for gun buyers, as Democrats pushed past Republican opposition to advance major gun safety measures after decades of congressional inaction. In two votes that fell largely along party lines, the House passed legislation that would require background checks for all gun buyers, and extend the time the F.B.I. has to vet those flagged by the national instant check system. Despite being widely popular with voters, the measures face what is expected to be insurmountable opposition in the Senate, where Republicans have resisted imposing any limits on guns, including stricter background check requirements."[517] Polling shows that over 80 percent of voters support the legislation, but the legislation joins a growing stack

---

514 Charlie De Mar, "With Gun Violence At Crisis Level In Chicago, Victims Hope Crackdown On Straw Purchases And Gun Trafficking Has An Impact," CBS2, September 6, 2021, https://chicago.cbslocal.com/2021/09/06/chicago-gun-violence-trafficking-straw-purchase-crackdown/.

515 Brian Knight, "State Gun Policy and Cross-State Externalities: Evidence from Crime Gun Tracing," *American Economic Journal: Economic Policy*, Vol. 5, No. 4 (November 2013), p. 200-29, https://www.jstor.org/stable/43189358.

516 Lisa Desjardins, "Congress has 110 gun bills on the table. Here's where they stand," *PBS NewsHour*," August 6, 2021, accessed August 18, 2021, https://www.pbs.org/newshour/politics/congress-has-110-gun-bills-on-the-table-heres-where-they-stand.

517 Catie Edmondson, "House Passes Gun Control Bills to Strengthen Background Checks," *New York Times*, March 11, 2021, updated June 18, 2021, accessed August 18, 2021, https://www.nytimes.com/2021/03/11/us/politics/biden-gun-control-bill.html?referringSource=articleShare.

of items on the liberal agenda that are widely popular with voters but appear destined to languish in the 50-50 Senate, where Democrats must win the support of ten Republicans to pass most major measures.[518]

Of course, the push for more gun control is not new. In 1991, Chicago police seized 6,729 guns, 2,000 more than the year before,[519] prompting calls for more gun control. Jump forward to some 2020 statistics and the number of people shot and number of guns seized soared: "Other numbers in Chicago also are markedly higher than a year ago: 4,115 people shot. 11,280 illegal guns seized. 7,236 gun arrests."[520] Though in fairness, it is notable that "[Of the more] than 41,500 people [who] died by gun violence this year [2020] nationwide, which is a record, according to the independent data collection and research group Gun Violence Archive [that] included more than 23,000 people who died by suicide."[521]

At midyear, Chicago is on track in 2021 "to recover 12,000 illegal guns by the end of the year, which would be a record, surpassing last year's 11,300 guns," according to Chicago Police Superintendent David Brown.[522]

The Small Arms Survey 2017 estimated that there were 120.5 guns (393,347,000 firearms) in private hands in the United States of America for every 100 persons in the U.S. (the U.S. population in 2017 was 326,474,000).[523] For perspective regarding the prevalence of U.S. gun ownership compared to the rest of the world, it is noteworthy

---

[518] Ibid.

[519] Wilson Ring, "Weapons seizure spurs a push for tougher gun laws," *Chicago Tribune,* May 6, 1991, Gierach notebooks, p. 511.

[520] "Behind the grim numbers on Chicago gun violence in 2020," *Chicago Sun-Times,* editorial, December 30, 2020,   https://chicago.suntimes.com/2020/12/30/22206618/chicago-gun-violence-homicides-policing-community-outreach-university-of-chicago-crime-lab-editorial.

[521] Grace Hauck, "'They're not forgotten': America's other epidemic killed 41,000 people this year," USA TODAY, December 12, 2020, accessed August 18, 2021, https://www.usatoday.com/story/ news/nation/ 2020/12/18/gun-violence-deaths-americans-2020/3906428001/.

[522] Sun-Times Wire, "78 people shot in weekend gun violence in Chicago, a third of them from four mass shootings," Sun-Times Wire, updated June 28, 2021, accessed August 18, 2021, https://chicago.suntimes.com/crime/2021/6/26/22551630/chicago-weekend-shootings-june-25-28-homicide-gun-violence-mass.

[523] *Wikipedia* s.v. "Estimated number of civilian guns per capita by country," https://en.wikipedia.org/ wiki/Estimated_number_of_civilian_guns_per_capita_by_country, accessed August 18, 2021.

that "Americans make up 4 percent of the world's population but owned about 46 percent of the estimated 857 million weapons in civilian hands at the end of 2017."[524]

Ballpark, the number of firearms in private hands in America is estimated to be 400 million guns. "The exact number of U.S. gun owners is unclear due to the fact that there is no federal registration requirement or similar regulation that would enable an official count. In fact, federal law prohibits a central registry of firearms owned by private citizens. About 40% of Americans say they or someone in their household owns a gun, and 22% of individuals (about 72 million people) report owning a gun, according to surveys from Pew and Harvard and Northeastern."[525]

Because the horse is already out of the barn, gun-control efforts to close the barn door seem a dubious solution to gun violence in America. Such a fix fails not only because of the great prevalence of firearms but also because Americans seem to love their guns as much as they love their drugs. Guns and drugs are everywhere. And if gun hardware is not problem enough, the new rage is so-called "ghost guns" that can be made with software on 3D-printers without metal and without affixing a serial number on the gun produced. They cost abounded $50 to $75 a piece.[526] Although the U.S. Congress has not acted to ban ghost guns after a bloody weekend of gun violence in April 2022, the bloodshed prompted President Biden and the U.S. Department of Justice to announce a new rule that will require ghost guns manufactured by businesses to have serial numbers and licensed gun dealers to do a background check

[524] Reuters Staff, "Americans own nearly half world's guns in civilian hands: survey," Reuters, June 18, 2018, accessed August 18, 2021, https://www.reuters.com/article/us-usa-guns/americans-own-nearly-half-worlds-guns-in-civilian-hands-survey-idUSKBN1JE220.

[525] Lisa Dunn, "How Many People In The U.S. Own Guns?" *American University Radio*, WAMU, 88.5, September 18, 2020, accessed August 18, 2021, https://wamu.org/story/20/09/18/how-many-people-in-the-u-s-own-guns/

[526] *Chicago Sun-Times*, editorial, "Untraceable 'ghost guns' are a growing threat, and it's time to ban them," August 29, 2021, https://paper.suntimes.com/html5/reader/production/default.aspx?pubname=&edid= aca06a 17-d39a-45a5-b99f-c0b2bddf1dfd, p. 34.

on purchasers of these weapons.[527] In May 2022, Illinois became the first Midwestern state to ban untraceable ghost guns.[528]

The Second Amendment protects American gun owners right to bear arms if no for their safety. In 2008, the U.S. Supreme Court decided in *District of Columbia v. Heller* that the Second Amendment protects an individual's right to possess a firearm unconnected with service in a militia, and to use that firearm for traditionally lawful purposes, such as self-defense within the home.[529]

The problem of gun violence, a corollary drug-war problem, is not just a United States problem. People are being shot everywhere, and nations, Mexico for one, are looking for answers. One strategy looks to the courtroom and monetary judgments as a recourse.[530] More directly aimed, Australia is a leader in gun policy reform following a mass killing.

In 1996, the Port Arthur Massacre[531] in Tasmania, Australia, featured one shooter, two automatic weapons, thirty-five killed, twenty-three wounded and led to the National Firearms Agreement (NFA). Tom Fischer, a proponent of the agreement called the agreement a "big cultural change" for Australians.[532] New laws enacted en masse by all Australian jurisdictions banned semi-automatic rifles and shotguns, required gun registration, and insisted that all gun-license applicants and gun purchasers have proof

---

[527] Tina Sfondeles and Frank Main, "Illinois Dems Join Biden In Taking Aim At Specter of Elusive 'Ghost Guns,'" *Chicago Sun-Times*, April 12, 2022, https://chicago.suntimes.com/politics/2022/4/11/23021035/illinois-democrats-president-biden-ghost-guns-crime-violence-republican-state-rifle-association?tpcc=email-breaking&utm_campaign=Chicago%20Sun-Times%20Breaking%20News&utm_content=20220415&utm_medium=email&utm_source=Revue%20newsletter.

[528] "What Are 'Ghost Guns', And Why Are They Now Banned in Illinois?" *NBCChicago*, May 18, 2022, https://www.nbcchicago.com/news/local/chicago-politics/what-are-ghost-guns-and-why-are-they-now-banned-in-illinois/2835952/.

[529] *Wikipedia* s.v. "District of Columbia v. Heller," https://en.wikipedia.org/wiki/District_of_Columbia_v._Heller, accessed August 18, 2021.

[530] E. Eduardo Castillo, "Mexico sues US gun manufacturers over arms trafficking toll," Associated Press, August 4, 2021, https://apnews.com/article/business-mexico-caribbean-gun-politics-8ed1a6e046e635d94f2ce61716752f7a.

[531] *Wikipedia*, s.v. "Port Arthur massacre (Australia), https://en.m.wikipedia.org/ wiki/Port_Arthur_massacre_(Australia), May 23, 2022.

[532] Elias Visontay, "How Australia's global gold standard on gun control is being eroded," *The Guardian*, April 24, 2021, https://www.theguardian.com/australia-news/2021/apr/25/how-australias-global-gold-standard-on-gun-control-is-being-eroded.

of a reason gun ownership was needed, and self-defense was not considered a reason.[533] The new law produced results: proponents of the reform wore body armor in response to threats of bodily harm, 650,000 guns were destroyed, the gun buyback price tag was $500 million, and gun deaths decreased in Australia from 516 in 1996 to 229 in 2019.[534] A quarter of a century later, gun interests are seriously eroding the reform. For example, gun club membership has become a popular and acceptable reason to own a gun in Australia. As a result, gun club membership jumped from 30,000 in 1996 to 200,000 in 2021.[535]

For these very real reasons, I think we must look beyond just better gun control to stop gun violence. Since the early 1990s, I have suggested Americans would have better success stopping violent crime by taking away the reason that people are shooting one another. As discussed in Chapter 4 above, the most preventable homicides are those caused ancillary to the prohibition drug trade.

Cul-de-sacs: Dead Ends as Effective Crime Curbs

In 1993, I wrote an article[536] that criticized politicians for failing to address the problem of drug prohibition and its adverse consequences head-on. Instead of directly, politicians try an endless litany of other inane to marginal programs in an effort to stymie the drug trade and stem the violence. Those efforts included an anti-loitering ordinance, callout-only pay phones, Chicago Housing Authority sweeps, more jails, longer prison sentences, a dozen Chicago night narcotics courts, gang membership computer banks, midnight basketball, random traffic barricades and vehicular searches for drugs and guns, a Chicago handgun sale ban, and construction of cul-de-sacs. The cul-de-sac idea sought to make it more difficult for drive-by shooters to get away. The cumulative import of these new programs evidence a willingness to try anything and everything other than challenge the drug monster head-on with programs aimed to undercut drug prohibition, the biggest root cause of the world's crime crisis, Chicago's too.

---

[533] Ibid.

[534] Ibid.

[535] Ibid.

[536] Gierach, James E., "Cul-de-sacs Are Dead End As Effective Crime Curbs," *Chicago Sun-Times,* January 30, 1993, https://jamesgierach.tumblr.com/post/674370431139053568.

Thirty years later, political and other community leaders continue the search for answers to the problems of violence, gangs, guns, carjackings, immigration, unaffordable healthcare, unsatisfactory policing, racism and so on. In doing so, all possible solutions are on the table, except not drug legalization. Drug prohibition remains a "Given." All other proposed solutions to these problems must be taken with the drug-prohibition poison pill. Drug legalization is never on the table as they attempt other solutions to these problems. Many of the other proposed solutions have merit and need to be part of the set of solutions, but the exclusion of the Silver Bullet from the solution mix is self-defeating.

Chapter 11 - Why Is It So Difficult to Reform Bad Drug Policy?

Many reasons contribute to the fact that it is nearly impossible to change drug policy or shake it loose from its drug-prohibition foundation. The following discussion will include seven such reasons, each reason by itself sufficient to make drug policy reform a Herculean task.

Reason 1: The Tangle and Complexity of the Global Drug Prohibition Mosaic

First, global drug policy is a complicated tangle of laws and rules.

Drug prohibition is state or regional law.

Why cannot local officials, say, in Los Angeles, Chicago, Detroit, New York, Madrid, Bogota, Kiev, Tokyo or Sydney try a new drug program, protocol or policy that would decriminalize drugs, legalize drugs or choose one of many variants? Consider for example a city, or like unit of local government located anywhere in the world, deciding to "legalize drugs for addicts only." Or suppose local authorities decided to experiment with licensing a limited number of local drug outlets, setting a legal age for recreational drug use, or requiring that drug businesses be conducted from fixed places of business only during certain hours, like local officials often do regarding liquor regulation and control. Such program and policy experimentation is simply not allowed, because, generally, state or regional law supersedes local law regarding the subject of drugs, and state or regional law prevents local public officials from experimenting with new drug policies, protocols and programs inconsistent with state or regional law.

Drug prohibition is national law.

But suppose lawmakers in some U.S. state wanted to authorize local public officials, in their discretion, to enact and implement an experimental legalization or decriminalization drug program or policy. State lawmakers could not do so, because federal law does not allow it.

Drug prohibition is international law.

But maybe the U.S. Congress or another country's national legislative body could, by law, authorize such experimentation. But no, the U.S. Congress and effectively every country's national legislative body are hogtied by drug prohibition international law. In the United States, with bipartisan and changing presidential leadership with the advice and consent of the U.S. Senate, two-thirds of those senators present and voting, the United States agreed to conform American drug laws, policies and programs to the dictates of the 1961 Single Convention. Nearly all nations, 186 nations by recent count, have likewise agreed to conform their national laws to the dictates of the 1961 Single Convention on Narcotic Drugs.

Crippling "Single Voice" Drug Policy

United Nations drug agencies — CND, INCB and UNODC — want all nations on the same page. These agencies want all nations speaking with a "single voice," each nation recognizing that all nations have a "common and shared responsibility" to support the three UN drug-control conventions that prohibit recreational drug use.[537]

Pearls of wisdom that might free the CND and INCB from sacrosanct, status-quo, prohibition quagmire are routinely trampled underfoot. Instead of drug-policy reform, the best the CND has to offer, always, is another gathering at the Vienna International Centre ("The VIC") in Austria. Dignitaries and delegates assemble there to speak with a stultifying single-voice, sprinkled with mundane and magical phraseology like "best-practice," "best-science" and "best-evidence," all just a bunch of "best-hooey" to the extent such terms hide the drug-prohibition killer from needed spotlight attention.

This legal straight jacket has unfailingly paralyzed drug policy reform globally for sixty years without a single nation, ever, filing with the UN Secretary-General a proposed amendment to UN drug-control treaties. The fact that drug-prohibition policy has made so much trouble for the world — boosted psychoactive drug invention, drug inundation and drug overdose, triggered more violent crime, and aggravated a dozen other crises — seems insufficient motivation for any nation to file a proposed amendment of those treaties. Filing such an amendment with the UN Secretary-General in accordance with the amendment provisions found in each of those treaties would trigger serious consideration of treaty amendment. Treaty reform talk is not treaty amendment filing.

[537] Gierach, James E., "United Nations Office on Drugs and Crime, the Minority Report," *Gierach Tumblr*, February 20, 2017, https://jamesgierach.tumblr.com/post/157477674599/united-nations-office-on-drugs-and-crime-the; and Gierach/LEAP "Proposed Amendment of United Nations Drug Treaties — 2014," Preface, p. 1, Failed Criminalization, Single-Voice Policy, https://www.unodc.org/documents/ungass2016//Contributions/Civil/Law_Enforcement_Against_Prohibition/LEAP_UN_Treaty_Amendment_2.26.1421-1.pdf.

United Nations recreational drug prohibition policy ties national drug policy into such a Gordian Knot that the least deviation from it draws predictable rebuke from the INCB, as in the case of Uruguayan cannabis legalization.[538] This is true despite the fact that cannabis (marijuana) has a history of benefit to humanity reaching back several millennia.

The tangle and complexity of the global, drug-prohibition mosaic obstructs experimentation with and development of better national and global drug policy choices. Various human rights landmarks and signposts contravene that result, one such signpost being the Universal Declaration of Human Rights.[539] Existing UN drug control-treaties run afoul of the protection of human rights in a multitude of ways as an Open Society Institute publication, "Human Rights and Drug Control Policies"[540] delineates. In addition, principles concerning national sovereignty, national constitutional supremacy, national laws and international laws regarding treaties such as the Treaty on Treaties,[541] and the Vienna Convention on the Law of Treaties 1969,[542] complicate the reform of drug treaties and drug policy. Recognizing these complexities — maybe

---

[538] "Uruguay is breaking the International Conventions on Drug Control with the Cannabis Legislation approved by its Congress," *United Nations Information Service*, December 11, 2013, https://incb.org/documents/Publications/PressRelease/PR2013/press_release_111213.pdf.

[539] "Universal Declaration of Human Rights 1948," United Nations, https://www.jus.uio.no/ lm/en/pdf/un.universal.declaration.of.human.rights.1948.portrait.letter.pdf.

[540] "Human Rights and Drug Control Policies," Open Society Institute, https://www.opensocietyfoundations.org/uploads/ee155943-41c6-4ccc-8a99-5e4bd2661231/humanrights-20110110.pdf,   accessed January 31, 2022.

[541] Richard D. Kearney and Robert E. Dalton, "The Treaty on Treaties," *Cambridge University Press*, March 28, 2017,   https://www.cambridge.org/core/journals/american-journal-of-international-law/article/abs/treaty-on-treaties/B2CB9F70D34D7F86568172B864E3F544.

[542] "Vienna Convention on the Law of Treaties 1969," https://legal.un.org/ilc/texts/instruments/english/conventions/1_1_1969.pdf.

it is time to cut through the red tape, erase the drug policy blackboard, set fear aside,[543] and recognize the power of the Silver Bullet Solution.

> *"The most effective way to defeat a moral evil is to allow it, debate it, and discredit it. Those who wonder if decriminalization would send the wrong message to kids about drugs ought to worry more [about] what signal we send to them when we pretend morality flows from the barrel of a gun."*
>
> — Commodities Trader Richard J. Dennis

Reason 2: The Supposed Morality Foundation of Drug War

An equally powerful obstruction to needed global, drug-policy reform is a perception that drug use is "evil." This moral judgment rivets many religious believers to a faulty drug-policy constructed — drug prohibition. Too often, evidence and reason are no match for *religious belief.* Belief is a "given," something that defies argument or rationality. Indeed, belief is more powerful in religious circles than Euclid[544] was in geometric circles which was one reason Earth was so flat for so long. There is just no fighting a given.

The predominant religion in the world is Catholicism,[545] a Christian-based religion with more than two billion believers. The roots of Christianity reach back nearly as far as the history of cannabis use. "The oldest known written record on cannabis use comes from the Chinese Emperor Shen Nung in 2727 B.C. Ancient Greeks and Romans were also familiar with cannabis, while in the Middle East its use spread throughout the Islamic empire to North Africa."[546] "People from a diverse range of cultures

---

[543] "An End to the UN As We Know It?," The fear of drug policy change is well expressed and exemplified by Dr. Peter van Wulffen Palthe in Vienna in 2015, attending the Commission on Narcotic Drugs, VIDEO, minute 5:02, *"Cannabis News Network,"* https://youtu.be/40vsGUxCbjc.

[544] *Wikipedia* s.v. "Euclid," https://en.m.wikipedia.org/wiki/Euclid, accessed March 17, 2023.

[545] Don Vaughan, "What Is the Most Widely Practiced Religion in the World?" *Encyclopedia Britannica,* https://www.britannica.com/story/what-is-the-most-widely-practiced-religion-in-the-world, accessed October 9, 2021.

[546] DEA Museum, https://museum.dea.gov.

have been using marijuana for thousands of years — in different forms and for different purposes."[547]

Two billion Catholic believers led by an infallible pope in matters of religion and morals is a lopsided tug-of-war against a mere 275 million drug users, the number of illicit drug users most recently estimated by UN sources. But there is more to it than the mere number of believers versus the number of drug users. "Catholicism maintains that the pope is infallible, incapable of error, when he teaches a doctrine on faith or morals to the universal Church in his unique office as supreme head. When the pope asserts his official authority in matters of faith and morals to the whole church, the Holy Spirit guards him from error."[548]

Pope Francis, Dr. Lochan Naidoo and Drugs

Pope Francis from Argentina worked as a bouncer in his youth.[549] On June 10, 2014, speaking at the 31st International Drug Enforcement Conference in Rome, supported by the Holy See, Pope Francis said, "*Don't legalize drugs.*" Making clear his opposition to drug legalization, Pope Francis pronounced, "Drug addiction is an *evil*, and with evil there can be no yielding or compromise."[550] The tone of those unyielding words mirrors the sentiments of Dr. Lochan Naidoo, a South African physician and former president of the International Narcotic Control Board, who said on March 3, 2015 in his Foreword to the Report of the International Narcotics Control Board 2014, "One of the most fundamental principles underpinning the international drug control framework, enshrined in both the 1961 Convention and in the Convention on Psy-

---

[547] Kyle Jaeger, "Health Study Documents Humanity's Use Of Marijuana Over 10,000 Years Of History," *Marijuana Moment*, January 26, 2019, https://www.marijuanamoment.net/study-documents-humanitys-use-of-marijuana-over-10000-years-of-history/.

[548] Rev. John Trigilio Jr. and Jr. and Rev. Kenneth Brighenti, "Is the Pope Really Infallible?" *Dummies*, March 26, 2016, https://www.dummies.com/article/body-mind-spirit/religion-spirituality/christianity/catholicism/is-the-pope-really-infallible-169671.

[549] Julia Marnin, "Fact Check: Was Pope Francis Once a Nightclub Bouncer?" *Newsweek*, March 5, 2021, https://www.newsweek.com/fact-check-was-pope-francis-once-nightclub-bouncer-1574178.

[550] Haroon Siddique and agencies, "Pope Francis says don't legalise drugs," *The Guardian*, June 20, 2014, https://www.theguardian.com/world/2014/jun/20/pope-francis-dont-legalise-drugs.

chotropic Substances of 1971, is the limitation of use of narcotic drugs and psychotropic substances to medical and scientific purposes. The legal obligation is absolute and leaves no room for interpretation."[551]

The attachment to perceived morality and the tone of "evil" used by Pope Francis in 2014 mirrors the tone of the 1961 Single Convention. "The Single Convention on Narcotic Drugs... aimed to replace the various multilateral treaties that existed in this field and merge them into a single document. The Convention arose in response to the concern for the '*physical and moral health* of humanity,' through the principle of limiting the use of narcotic drugs for medical and scientific purposes on the premise that 'addiction to narcotic drugs constitutes a *serious evil* for the individual and is fraught with social and economic danger to mankind,' asserting that signing parties should be 'conscious of their duty to prevent and combat this evil'."[552]

Pope Francis further said, "I would reaffirm what I have stated on another occasion — no to every type of drug use. It is as simple as that... But to say this no, one has to say yes to life, yes to love, yes to others, yes to education, yes to greater job opportunities. If we say yes to all these things, *there will be no room for illicit drugs, for alcohol abuse, for other forms of addiction*."[553]

Reading the news about Pope Francis' views regarding drug legalization in 2014, I wrote Pope Francis a four-page letter arguing against drug prohibition but received no acknowledgement or reply.

However, the moral incongruity of the Pope's pronouncement was not missed by others. A Washington Post journalist observed, "Today, Pope Francis denounced the Mafia and excommunicated its members from the Catholic Church. But just yesterday, he praised drug prohibition and refused to support any 'yielding or compromise' on the issue of legalization. There is an obvious tension between these two positions

[551] "Report of the International Narcotics Control Board for 2014," *International Narcotic Control Board,* https://www.incb.org/incb/en/publications/annual-reports/annual-report-2014.html, E/INCB/2014/1.

[552] Snapp et al., Chapter 12, "United States Drug Policy: Flexible Prohibition and Regulation," *Collapse of the Global Order on Drugs: From UNGASS 2016 to Review 2019,* Emerald Pub. Co., 2018, p. 253, emphasis added.

[553] Haroon Siddique and agencies, "Pope Francis says don't legalise drugs," *The Guardian,* June 20, 2014, https://www.theguardian.com/world/2014/jun/20/pope-francis-dont-legalise-drugs, emphasis added.

[since] the Sicilian Mafia – like many other organized crime and terrorist organizations – gets most of its revenue from the illegal drug trade."[554]

Argentina's "Successful" Drug Operations — 28,108 of Them

Since the Pope spoke, Martin Verrier, Argentina's Drug Enforcement Deputy Secretary of State between December 2015 and December 2019, wrote a police commentary, entitled "Cutting the Flow: Argentina as a Success Case against Drug Trafficking 2016–2019." In his commentary, he reports cocaine and marijuana seizures had increased. And "federal law enforcement forces arrested 31,820 individuals in 2018 for drug crimes, a 147% jump from the 12,853 arrests recorded in 2015. Anti-drug operations rose to 28,108 in 2018, an increase of 100% in comparison with the 14,065 registered in 2015.... Regarding synthetic drugs, in 2017, there was an increase, compared to 2014, of +236%. More units of this narcotic were seized in 2017 than in the last two years of the previous administration."[555]

Martin Verrier acknowledges that "... concerning the impact side of this policy in the first place, it is difficult to show a positive impact of the restriction of supply in demand for drugs. It is premature to try to identify any effect as the last consumption survey was completed in 2017, and the one before back in 2010. Still, the comparison between both reports shows an increase in consumption."[556]

With 31,820 individuals arrested for drug crimes and *28,108 successful anti-drug operations* in 2018, it is safe to conclude that there remains, as Pope Francis characterizes it, "room for illicit drugs" in Argentina, the Pope's home base. Furthermore, with regard to cocaine, the 2021 World Drug Report notes: "The cocaine trafficking route between South America and Europe is the second biggest in the world, and it is evolving. Supply chains once dominated by a few organized crime groups are changing, with many more groups involved.... The increased competition and efficiency of supply mean that cocaine is becoming more available and the quality is rising. The purity

---

[554] Ilya Somin, "Pope Francis denounces the Mafia, but praises drug prohibition – the main source of the Mafia's income," *The Washington Post*, June 21, 2014, https://www.washingtonpost.com/news/volokh-conspiracy/wp/2014/06/21/pope-denounces-mafia-but-praises-drug-prohibition-the-main-source-of-the-mafias-income/.

[555] Martin Verrier, "Cutting the Flow: Argentina as a Success Case against Drug Trafficking 2016–2019," *Journal of Illicit Economies and Development*, 2020, 2(1), pp.21–28. DOI: http://doi.org/10.31389/jied.61.

[556] Ibid.

of cocaine available in Europe has increased by 40 percent in the past decade, meaning that high-quality cocaine has, in effect, become cheaper per pure unit."[557]

Not only is there room for illicit drugs in Argentina, and the world, but the Taliban are doubling down on the profitability of a "drug-free" world. "The relative costs of heroin and methamphetamine make meth an attractive diversification for the Taliban, who are said to earn around $3 billion annually trafficking opium and heroin produced principally in southern Afghanistan."[558]

This manuscript section does not aim to criticize the predominant religion in the world, Catholicism, nor the nation of Argentina, and certainly not Pope Francis; rather the aim is to make the point that moral judgments regarding drug use and addiction are *beliefs and givens* that make drug policy change very difficult to accomplish. Regardless of how many people become addicted, afflicted or killed as a result of drug-prohibition policy, some goodhearted, religious leaders and followers continue to believe, mistakenly, that prohibiting drug use and drug sale is the right thing to do.

Pope Urban VIII and Flat Earth

But religious beliefs can and do evolve. Human understanding and belief can be altered by science, discovery and rationalism. Centuries ago, there was a reason why the top of the mainsail of a sailing ship would disappear incrementally as a sailing ship progressed into the yonder. Years ago, in 1633, Galileo ran afoul of Pope Urban VIII and was accused of heresy for contradicting flat-earth, religious gospel, thinking that the Earth circles the sun, a notion in conflict with Catholic orthodoxy. Galileo's belief and writing resulted in his trial, conviction and condemnation "to the prison of this Holy Office during Our will and pleasure regarding the idea that the Earth circles the sun."[559] Three hundred years later the Church righted its error.

However, Earth and religious belief are turning more quickly in the twenty-first century with a more **Richard Branson-** and **Jeff Bezos-like** view of the world from

---

[557] World Drug Report 2021, Booklet 1, p. 38.

[558] Lynne O'Donnell, "The Taliban Are Breaking Bad: Meth is even more profitable than heroin — and is turbocharging the insurgency," *Foreign Policy*, July 19, 2021, https://foreignpolicy.com/2021/07/19/taliban-expanding-drug-trade-meth-heroin/.

[559] History.com editors, "Galileo is accused of heresy," *A&E Television Networks*, November 13, 2009, updated May 19, 2020,

https://www.history.com/this-day-in-history/galileo-is-accused-of-heresy, accessed October 18, 2021

space.[560] Facts matter as much as ever, and if Pope Urban VIII were here today, he might agree — the Earth has a certain curvature to it.

Elsewhere in these pages is the Story of Float No. 62, a story of "Ministers Against the Drug War," religious leaders recognizing *the drug war accomplishes everything it aimed to prevent*. Clergy, too, can see the great harm and great evil caused by the War on Drugs, and some clerical leaders are beginning to amass and align their flocks against the Drug-War Harm Machine. One very constructive and recent evolution of religious drug policy thinking is found on the Internet.

Clergy for a New Drug Policy

Reverend Alexander E. Sharp has created a religious-based drug policy reform group called, "Clergy for a New Drug Policy."[561] The organization and collection of diversified religious leaders has adopted a succinct and powerful "Religious Declaration for a New Drug Policy" squarely grounded in truth and caring for one another. In part the declaration states: "As voices of faith, we call for an end to the War on Drugs which the United States has waged, at home and abroad, for over 47 years. This War has failed to achieve its stated objectives; deepened divisions between rich and poor, black, white, and brown; squandered over one trillion dollars; and turned our country into a 'prisoner' nation.... As clergy who oppose institutional racism, we have more than ample reason to seek alternatives to this Drug War on grounds of injustice. But our faith should take us even deeper. It should cause us to reject its very premise, based on our religious principles of compassion, healing, forgiveness, reconciliation, and love."[562]

Interestingly, despite some evolution of religious belief — the Pope, the Taliban, the DEA, politicians and the UN continue to support drug-prohibition policy for different and conflicting reasons. To the Pope it is a matter of *morals*;[563] to the Taliban,

---

560 Jackie Wattles, "Jeff Bezos and Richard Branson went to space. What's next?" *CNN Business*, July 21, 2021, https://www.cnn.com/2021/07/21/tech/jeff-bezos-richard-branson-space-what-next-scn/index.html.

561 Rev. Alexander E. Sharp, "Religious Declaration For A New Drug Policy," https://newdrugpolicy.org/." Date of access?

562 Ibid., emphasis added.

563 CNA staff, "Citing pope's warnings about drugs, Catholic bishops speak on ballot proposals," *Catholic News Agency*, October 28, 2020, https://www.catholicnewsagency.com/news/46392/citing-popes-warnings-about-drugs-catholic-bishops-speak-on-ballot-proposals, accessed February 1, 2022.

it is a matter of *money*;[564] to the Drug Enforcement Agency, it is a matter of *sworn duty*;[565] to politicians it is a matter of *votes*; and to the UN, it is a matter of protecting and keeping its drug-control *treaties inviolate*.[566]

Reverend Jesse Jackson's Call to "End the War on Drugs"

On the fortieth anniversary of the Nixon-declared War on Drugs, religious, civil rights and other leaders held rallies across America calling for "an end to the drug war." Perhaps one of the most famous and accomplished of those leaders was **Reverend Jesse Jackson, Sr.**, twice a candidate for president of the United States, supporter and understudy of Dr. Martin Luther King, founder of Operation Push and the Rainbow Coalition, and now insightful columnist for the *Chicago Sun-Times*.

But Reverend Jesse Jackson, Sr. was not always opposed to the War on Drugs. Like many religious leaders Reverend Jackson was *for* the War on Drugs before he was *against* it. Running for president of the United States in 1988, Reverend Jesse Jackson said: "I welcome Mr. Bush and Mr. Dukakis as lieutenants [in the War on Drugs], but *I am the general in this war to fight drugs*.... As president, I can stop the supply of drugs, but you must stop the demand.... No one has the right to kill our children, black or white... I won't take it from the Klan with a rope; I won't take it from a neighbor with dope. We must drive them out."[567]

Twenty-three years later as a columnist for the *Chicago Sun-Times*, Reverend Jackson had substantially reversed field regarding the War on Drugs, seemingly answering the question posed by this manuscript in Chapter 2 in the affirmative, "Is it Time to End the War on Drugs?" In his 2011 column titled, "It's time to end dismally failed 'war on drugs,'" *Chicago Sun-Times*, June 7, 2011,[568] Reverend Jackson writes: "Our neighbors to the south — Mexico and Colombia — are being torn apart by gang

---

[564] Hanif Sufizada, "The Taliban are megarich – here's where they get the money they use to wage war in Afghanistan," *The Conversation*," December 8, 2020, https://theconversation.com/the-taliban-are-megarich-heres-where-they-get-the-money-they-use-to-wage-war-in-afghanistan-147411.

[565] "DEA Mission Statement," *Drug Enforcement Agency*, https://www.dea.gov/about/mission.

[566] "Treaties," United Nations, *United Nations Office on Drugs and Crime*, https://www.unodc.org/ unodc/en/ treaties/index.html, accessed March 17, 2023.

[567] Cheryl Devall, "Jackson Calls Himself 'General' in Drug War," *Chicago Tribune*, May 23, 1988, https://www.chicagotribune.com/news/ct-xpm-1988-05-23-8801010475-story.html, emphasis added.

[568] Reverend Jesse Jackson, "It's time to end the failed 'war on drugs,'" *Chicago Sun-Times*, June 7, 2011, https://jamesgierach.tumblr.com/post/675061901582073856.

violence and corruption. Some 2.3 million now overcrowd America's prisons 25 percent of whom have been arrested for nonviolent drug crimes. Yet despite this, drugs are just as available and cheaper than they were 40 years ago.... The war on drugs turned, early on, into a new Jim Crow offensive against people of color: *Although whites abuse drugs at higher rates than African-Americans, African-Americans are incarcerated at 10 times the rate of whites for drug offenses.* We must use the 40th anniversary of a failed war to call that war into question.... Marijuana accounts for one-half of all drug arrests in the U.S.; decriminalizing it would save millions that could be used to treat addicts rather than arrest kids. Alternatives to incarceration should be preferred for those who pose no threat to others. Harsh mandatory and minimum sentences should be repealed. Why not take the drug addiction out of the criminal justice system and treat it in the public health system.... Ending the 'War on Drugs' doesn't mean we abandon the effort to *regulate* them, to teach children of their dangers, or to treat those who are hooked.... The drug war has been waged by both parties. Politicians have postured tough on crime, competing to invent the harshest punishments.... But now, 40 years later [this day, June 7, 2011, marking the 40th anniversary of the day Richard Nixon launched the second War on Drugs'], isn't it time to put aside the posturing, and have a fundamental debate about alternatives to this failed war?" (*Emphasis added*)

On April 24, 1995, I wrote a letter to Reverend Jesse Jackson and urged him to run for Vice President of the United States in 1996 on the idea of *drug policy reform*, making it "*the No. 1 issue...*" for without it nearly every American crisis he cared about "will just continue." I wrote, "Respectfully, you cannot be elected president when many Americans still notice that God made people in all shapes and colors, and the Bureau of the Census (1990) reports that the demographic diversity of America adds up to a 12.1 percent black population. Your previous presidential campaigns evidenced the point I pragmatically make: despite your notoriety, your middle ground position taken on issues, the most articulate and versatile presentation... and coalition-building efforts... the American public was not commensurately responsive.... Victory for you and your agenda, if it is to come at all, must be snatched with *the power of an idea.* Wholeheartedly, I believe that idea is drug policy reform.... For without drug policy reform — no man, no party, no coalition, no family value, no movement, no demonstration, no economic boycott can cleanse America of the sins and suffering caused by drug prohibition.... By welding your constituency to the idea of Drug Policy Reform — an idea that cuts across every economic, racial, and political strata — who knows *what miracle may ensue?* Incidentally, presidents die and vice-presidents are cloaked with a 'promotional preference.'"

My letter went unanswered. But over time Reverend Jesse Jackson's drug-war tune changed from that of a "general" to that of a civil-rights "activist."

But by the time Reverend Jackson wrote his 2011 column calling for an end to the war on drugs, it is critically important to notice — Reverend Jackson still did not use the words "*Legalize drugs.*" Even at that late stage (2011) and despite all the drug-war faults he itemized in his column, Reverend Jesse Jackson still did not equate ending the war on drugs with time to legalize drugs and license drug dealers, or time to regulate, control, inspect, label and tax drugs sold in legal markets. Is it time to do that?

Reverend Jesse Jackson, Pope Francis and religious leaders of every faith — Yes, it is time for a debate about alternatives to the failed War on Drugs. Yes, it is time to end it. Yes, it is time to legalize, regulate and control all popularly used recreational drug substances. Yes, legalize but, in my opinion, individuals of their own volition should choose not to use drugs, or at least not to excess.

What Does it Mean to "End the War on Drugs?"

In 2011, **Father Michael Pfleger**, Senior Pastor of Chicago's **St. Sabina** parish, a largely African-American Catholic parish, took the podium in the James R. Thompson Center to call for "an End to the War on Drugs." But like his friend, Reverend Jesse Jackson, he did not mean by that statement that drugs should be legalized. So, the words, "Ending the War on Drugs" has different meaning to different folks. Drug War causes endless violence, and for that reason, Father Pfleger wants to end the drug war. Pfleger is so obsessed with stopping Chicago violence in the Auburn-Gresham community where his parish is located that he sponsored weekly Friday night marches against it, invited Spike Lee to join him, handed out free book bags to kids going back to school, sponsored numerous no-questions-asked, gun buyback events, sponsored "Midnight basketball" for rival gang members, and much more. Organizing and leading a demonstration against violence, joblessness and poverty in 2018, he and his supporters forced the closure of the Dan Ryan Expressway, Interstate 94.[569] I joined him.

Like Reverend Jesse Jackson, his friend and colleague, Father Pfleger is not for legalizing drugs. Last time we talked, Father Pfleger told me he was not even for legalization of recreational marijuana. "Medical marijuana, okay," but he drew the line

[569] Patrick M. O'Connell, Jeremy Gorner and Megan Crepeau, "Anti-violence protesters shut down Dan Ryan: 'Today was the attention-getter, but now comes the action,'" *Chicago Tribune*, July 17, 2018, https://www.chicagotribune.com/news/breaking/ct-met-dan-ryan-pfleger-violence-protest-20180706-story.html.

here. Not only does Father Pfleger not want drugs legalized, he rejects the idea of an open meeting at St. Sabina to discuss its pros and cons, as I have repeatedly urged him over thirty years. Yet, he delivers great anti-drug war and anti-drug legalization speeches. "There is not a war on drugs, there is a war on the poor and a war on people of color!" huffed Pfleger,[570] whipping up the crowd back in 2011 on the fortieth anniversary of the War on Drugs.

Cook County Board President **Toni Preckwinkle** also spoke at the same Chicago End the Drug War rally as Reverend Jackson and Father Pfleger, and she effectively skewered the War on Drugs and called for its end. Incidentally, my request to speak at the event was denied.

President Preckwinkle said, "We all know that the war on drugs has failed to end drug use. Instead, it resulted in the incarceration of millions of people around the country, and 100,000 here in Cook County on an annual basis.... Drugs and the failed war on drugs have devastated lives, families and communities. For too long we've treated drug use as a criminal justice issue, rather than a public health issue, which is what it is."[571] In 2017, a courageous President Toni Preckwinkle joined me for a half-hour interview on CAN-TV, a Chicago cable series I hosted, called "Chicago's War on Drugs," sponsored by the nonprofit Azteca Baseball League.[572]

But again, what does it mean to "End the War on Drugs?" Does it mean legalizing all drugs, some drugs, or any drugs? Does it mean legalizing drugs for some people but not others — maybe addicts only?

Decriminalizing drugs is not legalizing drugs. Decriminalization removes penalties, incarceration, maybe even fines, but it *does not remove the black market in drugs.* And it is the black market that is needlessly killing us by overdose and gunfire. The black market is simply one more adverse consequence of drug prohibition. Drug prohibition is the common denominator to so many of our problems. In contrast, alcohol is legal. If you are of legal age, and old enough to know better, you can go to the store and buy alcohol.

---

570 P. Smith, "Rallies, Vigils Mark 40 Years of Failed Drug War," *Drug War Chronicle*, Issue #689, https://stopthedrugwar.org/chronicle/2011/jun/21/rallies_vigils_mark_40_years_fai.

571 Ibid.

572 Cook County Board Pres. Toni Preckwinkle, one of 13 guests on CAN-TV series, "Chicago's War on Drugs," broadcast June 6, 2017, with show host Jim Gierach, VIDEO, https://www.dropbox.com/ s/zas3zd pz1v17bjl/Chicago%20War%20on%20Drugs%20with%20Toni%20Preckwinkle.mp4?dl=0.

Is drug legalization what Jesse Jackson, Sr. was calling for in 2011? I think not. Neither did columnist Jacob Sullum who wrote, "Although that last line [of Jackson's column] suggests not just calling off the 'war' launched by Nixon but repealing the drug bans that the federal government began to impose in 1914, it's not clear exactly what policy Jackson favors. 'What if we treated drug addiction like alcohol addiction as a public health problem?' he asks. Well, if the government actually did treat drug addiction like alcohol addiction, drug users would not be arrested, and treatment would not be mandatory (except maybe in cases of drugged driving or other offenses that harm or endanger others). Furthermore, production, sale, and use of the currently prohibited substances would be legal. Is Jackson ready for that? It doesn't sound like it."[573] Sullum is right.

In my opinion, drug decriminalization is a weak-kneed effort to reduce some drug prohibition harm, but not the violence caused by it and gangs fighting over turf and control of the local drug prohibition franchise. If drug barons were forced to choose between drug legalization and drug decriminalization, they would universally pick the latter. Drug decriminalization and drug prohibition can cooperatively coexist, the former protecting illicit black markets and drug-gang profits.

Which begs the question that has haunted me since Jesse Jackson's presidential runs.

Why Hasn't Reverend Jesse Jackson Called for "Legalized Drugs?"

Why has Reverend Jesse Jackson never called for legalizing drugs to ameliorate the many crises he understood and articulated so well in his 2011 column? For decades, I have wondered. Now, right or wrong, I have formed an opinion.

Reverend Jesse Jackson is smart. He cares about the poor and downtrodden. I believe, he cares about all of us. He knows that revenues generated by illicit drug sales rain down on Black and minority communities like manna from heaven. He knew that if drugs were legalized it would take billions of dollars out of the Black and minority communities he cares so much about across America with little hope that that revenue stream would be replaced.

The struggle for fairness in cannabis social equity programs evidences the reasonableness of Reverend Jesse Jacksons's thinking, as I hypothesize it. "It's no secret that

---

[573] "Jesse Jackson Wants to End the War on Drugs," *Reason*, June 7, 2011, https://reason.com/2011/06/07/jesse-jackson-wants-to-end-the/.

the prohibition of cannabis disproportionately and adversely impacted people of color. To counter this, many states and cities have implemented what are called 'social equity programs' in connection with the legalization of medical or adult-use cannabis. Social equity deals with justice and fairness within social policy. These programs attempt to ensure that people of color, and those with marijuana offenses prior to legalization, be afforded an opportunity to participate, meaningfully, in this burgeoning industry."[574] Marijuana legalization in Illinois took more than a billion dollars a year off drug-dealer shelves with little social equity results to counter the loss.[575]

Drug-War Revenue Sharing

Reverend Jesse Jackson knows the War on Drugs serves as *"the employer of last resort."* If no one else will hire a convicted felon released from prison on return to their minority community with no job, no resources, minimal available family help, few skills and a criminal record, then the prohibition drug business always offers such folk an opportunity to work, eat and live. Dangerous, criminogenic, yes — but an opportunity to survive.

The War on Drugs is a form of unofficial societal **revenue sharing**.[576] It takes money from better-off, white communities and gives those funds to minority communities, enabling drug dealers to support their family members and loved ones. Magically, the War on Drugs facilitates that revenue transfer without raising taxes, without a War on Poverty, without paying reparations, and without the impossible approval of Republican Senate Majority Leader **Mitch McConnell** from Kentucky.

Senator Mitch McConnell and the Trump Administration believed the need for a war on poverty was over, a view supported by release of a 2018 report prepared by Donald Trump's Council of Economic Advisers. Those advisers "declared that the War on Poverty, introduced by President Lyndon Johnson in 1964, is 'largely over' and has been 'a success,' denied that homelessness is a 'meaningful problem,' declared

574 Robert Hoban, "The Critical Importance Of Social Equity In The Cannabis Industry," *Forbes*, August 31, 2020, https://www.forbes.com/sites/roberthoban/2020/08/31/the-critical-importance-of-social-equity-in-the-cannabis-industry/?sh=7e1c9e291a6d.

575 "Theory vs. Practice: The Trouble with Illinois' Cannabis Social Equity Program," *Cannabis Creative*, https://cannabiscreative.com/blog/theory-vs-practice-the-trouble-with-illinois-cannabis-social-equity-program/, accessed February 2, 2022.

576 Ronnie Lowenstein, "Federal Grants During the 1980s," *Federal Reserve Bank of New York*, May 1995, revised June 28, 1995. https://www.newyorkfed.org/medialibrary/media/research/staff_reports/research_papers/9508.pdf.

that 'reduced diet quality as a consequence of limited resources' isn't really hunger, and stated, in the face of problems in cities like Flint, Michigan, that 'almost all Americans have access to clean water.'"[577]

Regarding the War on Drugs and a Democratic bill to decriminalize marijuana at the federal level, a number of Republicans led by Senate Republican Leader Mitch McConnell (R-Ky.) opposed even marijuana legalization. "I do not have any plans to endorse the legalization of marijuana," McConnell said in 2018 when he announced his support for legalizing hemp, noting that they are "entirely separate plants."[578]

If my supposition regarding Reverend Jackson's aversion to legalized drugs is correct, Reverend Jesse Jackson smartly foresaw the loss of billions of dollars in illicit drug revenues that predominantly helped people living in Black and minority communities. In 2020, the first year that Illinois legalized marijuana sales, recreational pot was big business. "For the year, Illinois generated $669 million in recreational weed sales, with more than $331 million in medical sales through November."[579] In 2021, Illinois legal marijuana sales doubled, reaching $1.4 billion.[580] And "even as legal weed sales in Illinois continue to shatter records nearly 18 months after they kicked off, the illicit pot trade is still dominating a total statewide market some experts have valued at over $4 billion."[581]

Ministers Against the Drug War

In 2000, a Baptist Ministers Association led by Reverend Leonard DeVille, a former Chicago alderman, and I, sought to convey the idea that the War on Drugs was a two-edged sword, one edge an economic blessing and the other a deadly curse. To that end,

---

[577] Lesley Russell, "How America's War on Poverty became a war on the poor," *Inside Story*, August 17, 2018, https://insidestory.org.au/how-americas-war-on-poverty-became-a-war-on-the-poor/.

[578] Ashan Singh, Laura Coburn, Jessica Hopper and Allie Yang, "As legal marijuana booms, people push for justice for those impacted by war on drugs," *ABC NEWS*, June 2, 2021, https://abcnews.go.com/US/legal-marijuana-booms-people-push-justice-impacted-war/story?id=78028117.

[579] Robert Channick, "Illinois hits $1 billion in weed sales for 2020 with another record set in December," *Chicago Tribune*, January 4, 2021, https://www.chicagotribune.com/business/ct-biz-weed-illinois-sales-record-20210104-vay6ivrbmndefg2itqudtizrmu-story.html.

[580] Greg Bishop, "Illinois legal cannabis sales nearly $1.4 billion in 2021, double last year's total," *The Center Square*, January 3, 2022, https://www.thecentersquare.com/illinois/illinois-legal-cannabis-sales-nearly-1-4-billion-in-2021-double-last-years-total/article_dafe48f6-6cc3-11ec-a174-db1ea990d6c7.html.

[581] Tom Schuba, "Billions in black-market weed still selling in Illinois 18 months after marijuana legalized," *Chicago Sun-Times*, June 14, 2021, https://chicago.suntimes.com/cannabis/2021/6/14/22534079/illinois-dispensaries-illegal-legal-marijuana-cannabis-pot-bud-sale.

we created an award-winning float entry for Chicago's Bud Billiken Parade. The float depicted the idea that the drug war rained money on the Black community like manna from heaven, but at the same time its money-making, drug-prohibition feature poured violence and death on the same community. A rainbow emanating from a black "Drug War Cloud" poured money into a "Pot of Gold" while at the same time that same rainbow pushed up tombstones out of the grassy float floor-bed brandishing the message, "R.I.P." A wrought iron park bench rested on the green-grass float floor, providing seating for two African American mothers. One mother had lost her three-year-old son in gang crossfire as he played outside. The other mother had lost her teenage son as a combatant in Chicago drug-turf wars.

Drug Legalization and Its Transitional Pain

What happens when you take a billion-dollar revenue flow from street gangs in a metropolitan area like Chicago? Violence increases, carjackings spike, Chicago expressway shootings increase, Mag Mile and Near North robberies increase, catalytic converters disappear, and no one living in or entering Chicago feels safe.[582] Likewise, "Suburban killings so far this year are growing faster than the increase in Chicago. The gangs, guns and greed that have helped to make 2021, so far, Chicago's deadliest year in more than a decade are not confined to the city limits. Numbers provided by the medical examiner's office show there have been 100 homicides in suburban Cook County since January 1st, compared to 66 at this point last year and 63 in 2019. Many of the murders occurred in the south suburbs, including Harvey, which faces the same gang issues that Chicago Mayor Lori Lightfoot blames for two mass shootings that just occurred this past weekend."[583]

Why does this happen? Young drug dealers deprived of their customary drug-revenue stream endeavor to replace it. But no replacement criminal activity is nearly so rewarding; no replacement criminal enterprise offers the inflated price and profit margin offered by the illegal drug market. I suspect, the same violent dynamic is occurring

---

[582] Andy Grimm, "Mag Mile robbery crew took $43,000 in loot, seriously injured guard: police," *Chicago Sun-Times*, August 23, 2021, https://chicago.suntimes.com/crime/2021/8/23/22638436/mag-mile-robbery-michigan-avenue-security-guard-injuries-police.

[583] Mike Flannery, "Violence explosion: Killings in Chicago suburbs have increased 50% this year," *FOX32Chicago*, June 28, 2021, https://www.fox32chicago.com/news/violence-explosion-killings-in-chicago-suburbs-have-increased-50-this-year.

across America as the marijuana legalization movement steadily advances. In my opinion, the escalation of violent crime caused by marijuana legalization is a transitory crisis — temporary as my two Englewood friends wearing gold chains supporting a gold-gun and gold-dollar-sign jewelry adjust and learn how to make a living without drug prohibition or replacement criminal activity.

Weaning society off drug prohibition and transferring a US $500 billion drug trade from illegal to legal markets comes with transitional costs and withdrawal pain. During sixty years of recreational, drug-prohibition policy, a large segment of society became economically dependent on a prohibition economy. Regardless of the interim pain associated with change, society must kick its prohibition addiction. And it will.

Religious leaders who already say they want to "End the War on Drugs" must further modify their core beliefs and support the legalization of drugs to stop gang violence, prevent accidental drug overdose deaths, and eliminate the tempting, corrupting influence that drug-prohibition economic opportunity affords youth, today. This transformation and enlightened belief set will help dispose of the mistaken notion that drug war has a moral foundation. Or as attorney Brian A. Ford writes, "It is high time that the world realize that there is a moral obligation to end prohibition."[584]

Mistaken morality, again, explains why it is so difficult to change bad drug policy.

Reason 3: The Risk of Loss of Foreign Aid

As if a complex global legal construct and moral belief were not challenge enough for drug policy reform, the checkbook of the most powerful and richest nation in the world, the United States of America, and its use of foreign aid adds a sinister twist to the mix. America, armed with her vast riches and international influence inside and outside the United Nations, supported the War on Drugs far and wide. As if Harry Anslinger on the loose in international circles was not trouble enough, the United States began to annually certify cooperating nations in the drug-war orbit. The "ABCs of Drug War SIN" helped me remember the names of nations the United States determined years ago were not drug-war cooperative: Afghanistan, Bolivia, Colombia, Syria, Iran and Nigeria. As time passed, American anti-drug financial aid poured into Colombia, Mexico and Afghanistan with initiatives called "Plan Colombia," "the Mérida Initiative," and our War in Afghanistan and its poppy fields. That substantial

584 Brian A. Ford, "From Mountains to Molehills: A Comparative Analysis of Drug Policy," p. 35, https://www.academia.edu/3546783/From_Mountains_to_Molehills_A_Comparative_Analysis_of_Drug_Policy?email_work_card=thumbnail (2013).

drug-war funding bought and cemented drug-war cooperation and fealty of those nations, even as the funding stoked violence between national military forces and drug
cartel forces and as poisonous chemicals were sprayed incessantly on foreign lands in
an effort to kill drug produce.

A Congressional Research Service report explained: "One contentious issue has
been the congressionally mandated certification process, an instrument designed to
induce specified drug-exporting countries to prioritize or pay more attention to the
fight against narcotics businesses. Current law requires the President, with certain exceptions, to designate and withhold assistance from countries that have failed demon-
strably to meet their counternarcotics obligations."[585]

United States money and influence plied internationally continues to feed global
drug-war flames. British journalist Johann Hari wrote about the influence of America's
leading drug prohibitionist, Harry Anslinger, "Father of the Drug War"[586] and the
1930s head of America's Federal Bureau of Narcotics. In *Chasing the Scream,*[587] Hari
reported that Harry Anslinger attributed the failure of early American drug-prohibition policy to his mind, (Harry's) mind, to the notion that drug war must be global, a
worldwide policy in order to be effective.[588]

"Drug prohibition would work — but only if it was being done by everyone, all
over the world. So Anslinger traveled to the UN with a set of instructions for humanity: Do what we have done. Wage a war on drugs."[589] As Hari wrote, other nations
were reluctant to follow American's (Anslinger's) lead, "So Harry [Anslinger] started
twisting arms."[590] "One of [Harry's] key lieutenants, Charles Siracusa, boasted: 'I
found that a casual mention of *the possibility of shutting* off *foreign aid* programs,
dropped in proper quarters, brought grudging permission for our operations almost
immediately."[591]

---

[585] Perl, Raphael F., "International Drug Trade and U.S. Foreign Policy," July 21, 2006; Washington D.C.,
https://digital.library.unt.edu/ark:/67531/metacrs9497/: accessed October 30, 2021.

[586] Michael Weinreb, "The Complicated Legacy of Harry Anslinger," *Penn Stater Magazine,* January February
2018, https://www.case.org/system/files/media/file/Penn%20Stater%20Harry%20Anslinger.pdf, p.1.

[587] Johann Hari, *Chasing the Scream* (New York: Bloomsbury, 2015).

[588] "Introduction, Long Life of Service, Harry Jacob Anslinger," *DEA Museum,* https://museum.dea.gov/
exhibits/online-exhibits/anslinger/introduction, p.1, accessed March 17, 2023.

[589] Hari, supra, p. 43.

[590] Ibid.

[591] Ibid.

A Rule of Life: Don't Bite the Hand that Feeds You

It is a simple rule of international life and individual self-preservation: Don't bite the hand that feeds you. And there is a corollary rule: If you bite the hand that feeds you, expect trouble.

In some respects, little had changed between Anslinger's time and March 2015 when dignitaries assembled in Vienna for the 58th Session of the Commission on Narcotic Drugs. Two years earlier, in 2013, the president of Uruguay legalized recreational marijuana for his countrymen, making it the first country in the world to openly buck UN drug-control treaty mandates. In 2015, LEAP and the Czech Republic cosponsored a "side event," as they are called, at the 58th Session of the CND. I named the side-event topic: "Treaty Amendment: A Choice for Drug Policy Reform." Uruguayan Ambassador **Bruno Javier Faraone Machado**, permanent representative of Uruguay to the United Nations in Vienna attended my presentation at the side event calling for amendment of UN drug control treaties and an end to recreational drug prohibition.

In 2013, Uruguayan President Jose Mujica had just led his country to become the first nation in the world to defy the UN recreational drug prohibition edict.[592] That brave departure from the international prohibition norm regarded the world's most popularly used drug — "cannabis," alias "marijuana."[593]

After my LEAP-Cheque side event presentation on behalf of LEAP, Ambassador Faraone Machado asked to meet me later during the CND-week to ask me a question regarding Uruguayan leadership in international drug policy reform. The next day, we met in the "Hallowed Halls of World Drug Policy," the Vienna International Centre ("the VIC"), home of the Commission on Narcotic Drugs and International Atomic Energy Agency (IAEA).

---

[592] Steven Nelson, "Uruguay's President Quietly Signs Marijuana Legalization Bill," *U.S. News*, December 26, 2013, https://www.usnews.com/news/articles/2013/12/26/uruguays-president-quietly-signs-marijuana-legalization-bill.

[593] Anna Wilcox, "The Origin of the Word 'Marijuana,'" *Leafly*, March 6, 2014, https://www.leafly.com/news/cannabis-101/where-did-the-word-marijuana-come-from-anyway-01fb.

Ambassador Faraone Machado: Why Should Uruguay Lead World Drug Policy Reform?

Ambassador **Bruno Javier Faraone Machado** point-blank asked me, paraphrasing: Why should Uruguay want to lead global, drug-policy reform? He explained, "My president legalized recreational marijuana to help Uruguayans, not the world. When he did that there were many humanitarian programs jointly funded 50-50, half UN-funded and half Uruguay-funded. Many of those programs had nothing to do with drugs. Yet, all UN funding of those programs came to a halt without a word of explanation after my president legalized recreational marijuana. So I ask you, why should Uruguay want to lead global, drug-policy reform?"

My answer to the ambassador went something like this: "Somebody has to be the leader. It's too important to the world for Uruguay not to lead nations out of the UN drug-prohibition morass and out from under the myriad drug war-driven crises that accompany it...." My answer to the ambassador's question, I suspect, was less noteworthy than his question and the factual basis that prompted him to ask it.

Money — foreign aid and UN financial assistance — is habitually used to buy international cooperation for public policy. Whether those foreign-aid purchases aid or harm a well-intended objective, and whether "asking" for cooperation is commendable or despicable national behavior — that's how foreign affairs are dramatically influenced. Examples of national misbehavior — plying foreign aid and military aid to influence international affairs are commonplace.

President Donald Trump Withholds $400 Million In Ukrainian Military Aid

President Donald Trump's withholding of $400 million in military aid to war-torn Ukraine is a good example of military aid misbehavior. "The Washington Post first reported Monday night that Trump directed acting White House chief of staff Mick Mulvaney to hold back nearly $400 million in military funds for Ukraine at least a week before his summer conversation with Zelensky.... Trump on Monday afternoon denied that he offered an explicit quid pro quo to Zelensky, telling reporters: 'I did not ask for — I did not make a statement that you have to do this or I'm not gonna give you aid. I wouldn't do that. I wouldn't do that.'"[594] He did.

---

[594] Quint Forgey, "Trump changes story on withholding Ukraine aid," *Politico*, September 24, 2019, https://www.politico.com/story/2019/09/24/donald-trump-ukraine-military-aid-1509070.

Plan Colombia and The Mérida Initiative

Or take the action of America's first Drug Czar[595] Harry Anslinger's troops cited above, threatening the withholding of U.S. foreign aid unless foreign nations succumbed to U.S. demand for global drug-war cooperation; or contemplate the effect of hundreds of millions of dollars spent on Plan Colombia;[596] or consider the $1.6 billion spent on the Mérida Initiative;[597] or the on-going annual national certification process,[598] and the "List of Majors," a list of major drug-producing and major drug-transit nations, terms defined by the Foreign Assistance Act of 1961.[599] Disagreeing with United States drug-prohibition policies carries economic consequences.

As late as 2018, President Trump harangued other national leaders to support his call for renewed drug war.[600]

President Trump's "Global Call to Action on the World Drug Problem" did the exact opposite of what the United States and other nations should be doing to fix "the global drug problem" — repealing or amending UN drug-control conventions. The second paragraph of the Trump call to action said: "We reaffirm our commitment to implement the Single Convention on Narcotic Drugs, the Convention on Psychotropic Substances, the United Nations Convention against Illicit Traffic in Narcotic Drugs and Psychotropic Substances, and the United Nations Convention against

---

[595] *Wikipedia*, s.v. "Drug czar," https://en.wikipedia.org/wiki/Drug_czar. Date of access?

[596] *Wikipedia*, s.v. "Plan Colombia," https://en.m.wikipedia.org/wiki/Plan_Colombia#Expansion_under_Bush, accessed March 17, 2023.

[597] *Wikipedia*, s.v. "Mérida Initiative," https://en.m.wikipedia.org/wiki/Mérida_Initiative.

[598] Bill Spencer, "Drug Certification," *Institute for Policy Studies*, September 1, 1998, https://ips-dc.org/drug_certification/.

[599] "As defined in the Foreign Assistance Act of 1961, the terms 'major illicit drug-producing country' and 'major drug-transit country' refer to countries where illicit drugs — especially illicit crops of opium poppy, coca bush, and cannabis destined for the United States — are produced or trafficked. Each year, the President identifies which countries meet the statutory criteria for being listed as major illicit drug-producing and drug-transit countries and determines which countries on the so-called 'majors list' will not receive U.S. assistance... In September 2020, President Donald J. Trump identified 22 countries on the majors list for FY2021:..." ("The U.S. "Majors List" of Illicit Drug-Producing and Drug-Transit Countries," *Congressional Research Service*, February 25, 2021, https://www.everycrsreport.com/files/2021-02-25_R46695_3f0e06048b2d8b5716e0a 220f41b881241ecb74a.pdf.

[600] Samuel Oakford, "Trump Administration Plans U.N. Meeting to Ramp Up The International Drug War," *The Intercept*, September 18, 2018, https://theintercept.com/2018/09/18/un-drug-policy-trump-united-nations/.

Transnational Organized Crime."[601] President Trump's call mimicked UN-unflinching support for its own drug-war conventions, and the president's call urged continuation and protection of those failed policies a few months later at the 62nd Session of the CND in March 2019.[602] Oppose the will of the United States and risk the loss of its Golden Goose foreign aid, military aid, and friendship.

Reason 4: The Politics of Drug War: Voters Love Drug War

America's War on Drugs is a war fought with bipartisan support. For decades, Republicans and Democrats have tried to "out drug war" each other. "Tough on drugs" and "tough on crime" rhetoric sells well to voters. For that reason, the Anti-Drug Abuse Act of 1986 was adopted by overwhelming, bipartisan majorities with the law adopted

> *"The debate has now entered a political phase. Australia's drug policy has… continued despite its terrible outcomes because bad policy has been good politics."*
>
> — Australian Physician Alex Wodak

by a vote of 392-16 in the House and 97-2 in the Senate. To this day — despite the reality that public safety has fallen through the floor as drug sales and drug use has soared through the roof in response to decades of drug prohibition policies — voters starved for a little peace and quiet support drug prohibition policies. And with bipartisan support, American politicians still provide just that.

"The appearance of crack cocaine, the June 19, 1986 death of Len Bias (a University of Maryland basketball star) the morning after he signed with the NBA champion Boston Celtics, and the June 27, 1986 death of football safety Don Rogers, the Cleveland Browns 1985 Defensive Rookie of the Year, both from cocaine use, encouraged U.S. Rep. Thomas P. "Tip" O'Neill Jr. (D-MA), the Speaker of the House of Representatives, to mobilize the House Democratic leadership to assemble an omnibus anti-

---

[601] President Trump's "Global Call to Action on the World Drug Problem," https://s3.documentcloud.org/documents/4901223/Global-Call-to-Action-on-the-World-Drug-Problem.pdf, September 24, 2018.

[602] Gierach, James E., *Gierach Tumblr*, https://jamesgierach.tumblr.com/post/631789958084083712/former-ambassador-haley-pres-trump-and-broken-un.

drug bill that became the Anti-Drug Abuse Act of 1986." Republican President Ronald Reagan signed it into law.[603]

The Anti-Drug Abuse Act of 1986 included The Money Laundering Control Act of 1986 that criminalized money laundering for the first time in the United States. Along with the Comprehensive Crime Control Act of 1984, the 1986 Act substantially increased the number of drug offenses with mandatory minimum sentences, including a mandatory five-year sentence without parole for possession of five grams of crack cocaine or 500 grams of powder cocaine, the infamous 100:1 disparity that remained the law until adoption of the Fair Sentencing Act of 2010, reducing the disparity to 18:1; and authorized billions of dollars of spending to increase substance abuse treatment, drug counseling, drug-abuse prevention and education programs, AIDS research and international cooperation to limit drug production.[604]

Crime Increased with Enactment of the Anti-Drug Abuse Act of 1986

The U.S. crime rate was relatively flat in 1984, preceding adoption of the Anti-Drug Abuse Act of 1986.[605] But the crime situation worsened after adoption of the 1986 Anti-Drug Abuse Act consistent with my Chapter 5 conclusion — "Drug War Intolerance Means More Crime." Published in the *National Review of Public Health*, Alfred Blumstein, Frederick P. Rivara, and Richard Rosenfeld, each affiliated with respected universities and the National Consortium on Violence Research, observed that "A dramatic rise in homicide in the latter half of the 1980s peaked during the 1990s and then declined at an equally dramatic rate. Such trends in homicide rates can be understood only by examining rates in specific age, sex, and racial groups. The increase primarily involved young males, especially black males, occurred first in the big cities, and was related to the sudden appearance of crack cocaine in the drug markets of the big cities around 1985."[606]

---

[603] *Wikipedia, s.v.* "Anti-Drug Abuse Act of 1986," https://en.wikipedia.org/wiki/Anti-Drug_Abuse_Act_of_1986, accessed August 19, 2021.

[604] Ibid.

[605] "Violent Crime Stable in 1984, Overall Rate Down, U.S. Says," *The New York Times*, April 9, 1985, accessed August 19, 2021, https://www.nytimes.com/1985/04/09/us/violent-crime-stable-in-1984-overall-rate-down-us-says.html.

[606] Alfred Blumstein, Frederick P. Rivara, and Richard Rosenfeld, "The Rise and Decline of Homicide — and Why," *Annual Reviews*, Annual Review of Public Health, Vol. 21:505-541, Volume publication date May 2000, https://doi.org/10.1146/annurev.publhealth.21.1.505.

Speaking nine years before the Blumstein et al. publication in March 1991, Louis Sullivan, then U.S. secretary of health and human services, "noted that the leading cause of death for black males aged 15 to 34 is homicide... and that a black male teenager is 11 times more likely to be murdered with a gun than is his white counterpoint."[607] The month following Sullivan's note, discussing the prevailing level of urban violence and the tragic Black youth reality, a *Chicago Tribune* editorial writer powerfully and perceptively concluded that "what is at stake is not just individual lives, but the soul of our nation."[608]

Factors In Homicide Increase

Further excerpting from the Blumstein et al. source: "All of the increase in U.S. homicide rates that began in the mid-1980s resulted from large upswings in the victimization rates of those <25 years old." (Age Factors) "By 1993, the homicide rate for young adults was 2.5-fold that for the population as a whole... Since the early 1990s, the victimization rates for both juveniles and young adults have declined, although not to the levels of the early 1980s." "African Americans are exposed to a risk of homicide many times that of whites. The African-American victimization rate was 32/100,000 population in 1995, compared with 5/100,000 among whites." (Racial Factors) "The number of whites killed with firearms rose by 25% from a trough of 5875 in 1988 to a peak in 1993 of 7315.... The number of African-American firearm homicide victims, meanwhile, nearly doubled from a trough of 4786 in 1984 to a 1993 peak of 9394... (Firearm Factors) "Figure 7a illustrates that there was a dramatic change by 1993, with a very sharp increase at the younger ages and a very sharp peak at age 18. We also note that the rates for those over 30 had indeed declined." (Offender Trends)[609]

Let me interject my personal observation based on this data and my life experience. Ages thirteen to thirty years, approximately, seem to be violence-prone ages. I think, not coincidentally, the decline in male testosterone levels directly correlates with a natural reduced propensity for violence.[610] Unfortunately — like the rule that "You

---

607 "The stakes in urban violence," *Chicago Tribune*, editorial, April 1, 1991. Concluding "For humane reasons... America cannot continue to tolerate the kind of violence that Secretary Sullivan alluded to. For what is at stake is not just individual lives but the soul of our nation." Gierach notebooks, p. 487.

608 Ibid.

609 Blumstein, et al., supra, "The Rise and Decline of Homicide — and Why." Accessed March 17, 2023.

610 Archimedes Nardozza Júnior, et al. "Age-related testosterone decline in a Brazilian cohort of healthy military men," Figure 1, *International Braz J Urology*, 37 (5), October 2011, https://www.scielo.br/ j/ibju/a/ndhsKf34 nbVQFVzMwkDq7MN#.

can't get blood from a turnip"[611] — "You can't take testosterone out of a youngster." But we can take the profit out of the drug business that motivates some youngsters to enter the violent drug trade and deviate toward a gang lifestyle.

Continuing with the Blumstein, et al. report, "There is widespread recognition of the changing role of weaponry in young people's hands. Over the last decade the weapons involved in settling juveniles' disputes have changed dramatically from fists or knives to handguns, with their much greater lethality." (The Changing Role of Handguns...) "We also observe some important racial differences in the growth of handgun homicides, with the dominant growth being among African-American juveniles and young adults, both as offenders and as victims." (The Changing Role of Handguns..., part 6)

Finally, connecting the dots for me, Blumstein, et al. reported that "It is widely recognized that an important feature of the late 1980s was that *drugs, and especially crack cocaine, became an important part of life in many American inner cities.* This trend is reflected in the drug arrest rates..." (How Did the Young People Get the Guns: Links to Illicit-Drug Markets)[612]

Led by politicians from both political parties, American voters have had to take solace in violence solutions that ignored the greatest violence-driver — drug prohibition. Politically, drug prohibition is a non-debatable "Given." Rather than voters having to contemplate the unpleasant thought of legalizing drugs to attack violence and drug problems, voters had to take comfort, and still must take comfort, in the limited strategies offered by their respective political party leaders. Unfortunately, both mainstream political parties push, protect and preserve drug prohibition, substituting inadequate, sound-good strategies. These strategies included lock 'em up and throw away the key;[613] three-time loser laws;[614] harsh mandatory-minimum sentencing laws that typically "apply to gun and drug crimes and are based on only the type and weight of the drug involved or the possession or presence of a gun" and resulted in over "260,000

[611] A. Leverkuhn, "What Does It Mean 'To Get Blood from a turnip,'?" *Language Humanities Organization*, https://www.languagehumanities.org/what-does-it-mean-to-get-blood-from-a-turnip.htm, accessed July 31, 2022.

[612] Blumstein, et al., supra, emphasis added.

[613] Nathan, "Lock Em Up and Throw Away the Key," *Youth Voices*, January 10, 2018, https://www.youthvoices.live/lock-em-up-and-throw-away-the-key/.

[614] "10 Reasons to Oppose '3 Strikes, You're Out," *UCLA*, https://www.aclu.org/other/10-reasons-oppose-3-strikes-youre-out. Date?

people [receiving] mandatory minimums for a federal drug offense";[615] the Sentencing Reform Act of 1984 that "in essence, eliminated indeterminate sentencing at the federal level"[616] and established 43 levels of offense seriousness;[617] and construction of more prisons — lots more prisons — increasing the number of jail beds from 243,000 in 1970 to 915,100 in 2017.[618] Eventually, America's prison population would hit 2.3 million.[619]

America's Annual $70 Billion Incarceration Bill

American voters and taxpayers, who by their voting choices express love for the drug war, would rather not be reminded of the cost of being the world's largest jailer in "the Land of the Free." Nevertheless, as of a 2015 publication date, "It is estimated that there are now more than 6,000 jails and prisons nationwide in America. One in 100 American adults is incarcerated, and US taxpayers spend $70 billion each year keeping them behind bars. These people are disproportionately the poor and people of color."[620] And now — "At the end of March 2021, there were nearly 1.8 million people still incarcerated in the United States, down only 2 percent since June 2020 — there was a 9 percent decrease in the prison population, but that was offset by a 13 percent increase in the jail population."[621]

---

615 "Mandatory Minimums In a Nutshell," *Families Against Mandatory Minimum*, April 26, 2012, https://famm.org/wp-content/uploads/FS-MMs-in-a-Nutshell.pdf.

616 Lisa M. Seghetti, "Federal Sentencing Guidelines: Background, Legal Analysis, and Policy Options," *Congressional Research Service (CRS)*, March 16, 2009, https://www.everycrsreport.com/ reports/RL32766. html#_Toc225069429.

617 "An Overview of the Federal Sentencing Guidelines," *United States Sentencing Commission*, https://www.ussc.gov/sites/default/files/pdf/about/overview/Overview_Federal_Sentencing_Guidelines.pdf, accessed March 17, 2023.

618 Chris Mai, Mikelina Belaineh, Ram Subramanian, and Jacob Kang-Brown, "Broken Ground: Why America Keeps Building More Jails and What It Can Do Instead," *Vera Institute of Justice*, November 2019, https://www.vera.org/downloads/publications/broken-ground-jail-construction.pdf.

619 Pierre Thomas and Jason Ryan, "U.S. Prison Population Hits All-Time High: 2.3 Million Incarcerated," *ABCNews*, June 6, 2008, https://abcnews.go.com/TheLaw/story?id=5009270&page=1.

620 Josh Begley, "Aerial Photos Expose the American Prison System's Staggering Scale," *Wired*, January February 2015, https://www.wired.com/2015/01/josh-begley-prison-map/.

621 Jacob Kang-Brown, Chase Montagnet and Jasmine Heiss, "People in Jail and Prison in Spring 2021," *Vera Institute of Justice*, New York: Vera Institute of Justice, 2021, https://www.vera.org/ downloads/ publications/people-in-jail-and-prison-in-spring-2021.pdf.

America: Prison Capital of the World

Buying into popular, political, drug-war rhetoric comes with a high cost in terms of inmate lives, families undermined, and taxpayer dollars. "The United States has the largest prison population in the world, and the highest per-capita incarceration rate... In 2016, 2.2 million Americans have been incarcerated, which means for every 100,000 there are 655 who are currently inmates. Prison, parole, and probation operations generate an $81 billion annual cost to U.S. taxpayers, while police and court costs, bail bond fees, and prison phone fees generate another $100 billion in costs that are paid by individuals.... According to a 2014 Human Rights Watch report, 'tough-on-crime' laws adopted since the 1980s have filled U.S. prisons with mostly nonviolent offenders."[622] The stark facts about American incarceration rates beg the question: Are Americans really more criminalistic than the people of Russia, China, Bolivia, Belgium, Mongolia, Turkestan, Australia or the Philippines? No.

The U.S. War on Drugs: A Trillion Dollar Folly

Gierach Drug Policy Axiom No. 5 holds that "Everything in drug policy works in reverse; good drug policy is counterintuitive." My Drug Policy Axiom No. 6 holds that "The harder we try to suppress drugs, the more they flourish."[623] Sadly, proof of these simple axioms is overwhelming, mounting now for sixty years of UN drug-war and fifty years of United States drug-war. Connecting the dots leads one from drug prohibition policy to drug proliferation reality, accidental overdose and violent turf-war death. The dots and the costly "buck" stop here at the drug policy doorstep.

"Since 1971, America has spent over a trillion dollars enforcing its drug policy, according to research from the University of Pennsylvania. Yet many observers, both liberal and conservative, say the war on drugs has not paid off.... 'We are still in the midst of the most devastating drug epidemic in U.S. history,' according to Vanda Felbab-Brown, senior fellow at the Center for Security, Strategy, and Technology at Brookings Institution. In 2020, overdose deaths in the United States exceeded 90,000,

---

[622] *Wikipedia*, s.v. "Incarceration in the United States," https://en.wikipedia.org/wiki/Incarceration_in_the_United_States.

[623] Gierach Drug Policy Axioms, https://jamesgierach.tumblr.com/post/648356951735091200/gierach-drug-policy-axioms.

compared with 70,630 in 2019, according to research from the Commonwealth Fund."[624]

"Yet, the federal government is spending more money than ever to enforce drug policies. In 1981, the federal budget for drug abuse prevention and control was just over a billion dollars. By 2020, that number had grown to $34.6 billion. When adjusted for inflation, CNBC found that it translates to a 1,090% increase in just 39 years. According to the White House, the national drug control budget is estimated to hit a historic level of $41 billion by 2022. The largest increases in funding are requested to support drug treatment and drug prevention."[625]

Farmers Turned Jailers and "Dick and Jane Go to Jail"

As a grade school youngster, I read about Dick and Jane going to visit the farm, farming then representing the predominant occupation of members of the U.S. Congress. Not so today. Today, many Dick and Janes go to prison down on the farm. Tracy Huling wrote, "In the United States today there are more prisoners than farmers. And while most prisoners in America are from urban communities, most prisons are now in rural areas. During the last two decades, the large-scale use of incarceration to solve social problems has combined with the fall-out of globalization to produce an ominous trend: prisons have become a 'growth industry' in rural America."[626]

Concluding, she noted: "[T]he use of prisons as money-makers for struggling rural communities has become a major force driving criminal justice policy toward *mass incarceration of the urban poor* regardless of policy rationales like rising crime and prison overcrowding. As former New York State legislator Daniel Feldman observed 'When legislators cry "Lock 'em up!' they often mean 'Lock 'em up in my district!'" Indeed, the rural prison boom during the decade of the 1990s occurred at a time of falling crime rates and experience shows that the federal and state governments are reluctant to pull the plug on the many interests that now lobby for and feed off prisons. Allowed to continue, this cycle will have catastrophic consequences for the health and

---

624 Nathaniel Lee, "America has spent over a trillion dollars fighting the war on drugs. 50 years later, drug use in the U.S. is climbing again," CNBC, June 17, 2021, https://www.cnbc.com/2021/06/17/the-us-has-spent-over-a-trillion-dollars-fighting-war-on-drugs.html.

625 Ibid.

626 Tracy Huling, "Building a Prison Economy in Rural America," from *Invisible Punishment: The Collateral Consequences of Mass Imprisonment*, Marc Mauer and Meda Chesney-Lind, Editors (The New Press. 2002), https://www.prisonpolicy.org/scans/building.html.

welfare of individuals, families, and communities in urban and rural areas, and indeed for the nation."[627]

Recognition of this reality long ago, inspired the very unpopular notion embodied in Gierach Drug Policy Axiom No. 10: "The 'good guys' and the 'bad guys' are both aligned on the same side of the line of scrimmage, both in favor of drug prohibition.' The mix of good guy and bad guy drug prohibitionists includes such diverse actors as Al Capone and **William R. Brownfield**, former Assistant U.S. Secretary, Bureau of International Narcotics and Law Enforcement Affairs; Pablo Escobar and **Michael P. Botticelli**, former American drug czar; "El Chapo" Guzmán and **Yury Fedatov**, the late former executive director of the UN Office on Drugs and Crime; **Larry Hoover** and **Rahm Emanuel**, former Chicago mayor. Countless other such pairings seem just as odd and grotesque but drug policy harmonious. Both elements of society — good and bad — are in mutual symbiotic harmony, both feeding lavishly off prohibition stipends, riding what I call "the Drug War Gravy Train." Criminals and police, drug farmers and politicians, drug dealers and prison builders, drug cartel entrepreneurs and drug treaters, gang leaders and CND diplomats, drug soldiers and border patrol agents — all these players, and countless other persons holding drug-related jobs, are riding the same drug-war gravy train. However constructive the work of some of these employments, all drug-war players draw their pay from the same paymaster at the Drug Prohibition Pay Window.

Expressing Unpopular Ideas

Tom Angell, a marijuana legalization proponent and onetime Media Director for LEAP, warned me: If you make that point to LEAP audiences — the good guys and the bad guys are both riding the same drug-war gravy train — I won't give you LEAP speaking gigs. I did, and he didn't. Similarly, periodically I was a featured speaker at Roosevelt University in Chicago regarding drug policy topics. However, once **Kathie Kane-Willis** became director of the Illinois Consortium for Drug Policy at Roosevelt University, I only spoke there once more. Kathie had invited me to speak as a panelist. During the forum, I observed that the good guys (drug treaters, in that instance) and the bad guys (drug dealers) were on the same side of the line of scrimmage, both favoring drug prohibition. **Melody Heaps**, founder of "Treatment Alternatives to Street Crime" (TASC), now called "Treatment Alternatives to Safe Communities," was one

---

[627] Ibid., emphasis added.

of my co-panelists. I was never invited to speak there again, though I favored treatment over law enforcement approaches to the drug problem. And Kathie, in charge of who would speak at the 30th anniversary of America's War on Drugs rally in the Daley Center in 2001, did not allow me to speak there. Ironically, muffled by Kane-Willis, Melody Heaps told me that no judge in Cook County referred more criminal defendants to TASC than my father, Judge Will Gierach.

Be careful what you say, Jim.

Expressing an unpopular notion, ended my speaking career at Reverend Jesse Jackson's **Rainbow PUSH**, too. In 1993, I was invited to speak at one of its breakout meetings during its annual conference. I was speaking to a young, Black audience. I brought my "National Crisis Wheel" prop (p. 191), and I made the point that it was critical that youngsters get "their tools in their toolbox now," meaning get a good education and study, "because one day drugs would be legalized, and the drug business would no longer be a career choice." Never spoke there again. But I continue to maintain that an end to drug prohibition is inevitable. I admit its arrival is slower coming than I expected. Drug-war violence was so bad in the early 1990s, especially in Chicago, I thought the War on Drugs couldn't possibly last much more than a few more years. I was dead wrong.

Drug-Prohibition: A Popular Cancer Destroying Society

Reiterating, the fourth reason it is so difficult to change bad drug policy is because of the nature of politics and drug war: Voters Love Drug War. With bipartisan political support, shamefully supported by popular public opinion, America and the World have allowed this drug-prohibition cancer to feed on its institutions, character, values, virtues, health, safety and future, undermining society and modern civilization. This must stop.

The same intuitive, political, drug-prohibition dynamic cramps the individual's ability to think, reason, and reform. It is the same dynamic that transitioned Trump the Businessman Drug Legalizer into President Trump the Drug Warrior. To the drug dealer, prohibition means profit. To the politician, drug prohibition means votes.

As a candidate running for public office in 1992, Cook County state's attorney, I witnessed the power of intuitive, visceral disdain for drugs, even among progressives like myself. I was invited to speak and beseech the support of a progressive political group, **Independent Voters of Illinois-Independent Precinct Organization** (IVI-

IPO).[628] I delivered a fiery speech calling for drug policy reform to stop Chicago violence, but during the question and answer period, one independent voter asked, "Why don't we do like they do in Saudi Arabia and just cut off the hands of drug dealers?"

Without missing a beat, I fired back, "Good idea! The trouble is — what to do with all the hands?" The audience broke into laughter at my retort, and humor moved my audience's mood from intuitive thinking back toward the progressive side. Yet, the comment evidenced the frustration many voters understandably felt toward the untoward consequences of drug prohibition policy. After my presentation, IVI-IPO endorsed my candidacy for state's attorney.

Historically, voters love the drug war; they're all for it. Even when it is obvious that the drug war makes everything worse: more drugs, more gangs, more guns, more shootings, more overdoses, more police corruption and police brutality, more racist incarceration and contrary consequences, more unaffordable bullet-hole healthcare, more Central American citizens challenging U.S. immigration law, and more taxes. STILL, people love their drug war and refuse to do to drugs what Americans once did to alcohol. They L-E-G-A-L-I-Z-E-D it.

Reason 5: "Good Guys" & "Bad Guys" Both Riding "the Drug War Gravy Train"

Public sentiment against illicit drugs and drug-dealing — coupled with the power of lawmakers to leverage that sentiment — resulted in the enactment of laws, practices, appropriations and grants that financially benefit *the good guys* in their unending drug-war efforts. The good guys economically benefit from the War on Drugs just as surely as the same drug-prohibition laws and policies benefit drug dealers and drug cartels, effectively granting *the bad guys* exclusive, unlicensed control over the gigantic business of supplying mind-altering substances to willing consumers.

Third-Party Drug-War Beneficiaries: Federal, State, Local and Private Sectors

The good guys are a diverse and plentiful army of employees and third-party drug-war beneficiaries. Some work for federal agencies like the Drug Enforcement Agency, U.S.

---

628 *Wikipedia*, s.v. "Independent Voters of Illinois-Independent Precinct Organization," https://en.wikipedia.org/wiki/Independent_Voters_of_Illinois-Independent_Precinct_Organization, accessed March 17, 2023.

Customs, U.S. Border Patrol, the U.S. Postal Service, the U.S. Coast Guard, the Federal Bureau of Investigation, the Central Intelligence Agency, the U.S. Marshalls Office, the U.S. Bureau of Prisons, Alcohol, Tobacco, Firearms and Explosives, U.S. Immigration, the U.S. Department of Justice and U.S. Department of State, just to name a few.

Other drug-war good guys work for state and local police departments, state penitentiaries, county and city jails; others work in crime laboratories, drug courts, pretrial services; others work as probation and parole officers; and still others collect urine samples or administer drug tests. Other drug-war employees and benefactors work in the private sector in furtherance of a drug-free world like the builders of public and private prisons, their subcontractors and office staff, while others labor for drug-free workplace consulting and testing firms. Diplomats and drug-war academicians travel, attend drug conferences, and write papers and reports about drug-war statistics, strategies and successes. And failures.

Fighting the drug war is big business. "Since the War on Drugs began more than 40 years ago, the U.S. government has spent more than $1 trillion on interdiction policies. Spending on the war continues to cost U.S. taxpayers more than $51 billion annually."[629]

More Third Party, Drug-War Beneficiaries: Attorneys and Drug Counselors

Losing an election for Cook County state's attorney was no fun, but it had its bright moments. One such moment was a fellow attorney who told me, "Well, Jim, it was against my economic interests as a criminal defense attorney to vote for you, but I did, because you were right (regarding drug policy)."

Unfortunately, sometimes, the honor of being right can be personally disadvantageous. A few years later in 1997, I sought appointment to a Cook County judgeship. In a field of about 200 applicants, the final cut was made by three judges I knew reasonably well. A fellow prosecutor and then Chief of the Criminal Division of the **Circuit Court of Cook County Thomas R. Fitzgerald**, Chief of the Domestic Relations Division **Timothy C. Evans** and Chief Judge **Donald P. O'Connell**. Despite being

---

[629] Christopher J. Coyne and Abigail R. Hall, "Four Decades and Counting: The Continued Failure of the War on Drugs," *CATO Institute*, note 8, April 12, 2017, https://www.cato.org/policy-analysis/four-decades-counting-continued-failure-war-drugs.

found qualified by every screening bar association, I failed to make the cut. Later after his tenure as Chief Judge, Donald O'Connell explained to me the panel's decision. The Circuit Court of Cook County could not have a judge running around saying "legalize drugs." (It already had one with Judge Richard E. Neville.) Years later still — years filled with unending bad stories about gangs, drugs and violence — I bumped into retired Chief Judge O'Connell crossing a downtown Chicago street. Chief Judge O'Connell simply said, "Well, Jim, it looks like you were right." I replied, "I was." It was another bright spot on a long drug-policy reform road — often a lonely, contentious and disappointing road.

But back to the drug-war gravy train. And as already noted — I get in trouble saying this, but another big group of drug-war employees and benefactors are the drug treaters and counselors. How much money is enough money to spend on drug treatment and drug counseling? No amount of spending is enough. "More" is always the answer, no matter how much we spend. We need more money for drug prevention, drug treatment and drug education, no matter how big the present expenditure number. It is never enough. Incidentally, all politicians are in favor of drug treatment, prevention and education. Me too. That said, treatment dollars are the most productive drug-war dollars spent, but historically 70 percent of the drug-war dollar goes to "the drug soldiers," law enforcement, and 30 percent goes to "the drug saviors," the treaters and counselors.[630] Drug-war counselors and treaters are good people, caring about others, daily trying to rescue others, tirelessly working to help drug users regain self-control, self-respect, self-discipline, and get their lives back. Because this group of people see the voracious harm that drugs can do to individuals, their families and loved ones, drug treaters and drug counselors are one of the most difficult audiences to talk to about legalizing drugs. Drug counselors and drug soldiers, both are tough groups to address, especially if the discussion concerns getting smart about drug policy rather than getting tough.

Drug warriors and drug saviors are the good guys positioned on one side of drug-war gridiron line of scrimmage, and the drug dealers and street gang members are the bad guys positioned and perceived as being on the other side of the line of scrimmage. Yet, both sets of players, almost invariably, favor continuation of the drug war that feeds them in the seemingly endless, deadly drug-war "game," now in overtime. The

---

630 "The Federal Drug Control Budget: New Rhetoric, Same Failed Drug War," *Drug Policy Alliance*, February 2015, https://drugpolicy.org/sites/default/files/DPA_Fact_sheet_Drug_War_Budget_Feb2015.pdf, suggests a 55-45 split, though historically the split is recognized as 70-30.

players on both side of the line of scrimmage benefit from employment, travel, promotional opportunity and other economic benefits of drug-prohibition policy, including pensions for the good guys. Over the years, each side has grown and grown in numbers. Each year there are more and more combatants; each year monetary support and economic reward for each side grows. That must change. As "El Chapo" Guzmán observed, the drug business just grows and grows.[631] Each year too many people are addicted, too many overdose, too many are shot, too many are incarcerated, and too many die. Again, this mutually-rewarding, symbiotic, drug-war relationship must end.[632]

Civil Forfeiture Laws: A Form of Police Abuse

But how do we stop the abusive, gushing flow of drug money to the good guys? We need police. We need drug treaters. Always have, always will. With regard to law enforcement, the answer is not to defund the police. The answer is: remove the economic reward for drug-war policing. Firemen should not get a percent of the burning house they saved, and policemen should not get a cut of the drug money or other property they seized. Section 9, Article VII Local Government of the Illinois Constitutional Convention ended "fee offices," where an officer like a township collector kept a percentage of his tax collections as his fee. Harmfully, this reward norm incentivizes drug-war policing, justifies policing abuses and warps selection of policing priorities.

I hasten to note, elected governmental officials should be free to appropriate and spend as much money as they determine necessary and appropriate for policing services. But such appropriations should be made from the general revenue fund into which confiscated drug money and property should be deposited. Allocation of limited governmental resources for policing purposes should be a thoughtful budgetary decision made by elected officials, not a happenstance resulting from the interplay of incentivized special funds for policing activities with unpredictable revenue production, depending on decisions made by unelected police officials and impacted by whether the fishing for drug money was good in a particular year. Civil forfeiture is a related matter.

---

631 Rolling Stone video, https://www.rollingstone.com/politics/politics-news/watch-el-chapos-exclusive-interview-in-its-17-minute-entirety-35543/, January 12, 2016, accessed March 17, 2023.

632 Betsy Pearl, "Ending the War on Drugs: By the Numbers," *Center for American Progress*, June 27, 2018, https://www.americanprogress.org/article/ending-war-drugs-numbers/.

Police should not get a cut of the money that *might be* the product of the illicit drug business, seized, confiscated and subjected to civil forfeiture proceedings and practices. And the burden of proof of the origin of such confiscated money should be on the government and not the citizen. Use of the forfeiture tool invites recall of the equity court maxim, "Equity abhors a forfeiture." Fortunately, laws limiting and better regulating civil forfeiture practices are coming.[633]

Frontline, as part of its series on the War on Drugs, published an excellent article written by Kyla Dunn that discussed the ins and outs of law enforcement's use and abuse of the forfeiture tool. Kyla Dunn wrote, "It was the passage of the *Comprehensive Crime Control Act of 1984*, part of the Reagan-era ramp-up in the war on drugs, that first made this possible. At a federal level, the law established two new forfeiture funds: one at the U.S. Department of Justice, which gets revenue from forfeitures done by agencies like the Drug Enforcement Agency and the Federal Bureau of Investigation, and another now run by the U.S. Treasury, which gets revenue from agencies like Customs and the Coast Guard. These funds could now be used for forfeiture-related expenses, payments to informants, prison building, equipment purchase, and other general law enforcement purposes.

"But equally important, local law enforcement would now get a piece of the pie. Within the 1984 Act was a provision for so-called 'equitable sharing', which allows local law enforcement agencies to receive a portion of the net proceeds of forfeitures they help make under federal law — and under current policy, that can be up to 80%. Previously, seized assets had been handed over to the federal government in their entirety.

"Immediately following passage of the Act, federal forfeitures increased dramatically. The amount of revenue deposited into the Department of Justice Assets Forfeiture Fund, for example, soared from $27 million in 1985 to $644 million in 1991 — a more than twenty-fold increase. And as forfeitures increased, so did the amount of money flowing back to state and local law enforcement through equitable sharing.

"Some say that because of the resulting windfall, state and local law enforcement has become as addicted to forfeiture as an addict is to drugs — making property seizure no longer a means to an end, but an end in itself. In 1999 alone, approximately $300 million of the $957 million that the Treasury and Justice Department funds took in

---

[633] Anne Teigen and Lucia Bragg, "Evolving Civil Asset Forfeiture Laws," *NCSL, LegisBrief,* Vol. 26, No. 5, February 2018, https://www.ncsl.org/research/civil-and-criminal-justice/evolving-civil-asset-forfeiture-laws.aspx.

went back to the state and local departments that helped with the seizures. And *since 1986, the Department of Justice's equitable sharing program has distributed over $2 billion in cash and property*. Additional revenue comes from forfeitures done under state law, which adds to the total intake. According to a study by the Bureau of Justice Statistics, state and local law enforcement reported receiving a total of over $700 million in drug-related asset forfeiture revenue in 1997 alone with some departments single-handedly taking in several million dollars for their own use.

"Critics agree that the main problem with the civil asset forfeiture laws, before the recent reforms, was the low burden of proof required to seize property. A seizure could be made on the basis of mere suspicion, known as 'probable cause,' (sic) that the property was involved in a crime — and that is no more evidence than is required to obtain a search warrant. No arrest, let alone conviction, was needed. It was then up to the property owner to prove by 'a preponderance of the evidence,' a more difficult standard to meet (sic), that their money, or car, or home, was not bought with drug money or used to commit a drug-related crime, and should be returned.

"But on August 23rd, 2000, after a difficult seven-year campaign by Republican Congressman Henry Hyde from Illinois, the Civil Asset Forfeiture Reform Act finally went into effect — making it more difficult for the federal government to seize property without evidence of wrongdoing. It took a remarkable coalition of conservative and liberal lawmakers to change a law that everyone from the American Civil Liberties Union to the National Rifle Association has recognized as flawed. And while the reforms come too late to help Rudy Ramirez, [who innocently lost $6,000 confiscated from him] they will help to make cases like his rarer.

"Make no mistake about it, the recent reforms do not address the issue that many feel is central to most abuses of civil asset forfeiture: *the financial incentive for law enforcement to make seizures*. Still, the new law will help ensure that legitimate use of a powerful tool in the war on drugs violates the rights of fewer innocent people."[634]

From this review overall, it should be apparent that the drug-war gravy train is a powerful incentive for the good to be bad, a realization that again provides a big reason why it is so difficult to change bad drug policy.

---

[634] Kyla Dunn, "Reining In Forfeiture: Common Sense Reform in the War on Drugs," *Frontline*, part of Frontline's Drug Wars Series, https://www.pbs.org/wgbh/pages/frontline/shows/drugs/special/forfeiture.html, emphasis added, accessed March 17, 2023.

Reason 6: Fear of Change

Americans and voters the world over have insisted that their leaders wage a War on Drugs. In an elective democracy like America, the people get what they want — Drug War!

The Individual's Great Fear

Citizens of the world fear drugs will ruin the life of a loved one — a son, daughter, brother, sister or spouse. Life experience teaches us that drugs are addictive, and addiction can ruin lives. Therefore, drugs are bad. Therefore, outlaw drugs. So goes the thinking. The horror stories of drug addiction and blood-soaked violence associated with the drug trade fill seats in movie theaters and home recliners drawn near televisions.

The Politician's Greatest Fear

Politicians and candidates for public office fear losing election, or reelection, if their public decisions or positions are seen by voters as soft on drugs or crime. These labels instill fear in the hearts and minds of elected public officials like none other, because nothing is more important to a politician than retaining their seat, or so it seems.

The public's fear of the harm that drugs can do and the politicians' fear of the loss of election are parallel rails, never far apart, one rail a public sentiment and the other a public official priority. That fear is so great that politicians and voters have accepted extraordinary anti-drug measures to prevent drug use and sales. Those stomach-turning measures include: criminalization of millions of law-abiding citizens except for consensual, adult, drug behavior; revamping of the police mission from serving and protecting to morality policing; imposition of draconian prison sentences like the 100:1 crack cocaine versus powered cocaine sentencing disparity; adoption of three-time loser laws; acceptance of scared-straight[635] drug-treatment programs for kids; public service announcements like this is your brain on drugs; heavy-handed policing; and preservation of racial-disparity in the criminal justice system.

Drug fear is so powerful it justifies higher taxes for prisons and brings D.A.R.E. "how to do, what not to do" educational programs into our schools. Brutal policing and rough handling of druggies is okay because they're just junkies and addicts.

---

635 Derek Gilna, "'Scared Straight' Programs are Counterproductive," *Prison Legal News*, June 3, 2016, https://www.prisonlegalnews.org/news/2016/jun/3/scared-straight-programs-are-counterproductive/.

Shrinking constitutional rights, civil forfeiture of unexplained cash, shifting the burden of proof from the government to the individual to prove where a suspect got the money, no-knock police raids on homes, loss of an expectation of privacy in one's own car, militarized police departments, stop and frisk pat downs justified on suspicion alone, and police departments sharing drug-war spoils. It's all okay. This is war — drug war.

Fear of the Unknown: A New Drug Policy Paradigm

An international set of drug-war makers, enforcers, and reformers frequent Vienna, Austria, and regularly attend the doings of the Commission on Narcotic Drugs there. They have fears, too. "If we didn't have the UN drug conventions what would take their place?" some wonder. Would nations impose even more restrictive laws, harsher punishments, and even more human-rights intrusive drug policy paradigms? Would there be more death penalty, drug crime punishment? Fear of the unknown can be greater than fear of the known. And fear need not be rational, only palpable. Take the statement of a Vienna regular, who declared in 2015, "Cannabis is one of the most dangerous drugs."[636] The statement was sincerely made by **Per Johansson** who worked as a Secretary General for the National Association for a Drug-Free Society (RNS) since the early 1990s. Unfortunately, fear such as this protects and preserves unworkable UN drug conventions.

Somehow, the thoughtful work of knowledgeable and trained personnel at the WHO, who recommended the rescheduling of cannabis over two years ago, must displace the deep-seeded, fears of the less brave Vienna operatives. In the same video, another Vienna participant expressed fear of diverging from the known, however bad it may be. Dr. Peter van Wulffen of the Netherlands said, "If we are going to create new treaties today, it will be a long road and the outcome will be uncertain."[637]

President Franklin Delano Roosevelt stated the truth during his first inaugural address delivered on March 4, 1933, when he said, "So, first of all, let me assert my firm belief that the only thing we have to fear is... fear itself..." However, unlike Roosevelt's war assessment, today, we do have more to worry about than just fear itself. We have

---

[636] "An end to the UN as we know it?" *Cannabis News Network*, video, March 15, 2015, Commission on Narcotic Drugs, Vienna, Austria, YouTube, https://youtu.be/40vsGUxCbjc, first few seconds.

[637] Ibid., minute 4:59.

three UN drug conventions that guarantee more harm and more heartaches than all the harm-reduction strategies in the world can muster.

The world drug problem is UN-gospel codified into three, drug-prohibition conventions. Equally tragic, the same United Nations' gospel is at the core of many global crises. Hostility, inhumanity, intolerance, lawlessness, unfairness, hate, harm, affliction, addiction, death and hopelessness — all these cancers on civilization and humanity are encapsulated in the monolithic World War on Drugs — preserved and protected by fear.

Reason 7: Fourth Estate Leaders Are Just Like Us

There is a seventh reason it is difficult to change bad drug policy. The opinion-makers who sit on editorial boards across America and around the world use the power of the pen to change minds, collectively, public opinion. In some dimension, the power of the pen is more powerful than any army, president or preacher. And sometimes editorial thought is ahead of the crowd, introducing new ideas and views that may be still out of sight to many people. Doing so, newspaper leaders must not be so far ahead of the crowd that individuals in the crowd cannot see their leader to follow; beyond the horizon leadership is hard to follow. One of my shortcomings perhaps. Yet, editors and opinion-makers of the "**Fourth Estate**" are just people, too. Like you and I — they hold in their heads and hearts a set of beliefs, subliminal prejudices, a collection of life experiences and lessons learned, and possess a need for acceptance, understanding and a paycheck.

Within a number of years of my Chicago drug-policy reform political campaigns (1992-94), Chicago's two great newspapers, whether influenced by my efforts or not, both powerfully editorialized against the War on Drugs. Each newspaper bravely departed from then-prevailing public opinion. Did either Chicago newspaper call for the outright legalization of drugs? Well, no. Neither newspaper called for legalized drug markets, licensed drug dealers, drug sales from fixed places of business, government-inspected drugs or controlled, regulated and legal drug markets. But the editorial boards of each newspaper nudged their readers to new, higher ground. Each Chicago newspaper advanced the idea that the prohibition paradigm needed review and reform.

On January 29, 1996, the *Chicago Tribune* posited the question, "The war on drugs: Worth the price?" and suggested it was time for another Wickersham Commission like that which preceded the end of alcohol Prohibition. "The National Commision on Law Observance and Enforcement," more commonly known as the Wicker-ham Commission, was a committee established by the U.S. President Herbert Hoover, on May 20, 1929, in recognition that "evasion of the law was widespread and that prohibition had fueled the growth of organized crime."[638]

A *Chicago Tribune* editorial author, on January 29, 1996, pointed out that "suspicion grows that America is not only losing its war on drugs but the fighting of it is doing more damage to society than the harmful effects of the drugs themselves. Calls for a reappraisal now come from all points of the political compass, including such conservatives as Nobel laureate Milton Friedman and publisher William F. Buckley. Jr."

Equally bravely and awakening, on June 22, 2010, a *Chicago Sun-Times* editorial said, "When will we accept that America's war on drugs is over — we lost — and it's time to get real about our drug laws. Medical marijuana should be legalized. Pot more generally should be decriminalized. And the carnage in our streets and in Mexico begs that we rethink our national's approach to the sale and use of more serious drugs as well." ("Save marijuana for the ailing," *Chicago Sun-Times*, editorial, June 22, 2010)[639]

Bravo! I say, to both Chicago newspapers for broaching the obvious need to re-examine the World War on Drugs — twenty-five years ago for the *Chicago Tribune*, and eleven years ago for the *Chicago Sun-Times*. But who's carrying the ball now? Where's the follow-up?

---

[638] *Wikipedia*, s.b. "Wickersham Commission," https://en.wikipedia.org/wiki/Wickersham_Commission

[639] The Media Awareness Project, http://www.mapinc.org/drugnews/v10/n000/a018.html?1555.

Part Four - The Hard to Swallow
Silver Bullet Solution

Chapter 12 – Running for Public Office
Sounding Soft on Drugs

In 1992, I ran for state's attorney of Cook County that includes Chicago and its suburbs in a Democratic primary election on the idea of taking the profit out of the drug business to stop crime. Two years later, in 1994, I ran for governor of Illinois in a Democratic primary election on the same idea, among others. Several experiences during those campaigns struck me so powerfully, I'll never forget.

"Why Should that Housekeeper Vote for You?"

During my 1992 campaign for state's attorney, election law required that I collect the signatures of thousands of qualified voters to get my name printed on the primary ballot. I was collecting signatures on nominating petitions outside a Walgreens drug store about a mile from Reverend Jesse Jackson's Operation Push headquarters. A middle-aged, well-dressed, African American man approached me, and I reached out my hand and introduced myself: "Hi. I'm Jim Gierach. I'm running for state's attorney of Cook County to take the profit out of drugs to take crime off our streets." Expressionless and speechless, the man ignored my outstretched hand, turned and walked into the drugstore without a word.

Ugh. I thought to myself. *Not very friendly. Maybe he lost a loved one to drugs, or maybe he doesn't like white people. I'm the only white person around. Jim, maybe you should leave. No, I'm not leaving.* I continued collecting signatures wondering when that man would come back out of the store and how he would behave. It seemed he was in the store a long time. Finally, he came out, walked right up to me and said, "What did you say to me?"

I repeated my words verbatim, "I'm Jim Gierach. I'm running for state's attorney of Cook County to take the profit out of drugs to take crime off our streets."

"Let me ask you a question," he said. "A single woman, an African American mom with four kids works as a domestic and brings home $400 a week. Her oldest child is 16 sixteen years old, sells drugs, and brings home $600 a week that he gives to her. Tell me — why should that woman vote for you?"

Wow. I tried to fashion a good response but there was none, really. "It's dangerous for her son... there's no future in it... there has to be a better way to earn money." The man listened attentively, both of us unsatisfied with my answer, but he could see I cared. I wanted to help. I was trying to change the status quo. Concluding our brief exchange, he reached for my clipboard, said "Give me that," and signed my petition. "Thank you, sir." I was learning, understanding. Mulling over the experience, words of wisdom often spoken by my father, Judge Will Gierach, came to mind. "If you understand the economics of a situation, then you understand the politics of the situation."

"Hey, Man, What's We Gonna Do for A Living?"

Different day, same 1992 political campaign. I had just visited with Reverend Leonard DeVille, pastor of Alpha Temple Baptist Church located on Chicago's South Side and also a Chicago alderman. Leaving his church, I walked across a large athletic field, alone, in the high-crime Englewood community. It was daylight. A hundred yards in front of me, I saw two, African American young men coming directly toward me. I wondered — "Am I safe?" As the distance closed between us, I could see one youth was wearing a large, gold chain around his neck supporting a big, gold dollar sign. The other youth wore a matching gold chain but a large, gold gun replica hung from his chain.

"Hey man, what you doing here?" one youngster asked me as we met.

"Hi guys. I'm campaigning." Reaching out my hand, "I'm Jim Gierach. I'm running for state's attorney of Cook County to take the profit out of drugs, and crime off our streets."

"Hey, man, what's we gonna do for a living?" one of them replied.

"I don't know but something other than selling drugs. One day drugs will be legalized, and you'll have to find something else to do to earn a living anyway."

Once we started chatting, they weren't afraid of me, and I was not afraid of them. Initially, they probably thought anybody out there in Englewood saying something like that had to be touched in the head. I recognized they asked me a reasonable, thoughtful question. Like my Walgreens' petition-signer, the reality was: drug prohibition offered an opportunity to make money, more money than the alternatives, and very few other opportunities existed there.

The 1993 Chicago Gang Summit

A third campaign experience equally daunted me. Two years later, I was running for governor of Illinois. Not unexpectedly, I lost my primary election for Cook County state's attorney in March 1992. But still — the power of a good idea (drug policy reform) is supposed to prevail. In the surreal realm of poetry it is written, "How weak an arm may turn the iron helm of fate"[640] and "The pen is mightier than the sword."[641] On the streets of the gun-laden, real world, it needs to be written, "Drug legalization stops violent crime."

John Flood, union head of the Combined Counties Police Association, came to me after my 1992 defeat and said, "You were right about drugs and crime. Your problem — you were advocating too big an idea for such a low-level office. You needed a bigger platform. You should run for governor on your drug policy reform agenda." I knew John because his union newspaper, *Illinois Police and Sheriff's News,* often published my drug policy articles.[642]

I told John Flood it was preposterous to think I could run for governor. I lacked any of the essentials that media gatekeepers look to when deciding whether a candidate is electable. Failing that credential — regardless of message — a candidate can expect little campaign coverage. I had no campaign chest, held no public office, controlled no government contracts, could tout no bigwig politician endorsements, lacked an identifiable political base, and possessed meager name recognition though I had just collected a **Ross Perot**-like 14-percent of the vote in a four-way race for state's attorney. It was surprising I did as well as I did given that just days before the election, the *Chicago Sun-Times* told Cook County voters on page one that I would receive 1 percent of the vote according to polling. It made no sense to run for Illinois governor in the March 1994 Democratic primary election.

[640] James Russell Lowell, "The Present Crisis," https://poets.org/poem/present-crisis.

[641] *Wikipedia,* s.v. "The pen is mightier than the sword," https://en.wikipedia.org/wiki/ The_pen_is_mightier_than_the_sword.

[642] E.g. Gierach Blogs, *Tumblr,* https://jamesgierach.tumblr.com/post/672663834211876864/illinois-police-and-sheriffs-news-published-by.

But late October 1993 horrific violence continued to enshroud Chicago. Nationally, violent crime was so bad that gang members organized a series of national gang summits to bring rival gang factions together to discuss their future concerns and advance their interests. Upper echelon gang leaders realized that violence was bad for the drug business. Chicago hosted one such gang summit as reported in the Washington Post.[643] *The New York Times* also covered the story along with a photo taken by its reporter Steve Kagan who caught me talking with gang members in Chicago.

At the time of Chicago's 1993 gang summit, Chicago was regularly experiencing more than 900 murders per year,[644] a major factor prompting my state's attorney run and my advocacy of drug policy reform to stop it. Continuing bloodshed got the better of me, and I decided to follow John Flood's advice and run for governor and take my message to the people of Illinois.

Just months before the October Chicago gang summit in March 1993, *USA Today* published my call to Take "profit out of drug dealing" (*USA TODAY,* March 8, 1993)[645] and in May 1993, the American Bar Association Journal published my proposal for "An Economic Attack on Drugs" *ABA Journal,* May 1993 and an opposing view, "Drug Policy for Results," by Roger Conner.[646]

The Chicago gang summit provided a perfect opportunity for me to take my anti-drug economic message to the lion's den. Predictably, politicians stayed as far removed as possible from the October 1993 national gang summit held in Chicago, but I was drawn to it. These were the people who I wanted to reach, redirect and put out of an illegal business. I made a one-page handout, one side displayed the *USA Today* article and the other side my proposed "Economic Attack on Illicit Drugs," and I headed to the gang summit held at Reverend Jesse Jackson's, Operation Push headquarters. Reporter Steve Kagan's photo of me working the gang summit caught the irony of what I was doing — taking a drug legalization message to a drug-dealer convocation.

---

643 Lynne Duke, "Summit Brings Together Gang Members, Black Elders," *The Washington Post,* October 24, 1993, https://www.washingtonpost.com/archive/politics/1993/10/25/summit-brings-together-gang-members-black-elders/a8abc997-4b37-4367-ab64-0e76ef6ccd47/.

644 Andy Grimm and Tom Schuba, "Murders At 25-Year High: 'It Feels Different Now,'" *Chicago Sun-Times,* January 3, 2022, https://chicago.suntimes.com/crime/2022/1/3/22858995/chicago-violence-dangerous-murders-per-capita-2021-2020-surge-garfield-park-police-lori-lightfoot.

645 Gierach, James E., "Take the profit out of drug-dealing," https://jamesgierach.tumblr.com/ post/67535 8022616367104.

646 Gierach, James E., "An Economic Attack on Illicit Drugs," *ABA Journal,* Vol. 79, No. 5 (MAY 1993), p. 95, https://www.jstor.org/stable/27832980?refreqid=excelsior%3A245f1107600dce8270bae874a9085d59.

The Chicago gang summit provided me a third unforgettable campaign interaction.

Inside Operation Push crowded with gang members, I passed out my handout and visited with young gang members. Eventually, I ran across a handsome, successful looking, Black man in his thirties or forties. I introduced myself and gave him a copy of my handout. The man carefully examined it front and back, locked his eyes on me and proceeded to tear my handout in half, then in four quarters, then eights and dropped the pieces to the floor never blinking or losing his penetrating eye-contact with me. Not a further word was exchanged. But if a look could kill, I'd have been dead. The interesting facet of the interaction to me was that he knew, and I knew, the economic power of the idea I was advocating and what it meant for the future of illicit drug-dealing. But was America unique in its reaction to my new societal, prohibition/economic rules?

Afghan, Colombian, Peruvian and Bolivian Farmers in the Same Boat

Now, thirty years later and seasoned by some first-hand, UN international drug experience, I realized that the indigent farmer planting poppies in Afghanistan and the coca plant in Colombia, Bolivia and Peru, could give very similar explanations for their chosen work. Drug prohibition creates a new set of rules and economic realities that steer the life and livelihood of many people. But politically for me in the 1990s, as now, drug policy reform — the Silver Bullet Solution — was a tough sell. And it was equally tough getting help from the press to deliver my message.

Although I was able to buy some television time in my 1992 race for Cook County state's attorney and command 14 percent of the vote in a four-way race, that advantage and degree of voter recognition — like my part in writing the 1970 *Illinois Constitution* as the youngest elected delegate to the Sixth Illinois Constitutional Convention — would not get me into the first televised gubernatorial debates in 1994. In both my state's attorney and gubernatorial races — it was a continuing struggle to attract public attention or media coverage.[647]

---

[647] Greg Hinz, "Snob Appeal, In Its Non-coverage of Fringe Candidate, the *Trib* Didn't Do As It Said," *Chicago*, May 1994, https://jamesgierach.tumblr.com/post/675360404480950272.

Can We Expect Armed Raids on the Suburbs?

As a state's attorney candidate in 1992, there was only one question I feared some smart reporter would ask me. "Well, Mr. Gierach, if drugs were legalized and we took the profit out of drugs, as you advocate, can we expect roving bands of armed, black gang members striking in the white suburbs? Are these armed, Black and brown gangbangers and uneducated drug dealers — accustomed to fat rolls of cash, flashy cars, pretty girls and the good life — coming to the suburbs to replace their lost drug revenues with plunder from armed robberies and home invasions?"

The question never came. The question still plays in my mind in 2022 as much of America removed marijuana revenues, billions of dollars — from drug dealer shelves. Escalating crime in well-to-do neighborhoods has me wondering. Witness the numbers of carjackings, Mag Mile robberies, expressway shootings and catalytic converter thefts. Is marijuana legalization a factor in increased nice-neighborhood crime? Is the scenario I contemplated thirty years ago and feared a reporter would ask then coming home to roost in reality now?

My Personal Safety

Speaking of fears — as a candidate talking about taking the profit out of drugs — I occasional thought about my personal safety. Are drug dealers fearing drug legalization destroying their business going to shoot me? I told my friend Reverend Leonard DeVille about my thought the day of the **Bud Billiken Day Parade** in Chicago. For hours I screamed admonitions to a million parade attendees over a bullhorn as I led Float No. 62 (p. 260) south down Martin Luther King Drive — "Stop the killing. Bankrupt drug dealers. Legalize Drugs. Send the kids back to school. Let's take the profit out of drugs..." Unconstrained rap without a musical background — communication — just Jim speaking directly to mankind lining the roadways for hours. No media gatekeepers. No filters. Freedom to speak and an opportunity for my hopeful message to be heard. Repeatedly, the message was greeted with much applause, shouts and smiles. Like my 1992 appearance at a Chicago West Side church filled to overflowing capacity with political leaders and parishioners, where my handler/driver Jim Exum (phonetic) observed on our leaving — "Do you realize you [my drug policy message actually] received a bigger round of applause than Carol Moseley Braun, a popular U.S. senate candidate, and soon to become the first African-American U.S. senator?"

People know the truth when, and if, they get to hear it.

The "Ministers Against the Drug War" float I conceived, built, and led down Dr. Martin Luther King Drive won an award. And I wasn't shot. Sagely, Reverend DeVille said, "You don't have to worry about your safety. You have no power. You can't hurt drug dealers. If you were U.S. Congressman Bobby Rush, and you said what you say, then maybe you'd have something to worry about." Reverend DeVille was right. I was never in any danger.

The Illinois Governor's Race

In March 1994, I lost my primary race for Illinois governor. I ran on a platform of drug policy reform to stop the violence, defund gangs, regain control of drugs, stop building prisons, increase school funding, and start making illicit drugs legally available to drug addicts only — the latter campaign plank premised on the idea that addicts reportedly represented 80 percent of the illicit drug business.[648] My advocacy for "the British system" (Dr. John Marks heroin maintenance program operated in Liverpool, England, a medical program where heroin was dispensed to clientele addicted to it) and "legalized drugs for addicts only" recognized that the public was frightened of drugs and looked askance on anyone brandishing soft on drugs political rhetoric. But I thought it was a good idea, politicly brave — yet far short of calling for the outright legalization of drug markets for all adults.

Drug policy expert **Mark Kleiman**, who would later shepherd the state of Washington's marijuana legalization program,[649] asserted that persons addicted to drugs represented 80 percent of the illicit drug business. If that were true — by legalizing drugs for addicts *only*, I could remove 80 percent of the money from illicit drug markets without exposing the general adult population to the perceived risk of legalized drugs.

Ten years or more after my gubernatorial run, as a speaker volunteering for LEAP, I debated Mark at a University of Maryland forum. Then advocating "legalized drugs for addicts only," I used the statistic from his book to demonstrate that illicit drug consumption by persons addicted to drugs accounted for the lion's share of the illicit drug business. In 1992, he wrote, "As a rule of thumb, 20 percent of the users of any given drug account for 80 percent of the volume." By Mark's formula and some estimates of the global drug trade at $500 billion annually, my middle-ground drug policy

---

[648] Mark A.R. Kleiman, *Against Excess: Drug Policy for Results* (New York: Basic Books, 1992), p. 391.

[649] Christopher Hurley, "Professor advises Washington state in regulation of marijuana," *Daily Bruin*, September 3, 2013, https://dailybruin.com/2013/09/03/professor-advises-washington-state-in-regulation-of-marijuana.

idea would take $400 billion out of the hands of local dealers and transnational drug cartels without legalizing drugs for the general population and sending kids the "wrong message" that drug use was okay.

Nevertheless, whether my "Silver Bullet" idea was a great idea, or not — to stop the violence, defund gangs, regain control of drugs, stop building prisons, and start making illicit drugs legally available to drug addicts only — it was a difficult message to sell to voters and opinion-makers. Nevertheless, I branded myself, "Illinois' First Drug Policy Reform Governor,"[650] a label more successfully worn by Governor J.B. Pritzker who would lead Illinois to legalize recreational marijuana twenty-six years later.[651]

Good Publicity: Key to Political Success

Newspapers spread the news of my candidacy with headlines like: "Plan to legalize drugs exiles Gierach to 'fringe' status,"[652] and, two years earlier, "Candidate urges giving drugs to criminals,"[653] and "Give addicts drugs to stop crime, says candidate."[654]

Despite the fun some columnists and headline writers had with my advocacy, some positive words about my candidacy reached the public. Ray R. Coffey, a *Chicago Sun-Times* columnist, wrote: "'Gierach the Unknown' has come up with what strikes me as the brightest, freshest, most welcome idea I've heard yet in this campaign season,"[655] a proposal for a "Yes" or "No" debate with candidates asking each other questions. And columnist **Jack Mabley** wrote "The best speech... was by a man who doesn't have a chance of winning the nomination. He is James E. Gierach a municipal attorney from the south suburbs." Regardless of some good press and receiving 14 percent of the Democratic Cook County vote two years earlier, I was excluded from televised

---

650 Campaign photo, Gierach "Illinois' First Drug Policy Reform Governor," https://jamesgierach.tumblr.com/post/675368392537112576.

651 Robert McCoppin, "Legal marijuana is coming to Illinois as Gov. Pritzker signs bill he calls an 'important and overdue change to our state,'" *Chicago Tribune*, June 25, 2019, https://www.chicagotribune.com/news/breaking/ct-governor-to-sign-recreational-marijuana-law-20190624-ee2bswlsq5eqvkcbuq6oz6id5i-story.html.

652 Thomas Hardy, "Plan to legalize drugs exiles Gierach to 'fringe' status," *Chicago Tribune*, December 19, 1993.

653 Thomas Hardy, *Chicago Tribune*, "Candidate urges giving drugs to criminals," October 15, 1991.

654 Lynn Sweet, *Chicago Sun-Times*, "Give addicts drugs to stop crime, says candidate," November 19, 1991.

655 Ray R. Coffey, "Ok, Pols, Let's Have A Simple Yes or No," *Chicago Sun-Times*, January 17, 1994, press release date.

debates and locked out of the state capitol where a multicast gubernatorial debate was being held and sponsored by Illinois News Network.[656] *Chicago Tribune* columnist Jon Margolis wrote about my exclusion.

Gierach Excluded from Television and Radio Debates

Margolis wrote: "Okay, as outrages go this one will not shake the pillars of Western Civilization. Still, an outrage is an outrage, and we have one right here in Illinois. As are so many outrages, this one is being perpetrated by proper and respectable people. In fact, the next installment, scheduled for this evening, is being perpetrated by a news agency.... [W]hen [private organizations] [**Illinois News Network** in this case] choose to sponsor candidate debates, they take on a quasi-official responsibility. They become the major conduit through which the candidates make themselves and their views known to the electorate.

"That's why it was wrong for the Chicago Bar Association [CBA] to cancel its debate last week rather than allow James Gierach to join Attorney General Roland Burris, Comptroller Dawn Clark Netsch and Cook County Board President Richard Phelan in a candidate forum. And it is why the Illinois News Network is even more wrong to insist on keeping Gierach from the stage tonight, complete with threats of tight security — What are they afraid of? An unconventional idea? — designed to bar him from the hearing room in the state Capitol, which is his as much as the network's.

"Gierach is not an irresponsible person. He's a lawyer, the municipal attorney for some local governments and the author of articles that have appeared in respected magazines and newspapers. Nor, with one exception, are his views out of the main-stream. The exception is his contention that the drug laws ought to be changed so that drug use is treated as a problem, not a crime."[657]

The crescendo of media support to let Gierach debate — akin to Jean Harlow's shoutout for "Mr. Smith" played by Jimmy Stewart, "Let him speak!"[658] — was heart-warming but a sidelight to the drug policy reform message of my campaign, and less than sincere in action than in words.

---

[656] Thomas Hardy and Peter Kendall, "Quinn comes to the aid of Gierach," *Chicago Tribune*, February 21, 1994, https://www.chicagotribune.com/news/ct-xpm-1994-02-21-9402240002-story.html.

[657] Jon Margolis, "Democratic hopefuls' debate ought tone more democratic," *Chicago Tribune*, February 22, 1994.

[658] *Mr. Smith Goes to Washington*, "Let him speak!" https://youtu.be/rPvbHeufC9Q.

Chicago columnist Greg Hinz hit the nail on the head writing later about the hypocrisy and missed message.[659] He wrote, "On February 22nd, the state's leading newspaper went into full snit over the fact James Gierach, a drug policy zealot and then candidate for the Democratic nomination for governor, was being barred from the night's Illinois News Network radio debate on grounds of his low standing in the polls.... How did the *Tribune* follow its own advice? Mostly by ignoring it. In their February 23rd story on the INN debate, *Trib* reporters Peter Kendall and and Rick Pearson devoted four paragraphs out of 35 to Gierach. All four were about his attempt to crash the event; not one word was written about Gierach's views on drugs or anything else. The next day after another debate, this on WBBM-TV, *Trib* political writer Thomas Hardy didn't even mention Gierach. Gierach was shut out of that event, too, but Hardy's lead paragraph referred to only 'the three Democrats competing for the Democratic nomination.' On Sunday March sixth, the *Tribune* endorsed Illinois comptroller Dawn Clark Netsch for governor. The editorial discussed her strengths and flaws, as well as those of Illinois attorney general Roland Burris and Cook County Board president Richard Phelan. Gierach's name and views somehow didn't come up at all."

Greg Hinz asked *Tribune* editorial page editor N. Don Wycliff about the certain contradiction between what the *Trib* said and what it did. Wycliffe chuckled and said, "I don't want to talk about it," to which Hinz commented, "Sometimes there is nothing you can say."[660]

Initially, I was included in the first televised debate sponsored and run by the Chicago Bar Association (CBA), but a few days before in another CBA non-televised forum where all gubernatorial candidates participated, I referred to Cook County Board President Phelan as "Mr. Tax." I so dubbed him because of the ambitious Cook County Jail construction program occurring on his watch that had doubled the bonded indebtedness of Cook County. Within an hour of the debate and before I could drive back to my suburban law office, the CBA notified my office that the CBA televised debate scheduled for a few days later was canceled, would be rescheduled, and I was no longer invited. Incidentally, Richard Phelan was a former president of the Chicago Bar Association (CBA).

---

[659] Greg Hinz, "Snob Appeal, In Its Non-coverage of Fringe Candidate, the *Trib* Didn't Do As It Said," *Chicago*, May 1994, https://jamesgierach.tumblr.com/post/675360404480950272.

[660] Ibid.

Gierach Views Mainstream with One Exception

As a candidate pushing to the fringe by the media at a time in the early 1990s when anything other than hang 'em high and get tough on crime and drugs was radical, I complained to the *Chicago Sun-Times* about poor coverage of my gubernatorial race. **Mark Hornung**, then editor of its editorial page, good-naturedly advised me, "If you don't like it, buy your own newspaper." I made the same complaint to **Jack Fuller**, Editor of the *Chicago Tribune* and who would later become head of Tribune Publishing, part of **Tribune Media**, explaining I was trying to get an idea out to the public regarding drug policy reform. Memorably, he advised, "An election is the worst time to get an idea out. Voters think you're just saying that to get votes." Lol (laughing out loud). Oh, the fun and insight offered by the world of politics and media. Who in their right mind, politically in the early 1990s, would think they could "get votes" by calling for an increase in the state income tax to better fund education, advocating a moratorium on prison construction, and endorsing some version of drug legalization?[661]

Well, there are many, many more stories to my two years of running for public office on the idea of drug policy reform in Chicago, Cook County and Illinois, but I won't digress further. The purpose of this manuscript is to arouse public opinion against the war on drugs, because of its futility, failings, and counterproductive harm generation. The purpose is to inform and instigate drug policy reform. I would simply say that from about 1990 to 2012, I spent my life trying to arouse public opinion against the failed and counterproductive War on Drugs. I utilized every lever and idea that came to mind. I sowed seeds in political venues, business and professional organizations, college and university classrooms, and student groups with audiences often provided by LEAP and Students for a Sensible Drug Policy (SSDP). I did guest interviews on "Top 100" talk radio shows often arranged by Whitney Garlinghouse, an energetic and very able LEAP volunteer. I wrote frequent articles, columns and letters

---

[661] Repeatedly, I implored Chicago's two great newspapers to take up the drug policy reform cause earlier, writing to their publishers and editors occasionally. And in one August 1993 instance, letters provoked a thoughtful response from John W. Madigan, publisher and president of the *Chicago Tribune,* https://www.tumblr.com/jamesgierach/675378572673875968.

to the editor that were published in many U.S. venues and elsewhere in several languages. I utilized various other initiatives and strategies, including float-building,[662] parade-marching, designing of a large "End the Drug War To Stop the Killing" banner,[663] a billboard,[664] poetry,[665] debates, a Gierach-hosted cable television series,[666] a blog,[667] and creation of the "The Drug Corner," a nonprofit organization whose "Statement of Purpose" espoused laudable drug policy reform objectives supported by responsible directors and credible people.[668] My efforts, letters and articles were often directed to, and sometimes aimed at, political and religious leaders. I encouraged many leaders, including popes, cardinals and priests, editors, broadcasters, columnists, politicians, and candidates for president of the United States, to take up the drug policy issue.[669] Always, the aim of my efforts was to mount public opinion against the War on Drugs, the heart of so many crises. Until 2012, my efforts were limited to changing domestic drug policies of the United States.

However, in 2012 my drug policy orientation shifted from national to international. Thanks to opportunities afforded me by LEAP, **México Unido Contra la Delincuencia** (MUCD), Michael Krawitz, the **Transnational Radical Party** (a human rights NGO), the ACLU, and others. Quickly, I learned that the root-cause of bad drug policy, globally, was UN "drug-control" conventions. Three UN drug conven-

---

[662] Parade Float, State's Attorney Race, see photo section; and Bud Billiken Day Parade Float, "Ministers Against the Drug War," see photo section.

[663] Banner, "End the Drug War To Stop the Killing," https://jamesgierach.tumblr.com/ post/6533421 46776170496.

[664] Billboard, "Schools Not Jails — End the Drug War," https://jamesgierach.tumblr.com/ post/67542366 3305162752.

[665] Poetic Effort, Gierach, James E., "Stop the Killing," 2007, update in 2010, https://jamesgierach.tumblr.com/ post/675380421887934464.

[666] "Chicago's War on Drugs," CAN-TV, 13 weekly shows produced and hosted by Jim Gierach with guests, e.g. Cook County Board President Toni Preckwinkle, https://jamesgierach.tumblr.com/post/ 675064155419623424/chicago-war-on-drugs-with-toni-preckwinklemp4.

[667] "Gierach Blogs," opinion, thought and cross-examination, https://jamesgierach.tumblr.com/page/2.

[668] "Statement of Purpose," The Drug Corner, an Illinois not-for-profit organization, https://jamesgierach. tumblr.com/post/667933174743154688.

[669] Gierach, James E., "Presidential Aspirants, A Question Please," October, 1995, https://jamesgierach.tumblr. com/post/675379907969302528; Pres. Clinton letter, December 28, 1994, https://jamesgierach. tumblr.com/ post/673207829595914240.

tions afflicted the world with the worst of all possible drug policy choices — prohibition, a policy deeply rooted in intolerance, criminalization, incarceration and assorted harms. I was learning that kids across America were being shot long-distance with bullets (policy decisions) fired from Vienna, Austria, home of the Commission on Narcotic Drugs and other UN drug-prohibition agencies. Startlingly, the incentive to make drug-prohibition bullets globally emanated from bad drug policy guarded by the United Nations. I was learning that UN drug conventions were the foundation and fountainhead of "The World War on Drugs." It was an eye-opening discovery.

Part Five - An International Effort to "End the War on Drugs"

Chapter 13 - Mexico City 2012, MUCD

On February 15, 2012, at the invitation of **México Unido Contra la Delincuencia (MUCD)**, a respected Mexican NGO, I was a guest speaker in Mexico City. About thirty drug policy speakers were assembled from around the world to discuss global drug policy and its untoward consequences, because lawlessness held a death grip on the people of Mexico, evidenced by over 100,000 people murdered and tens of thousands of people missing. The Associated Press noticed. "Ten years after Mexico declared a war on drugs, the offensive has left some major drug cartels splintered and many old-line kingpins like Joaquin 'El Chapo' Guzmán in jail, but done little to reduce crime or violence in the nation's roughest regions. Some say the war has been a crucial, but flawed, effort. Others argue the offensive begun by then-President Felipe Calderon on Dec. 11, 2006, unleashed an unnecessary tragedy with more than 100,000 people dead and about 30,000 missing - a toll comparable to the Central American civil wars of the 1980s."[670]

The War on Drugs: the U.N./Al Capone Drug Policy Paradigm

The auditorium where the Mexico City event was held was filled with people who had traveled from near and far across Mexico, and far beyond, in hopes of finding a strategy to stop the killing and disappearance of people. Because this was my first opportunity to speak outside the United States regarding the failings of global drug policy, it was the first time I tied the horrific consequences of global drug prohibition policy to the United Nations, connecting its policy of lawless prohibition to the Al Capone/Alcohol Prohibition Era. The huge backdrop illuminating the auditorium stage during my

---

[670] "100,000 dead, 30,000 missing: Mexico's war on drugs turns 10," *The Associated Press*, December 11, 2016, republished by CBS News, https://www.cbsnews.com/news/100000-dead-30000-missing-mexico-war-on-drugs-turns-10/.

presentation was entitled, "The War on Drugs: the U.N./Al Capone Drug Policy Paradigm."

Speakers were grouped into panels, each with a moderator. On stage with me were fellow panelists Sergio Ferragut, an author and expert in the prevention of bank and retail money laundering, **Antonio L. Mazzitelli**, UNODC Regional Representative, Mexico City, and moderator Judge **James P. Gray** from California. Mr. Mazzitelli criticized my idea of legalizing drugs to stop Mexican violence, arguing that doing so would make drugs more available, increase drug consumption and worsen drug-related problems. In rebuttal, I pointed out to Mr. Mazzitelli that just days earlier Mexican authorities seized fifteen tons of methamphetamines valued at $4 billion in Mexico. U.N. prohibition drug policy was succeeding in making drugs more available, hugely more available.[671] "Mexican authorities announced their largest methamphetamine seizure ever late Wednesday: 15 tons, found in pure powder form at a ranch outside Guadalajara. It was about 13 million doses worth $4 billion — more than double the size of all meth seizures at the Mexican border in 2011. But while the authorities proudly showed off the seizure to local reporters, the sheer size of the find set off alarm among experts and officials from the United States and the United Nations. It was a sign, they said, of just how organized, efficient at manufacturing and brazen Mexico's traffickers had become even after expanded efforts to dismantle their industry."[672]

From the auditorium stage I suggested to Mr. Mazzitelli that he return to the UN and advise leaders there that drug prohibition was not working. In fact, UN drug policy was responsible for the success of many Mexican drug cartels, including the **Gulf Cartel**, **Los Zetas**, the **Sinaloa Cartel** and a number of others that I named in my rebuttal, increasing drug availability and triggering prolific Mexican violence. The U.S. Drug Enforcement Agency (DEA) prepared a map that portrayed areas of dominant Mexican cartel presence as of April 2015.[673]

---

[671] Damien Cave, "Mexico Seizes Record Amount of Methamphetamine," *The New York Times*, February 9, 2012,   https://www.nytimes.com/2012/02/10/world/americas/mexico-seizes-15-tons-of-methamphetamine. html?referringSource=articleShare, emphasis added.

[672] Ibid.

[673] Aleszu Bajak, "Visualizing Mexico's drug cartels: A roundup of maps," *Storybench*, January 12, 2016, https://www.storybench.org/visualizing-mexicos-drug-cartels-roundup-maps/.

Enigmatic and Elusive Global Mass Killer Identified

For the first time in about twenty-two years of drug-policy reforming, my riveting MUCD-experience in Mexico City refocused my attention and elevated my vantage point to much higher ground, ground from where I could see and appreciate the culpability of UN drug policy for the global drug war disaster. Prohibition simply caused awful, collateral unintended consequences. From January 2012 forward, I realized I had spotted and identified the enigmatic and elusive global mass killer, destroyer of millions of human lives, thousands of communities, and the futures of countless human beings. The killing was accomplished with the best of intentions through an ethos of drug intolerance and punishment. As it turned out, the killer was not a **crime boss** nor a drug cartel. Rather the global killer was a UN-promoted prohibition drug policy, the culprit that always escaped scrutiny and always got away. The stealth killer simply coupled intolerance and punishment into a transnational system of mass criminalization, mass incarceration, forced drug rehabilitation through abusive, forced labor camps as found in China, and private prison proliferation as countenanced in the United States.

China's Forced Labor Camps for Drug Users

Human rights abuses in China labor camps are routine with half a million examples. "Chinese authorities are incarcerating drug users in compulsory drug detention centers that deny them access to treatment for drug dependency and put them at risk of physical abuse and unpaid forced labor, Human Rights Watch said in a new report released today. Half a million people are confined within compulsory drug detention centers in China at any given time, according to the Joint United Nations Programme on HIV/AIDS (UNAIDS). The 37-page report, 'Where Darkness Knows No Limits,' based on research in Yunnan and Guangxi provinces, documents how China's June 2008 Anti-Drug Law compounds the health risks of suspected illicit drug users by allowing government officials and security forces to incarcerate them for up to seven years. The incarceration is without trial or judicial oversight. The law fails to clearly define mechanisms for legal appeals or the reporting of abusive conduct, and does not ensure evidence-based drug dependency treatment."[674]

---

674 "China: Drug 'Rehabilitation' Centers Deny Treatment, Allow Forced Labor, Anti-Drug Law Perpetuates Rights Abuses," *Human Rights Watch*, January 6, 2010, https://www.hrw.org/news/2010/01/06/china-drug-rehabilitation-centers-deny-treatment-allow-forced-labor.

The temptation to forgo human rights and constitutional rights looms large while the drug war endlessly fails to fix the drug problem. Leroy Martin, Chicago's former police superintendent, was so enamored by his visit to China in 1991, he observed "The sanitary facilities [in the Chinese prison system] are a bucket. The prisoners are given a bowl of rice and a Thermos bottle of tea. And then they're locked down.... He noted that drug dealers were sentenced to execution by firing squad, adding, we give drug dealers I-bonds [bonds without posting any cash] here, and what do they do? They go back out and sell more drugs.'"[675]

America's Proliferation of Capitalistic Private Prisons for Profit

America's record on human rights abuses, drug intolerance and peonage labor practices accomplished through privately-owned, capitalistic prisons and public prisons is not much better than China's forced labor camps. "The War on Drugs and harsher sentencing policies, including mandatory minimum sentences, fueled a rapid expansion in the [American] prison population beginning in the 1980s. The resulting burden on the public sector led to the modern emergence of for-profit private prisons in many states and at the federal level. The United States has the world's largest private prison population. Of the 1.5 million people in state and federal prisons in 2016, 8.5 percent, or 128,063, were incarcerated in private prisons. Another 26,249 people — 73 percent of all people in immigration detention — were confined in privately-run facilities on a daily basis during fiscal year 2017. From 2000 to 2016 the number of people housed in private prisons increased five times faster than the total prison population. Over a similar timeframe, the proportion of people detained in private immigration facilities increased by 442 percent. The federal government and 27 states utilized private prisons operated by for-profit and non-profit entities during 2016."[676] American incarceration practices took not only freedom from masses of people but the value of their labor as well.

"The stated aim of penal labor in the United States is to mitigate recidivism risks by providing training and work experience to inmates; however, some prison labor is involuntary, with noncompliance punished by means including solitary confinement.

---

[675] Robert Blau and William Recktenwald, "Let's fight crime as Chinese do, Martin says," *Chicago Tribune*, July 12, 1991. Gierach notebooks, p. 550.

[676] Kara Gotsch and Vinay Basti, "Capitalizing on Mass Incarceration: U.S. Growth in Private Prisons," *The Sentencing Project*, August 2, 2018, https://www.sentencingproject.org/publications/capitalizing-on-mass-incarceration-u-s-growth-in-private-prisons/.

Penal labor is economically important due to it being a source of cheap labor, with base pay being as low as 60 cents per day in Colorado, and in Texas there is no compensation for prison labor whatsoever."[677]

After my Mexico City experience, my drug policy reform focus was no longer hemmed in by United States borders. I was now stalking the enigmatic and elusive global mass killer, drug prohibition, internationally.

---

677 *Wikipedia*, s.v. "Penal labor in the United States," https://en.wikipedia.org/wiki/Penal_labor_in_the_United_States, accessed March 17, 2023.

Chapter 14 - Vienna 2012 and my Discovery of the United Nations Commission on Narcotic Drugs

As of March 2012, LEAP, an international, educational, nonprofit organization consisting of active and retired law enforcement officers, prosecutors, judges, and other law enforcement officers, had not acquired what is called "special consultative status" regarding drugs, a status awarded by the United Nations Economic and Social Council (ECOSOC). As such, LEAP board members such as myself, Board Secretary at the time, could not attend or even enter the VIC, again, the home of the CND and the IAEA. Fortunately, other NGOs with such consultative status like the **ACLU**, **Transform Drug Policy Foundation**, and the **Transnational Radical Party** had such status and had extra coveted passes that enabled me and other LEAP members to gain admission to the VIC and the CND in 2012, and again in 2013. By 2014, I had helped LEAP attain special consultative status regarding drugs. Kindly, Andrei Abramov, Chief of the NGO Branch, Office for ECOSOC Support and Coordination and other LEAP directors helped.

My first impression of the CND in 2012 was that of a meeting ground with high security, prearranged admission screening, photographing and badges. Members of the press or public could not just walk in or wear shirts sporting reform messages like LEAP's familiar T-shirt, "Cops Say Legalize Drugs" and on the reverse side, "Ask Me Why." I felt a little like I was behind the Iron Curtain, observing, and trying to sneak word out to the rest of the world what was happening there — which was not much.

The Centennial Celebration of the Hague Opium Convention of 1912

For a week in Vienna, Austria, March 12-16, 2012, I witnessed the United Nations Commission on Narcotic Drugs at work. Ministers, diplomats, delegates and national representatives were assembled in a large room with a high-vaulted ceiling in the Vienna International Centre, the room crammed with row after row of tables and chairs, microphones, country name tags, and a gigantic computer screen stretched across the front of the room that displayed a resolution draft. Day after day the dignitaries busied themselves negotiating and finalizing the wording and sentence structure of a hortatory resolution commemorating the centennial anniversary of the first international drug-control treaty.

National representatives took turns addressing word choice and other trivialities. Resolution whereas-clauses affirmed that drugs were still a problem, appreciated the first international treaty endeavor to control drugs, and climaxed with apparent unanimous support for the resolution and three UN drug-control treaties underlying global drug policy. I say, "apparent unanimous support" because no votes are taken. All CND-business is accomplished by harmonious acclamation. The three international UN drug-control treaties underlying global drug policy were: The 1961 Single Convention on Narcotic Drugs, the 1971 Convention on Psychotropic Substances, and the 1988 United Nations Convention Against Illicit Traffic in Narcotic Drugs and Psychotropic Substances. These three UN drug-control treaties superseded The Hague Opium Convention of 1912, and all other international drug treaties,[678] and became the "Gospel of Global Drug Control" that, according to all CND-attending national representatives, warranted universal acclaim, fealty and continued support.[679] One of the three treaties, the 1961 Single Convention, preserved the idea of the prohibition of recreational drug-use taken from The Hague Opium Convention of 1912.[680] The 1912 Hague Opium Treaty went into effect globally in 1919 when it was incorporated into the Treaty of Versailles.[681]

In fairness, lots of other work, reports, statements, speeches, side events and business occupied the week, evidenced by a Report of Proceedings and a List of 55th Session

---

[678] For an excellent Historical Overview of the International Drug Control System, *see* John Collins, *Legalising the Drug Wars* (Cambridge, Cambridge University Press, 2022), p. *xiv-xvi*, and for a comprehensive and thorough history of International Drug Control, *see* his book. Collins argues at p. 205, "The 'war on drugs' was not a creation of any UN framework or treaty. It was certainly facilitated by the UN and the international drug control system, but it represented a far more complex phenomenon, driven by a mixture of national, bilateral, regional and international efforts." Collins' highlights in his book at p. 2-3 "the fundamental historical inaccuracy of the U.S.-led prohibition regime narrative. It instead points to the regulatory complexity of the system, built on an intersection of member state interests and agendas, of which the U.S. is only a part." At p. 223-24, Collins' book "argues that the 1961 Single Convention was ultimately a compromise, a regulatory system with prohibition aspects. However, in the short term, the Single Convention represented a victory for the regulatory stand and UK-led coalitions over the U.S.-led prohibitionist stand." At p. 224, looking forward, Collins observes "recent trends of system fragmentation and the emergence of a drug control regime complex." He writes, "The goal of a 'drug-free world' has undoubtedly been shown as a weak and simplistic strategic goal for a complex global phenomenon. Better managing and regulating licit and illicit drug markets will be key to move beyond the many failures of the 'war on drugs' era and establish a future of drug policy grounded in UN principles of cooperation, pragmatism, rule of law, socio-economic development and human rights."

[679] "100 years of narcotics control," *United Nations Office on Drugs and Crime*, March 14, 2012, https://www.unodc.org/unodc/en/frontpage/2012/March/100-years-of-narcotics-control.html.

[680] Desmond Manderson, "The Trojan Horse of the global drug wars: from Canberra to Sinaloa," June 9, 2022, https://www.canberratimes.com.au/story/7774264/the-trojan-horse-of-the-global-drug-wars/.

[681] *Wikipedia*, s.v. "International Opium Convention," https://en.wikipedia.org/wiki/International_Opium_Convention, accessed March 17, 2023.

CND Documents.[682] But it would also be fair to note that at no time during the week were any of the three UN drug control treaties at risk of serious review, discussion or amendment. Moreover, national representatives to the CND 55th Session ignored critical, fundamental drug policy questions like: Does UN recreational, drug-prohibition policy do more harm than good? Outside the "VIC Hallowed Halls," the world was and is, at war with itself. The good guys versus the bad guys, drug cartel versus drug cartel, street-gang versus street-gang, and innocent drug users versus intolerant governmental authorities. Often civilian bystanders, too, supply a source for the drug war's quick and the dead,[683] because of awful drug policy conceptualization and metrics. In Mexico, 100,000 people were dead and 30,000 missing. Yet, drugs were seized and mounded by the ton, while many unwary and unwarned drug consumers overdosed, became sickened with needle diseases and died needlessly.

Earlier Recognition of the Need for Treaty Amendment

An enlightening 2009 article, written by Tom Blickman and Martin Jelsma three years before the 55th CND session, discussed many unfortunate consequences flowing from antiquated UN drug conventions and its intolerant prohibition base. It discussed growing support from various nations that favored harm reduction-oriented drug policies and programs, and evolving recognition of the importance of human rights considerations alongside drug policy.[684] The following article excerpts enlighten still:

"The last decade was characterized by major advances in harm reduction programs, particularly among injecting drug users, aimed at decreasing the spread of diseases like HIV/AIDS and hepatitis. According to UNAIDS, there are about 16 million injecting drug users, and around 3 million of them are infected with HIV. In 77 countries some

---

[682] "The 2012 Commission on Narcotic Drugs Report of Proceedings," *International Drug Policy Consortium*, April 2012, http://fileserver.idpc.net/library/CND-Proceedings-Document-2012.pdf, 32 pages; and "List of documents before the Commission at its fifty-fifth session," E/CN.7/2012/CRP.8, *Commission on Narcotic Drugs*, 12-16 March 2012, https://www.unodc.org/documents/commissions/CND/CND_ Sessions/CND_55/ E-CN7-2012-CRP8_V12522831_E.pdf.

[683] *Merriam-Webster*, s.v. "Quick: read this!" — etymology of "the quick and the dead," https://www.merriam-webster.com/words-at-play/quick-word-history.

[684] Tom Blickman and Martin Jelsma. "Drug Policy Reform in Practice: Experience with Alternatives in Europe and the U.S.," *Nuevo Sociedad Nro. 222 Julio-Agosto 2009*, https://www.academia.edu/3313032/ Drug_ policy_reform_in_practice?email_work_card=thumbnail.

level of needle and syringe exchange programs are running and about one million people in 63 countries are receiving substitution treatment with methadone or buprenorphine."[685]

"The prison population throughout most of the world has exploded these last twenty years, partly due to the tightening of anti-drug laws, under the influence of the 1988 Convention. The Convention makes it mandatory for the signatory countries to 'adopt such measures as may be necessary to establish as criminal offences under its domestic law' (art. 3, §1) all the activities related to the production, sale, transport, distribution, etc. of the substances included in the most restricted lists of the 1961 and 1971 conventions. Criminalization also applies to the 'cultivation of opium poppy, coca bush or cannabis plants for the purpose of the production of narcotic drugs'. The text distinguishes between the intent to traffic and personal consumption, stating that the latter should also be considered a criminal offence, but 'subject to the constitutional principles and the basic concepts of [each country's] legal system' (art. 3, §2)…. In the US, Russia and China, massive imprisonment is practiced, and the majority of European and Latin American countries have also seen a major increase. The resultant prison crisis and lack of positive impact have prompted various depenalisation and decriminalization reforms."[686]

These transformative drug policy observations expressed by authors Tom Blickman and Martin Jelsma were evident in Europe, the United States, the Netherlands, and across much of Latin America. These progressive authors and thinkers concluded, "*After 50 years, it is time to modernize the system and establish a coherent Single Convention to replace the three existing treaties.* If a better balance between protection and repression is to be established legislators will have to shed the political fear that paralyzes them. The conventions are not sacred, but must be seen as outdated instruments, full of inconsistencies…. The Executive Director of UNODC, Antonio Maria Costa, affirmed 'there is indeed a spirit of reform in the air, to make the conventions fit for purpose and adapt them to the reality on the ground that is considerably different to the time they were drafted.'"[687]

---

[685] Ibid.

[686] Ibid.

[687] Ibid., emphasis added.

The First Successful Challenge to the 1961 Single Convention

One of the highlights of my 2012 CND experience, and the next year as well, was meeting **Martin Jelsma** and twice hearing **Evo Morales**, then president of Bolivia, speak regarding the need for a Bolivian reservation to the 1961 Single Convention ban on coca bush production. His request for a reservation was based on correcting what he termed "an historical accident." Bolivia initially acceded to the 1961 Single Convention treaty prohibition when it was a dictatorship and not a free country. And secondly, President Morales argued that since the new Bolivian constitution was popularly adopted in 2009, it became the president's responsibility to protect the cultural and practical importance of the coca leaf in Bolivia.

One important change in Bolivia's **new constitution** was the introduction of an article concerning **coca**. Article 384 states: "The State shall protect native and ancestral coca as cultural patrimony, a renewable natural resource of Bolivia's biodiversity, and as a factor of social cohesion; in its natural state it is not a narcotic. Its revaluing, production, commercialization, and industrialization shall be regulated by law." In 2011, Bolivia withdrew from the 1961 Single Convention.[688] It then sought re-accession to the 1961 Single Convention subject to a reservation regarding the coca bush and coca-leaf chewing. In 2013, Bolivia successfully re-acceded to the convention with the stated reservation.[689] In 2013 at CND, I inquired who brainstormed and engineered the successful legal strategy that led to Bolivia's success. I was told it was the work and strategizing of Martin Jelsma of the Transnational Institute. Learning that, in 2013 I sought out Martin Jelsma and arranged to meet with him and other CND-attendees who agreed the UN drug-control treaties needed amendment. Mr. Jelsma listened attentively as I made the case for more comprehensive and aggressive amendment of UN drug-control treaties. A photograph of the 2013 Jelsma-Gierach CND-meeting in progress captured my impression of it. I dutifully pleaded my case for treaty amendment as the way forward, and Martin Jelsma looked on thoughtfully and intrigued, but skeptical.

---

[688] "Bolivia Withdraws from the UN Single Convention on Narcotic Drugs," *TNI/WOLA* press release, June 30, 2011, https://www.hr-dp.org/print/89.

[689] "Bolivia to re-accede to UN drug convention, while making exception on coca leaf chewing," *UNODC*, https://www.unodc.org/unodc/en/frontpage/2013/January/bolivia-to-re-accede-to-un-drug-convention-while-making-exception-on-coca-leaf-chewing.html.

PHOTO. Jelsma-Gierach Meeting at CND 2013, discussing the need for comprehensive UN drug treaty amendment. Other meeting attendees included Czech drug czar Jindrich Voboril and LEAP and ENCOD representatives.

It was eye-opening to me — shocking really — transitioning from urgent and horrific stories of life and death tragedy on parade in Mexico City in February 2012 to a leisurely, hortatory resolution drafted in an antiseptic, academic and removed Vienna meeting hall in March 2012. The resolution supported more of the same deadly drug policies that afflicted Mexico, American cities and Central and South America, but not those countries or cities exclusively. Sadly, the meat and potatoes of drug policy reform never reached the plates of CND actors — just acquiescent CND attendees, really.

Chapter 15 – Vienna 2013, The Commission on Narcotic Drugs

Recognizing that CND, drug-policy players in Vienna were missing or intentionally avoiding the opportunity to save the world from the horrible United Nations prohibition drug policy, I decided to compose a "Letter to World Leaders"[690] to be signed by **Neill Franklin**, the Executive Director of LEAP and distributed the week before the convening of the 2013 CND-session. The letter was distributed to all nations through the UN mail system at its New York headquarters. The letter urged national and world leaders to authorize and encourage their respective Vienna representatives at the CND to address and discuss five fundamental drug-policy questions, as follows:

Does the UN policy of drug prohibition do more harm than good?

Does drug-prohibition policy itself cause increased drug availability, potency, use, abuse, addiction, disease and death?

Does drug prohibition also cause turf-war crime, violence, corruption, addict crime and injustice; does it erode freedom, liberty and human rights; and does it tear at the moral fabric of mankind worldwide?

Has massive drug-war spending compromised the role of the responsible elements of society (police, military, intelligence agencies, government, business, academia, media and international organizations) and aligned those elements with the interests of irresponsible drug purveyors and drug cartels, both sides supporting the continuation of drug prohibition for economic gain?

What drug policy should replace the UN/Al Capone-style drug-prohibition paradigm?

Regrettably, no nation was inspired to follow LEAP's lead, and no nation addressed any of the five questions proffered. Disappointed, I wrote and reported on my experience, titling the piece, "United Nations Drug War 2013,"[691] paraphrased in part below. The good news was that in the process, I ran across an article written by the experienced voice of **Cindy S.J. Fazey**, a former high-ranking CND official, written ten years before CND 2013. Her article explained what CND annual sessions were

---

[690] Gierach/LEAP "Letter to World Leaders," 2013, https://jamesgierach.tumblr.com/ post/67563040197 3288960/gierach-drafted-neill-franklin-signed-letter-to.

[691] Gierach, James E., "United Nations Drug War 2013," *Gierach Tumblr,* https://www.dropbox.com/ s/l590tz 7i81r4qov/JEG%20final_%20CND%202013_3%2024%2013.docx?dl=0.

and were not, and what could and could not be accomplished at them. Her analysis helped me understand the proceedings, their practical limitations, and served to assuage my disappointment.

Cindy S.J. Fazey's article noted that proceedings of the Commission on Narcotic Drugs are not a forum for debate and change. "UN conferences are like plays where all roles are carefully defined and the scripts written in advance. They are not places for debate but for statements of position, where any potential conflict has been headed off months before through a series of preliminary discussions and preparatory meetings,"[692] She further explained that "In the Commission... no votes are taken. Everything is settled by consensus.[693] This is because in the original charter for the UN only those countries that are fully paid-up members can vote. Since the USA is behind with its dues, there is an informal agreement that nobody votes."[694]

Although the USA paid a part of its debt to the UN in 1999 pursuant to the Helms-Biden legislation, the USA still owes the UN over $1.3 billion. Of this, $612 million is payable under Helms-Biden. The remaining $700 million result from various legislative and policy withholdings; at present, there are no plans to pay these amounts.[695] The Commission on Narcotic Drugs (CND) is comprised of fifty-three UN Member States,[696] and most of the funding for the Commission comes from seventeen major donors who for practical purposes, Fazey wrote, have "decisive influence over both the CND and the UNDCP [United Nations Drug Control Program]." The Commission annually adopts resolutions regarding drug policy. "If any member of the

---

[692] Cindy S.J. Fazey, "The Commission on Narcotic Drugs and the United Nations International Drug Control Programme: politics, policies and prospect for change," *The International Journal of Drug Policy*, Received 3 November 2002; received in revised form 7 December 2002; accepted 16 January 2003, C.S.J. Fazey / International Journal of Drug Policy 14 (2003) 155⊠/169, http://www.undrugcontrol.info/images/ stories/documents/Fazey-Commission_on_Narcotics-2003.pdf.

[693] *But note*, "It will be recalled that scheduling decisions are rare within the CND since they are decided by votes rather than consensus." The 2017 Commission on Drugs Report of Proceedings," *IDPC*, http://www.respadd.org/wp-content/uploads/2017/08/CND-Proceedings-Report-2017_ENGLISH.pdf.

[694] Fazey, *IJDP*, supra.

[695] *Wikipedia*, s.v. "United States and the United Nations," the U.S. Arrears Issue, https://en.wikipedia.org/wiki/United_States_and_the_United_Nations. Date of access?

[696] Commission on Narcotic Drugs, *UNODC*, https://www.unodc.org/unodc/en/commissions/CND/index. html.

Commission were against a particular resolution, it would not go through," Fazey continued.[697]

Analyzing why the Commission is unable to extricate itself from the status quo (deep, drug-prohibition ruts), Fazey commented on the nature of the delegates to the Commission.

She said, "[The] preponderance of diplomats and law enforcement representatives militates against change and helps to perpetuate inertia within the Commission.... Any changes achieved have never occurred through debates on the floor of the Commission."[698]

Finally, Fazey observed that "The majority of UN Member States have long opposed any change of the Conventions.... [T]he three most vociferous opponents of change and slackening of the interpretation of the Conventions are the USA, Sweden and Japan. Other countries that support this approach fall roughly into two categories: previous USSR states and dictatorships."[699] ECOSOC, revisiting the subject of its power regarding global drug policy, has the power to elect nation states to serve on the Commission on Narcotic Drugs, comprised of fifty-three nations.[700] Some of those fifty-three nations must be more amenable to UN drug policy reform, we should hope, than the three drug-regressed prohibitionist countries Fazey named.

---

[697] Fazey, *IJDP*, supra.

[698] Ibid.

[699] Ibid.

[700] "The CND has 53 member States that are elected by ECOSOC and is chaired by a Bureau, including one member per Regional Group," *UNODC*, "Commission on Narcotic Drugs," https://www.unodc.org/unodc/en/commissions/CND/index.html, accessed March 17, 2023.

Chapter 16 – The Gierach/LEAP "Proposed Amendment of United Nations Drug Treaties – 2014"

Daunted but unbowed, I headed home from Vienna in 2013 motivated to read and study the three UN drug-control conventions that occupied such a revered place at CND in Vienna. Seemingly, the conventions were written in indelible ink though unquestionably the cause of so much harm to so many people the world over. I had only a passing familiarity with their contents before 2013. Studying the treaties was another eye-opener for me, making it crystal clear that these treaties were the foundation and fountainhead of global, drug prohibition policies. These treaties were the heart of "the world drug problem," and a dominant cause and exacerbation of a dozen global harms and human rights degradations.

Over several months I studied and pondered. Obviously, the Commission on Narcotic Drugs and its partners in prohibition were incapable of proposing changes to fix antiquated UN drug-control treaties. Any breath of treaty amendment was ignored or beaten down in a chorus calling for unity and admonition that all nations must speak with a single voice. So, I asked myself, "Jim, if you were all powerful and could rewrite UN drug-control treaties, what would they say?" It was not an easy question to answer. But at least I did not have to figure it out "by committee" with guidance from "expert panels," or a need to compromise the end product to attain acclamation and satisfy competing national self-interests. If I could just get "me, myself and I" to agree, maybe, "we" would have a good, new single convention regarding mind-altering substances. I spent months studying the treaties and thinking. Finally, I began drafting, starting with the Preamble.

New Preamble Additions and Subtractions: Elimination of the Moralistic "Evil" of Drug Use and Addiction, Recognition of the Benefit of Medical Marihuana, and Addition of Regulation of Tobacco and Alcohol

I removed some old preamble clauses, added some new ones, and rewrote still others. All additions and modifications of preexisting preambles from the three UN drug-control treaties were footnoted, identifying the source of the clause, and whether it was new, modified or unchanged. Philosophically, the moralistic bent of drug use and addiction as an "evil" was removed. Preamble clause four regarding the medical use of marijuana was new. It provided, "*Recognizing further* that the medical use of cannabis can be an indispensable alternative treatment for the relief of pain and suffering and therapeutic treatment for myriad other illnesses, such use often decreasing patient dependence on the use of more dangerous and addicting narcotic drugs,..."[701] And Preamble clause six modified clause three of the 1961 Single Convention by adding *nicotine* and *alcohol* to the categorization of mind-altering psychoactive substances that "can constitute a serious health issue for the individual,..."[702]

New Preamble Concepts: Introduction of Lawful Recreational Drug Use, Harm Reduction, National Freedom to Experiment with New Drug Policies, and Recognition of the Negative Role of Drug Prohibition Policy

Clause five of the 1988 United Nations Convention Against Illicit Traffic in Narcotic Drugs and Psychotropic Substances ("the 1988 Anti-Drug Trafficking Convention")[703] provided:

"*Aware* that illicit traffic generates large financial profits and wealth enabling transnational criminal organizations to penetrate, contaminate and corrupt the structures of government, legitimate commercial and financial business, and society at all its levels,..." The revised Gierach/LEAP proposed amendment replacement clause recognized the role that drug prohibition plays in the illicit drug-trafficking equation. Drug prohibition dramatically affects drug prices, supply and demand, providing great economic incentive to transnational criminal organizations to do the wrong thing. The new, replacement clause nine, provided: "*Aware* that illicit, prohibition-driven and uncontrolled narcotic and psychotropic drug-traffic[king] generates huge financial profits and wealth, enabling transnational criminal organizations to penetrate, contaminate and corrupt the structures of government, legitimate commercial and financial business, and society at all levels...,"[704]

New Preamble clause eleven recognized that *recreational* drug use was an inevitable and foreseeable drug use, providing as follows: "*Recognizing* that new measures and a

---

[701] Gierach/LEAP "Proposed Amendment of United Nations Drug Treaties — 2014," Preamble, p. 8, Clause 4, https://www.unodc.org/documents/ungass2016//Contributions/Civil/Law_Enforcement_Against_Prohibition/LEAP_UN_Treaty_Amendment_2.26.1421-1.pdf, English; https://www.unodc.org/documents/ungass2016// Contributions/Civil/Law_Enforcement_Against_Prohibition/FINAL-3-Spanish_LEAP-Treaty-Amendment_5.27.14-1.pdf, Spanish.

[702] Ibid., p. 8.

[703] "1988 United Nations Convention Against Illicit Traffic in Narcotic Drugs and Psychotropic Substances," Preamble, Clause 5, *UNODC*, https://www.unodc.org/pdf/convention_1988_en.pdf, p. 1.

[704] Gierach/LEAP Proposed Amendment, supra, p. 9.

new international framework are necessary to effectively control and regulate the inevitable and foreseeable use, misuse and abuse of, mind-altering substances like alcohol, tobacco, narcotic and psychotropic drugs intended for medical, scientific and *recreational* purposes,..." This concept challenged the unrealistic and delusional 1961 Single Convention principle that disallowed recreational drug use, a major use, if not the dominant use of drugs over millenniums. Similarly, the Gierach/LEAP amendment proposal repudiated the UN criminalization and penal model of drug control. Clause nineteen, also a new provision, provided: "*Discovering* that harsh and extreme drug regulation represented by zero tolerance and harsh criminalization is as counterproductive to the control of drug abuse as the other extreme represented by no control, or total deregulation of all substances as if all drugs and substances posed identical risks of bodily harm, addiction and popularity,..."[705]

Lastly, though other attitudinal changes are replete throughout the Gierach/LEAP Preamble, clause twenty importantly recognized nations need to retain their sovereignty and the latitude to experiment with new drug policy models that recognize and practice harm-reduction principles and protect human rights. Clause twenty provided: "*Nevertheless believing* that effective measures aimed at dissuading the use and abuse of alcohol, tobacco, narcotic, psychotropic and other mind-altering drugs and substances require international cooperation within a framework that permits sovereign nations to *experiment* with new drug policy models based upon sound economic principles and good health strategies, including, but not limited to, regulated drug markets, drug maintenance programs, treatment on demand protocols, clean needles and other *harm-reduction* methods,..."[706]

---

[705] Ibid., p. 10. The Gierach/LEAP proposed treaty amendment was published in pamphlet form. The pamphlet back cover included the "LEAP Statement of Ten Principles." Principle 10 provided: "LEAP recognizes that different 'illicit drugs' pose differing risks of harm. As such, in a post-prohibition world, LEAP recognizes than an appropriate set of regulations and control for one substance may not be a suitable or sufficient regulation and control for another substance. LEAP believes that the nation states of the world and various states in the United States must be given the regulatory latitude to try new models that wisely balance the notions of freedom over one's own body with the need for common sense regulation of drugs to reduce death, disease, addiction and harm." *See the* full set of principles here, https://jamesgierach.tumblr.com/post/675718148708810752/law-enforcement-against-prohibition-2013.

[706] Gierach/LEAP Proposed Amendment, https://www.unodc.org/documents/ungass2016// Contributions/ Civil/Law_Enforcement_Against_Prohibition/LEAP_UN_Treaty_Amendment_2.26.1421-1.pdf,   p.10, emphasis added.

The New, Proposed "Single Convention on Drugs" Abandoned the Notion of a "Drug-Free World," Eliminated the Flawed "Estimates System," and Replaced the "One-Size-Fits-All" Drug Paradigm with a National Right to Drug Experimentation

I combined the three UN conventions into one, much as was done in 1961 to arrive at the 1961 Single Convention on Narcotic Drugs. In doing so, I embraced several overarching principles. I concluded that a "one-size-fits-all approach"[707] fits no nation, and such an approach tended to stymie sovereignty and individual national experimentation with decriminalization, legalization and medicalization approaches tailored to fit a country's particular drug problem or problems which can evolve from year-to-year and decade-to-decade. I thought the scope of the new "Single Convention on Drugs" should include alcohol and tobacco, because these two mind-altering substances kill the most people and are currently excluded from the trilogy of UN drug-policy gospel.

Then, of course, drug prohibition, the heart and worst of all drug policy choices had to go. This meant an end to the penalty Article 36, and an end to the 2009 Political Declaration and Plan of Action, make-believe, *drug-free world* nonsense. Then too, the delusion that mind-altering substances should only be lawful for medical or scientific purposes had to go. Probably, the most common use of mind-altering substances is other than for medical or scientific purposes. Personally, I never ingested a beer for scientific or medical purposes. Ah, but rules always have their exceptions. I recall an instance of impacted, wisdom-tooth removal, pain and a choice of narcotic pills or a beer. Medically motivated, I drank a beer, forgoing narcotic pills. My sore tooth, my choice of medicine.

Then too, I realized the criminalization and penal approach of UN treaties should instead be a *medical, harm-reduction and human rights-based treaty*. The prohibition paradigm incarcerated millions, risked the arrest of 275 million (Chapter 2), corrupted the mission of law enforcement, fed the black-market drug trade, and forced drug use underground, leading to contaminated substances, dirty needles, and drugs that always avoided inspection, labeling and warnings, leading to commonplace overdose and death. Hello... fentanyl.

---

[707] Ibid., Preface, p. 1, "Principal among the many reasons for proposing this amendment is the indispensable fact that the prohibition, criminalization, top-down, one-size-fits-all drug policy paradigm has failed for over 50 years."

The failed and flawed "estimates system" also had to go. The estimates system by which someone other than a sovereign country was overseeing the narcotic need of a particular country proved certain to deprive many countries of reasonable access to necessary medicines for its citizenry. Oh, and the subject of cannabis, the most benign of drug substances according to Harvard Medical School icon, Dr. Grinspoon (Chapter 22), and the most commonly used illicit substance — "Out!" Is it mind-altering? Yes, should it logically be included? Yes, but no, "Out." Why? Kind of like reparations for bad law inclusion for so long.

What remained then of global drug policy according to Jim?

Drug use was a medical problem, not principally a law-enforcement matter. Countries were free to experiment with decriminalization and legalization drug protocols. Pursuant to Article 7 of the new, amended single convention, it would become the duty and responsibility of international drug agencies to keep track of harm reduction programs and guard against human rights infringement related to drug laws. In short, the Gierach/LEAP proposed amendment of UN drug treaties would turn night into day; drug use would come out of the closet; transnational criminal organizations would need to hope for a new prohibition of some other sort; police would again become a friend and helper of communities and citizens; corruption would have largely lost its drug-war pay window; and people could start caring about one another again, whether they used some organic or synthetic substance or not; and twenty-first century society and civilization could heal as the World War on Drugs melted away with the trashing of Anslinger's, sixty-year-old, treaty poison.

In sum, the Gierach/LEAP proposed amendment of UN drug-control treaties envisioned a better and kinder drug policy paradigm, a "displacement of the prohibition drug policy paradigm with a new model based upon regulated markets, innovative programs, international cooperation and voluntary national regulation and control of mind-altering substances commensurate with the relative danger, or lack thereof, posed by each drug or substance. This proposed course of action would better control drug use and abuse, improve public health and safety, undermine the profit motive that drives the illicit drug industry, free some nonviolent offenders, reunite families, save lives, prevent disease, rejuvenate respect for judicial systems and government, redirect the resources of law enforcement, save money, and broadly restore freedom, tolerance, fairness and human rights."[708]

---

708 Ibid., Preface, p. 6.

Chapter 17 - Civil Society Reaction to the Gierach/LEAP Proposed Amendment

The 2014 reception to the Gierach/LEAP proposed amendment of UN treaties by civil society[709] (nongovernmental organizations) was cool at best. Several able, honorable and vintaged drug policy NGO leaders resisted the GIERACH/ LEAP invitation to support the first comprehensive proposed amendment of UN drug conventions in over five decades. Unfortunately, Gierach and LEAP were left largely alone calling for UN treaty amendment at the upcoming CND session in March 2014. The largest of the reform NGOs and affiliates did not support the initiative. I suspect and hasten to add that **ENCOD**, the European Coalition for Just and Effective Drug Polices, and other NGOs were sympathetic to the initiative, but the critically important work of amendment of UN drug conventions is yet to be accomplished.

Civil Society Resists Comprehensive Amendment of UN Treaties

Without intending to attribute fault, criticism or blame here — simply reporting — several leaders of long-established civil society organizations concerned with drug policy, human rights and harm reduction were unable to support the Gierach/LEAP proposed amendment for various reasons including its timing and manner of development. One of those leaders, **Damon Barrett**, had this to say.

"You didn't include us in planning, strategy and content... Treaty amendment doesn't work like that... years of trust and relationship building, working resolutions and initiatives is necessary, work on the wording must include them (nations) and they need to know they are leading... A wholesale draft presented up front just won't work. No state will file such a proposal alone; other states must join them... I don't like including alcohol or tobacco... You offer nothing to replace the estimates system... I don't necessarily support a national sovereignty-based approach... There's nothing in the proposal on access to essential medicines... and the INCB responsibilities of Article 7 exceed its budgetary capacity... There is no definition of "mind-altering substance" or "drug abuse," and I don't like the term "addict"... Most people do not know who Al Capone is... I disagree with the tact and the draft as written."

---

[709] Penelope Hill, Orsi Fehér & Jamie Bridge, "International drug policy: The impact of civil society and opportunities for addiction professionals to engage," *IDPC*, April 28, 2021, https://idpc.net/publications/2021/04/international-drug-policy-the-impact-of-civil-society-and-opportunities-for-addiction-professionals-to-engage.

Another respected international NGO leader, **Ann Fordham**, noted: "There hasn't been sufficient consultation with civil society partners... notice is too short... important and nuanced strategic decisions need to be made in careful consultation with our allies within government... potentially counterproductive to push this kind of initiative too strongly from outside. It needs to be borne out of constructive dialogue between civil society and like-minded government officials."

And a thirdly, an equally respected and able international NGO operative, **Steve Rolles**, consulted with like Vienna CND-regulars and observed: "We have concerns about the project. The primary one is that both the document itself, and the political strategy around it have been developed without our collaboration or input.... Your initiative overlaps various collaborative publications and political strategies already published and in play by other NGOs... Our outputs aren't necessarily in sync... In terms of the political strategy for the document at the CND – it's important to understand that we have been working with various organisations and governments for many months (in some cases, years) on a range of initiatives related to drug policy, law and convention reform... The initiative arrived with only a couple of weeks to go before HLS/CND, and potentially throws something of a spanner in the works of some of these various plans... Little time to discuss and no opportunity to input into... My suggestion would be that you hold off a full-blown launch... recast it - along with a revised letter... position LEAP in the on-going collaborative process, without potentially stepping on toes of other organisations who already have specific plans in play around convention reform... In the international arena, particularly in the rather bizarre and rarified world of the UN and CND, it's really important that we work collaboratively on both content and strategy so we can maximise the impact of our collective expertise and resources."

Several powerful civil society organizations, one a conglomerate with nearly 200 drug policy reform NGOs at its disposal, refused to electronically circulate the proposed amendment among its affiliated organizations for their thought and input.

Wide Dissemination of Amendment Proposal Accomplished, CND 2014

Despite resistance and the misgivings expressed by several CND-recognized NGO powerhouses, LEAP operatives, including myself, widely and enthusiastically disseminated the pamphlet containing our treaty amendment in English and Spanish at CND 2014. The document generated much discussion and powerfully jarred the Vienna status quo. This brazen shot across the bow of UN drug agencies and its foundational treaties by a CND-newcomer to the rarified world of international drug policy was not the typical, gradualist approach utilized by established civil society. Instead, the Gierach/LEAP proposed amendment was a head-on assault and confrontational approach to global drug prohibition. Dr. Martin Luther criticized the "... tranquilizing drug of gradualism" in his famous "I have a Dream" speech, and he "worried that by merely chipping away at injustice, we were lulled into a sense of advancement when very little was actually being accomplished."[710] For once, the Gierach/LEAP initiative proposed a concrete, written, comprehensive, dynamic, 180-degree change in UN drug policy.

The Comprehensive Amendment Triggered Meaningful Responses

Ecuador Invited Gierach to Present Proposed Amendment of UN Drug Treaties

Reading the Gierach/LEAP proposed amendment of UN drug treaties so enamored **Rodrigo Vélez**, then-drug czar of Ecuador, that he promptly invited me at state expense to Ecuador to present my proposed treaty amendment to Ecuadorean leaders and the press. The press from at least half a dozen countries including Guatemala, Peru, Ecuador, Canada, Cuba and more were also invited to hear my treaty amendment proposal and to also consider Ecuador's sustainable development projects designed to displace drug-trafficking. The three-day press event included my presentation and an on-site inspection of two parcels of land seized from drug traffickers and turned over to local communities to facilitate sustainable development projects. One parcel of land became a shrimp farm and the other a cornfield, both located between Quito and Guayaquil. While in Ecuador, I was introduced to the team of attorneys assigned to transform the Gierach/LEAP proposed amendment into the "Ecuadorean Proposed Amendment of United Nations Drug Treaties." Discussions included the timing of the filing of the amendment with the UN secretary-general. That filing — that act — was the trigger that by the amendment terms of the 1961 Single Convention would start the CND and Secretary-General amendatory machinery.

Close but no cigar. As fate would have it, and as doubtful civil society leaders had hypothesized and forewarned, generally, a progressive drug czar like Rodrigo Vélez could not secure national permission for the filing of an Ecuadorean proposed treaty

---

[710] Steven Dennis, "The Tranquilizing Drug of Gradualism," https://stevenpdennis.com/2020/01/13/the-tranquilizing-drug-of-gradualism/.

amendment. Yet, I was able to share my message with the assembled press and Ecuad-orean leaders regarding the critical, global need to amend UN drug-control treaties by ending drug prohibition.[711] UN drug conventions were the foundation for global drug prohibition, and drug prohibition policy had two principal failings: 1) It didn't work, and 2) It was the heart of many global crises regarding such subjects as violence, gangs, guns, corruption, public health, human rights, and so forth. The press was receptive and carried my message beyond Ecuador.[712]

INCB President Attempted to Rebut Contentions of the Gierach/LEAP Proposed Amendment

Perhaps the most telling saga regarding the positive impact of the distribution of the proposed amendment of UN drug treaties on United Nations officialdom was the defensive position in which the INCB president found himself. Dr. Lochan Naidoo spent his entire CND-plenary address the following year (2015) attempting to rebut the contentions and proposals made in the 2014 comprehensive proposed treaty amendment, point by point. However, his rebuttal failed to persuade thinking minds. In fact, a new annual set of depressing stats on global drug use and drug-trafficking from the Secretariat to CND confirmed more drug-war futility and failings, just like every year.

Czech Republic Joined Gierach and LEAP in a 2015 CND Side Event

Jindrich Voboril, drug czar of the Czech Republic in 2014 and 2015, was also supportive of the Gierach/LEAP proposed amendment of UN drug conventions. He obtained permission from his country to cosponsor with LEAP a 2015 CND-side event called, "Treaty Amendment: A Choice for Drug Policy Reform." This event attracted the attendance of the Uruguayan ambassador in Vienna, and from him we learned the punishing cost of resisting UN drug-war dictates. *See* Chapter 11, Reason 3, Uruguayan Ambassador **Bruno Javier Faraone Machado**.

---

711 Video, Hispanicroots, 2014, Gierach in Ecuador, "CONSEP 4, Segment 4," HISPANIC ROOTS de Canada, YouTube, https://youtu.be/kBGAszqKnDQ, June 11, 2014.

712 Videos, Hispanicroots, 2014, Gierach, James E., "CONSEP 5, Segment 5," https://youtu.be/DQl_beAckak; "CONSEP 11, Segment 6," https://youtu.be/vRGwDKKP3uE; and "CONSEP 12, Segment 7," https://youtu.be/n9wjpAv3JMw, June 11, 2014.

Chapter 18 – LEAP Expels Gierach and Abandons Treaty Amendment

After eleven years of voluntary service on behalf of LEAP, my unrelenting and energetic pursuit of the amendment of UN drug treaties stepped on the toes of too many other organizations, LEAP included. UNGASS 2016 — a United Nations General Assembly Special Session regarding the world drug problem — was scheduled for April 2016. I was a LEAP Board director and chair of its UNGASS 2016 committee. Despite this important international drug policy opportunity for change — on September 29, 2015, the LEAP Board of Directors called a Special Meeting for the single purpose of removing me as its Executive Board vice chair and as Director. A majority of a split board removed me, and, in response, I resigned as a LEAP speaker. Soon thereafter LEAP dropped what some considered the critical words "Against Prohibition" from its name and removed all reference from its website and its *Wikipedia* history, identity and activities of its unanimously adopted proposed amendment of UN drug treaties.

The newly conceptualized LEAP was renamed "Law Enforcement Action Partnership," preserving its nationally and internationally well-recognized acronym, LEAP. My criticism was that the new LEAP was diluting the old LEAP core reason for its creation and existence — law enforcement "Against Prohibition." In my opinion, the transformed NGO now promoted many constructive initiatives but so many that the old, core message — Against Prohibition — was upstaged. Those initiatives included bail reform, police reform, harm reduction, and many other worthwhile causes. But theretofore all those causes were secondary and incidental to the core LEAP message, "Against Prohibition."

Because I viewed UNGASS 2016 as such a unique opportunity to raise the need for the amendment of UN drug treaties before the United Nations General Assembly itself, though expelled and with the thanks of LEAP's executive director and friend, Neill Franklin, I drafted my fourth and last annual letter to "World Leaders." As always, my letter went out over the signature of LEAP's Executive Director.

Gierach's Last Letter to World Leaders for LEAP, 2016

My last letter to "World Leaders" on behalf of LEAP, dated January 22, 2016, concerned UNGASS 2016, scheduled for April 19-21, 2016 in New York City at UN headquarters. The subject line read: "A Rare Opportunity for Meaningful Drug Policy Reform,"[713] and the letter said in part:

"Dear World Leader:

"How can we defend the status quo represented by the foundational 1961 Single Convention on Narcotic Drugs and yet nudge world drug treaties and policies flowing from them into a better twenty-first century?

"The words of Joaquin 'El Chapo' Guzmán are instructive: 'When I no longer exist there will be no decrease in the level of world addiction to drugs. It is true that consumption, day after day, becomes bigger and bigger. So it sells and sells.' He spoke of the drug business environment that he knew so well, an environment that we nations made for him. Well-intentioned but mistakenly, we nations, through the United Nations, resurrected the criminalization of recreational drug use, the "Al Capone prohibition model.""...

"Avoiding the obvious with talk of how 'flexible' UN drug conventions are is an abuse of the meaning of language and, importantly, an evisceration of the rule of law. The tenets of the conventions unavoidably clash with the principles of the 1948 Universal Declaration of Human Rights, as evidenced by the collateral damage they cause globally to life and freedom. Talk of 'flexible construction' of the conventions is an untenable proposition as noted by then-INCB president Dr. Lochan Naidoo, a year before. World leaders must not squander the UNGASS 2016 drug-policy-reform opportunity. It's one thing to talk about reform, as is done annually at the sessions of the CND in Vienna, but quite another to act out reform by changing treaty foundational rules....

"The starting point for action is for each nation to utilize the amendatory process of the existing drug conventions. Each nation should determine what treaty provision or aspect is most counterproductive to sensible drug control, and public health and safety in their country and file with the UN Secretary-General a proposed amendment to change it. The precious little time available between now and UNGASS in April should not be spent drafting 'outcome documents,' but rather detailed, concrete proposed treaty amendments that can serve as specific reforms capable of meaningful de-

---

713 Gierach, James E., LEAP letter, January 22, 2016, unabridged, *Gierach Blogs, Tumbler*, https://www.tumblr.com/jamesgierach/712058554969997314.

bate regarding devilish details. Written, concrete and filed proposals for treaty amendment are not written in stone, nor does the mere act of filing a proposal tie the hands of the proposing nation. Filed proposals simply serve as an invitation for many voices to be heard, provoking thought in forging opportunity for new consensus. The past four years, Law Enforcement Against Prohibition has encouraged you to consider the most fundamental drug policy question: Does the war on drugs cause more harm than good? LEAP believes the evidence is overwhelming that the intolerant and prohibitionist war on drugs, promoted by UN drug conventions, makes the global drug problem worse. LEAP further believes that the intolerant, prohibitionist paradigm exacerbates existing problems in many facets of human life and depreciates human rights.

"As a world leader, please ponder your nation's drug and associated problems, craft specific proposed treaty amendments to deal with them, and file those proposed amendments with the UN Secretary-General as soon as possible, hopefully in time to enable distribution and consideration by other nations before UNGASS 2016...

Sincerely, LEAP Executive Director [The end]

Chapter 19 - Failed Opportunities: UNGASS 2016 and High-Level Ministers Segment CND 2019

On April 19, 2016 in New York City, UN drug policy agencies and their leaders, along with drug treaty Member States, civil society and world leaders drew open the curtain of hope on the possibility of global drug policy reform. The drug problem and drug policy consequences were deemed so bad that three drug-treaty Member States — Mexico, Guatemala and Colombia — successfully convinced UN General Assembly authorities to take up the subject of what was called "the world drug problem" (inherently including "the world drug policy problem") three years ahead of schedule at UNGASS 2016.[714] Three days of open discussion and debate offered the opportunity to revise an intolerant, prohibitionist, war-fashioned, criminalistic and penal UN drug policy paradigm that had cursed the world since 1961. It was a once-in-a-decade opportunity to discuss written, concrete and pre-filed amendment proposals of UN drug treaties. Hope was alive. However, as preparations for UNGASS 2016 got underway, hope started to fade. Martin Jelsma of the Transnational Institute explained.

"After long negotiations in the CND on the modalities for the UNGASS, the decision was made that the CND should 'lead this process' while the President of the General Assembly (PGA) was invited 'to support, guide and stay involved in the process'. In order to 'ensure an adequate, inclusive and effective preparatory process' in December 2014 the CND put an 'UNGASS Board' in charge of all preparations, including drafting the UNGASS outcome document. The [UNGASS] Board, chaired by the Egyptian Ambassador Shamaa, requested inputs from regional groups for the drafting process... UNODC created a special website to collect all those inputs, plus those coming from civil society.

"In the course of the negotiations, however, most of those other inputs [were] ignored and the ungass2016.org web depository, rather than serving as a source of inspiration for the drafting of the outcome document, became a sorry substitute for meaningful participation. In fact, the drafting and negotiations process became a rather obscure process tightly controlled by the UNGASS Board, lacking transparency and drawing much criticism from reform-orientated countries and civil society.... The

---

714 Zara Snapp and Jorge Herrera Valderrábano, "United States Drug Policy: Flexible Prohibition and Regulation," *Collapse of the Global Order on Drugs, From UNGASS 2016 to Review 2019* (Bingley, United Kingdom: Emerald Publishing, 2018), Ch. 12, p. 256.

Board applied a strong filter, not allowing any language to enter the draft text that could complicate its main aim to avoid controversy as much as possible and to reach a political consensus well in advance of the UNGASS. Proposals for new paragraphs that were considered too problematic ended up in a 'parking lot' that in the end proved to be the burial ground for any contentious language about new challenges, abolishing the death penalty, harm reduction, or the establishment of an expert advisory group."[715]

UNGASS 2016: A Sham

Then, crushing hope like a bug under foot, UNGASS 2016 powers adopted the so-called "Outcome Document" as the first order of business before any substantive discussion of the world drug problem, or solutions to it. The proceeding was a sham, a hoax, window-dressing for the *status quo* sprinkled with intermittent more progressive statements by some nations and some NGOs. Like annual March sessions of the Commission on Narcotic Drugs in Vienna, there were no open debates, no concrete, written, filed proposed amendments of UN drug conventions, and no crack in the bedrock prohibition foundation of global drug policy.

Equally upsetting, the Special Session of the UN General Assembly still failed to answer the fundamental drug policy questions I posed to World Leaders three years earlier: "Does the UN policy of drug prohibition do more harm than good? Does drug-prohibition policy itself cause increased drug availability, potency, use, abuse, addiction, disease and death? Does drug prohibition also cause turf-war crime, violence, corruption, addict crime and injustice; does it erode freedom, liberty and human rights; and does it tear at the moral fabric of mankind worldwide?" The obvious answer to all those questions is an emphatic, "Yes!"

In the introduction to an anthology written by Axel Klein and Blaine Stothard, *Collapse of the Global Order on Drugs, From UNGASS 2016 to Review 2019*, they observed: "The run-up to the 2016 United Nations General Assembly Special Session (UNGASS) was therefore accompanied by great anticipation within the reform community that led to an equally great sense of disappointment at the end of the United Nations General Assembly Special Session on Drugs (cite). After the build-up to what some commentators thought of as a paradigm shifting event (cite), what transpired was

---

[715] Martin Jelsma, "UNGASS 2016: Watershed event or wasted opportunity?" *TNI*, 2016, https://www.tni.org/my/node/22954?content_language=en.

more akin to re-affirmation of the established system, where the drug control conven-tions remain the central international drug policy reference point, with the drive of the 'Vienna Institutions' (CND, UNODC and INCB) shored up and their mandates extended. There is no explicit reflection on [the] impact [of United Nations drug pol-icy], no concern over unintended consequences, no acknowledgement that the policies themselves have been the cause of any harm. Instead the Outcome Document attrib-utes the high price paid by societies to the postulated 'world drug problem' and in an explicit endorsement of the prevailing repressive approach pays the first tribute to 'law enforcement and judicial personnel' (cite)."[716] And there were other criticisms and critics.

"Immediately following the adoption of the document, there were nine statements from governments and regional groups to express dissatisfaction with the outcome document noting the issues that had not survived the negotiations such as the abolition of the death penalty for drug offenses, decriminalization and reference to allowing traditional use (cite)."[717]

The Givens: Recreational Drug Prohibition/ No Convention Amendments

Recreational drug prohibition was an UNGASS 2016 given, just as it was a given that no nation would dare file a proposed amendment of UN conventions. Instead, nations and NGOs just read prepared statements, much as described by Cindy S.J. Fazey (su-pra, pages 268-270) "[M]eetings of the Commission on Narcotic Drugs (CND) are no forum for debate and change. . UN conferences are like plays where all roles are carefully defined and the scripts written in advance. They are not places for debate but for statements of position, where any potential conflict has been headed off months before through a series of preliminary discussions and preparatory meetings."

True, the so-called "Vienna consensus"[718] had been shattered and more and more nations and NGOs were loudly calling for reform, calling for a health-based drug pol-icy paradigm, a people-based rather than substance-based paradigm, a human rights-

---

[716] Axel Klein and Blaine Stothard, *Collapse of the Global Order on Drugs, From UNGASS 2016 to Review 2019* (Bingley, United Kingdom: Emerald Publishing, 2018), "Introduction," p. 2, emphasis added.

[717] Ann Fordham and Heather Haase, "A Catalyst for the Drug Policy Reform Movement," *Collapse of the Global Order on Drugs*, Ch. 1, p. 38, emphasis added.

[718] Zara Snapp and Herrera Valderrábano, "United States Drug Policy: Flexible Construction and Regulation," *Collapse of the Global Order on Drugs* (Bingley, UK: Emerald Publishing, 2018) Ch. 12, p. 262.

and harm reduction-based drug policy rather than more nonsensical clatter about an imaginary "drug-free" world. But not one nation and not one NGO (other than my LEAP-drafted letter to world leaders) called for the amendment of UN drug conventions at UNGASS 2016. So, all the statements and all the talk still missed the bullseye. Recreational drug prohibition and the criminalization of offending parties remained UN drug policy without even a challenge.

The UNGASS 2016 General Assembly adopting an Outcome Document as a first order of business is like a jury rendering its verdict before the presentation of any evidence. The proceeding more resembled a cart-before-the-horse cartoon than an open debate. Why the failure?

Understanding the Continuous "Drug War Tug-of-War"

The plenipotentiary conference of seventy-three nations that met for more than eight weeks in 1961 to hammer out a single convention on narcotic drugs was known as "the United Nations Conference on Narcotic Drugs" and the product produced was called "the 1961 Single Convention on Narcotic Drugs." The seventy-three nations organized themselves into five distinct caucuses according to their differing interests. The "organic states group" represented a group of states that produced coca, opium and cannabis and because of centuries-old socio-cultural experience with organic drugs were more open to drug use; the "manufacturing states group," consisting of the United States and other industrialized countries who had no cultural affinity for organic drug use, yet being faced with the effects of drug abuse on their citizens, advocated stringent controls on the production of organic raw materials and on illicit trafficking, but also sought to protect the interests of medical research and domestic, synthetic drug manufacturers; the "strict control group," non-producing and non-manufacturing states with no direct economic stake in the drug trade, like France, Sweden, Brazil, and the Republic of China, but culturally opposed to drug use and suffered from abuse problems, that favored restricting drug use to medical and scientific purposes and were willing to sacrifice a degree of national sovereignty to ensure the effectiveness of supranational control bodies; the "weak control group," led by the Soviet Union and others states in Europe, Asia and Africa that considered drug control a purely internal issue and adamantly opposed any intrusion on national sovereignty; and "the neutral group," a diverse group including most of the African countries, Central America, sub-Andean South America, Luxembourg and the Vatican that had no strong interest in the issue apart from ensuring their own access to sufficient drug supplies.[719]

These diverse groups produced a convention document that limited the legitimate use of drugs to *medical and scientific purposes* and *provided for criminalization and punishment* for deviation through a treaty mandate that required all member states to adopt legislative laws and administrative rules that would implement the 1961 Single Convention.

Over time the circumstances and interests of states evolved. For example, Afghanistan became the producer of more than 80 percent of the world's opium;[720] China became, according to unequivocal US officials, "the main source for fentanyl and similar drugs;"[721] and cannabis potency, production and popularity led the array of "scheduled and branded" substances used for illicit, non-medical and nonscientific drug purpose. "In 2013, between 128 and 232 million people used cannabis (2.7% to 4.9% of the global population between the ages of 15 and 65). Cannabis is by far the most widely used illicit substance. Marijuana or marihuana (herbal cannabis) consists of the dried flowers and fruits and subtending leaves and stems of the female Cannabis plant. This is the most widely consumed form, containing 3 percent to 20 percent THC, with reports of up to 33 percent THC.[722]

Transit-nations became producing-nations, and producing nations became consuming nations.[723] And the ever-changing, catalytic influence and dynamics of drug prohibition on drug production, invention, marketing, money laundering, transit, sale

---

[719] Paraphrased and abbreviated from *Wikipedia, s.v.* "Single Convention on Narcotic Drugs," History, https://en.wikipedia.org/wiki/Single_Convention_on_Narcotic_Drugs. But also see John Collins, Legalising the Drug Wars (Cambridge: Cambridge University Press, 2022), p. 4, arguing "that international drug control efforts between the collapse of the League of Nations system and the coming into force of the 1961 Single Convention are best understood as a triangulation of three blocs: control advocate states, led by the US; producing states and their non-interventionist allies, led by Turkey and the Soviet Union; and moderate manufacturing and consuming countries, led by the UK. In this triangulation process, the US and UK remained the core actors in international drug diplomacy and the two main policy strands within the system: prohibition and regulation, respectively."

[720] Reality Check team, "Afghanistan: How much opium is produced and what's the Taliban's record?" *BBC*, August 25 [2021], accessed November 10, 2021, https://www.bbc.com/news/world-asia-58308494.

[721] Reality Check team, "Fentanyl crisis: Is China a major source of illegal drugs?" *BBC*, September 24, 2018, https://www.bbc.com/news/world-45564744.

[722] *Wikipedia, s.v.* "Cannabis (drug)," https://en.wikipedia.org/wiki/Cannabis_(drug), accessed March 17, 2023.

[723] Héctor Silva Ávalos, "Honduras Goes From Transit Nation to Cocaine Producer," *Insight Crime*, March 19, 2020, https://insightcrime.org/news/analysis/honduras-transit-nation-cocaine-producer/.

and use continued its overwhelmingly and universally negative impact. Unquestionably, the negative impact of drug prohibition policy was drugogenic, criminogenic and corruptogenic, as discussed earlier. (Chapters 4-6, supra).

A much earlier session of the UN General Assembly held in 1989 also evidenced negative treaty prohibition consequences for many countries. Statements made by national representatives in 1998 evidenced spreading drug-prohibition conundrums. "Abdurrahman Fachir (Indonesia) said the latter half of this century had witnessed a staggering growth in organized transnational crime, generating such profit as to overwhelm national law enforcement mechanisms." "Zamira Eshmambetova (Kyrgyzstan) said: Although drug abuse was not widespread in Kyrgyzstan, there had been a huge increase in drug-related crime." "Kaba Camara (Cote d'Ivoire) said the globalization of the world had also brought liabilities such as international organized crime. Such liabilities had destroyed social tissues, health programmes, human dignity and were not things of the past.... For African countries, one key problem was the porous nature of borders and a lack of resources to fight the scourge of drugs." Ahmet Arda (Turkey) said that "according to the Single Narcotics Convention of 1961, his country was one of the two leading poppy straw producers.... Turkey was on the main drug transit route, he said, adding that with limited resources, law enforcement agencies had tried to prevent trafficking." Pe Thein Tin (Myanmar) "reiterated his country's commitment to undertake its share of the global illicit drug burden and cooperate with the international community. Myanmar was determined to achieve success in the total elimination of poppy cultivation and opium production in the country. In 1996, Myanmar had undertaken a 15-year narcotics elimination plan, by which the country would be totally free of narcotic drugs by the year 2011."[724]

Then, as the world drug problem worsened under the drug-prohibition paradigm, pressure to escape its deleterious consequences resulted in calls from some Member States and civil society for experimentation with harm-reduction programs and human rights inventions, even decriminalization of all drugs as in Portugal.[725] And in two

---

[724] Press Release, "Plight of Transit Countries Highlighted in Third Committee Debate on International Drug Control," *United Nations, General Assembly, Third Committee*, October 12, 1998, https://www.un.org/press/en/1998/19981012.gash3470.html.

[725] "Drug Decrminalisation in Portugal: Setting the record Straight," *Transform Drug Policy Foundation*, May 13, 2021, https://transformdrugs.org/blog/drug-decriminalisation-in-portugal-setting-the-record-straight, accessed February 10, 2022.

countries that pressure led to the outright legalization of marijuana for recreational purposes, Uruguay and Canada.

Yet, bad drug policy is habit-forming. So even as national interests vis-à-vis drug production and use changed from their 1961 orientation, old intolerances continued to resist change. Yes, sharing dirty needles spread HIV and hepatitis; and yes, untested and unlabeled street drugs caused many unnecessary accidental overdose deaths; and yes, punitive and intolerant drug laws made for unaffordable and racially discriminatory mass incarceration; and yes, recreational drug prohibition surrendered control of illicit drugs to transnational criminal organizations that thereby earned incredible wealth and unimaginable power and influence. But drugs are "bad," drug addiction is "evil," and "what message would it send" if states became tolerant of safe injection facilities, overdose prevention programs, naloxone mandatorily sold with every opioid sale, persons addicted to a substance granted inexpensive access to the substance to which they were addicted? How could elected public officials face their constituencies with "soft on drugs" and "soft on crime" messaging? Such softness is politically unimaginable in a drug-prohibition world.

The Drug Policy Continuum

Over these sixty years of recreational drug prohibition, nongovernmental organizations and nations took their respective positions on a *drug policy continuum*, a continuum that at one end insisted on a drug-free world,[726] demand and supply reduction, and "Just say no" intolerance with harsh penal enforcement (Chapter 3, supra). And that continuum stretched all the way to what seemed like another world, where all drugs should be legal, and no one should be imprisoned or forced into drug treatment because of drug possession or recreational drug use.

This drug policy tug-of-war (the status quo versus reform) plays out endlessly at annual sessions of the Commission on Narcotic Drugs in Vienna; it played out preparatory to and at UNGASS 2016 in New York City; and it played out at the High-Level Ministers Segment of CND in 2019. The tug-of-war is also played out at countless other meetings, seminars, thematic midsession meetings, and events around the world. Victory for the reform end of the continuum is seen as a nation or NGO that made a powerful statement supportive of harm reduction, alternatives to incarceration,

---

[726] e.g., 2009 CND Political Declaration and Plan of Action, *UNODC*, https://www.unodc.org/ documents/ commissions/CND/CND_Sessions/CND_52/Political-Declaration2009_V0984963_E.pdf.

an end to the death penalty for drug offenses, a call for drug decriminalization, greater accessibility to narcotic medicines, and so on. Other NGOs or nations representative of the other end of the tug-of-war rope would applaud delivery of a contrary statement, one supportive of the 2009 Political Declaration and Plan of Action, talk of an illusory and utopian drug-free world, or a "successful" seizure of drugs in some corner of the world, or a new precursor initiative, or a new drug laboratory resource.[727]

This tug-of-war plays out over and over, but always on a playing field impregnated with ingrained, foundational and inviolate UN drug-control conventions — the recreational drug prohibition "Ace in the hole."

UNGASS 2016: the "Status Quo" Outcome and "Paragraph 8 Poison"

I didn't see it. I wasn't there. Thank goodness the LEAP Board of Directors excused me from my LEAP UNGASS 2016 committee chairmanship six months before the UNGASS charade (April 19-21, 2016) and months before apparent abandonment of its own 2014 call for amendment of UN drug treaties. What was the UNGASS outcome? No nation filed a proposed amendment of UN drug conventions. The diligent efforts of Mexico, Guatemala and Colombia provoked the UN General Assembly to take up "the world drug problem" in special session three years ahead of its scheduled 2019 date, but none of the three countries filed a proposed amendment of UN drug treaties with the UN secretary-general in advance of the special session. Any country talking about drug policy reform without first filing a proposed treaty amendment to fix the problem is not serious about reform. It's just talk.

Therefore, at UNGASS 2016 there was no need to plan for discussion of a proposed treaty amendment, and there was no opportunity to discuss one. As such, there was no need to negotiate the wording of its fate in an outcome document. The failure of any country to file a proposed amendment of UN drug treaties, the cornerstone of UN drug policy, was absolutely fatal to systemic, global, drug policy reform. For whatever reason (see Chapter 11, "Why Is It So Difficult to Reform Bad Drug Policy?"), no nation called out the conservative, status quo, prohibition stalwarts. Not one! Instead, the defeat of reform at UNGASS 2016 was reported in a single paragraph of the UNGASS Outcome Document.

---

[727] "Laboratory and Forensic Science Service," *UNODC*, https://www.unodc.org/unodc/en/ scientists/lab/index.html.

Paragraph 8 of the adopted UNGASS Outcome Document said, "We underscore that the Single Convention on Narcotic Drugs of 1961 as amended by the 1972 Protocol, the Convention on Psychotropic Substances of 1971, the United Nations Convention against Illicit Traffic in Narcotic Drugs and Psychotropic Substances of 1988 and other relevant international instruments constitute the cornerstone of the international drug control system;..."[728] By God they do, but I wish they didn't.

The UNGASS 2016 Outcome Document is thirty-two pages long,[729] but the essential outcome of UNGASS 2016 is fully embraced by the paragraph eight declaration. There is no need to read any preceding or succeeding paragraphs, really. Although the Outcome Document contains some reform-minded and constructively aimed verbiage seemingly impeaching the UN drug prohibition paradigm, paragraph eight "trumps" that verbiage. Paragraph eight assures that the United Nations' harm-making, human-rights crushing, recreational drug use and sale condemnation, intolerance, discrimination and mass incarceration will continue unabated. As over half a century of experience demonstrates: the harm-making and human rights-crushing capacity of UN drug prohibition drug conventions is more powerful than any sanctuary afforded by harm reduction and human rights initiatives, individually or collectively.

UNGASS 2016 was simply a reaffirmation of the prohibition of recreational drug use as the 1961 Single Convention mandates, and that's the end of the story. Before UNGASS 2016, the only legitimate use of drugs was for medical and scientific purpose, and after UNGASS 2016, the same. Reform lost; the status-quo won.

The 2019 CND High-Level Ministers Segment and Its "The Paragraph 6 Declaration"

The 2019 CND High-Level Ministers Segment (HLMS 2019) disposed of meaningful, global, drug policy reform in its Ministerial Declaration in the same manner as UNGASS 2016, but it did so two paragraphs sooner than the UNGASS 2016 Outcome Document. Paragraph six of the HLMS 2019 resolution declaration provided: "We underscore that the Single Convention on Narcotic Drugs of 1961 as amended by the 1972 Protocol, the Convention on Psychotropic Substances of 1971, the United Nations Convention against Illicit Traffic in Narcotic Drugs and Psychotropic

---

[728] "Outcome Document of the 2016 United Nations General Assembly Special Session On The Drug Problem," 13th Special Session, April 19-21, 2016, *United Nations Office on Drugs and Crime*, https://www.unodc.org/documents/postungass2016/outcome/V1603301-E.pdf, p. 2.

[729] Ibid.

Substances of 1988 and other relevant instruments constitute the cornerstone of the international drug control system...”[730] Again, story over; the drug-prohibition killer cornerstone escaped, again.

As the 2019 CND High-Level Ministers Segment evidenced — and UNGASS 2016 before it — global, UN, recreational drug prohibition policy acts upon civilization like a low-level dam acts upon unsuspecting swimmers and boaters. The harmless-looking and sounding low-level dam creates a washing-machine effect that continually sucks people under the water to drown with no escape.[731] Nothing can stop the killer effect of low-level dams or drug-prohibition policies, except removal of low-level river dams and the drug-prohibition policies.

The Hard and Tireless Work of Civil Society

The hard work of civil society leaders at UNGASS 2016 reflected the Global Civil Society Forum and the consensus declaration agreed to by 300 civil society representatives in 2008. The consensus statement said: “Reform groups welcomed the commitment to harm reduction, to human rights issues, the need for a culturally appropriate response, the inclusion of the most affected communities, as well as improved access to controlled medicines and alternatives to incarceration.”[732]

The UNGASS 2016 Outcome Document included mention of the term “human rights” twelve times and the word “naloxone” once, but the term “harm reduction” escaped the thirty-two-page document entirely. The document also made no mention of the elimination of the death penalty for drug offenses.[733] For these and many other reasons, I have difficulty finding much meaningful reform in the 2016 Outcome Document, especially since it steadfastly supports the status-quo treaty gospel and still subscribes to its “Paragraph eight poison.”

---

[730] “Ministerial declaration on strengthening our actions at the national, regional and international levels to accelerate the implementation of our joint commitments to address and counter the world drug problem,” *IDPC*, http://fileserver.idpc.net/misc/Ministerial_Declaration.pdf.

[731] Alicia Stice, “Experts call them ‘drowning machines.’ So why are they on the Poudre?” *The Coloradoan*, June 24, 2017, https://www.coloradoan.com/story/news/2017/06/24/experts-call-them-drowning-machines-so-why-they-poudre/419579001/.

[732] Ann Fordham and Heather Haase, “The 2016 UNGASS on Drugs: A Catalyst for the Drug Policy Reform Movement,” *Collapse of the Global Order on Drugs* (Bingley, UK: Emerald Publishing, 2018), Ch. 1, p. 27.

[733] Gen Sander and Rick Lines, “The Death Penalty for Drug Offences,” *Collapse of the Global Order on Drugs*, supra, Ch. 2, p. 58.

However, opinions regarding the merit and usefulness of the UNGASS 2016 Outcome Document varied greatly. "The UNGASS 2016 met with mixed approval with some lauding it as a progressive move towards public health, harm reduction and development (cite), while others feel it has proved a missed opportunity to overhaul and modernize the global drug control system."[734]

One final sad point. Just as the UN Vienna Drug Institutions (INCB, CND and UNODC) partnered to defend and protect UN drug conventions from critical review and amendment, these same bureaucratic institutions and assembled gravy-train riders will continue to control the direction of upcoming opportunities for change in Vienna. The multimillion-dollar meal ticket that feeds UNODC programs is just for starters.[735] The biennium budget for the United Nations Crime Prevention and Criminal Justice Fund for 2020-2021 projects revenues of $377,277,300 USD.[736]

In my opinion: We should not only take the profit out of drugs to defund criminals. We should also take the profit out of drug prohibition to defund drug-war, gravy-train riders (other than treaters).

It is difficult for me to respect the actions and decisions taken by the UN General Assembly at UNGASS 2016, just as it is the actions and decisions taken at the 2019 CND High-Level Ministers Segment. In both instances the status quo prevailed. Yet, a respected drug policy collective like the International Drug Policy Consortium

---

[734] Caroline Chatwin, "The European Union in Panglossian Stagnation," *Collapse of the Global Order on Drugs*, supra, Ch. 11, p. 243.

[735] The Commission on Narcotic Drugs, Resolution 62/9, "Budget for the biennium 2020–2021 for the Fund of the United Nations International Drug Control Programme," https://www.unodc.org/documents/commissions/FINGOV/Background_Documentation_2019-2021/CND_Resolution_62_9.pdf.

[736] The Commission on Crime Prevention and Criminal Justice, Resolution 28/4, "Budget for the biennium 2020–2021 for the United Nations Crime Prevention and Criminal Justice Fund," *The Commission on Crime Prevention and Criminal Justice*, https://www.unodc.org/documents/commissions/ CCPCJ/Crime_Resolutions/2010-2019/2019/CCPCJ_Resolution_28-4.pdf, p. 4. UNODC's historic share of the pot was discussed in 2017: "As such, deliberations within the Plenary were predicated on the fact that, once again, the UNODC was dealing with not only reduced funding relative to workload and donor-supported programmes, but also an increasingly precarious situation vis-à-vis generated al-purpose funding; that is to say monies not earmarked for specific projects. According to the information provided to delegates, revised cost estimates and resource projections for the biennium 2016-2017 came to a total of $606.1 million. This comprised $9.6 million in general-purpose funds, $513.3 million in special-purpose funds, $45 million in programme support costs funds and $38.2 million from the UN's regular budget. Overall, this marked a significant decrease on the overall projection on the consolidated budget for biennium 2014-15, but also represented a $37 million and an estimated $1 million reduction in the special-purpose fund budget endorsed by the CND in previous years and support cost funds respectively. Such figures reflected the Office's attempts to maintain a balanced budget in relation to income projection." "The 2017 Commission on Narcotic Drugs, Report of Proceedings July 2017," IDPC, http://www.respadd.org/wp-content/uploads/2017/08/CND-Proceedings-Report-2017_ENGLISH.pdf, p. 30.

(IDPC), founded in 2006, which produced the wonderful "Shadow Report," can somehow patiently, respectfully and seriously report and discuss the UNGASS 2016 charade in a "Report of Proceedings" regarding the subsequent 60th Session of the Commission on Narcotic Drugs.[737]

For example, IDPC reported that INCB president Werner Sipp, speaking at the 60th Session, applauded the UNGASS 2016 work. But regarding the need for drug treaty convention revision or reform, Mr. Sipp asserted that the conventions were flexible enough, in the view of INCB, "for their implementation at the national level but this flexibility does not in any way extend to any legalization or regulation of non-medical use of narcotic drugs or psychotropic substances."[738] That view is incongruous and ludicrous.

[737] "The 2017 Commission on Narcotic Drugs Report of Proceedings, July 2017," *IDPC*,

http://www.respadd.org/wp-content/uploads/2017/08/CND-Proceedings-Report-2017_ENGLISH.pdf.

[738] Ibid., p. 18.

Part Six – The Way Forward: Treaty Amendment, Gradual Incremental Reform, or Swooping Change in Public Opinion Regarding Drug Policy

Chapter 20 – Sudden Treaty Amendment or Incremental Reform

What is the best way forward from here? How can we best and most quickly end "The Curse of Solomon: The World War on Drugs." Finding a country willing to file a proposed amendment of UN drug-control treaties would certainly be the quickest and most direct means to open the debate and hopefully tear the evil out of the World War on Drugs, but what nation can afford to risk the loss of U.S. foreign aid or withstand a financial blow like that suffered by Uruguay at the hands of the United Nations over its legalization of cannabis? Maybe slow-moving, trust-building, incremental reform like that cautioned by several NGO leaders in response to the Gierach/LEAP "Proposed Amendment of United Nations Drug Treaties — 2014" is the better way forward to transition out of the "Jurassic," "frozen in time" UN drug policy straitjacket.[739]

Longtime drug policy reformers, harm reductionists and human rights activists working through NGOs and laboring in the fields of the Vienna Commission on Narcotic Drugs deserve great credit. There was a time when their work was misunderstood as that of the "pro-drug lobby,"[740] and there were days when civil society was given a last-place chance to speak at CND thematic sessions and intercessional meetings, if time did not run out first. And more recently, hundreds of civil society members were denied access to a civil society meeting the day before the UNGASS 2016, and other civil society, side-event speakers were denied access to the events at which they were to

---

[739] Tom Blickman, "The Elephant in the Room," *Collapse of the Global Order on Drugs*, supra, ch. 5, p. 107, 117.

[740] Ann Fordham and Heather Haase, "A Catalyst for the Drug Policy Movement," *Collapse of the Global Order on Drugs*, Ch. 1, supra, p. 24.

speak.[741] Civil society has not had an easy time gaining the respect and appreciation it deserves for its drug policy insight, experience, and perseverance.

Despite earlier difficult days, civil society has exerted a constant, constructive and reformist presence and influence on UN drug agencies and global drug policy. Yet, despite those invaluable contributions and influence, drug prohibition lives. Despite sixty-two years of unequivocal failure, UN drug treaties still underscore global drug policy.

I arrived late on the Vienna scene in 2012. But upon my arrival it was very soon obvious to me that UN recreational drug prohibition was at the heart of nearly every drug-policy failing and human rights abuse. And like the proverbial bull in the China shop, I wanted abrupt, comprehensive change in all the teacups, now. In contrast, civil society sought by incremental change to address these many failings: e.g., cannabis reform, incarceration diversion, better access to medicines, decriminalization,[742] an end to the death penalty for drug crimes, clean needles, safe injection sites, drug maintenance, naloxone, and so on. But the one thing that civil society failed to do was spearhead a drive to end recreational drug prohibition by comprehensive treaty amendment. Instead, in my opinion, respectfully, its gradualist approach to reform has been too patient, too incremental, too indirect, too laborious, too gradual, too cooperatively consensual, and too slow.

Every day, people are overdosing, dying, being shot, fumigated, arrested, incarcerated, humiliated and stigmatized. Gradual, incremental, global drug policy reform is unsatisfactory, because it is too slow a reform process. Life events and news make UN drug treaties more and more obsolete and irrelevant, daily. Years ago, Dr. Martin Luther King criticized the "… tranquilizing drug of gradualism" in his famous "I have a Dream" speech. He "worried that by merely chipping away at injustice, we were lulled into a sense of advancement when very little was actually being accomplished." Dr. King's criticism of the gradualist and incremental approach epitomizes civil society's major failing at the Commission on Narcotic Drugs in Vienna. It has taken sixty years

[741] Fordham and Haase, Ibid., p. 37.

[742] For example, see Steven Rolles, *Legalizing Drugs: The Key to Ending the War* (Oxford, UK: New Internationalist Publications, Ltd., 2017), "[Decriminalizing of people who use drugs, sometimes confused with legalization…] is one of the most important steps on the incremental journey towards legalized regulation, and it is a reform that is increasingly widespread across the world." p. 73.

and a rescheduling recommendation by the WHO, plus two years, to reschedule cannabis. And still — recreational cannabis is outlawed in Vienna for the world by UN prohibition forces.

Nation by nation, reform by reform, crisis by crisis, precursor by precursor — UN drug conventions are becoming inconsequential, irrelevant and ignored. United Nations "Jurassic" cannabis policy is a great example. The hopelessly regressed CND attitude is well reflected by the close vote regarding the begrudged cannabis rescheduling and Russian foot-dragging.

"The UN Commission on Narcotic Drugs voted to reclassify cannabis Wednesday, taking it off the strict Schedule IV list that includes dangerous and highly addictive drugs such as heroin. The UN still deems cannabis a controlled substance. But the move, which the U.S. supported, could ease restrictions on research into marijuana's therapeutic use. The 53-member commission approved the change in a close vote, by 27-25, with 1 abstention. Russia was a vocal opponent of the move, calling cannabis 'the most abused drug globally.'"[743] True to its radical view, today, Russian authorities sentenced basketball great Brittney Griner to nine years in prison for possessing cannabis oil.[744]

Creative "Inter Se" Agreements and "Fifth Stage Interpretive Fora" Alternatives Inadequate

Some of the best civil society leaders have racked their brains trying to develop new strategies to circumvent the harms implicit in UN drug prohibition treaties. In a scholarly work, *Drug Control and Human Rights in International Law*,[745] Dr. Richard Lines suggests a new, "fifth stage" of drug control. He described the first stage as the "pre-multilateral era" when a few nations attempted to control drugs nationally or bilaterally; a second stage as the "multilateral effort" exemplified by the International Opium Convention of 1912; a third stage as the 1920 League of Nations cooperative efforts to control opium and other dangerous drugs; and a fourth stage, beginning with

---

[743] Bill Chappell, "U.N. Commission Removes Cannabis From Its Most Strict Drug Control List," *NPR*, December 2, 2020, https://www.npr.org/2020/12/02/941283185/u-n-commission-removes-cannabis-from-its-most-strict-drug-control-list.

[744] Dina Zaru, "Brittney Griner found guilty in Russian drug trial, sentenced to 9 years in prison," August 4, 2022, *ABC News*, https://apple.news/Ab65Dog1rR3CWnYiZyQtCfA.

[745] Richard Lines, *Drug Control and Human Rights in International Law* (Cambridge: Cambridge University Press, 2017)

1945 and United Nations efforts to control drugs via its three drug-control treaties, marked by increasingly penal efforts to suppress drugs.[746] Dr. Lines writes of the existing stage-four drug policy: "According to the UN Office on Drugs and Crime, the negative unintended consequences of this fourth stage regime are many including the creation of huge criminal markets for drugs, controlled by cartels that often use violence and the corruption of State officials to maintain their vast profits, destabilising weak States; untold billions of dollars spent each year in largely ineffective drug interdiction efforts, at the expense of public investment in health, education and social services; exploding prison populations in many parts of the world, often driven by prosecution of drug-related offences; and millions dead from, and many millions more infected with, HIV as a result of sharing of syringes for injecting drug use."[747]

Dr. Lines' way-foreword suggestion is a fifth stage of drug control, one where penal, drug-control enforcement gives way to concerns regarding human rights by means of interpretive avoidance of what UN drug treaties say. In Dr. Lines' words, he proposes "an interpretive approach to resolving tensions and conflicts between drug control law and human rights law to prevent such abuses. Through this process, [he] propose[s] a framework and possible interpretive fora for the development of a 'fifth stage' of drug control, one that ensures obligations enshrined within international drug control law are carried out in a manner that is human rights compliant."[748]

But is creative construction of UN drug conventions to reach a constructive result any less damaging to respect for "the law" than drug-dealing in illicit markets or unbridled drug-war law enforcement. To construe UN drug treaties to mean what they do not say is an unsatisfactory way forward. How can one construe a treaty provision that clearly limits drug use to medical and scientific purpose to permit recreational drug use? Interpretation cannot have it both ways. In my opinion, a better choice for the fifth stage of drug control is to trash UN drug conventions. Amend them or repeal them. Nothing good would be lost, and much good could be gained by meeting bad drug conventions head-on rather than obliquely in an interpretive fog.

Martin Jelsma is another, well-respected, accomplished leader of Civil Society, who masterfully helped engineer the Bolivian coca strategy to withdraw from the 1961 Single Convention and re-accede to its terms, except with a reservation that allows for

---

[746] Ibid., pp. 1-4.

[747] Ibid., p. 4.

[748] Ibid., p. 273.

Bolivian indigenous, cultural and constitutionally protected use of the coca leaf. Reiterating, "The government of Bolivia withdrew from the 1961 Convention after its effort to amend the [1961] Single Convention by deleting its provision requiring that 'coca leaf chewing must be abolished' within 25 years (Article 49) failed. Bolivia then followed established procedures to leave and return as a party to the convention with the new reservation on the coca leaf."[749]

Mr. Jelsma has also taken a stab at devising a way forward to reach the goal of better drug policy, policy respectful of human rights, harm-reduction, and tolerance consonant with indigenous culture and individual rights, despite continued existence of archaic UN treaties. He proposes the avoidance of these UN drug treaty deficiencies and strictures by allowing nations to experiment with new drug policies by use of "*inter se*" agreements between agreeable, 1961 Single Convention, Member States. The bilateral or multilateral inter se agreements would enable "inter se partners" (nations) to do what UN treaties disallow. A Transnational Institute paper explained "An inter se modification would mean that the provisions in the treaties that are not part of the modification continue to be in force.[750]

Tom Blickman, a Transnational Institute colleague of Martin Jelsma, succinctly capsulized the way forward with the few choices available for meaningful drug policy reform: "If human rights overrule the drug control obligations that would be a strong argument for breaching them, but it would still only be in accordance with international law if the breaching party subsequently changes its obligations under the drug conventions, via reservation, inter se modification or amendment."[751]

Rather than an "interpretive fora," "inter se" agreements or continued civil society gradualism as a way forward to avoid the terms of rusty, unworkable and counterproductive UN drug conventions, just junk them. A two-page proposed amendment, already-drafted, could entirely remove cannabis from UN drug-control treaties,[752] or

---

[749] Coletta Youngers, "Bolivia Officially Returns as a Party to the 1961 Single Convention on Narcotic Drugs," *WOLA*, February 12, 2013, https://www.wola.org/analysis/bolivia-officially-returns-as-a-party-to-the-1961-single-convention-on-narcotic-drugs/.

[750] Zara Snapp and Jorge Herrera Valderrábano, "United States Drug Policy: Flexible Prohibition and Regulation," *Collapse of the Global Order on Drugs* (Bingley, UK: Emerald Publishing Inc, 2018), Ch. 12, p. 255.

[751] Tom Blickman, "The Elephant in the Room," *Collapse of the Global Order on Drugs*, supra, Ch. 5, p. 123

[752] Gierach, James E., "Cannabis Amendment: UN Drug Treaties," *UNODC site*, proposed, 2014, https://www.unodc.org/documents/ungass2016//Contributions/Civil/Law_Enforcement_Against_Prohibition/ CANNABIS_AMENDMENT_UN_DRUG_TREATIES.pdf.

another proposed amendment, already-drafted, would decriminalize drug use by eliminating mandated criminal penalties.[753] More comprehensively, all three UN treaties
could be consolidated and amended as discussed herein ("The New Single Convention
on Drugs," Chapter 16, supra).[754]

Civil Society Must Speak with a Single Voice

Drug prohibition has had a long and successful run by admonishing nations to speak
with a single voice. Caroline Chatwin, a harm reductionist, wrote that the "Drive to
Speak with One [Prohibition] Voice" is, and always has been, a problem. "Drug policy
is, inherently, an international issue and the EU has been active in this area since the
late 1980s. Seeking to build on *the United Nations' success in gaining near global
agreement to the prohibition of drugs,* illicit drug policy was quickly earmarked as an
area for 'ever closer union' within Europe."[755] She recognized the importance of a single voice in global drug policy, but unfortunately that voice has supported the cause
of the world drug problem, namely, drug prohibition.

   Civil society should mimic drug prohibition's enduring success by speaking with a
single voice, only this time, **"AGAINST PROHIBITION."** The secret strength of
LEAP was the simple rule that LEAP speakers under the leadership of cofounder Jack
A. Cole were at liberty to advocate freely whatever replacement drug policy he or she
favored, provided the LEAP speaker was against prohibition. Additionally, a LEAP
speaker was required to advise his or her audience that the prohibition-replacement
proposal he or she favored was just his or her opinion and not that of LEAP. Maybe it
was the individual LEAP speaker's view to replace prohibition with drug decriminalization, or drug medicalization, or drug legalization, or the legalization of one drug.
But the binding thread was this: All LEAP Speakers were against prohibition.

---

[753] Gierach, James E. "Decriminalization Amendment: U.N. Drug Treaties," *UNODC site,* proposed, 2014,
https://www.unodc.org/documents/ungass2016//Contributions/Civil/Law_Enforcement_Against_Prohibitio
n/DECRIMINALIZATION_AMENDMENT_UN_DRUG_TREATIES_.pdf.

[754] Gierach/LEAP "Proposed Amendment of United Nations Drug Treaties — 2014," English,
https://www.unodc.org/documents/ungass2016//Contributions/Civil/Law_Enforcement_Against_Prohibition/
LEAP_UN_Treaty_Amendment_2.26.1421-1.pdf, Spanish, https://www.unodc.org/documents/ungass2016//
Contributions/Civil/Law_Enforcement_Against_Prohibition/FINAL-3-Spanish_LEAP-Treaty-
Amendment_5.27.14-1.pdf.

[755] Caroline Chatwin, "The EU in Panglossian Stagnation," *Collapse of the Global Order on Drugs,* supra, Ch.
11, p. 235, emphasis added.

Civil society should be speaking with a strong, single, unwavering voice **Against Prohibition**. Ideally, in my opinion, it should call for an end to recreational drug prohibition and drug criminalization, as well as for a comprehensive amendment of UN drug-control conventions. Alternatively and justifiably, civil society could call for the repeal of UN drug-control conventions entirely. No choice of international drug policy could be worse than existing UN drug-control treaties, even a world devoid of any UN drug conventions. But unfortunately, civil society has been unable or unwilling to take that step. For too long, civil society and leading, drug policy reform organizations — like the Drug Policy Alliance — have been afraid of the words — "*LEGALIZE DRUGS.*" But those words are the elusive, universally overlooked Silver Bullet Solution to fix a dozen crises, globally and in America. (*See* Chapters 4-6, 8 and 9 herein.). Legalized drugs and legal drug markets are not the answer to everything, but nearly every drug problem and collaterally aggravated prohibition crisis will continue to defy solution without inclusion of *the essential, legalize-drugs ingredient* in the solution mix.

The Drug Policy Alliance Invited to Catalyze A "Single Voice" Call Against Drug Prohibition

In 2017, I encouraged the Drug Policy Alliance (DPA), still at that time under the able leadership of drug-policy reform stalwart Ethan Nadelmann, to use the DPA biennial conference being held in Atlanta, Georgia, to start the single-voice ball rolling. The DPA was in a position with experts and activists gathered from around the world to attempt to change public opinion regarding drug policy. I supplied a draft resolution (set forth here in full) that would do so, to wit:

"RESOLUTION SUPPORTING NATIONAL AND INTERNATIONAL DRUG POLICY REFORM"

Whereas, the undersigned Conferees of the Drug Policy Alliance Conference 2017, Atlanta, Georgia, USA, find and believe that the 1961 Single Convention on Narcotic Drugs[1] (hereinafter "the Single Convention") is the foundation and fountainhead for the fifty-six-year-old, failed "World War on Drugs"; and

Whereas, Article 4 of the Single Convention limits the use of drugs exclusively to medical or scientific purposes and imposes upon the parties thereto the general obligation to take legislative and administrative measures, inter alia, to criminalize, punish and deprive offenders of their liberty for serious offenses; and

Whereas, the magnitude of the 1961 treaty mistake and misconception is powerfully evidenced, according to the United Nations' Report of the Secretariat to the

Commission on Narcotic Drugs (CND), by this statement: "In 2012, 3.5 to 7 percent of the people aged 15-64 were estimated to have illicitly used drugs at least once in the preceding year"[2]; and

Whereas, according to World Bank data[3], in 2015 there were 2.5 billion males and 2.4 billion females aged 15-64, or 4.9 billion people combined, and 3.5% equals 171.5 million people and 7.0% equals 343 million people using drugs illicitly, annually; and

Whereas, most mind-altering substance use – including alcohol, tobacco, chocolate, caffeine, licit and illicit drugs – is for recreational purpose, or purposes other than medical or scientific; and

Whereas, the world prison population is estimated to be nine million people;[4] and

Whereas, criminalizing, incarcerating and punishing people who use illicit drugs has proven to be counterproductive rather than a constructive, realistic or affordable drug policy paradigm; and

Whereas, the World War on Drugs has not only failed to control the production, cultivation and processing of organic drugs, but it has also effectively encouraged the invention and proliferation of new synthetic substances at an ever-accelerating rate; and

Whereas, at the end of each day, the World War on Drugs facilitates the transportation, delivery, sale, use, abuse and misuse of all mind-altering drugs, licit and illicit; and

Whereas, the urgency of the need for drug policy reform in the United States is well-exemplified by the attention now being given to the so-called "Opioid Epidemic," a mix of legal and illegal opioid use, including physician-prescribed opioid medications such as OxyContin, and illegally-concocted, prohibition-encouraged, organic heroin and synthetic fentanyl; and

Whereas, the U.S. opioid epidemic did not exist in 1961 when the UN Single Convention was adopted, just as the crack cocaine, PCP, LSD, Ecstasy, methamphetamine and cannabis "epidemics" did not exist in 1961; and

Whereas, the well-intended, United Nations-encouraged World War on Drugs has not only failed to control drugs but has also caused myriad harms and pervasive collateral damage to people, human rights and institutions in many forms; and

Whereas, that damage and those harms include, but are not limited to, the following: transnational crime, addict crime, gang turf-war crime, retaliatory crime, mass incarceration, selective and disparate racial arrest, prosecution and incarceration, over-dose, disease, death, corruption, police abuses and distorted mission, trade imbalance, fear, flight, migration and human trafficking; and

Whereas, harm reductionists, drug policy reformers and advocates for human rights pursue, endlessly, as many harm-reduction initiatives and programs as the World War on Drugs causes by its enshrinement of drug intolerance embodied in the Single Convention, UN drug treaty, prohibition paradigm; and

Whereas, most, if not all, DPA Conference 2017 sessions are constructively aimed at reducing diverse and prolific drug prohibition-driven harms and collateral damage; and

Whereas, there can be no end to drug and drug-prohibition harms and damage confronting the world without an end to the prohibition-styled World War on Drugs itself that cause them; and

Whereas, the April 2016 United Nations General Assembly Special Session (UN-GASS 2016) regarding "the drug problem" provided an opportunity for major, world-wide, comprehensive drug policy reform, but that convocation failed to galvanize or articulate the dominant and prevailing thought of serious reformers, everywhere, namely, that drug prohibition must end if its harms and damage are to be ameliorated; and

Whereas, instead, the United Nations General Assembly by adoption of its "Out-come Document" (UNGASS 2016)[5] paid homage to the sacrosanct and seemingly indelible status of UN drug control treaties that drive nations, individually and collec-tively, to preserve and protect their adoption and enforcement of home-grown, self-defeating World War on Drugs policies and laws; and

Whereas, this DPA Conference 2017 aims to do more than just hear session after session of harm reduction[6] ideas and talk of reform without collective Conferee or DPA Conference Resolution; and

Whereas, this DPA Conference 2017 aims to identify, galvanize, and articulate the essential prerequisites to drug peace and advancement of the best overall harm-reduc-tion strategic plan, to-wit:

(1) End the World War on Drugs; and

(2) Amend or Repeal the United Nations 1961 Single Convention on Narcotic Drugs, and Its Progeny, That Encourage the "World Drug War" Paradigm; and

(3) Replace Existing National and International Drug Prohibition Laws, Policies and Treaties with Public Policy Models That Are Constructive, Tolerant, Health-Based, Public

Safety-Oriented, Human Rights-Friendly and Regulated Drug Market-Savvy; and

Whereas, opinions of DPA 2017 Atlanta Conferees may vary as to the specifics of the drug policy model that should replace prohibition, but there is overwhelming unanimity among harm reductionists, drug policy reformers and human rights advocates here assembled that the UN Single Convention prohibition-fashioned model must be replaced, and soon, and in no event later than the United Nations 2019 [Commission on Narcotic Drugs High-Level Ministers Segment regarding] World Drug Policy.

NOW, THEREFORE, BE IT RESOLVED BY THE UNDERSIGNED CONFEREES ASSEMBLED FOR THE DRUG POLICY ALLIANCE CONFERENCE 2017, Atlanta, Georgia, USA as follows:

A. SINGLE VOICE CALL TO ACTION

1. We call upon World and National Leaders to end the World War on Drugs.

2. We call upon World and National Leaders to amend or repeal the United Nations 1961 Single Convention on Narcotic Drugs, and related UN "drug control" treaties that encourage and protect bad, often cruel, sometimes deadly and always counterproductive international and national drug prohibition laws and policies.

3. We call upon World and National Leaders to replace the "World War on Drugs" paradigm with a more constructive, affordable, wiser, drug-tolerant, health-oriented and public safety-oriented drug policy paradigm with regulated legal drug markets, the essential prerequisite to comprehensively ameliorate the myriad and pervasive harms, collateral damage and human rights abuses inherent in the criminalization and drug prohibition paradigm.

B. TIMEFRAME FOR ACTION

This Call to Action needs to be converted into Action by leaders everywhere as soon as possible, but in no event later than the 2019 United Nations [Commission on Narcotic Drugs High-Level Ministers Segment regarding] World Drug Policy and Treaties.

C. DISSEMINATION OF THIS RESOLUTION

Copies of this Resolution shall be widely and boisterously distributed to the world press, the people of the world, and leaders everywhere, specifically including the following:

1. The Secretary-General of the United Nations

2. The President of the United Nations General Assembly

3. The Executive Director of the United Nations Office on Drugs and Crime

4. The President of the United States (POTUS)

5. The Leaders of the U.S. House of Representatives and Senate

6. Leadership of The World Health Organization (WHO)

7. The President of the International Narcotic Control Board (INCB)

8. To All Member Nations of the United Nations

[Footnotes:]

1. 1961 Single Convention on Narcotic Drugs

2. Report of the Secretariat, "World Situation with regard to drug abuse," E/CN.7/2015/3

3. World Bank staff estimates based on age/sex distributions of United Nations Population

Division's World Population Prospects, https://data.worldbank.org/indicator/SP.POP.1564.FE.IN

4. World Prison Population (5th edition), http://www.csdp.org/research/r234.pdf

5. OUTCOME DOCUMENT OF THE 2016 UNITED NATIONS GENERAL ASSEMBLY

SPECIAL SESSION ON THE WORLD DRUG PROBLEM,

https://www.unodc.org/documents/postungass2016/outcome/V1603301-E.pdf, excerpt from

page 2, "We underscore that the Single Convention on Narcotic Drugs of 1961 as amended by

the 1972 Protocol, the Convention on Psychotropic Substances of 1971, the United Nations

Convention against Illicit Traffic in Narcotic Drugs and Psychotropic Substances of 1988 and

other relevant international instruments constitute the cornerstone of the international drug

control system;" (Emphasis supplied)

6. DPA Conference 2017 Program, http://www.reformconference.org/conference-program

PREPARED, PROPOSED AND CIRCULATED BY:

James E. Gierach, former Chicago prosecutor; former Speaker, Director and Executive Board Vice Chairman of Law Enforcement Against Prohibition (LEAP), now known as Law Enforcement Action Partnership; Draftsman of LEAP's "Proposed Amendment of United Nations Drug Treaties – 2014," and two less comprehensive, proposed, Alternative Amendments of UN Drug Treaties.

See http://www.unodc.org/ungass2016/en/contributions/ngos/leap.html

Contact Information:

James E. Gierach

Palos Park, IL 60464 USA

Phone: 1-708-951-1601

Blog: www.jamesgierach.tumblr.com

Email: drugnews1@yahoo.com

Note: James E. Gierach will not be in attendance at the DPA Conference this year. Readers of this draft Resolution are invited to share, publish, forward, use, circulate and encourage its adoption in Atlanta and elsewhere.

[End Resolution and DPA communique.]

Unfortunately, the Drug Policy Alliance chose to ignore my suggestion, and 2017 Atlanta DPA attendees never heard nor saw anything of the Resolution or "Single Voice Call to End Drug Prohibition." Thus, the job is yet to be accomplished.

"Marijuana is effective at relieving nausea and vomiting, spasticity, appetite loss, certain types of pain, and other debilitating symptoms. And it is extraordinarily safe — safer than most medicines prescribed every day. If marijuana were a new discovery rather than a well-known substance carrying cultural and political baggage, it would be hailed as a wonder drug."

— Psychiatrist Lester Grinspoon

Part Seven – Marijuana: A Big Crack in the Drug-War Monolith

The sixty-two-year-old World War on Drugs serves as a monument to human intolerance of fellow human beings — intolerance based on superficial differences, foibles, and life choices whether made in the pursuit of happiness or subsistence. Enduring for decades, unscathed by its failure to control drugs and guarantee to cause trouble — unending violent crime, corruption, overdose, drug invention, inaccessible medications, mass incarceration, addiction, disease, racial profiling and abusive punishment — drug prohibition lives. Drug prohibition (the World War on Drugs) became like *a universal world religion* of sorts with revered drug dogma and pulsating drug intolerance. That dogma and intolerance was capable of hurdling national boundaries, vast differences in cultures, laws, mores, practices, customs and beliefs while also suppressing innate human empathy for one another — our respective troubles, needs, circumstances and shoes. The staying power of the drug prohibition monolith despite its colossal failure is truly a wonderment, a twentieth and twenty-first century, societal and civilization Wonder of the World.

However, thanks to marijuana, there is a big crack in the drug-war monolith.

Chapter 21 – Drug-War Incongruities

Because the War on Drugs suit never fits, and because its ill-tailored cloth wears so uncomfortably in every climate and region — bringing us more drugs, crime and corruption — drug-policy incongruities continue to sprout around the world. Examples abound.

In 2001, despite UN drug conventions, Portugal decriminalized the possession of all drugs for personal use.[756] Importantly, drug use and crime did not increase in response as officials elsewhere expected. Instead, the radical program proved to be a huge success,[757] and Portugal's former prime minister at the time of its drug-decriminalization rebellion became and serves as Secretary-General of the United Nations today.

In 2013, again in contravention of UN conventions, Uruguay became the first nation to legalize recreational marijuana; Canada followed suit in 2018; and Mexico is expected to follow soon.[758] Legalizing drugs reduces the value of drugs. In Mexico as everywhere, if taxes are not so high as to become confiscatory, the price of illicit drugs, now licit, will fall. This economic reality reduces the profiteering motivation to supply and deal drugs. Illustrating the power of drug policy on prices, Mexican "[g]rowers expect the price of marijuana to drop further and think their trade will become economically unfeasible. They say in the *past five years, the price they get has been halved*. Everyone is waiting to see how the drug capos will respond to a new legal business. Meanwhile, half of María's crop sits unsold. Marijuana has become less lucrative each day compared to the cartels' revenue from synthetic drugs like fentanyl. Demand and the price for pot fell when several states in the U.S. legalized it, though Mexico is still the top foreign supplier to U.S. consumers, according to a recent report by the U.S. Drug Enforcement Administration."[759] "Taking the profit out of drugs"

---

[756] Naina Bajekal, "Want to Win the War on Drugs? Portugal Might Have the Answer," *Time*, August 1. 2018, https://time.com/longform/portugal-drug-use-decriminalization/.

[757] Susana Ferreira, "Portugal's radical drugs policy is working. Why hasn't the world copied it?" *The Guardian*, December 5, 2017, https://www.theguardian.com/news/2017/dec/05/portugals-radical-drugs-policy-is-working-why-hasnt-the-world-copied-it.

[758] Zara Snapp, *Filter*, "Mexican Lawmakers Could Finally Legalize Marijuana Sales Next Month (Op-Ed)," *Marijuana Moment*, August 3, 2021, https://www.marijuanamoment.net/mexican-lawmakers-could-finally-legalize-marijuana-sales-next-month-op-ed/.

[759] María Verza, "Growers fret as Mexico moves to legalize marijuana," *AP News*, April 15, 2021, https://apnews.com/article/mountains-marijuana-latin-america-mexico-b607acdb6ffe72c24b83f683b4dda1d9, emphasis added.

is the economic weapon powerful enough to severely drain the lifeblood of gangs,[760] and drug legalization remains the most effective means to reduce the value of illicit drugs, as Mexico marijuana producers and dealers are discovering. Other incongruities appeared.

In 1996, despite UN drug conventions, California became the first U.S. state to legalize medical marijuana and many American states followed California's medical marijuana lead. Then, in 2012, Colorado and Washington state became the first U.S. states to legalize marijuana for recreational use.[761]

The following years, state after state and voter-referendum after voter-referendum approved recreational marijuana. "In 2018, Vermont became the first state to legalize marijuana for adult use through the legislative process (rather than a ballot initiative.) Vermont's law went into effect July 1, 2018,"[762] followed by Illinois in 2020. In 2021, Illinois' legal recreational marijuana sales hit $1.38 billion, double the 2020 sales.[763]

As of 2021, eighteen U.S. states have legalized recreational marijuana.[764]

Yet, Dr. Naidoo, then-president of INCB, said during the annual session of the Commission on Narcotic Drugs in 2015, that the "legalization of cannabis for non-medical and nonscientific purpose contravenes international drug-control treaties." He further said, "I find it very difficult to understand that [with] so many millions of dollars, and pounds and yen and with so many great minds applying themselves to find a solution for the world drug problem and everyone comes up with the same

[760] Gierach, James E., "Take profit out of drug dealing," *USA Today*, March 8, 1993.

[761] Keith Speights, "A Guide to Marijuana Legalization in the United States," *The Motley Fool*, updated August 2, 2021, accessed October 13, 2021, https://www.fool.com/investing/stock-market/market-sectors/healthcare/marijuana-stocks/marijuana-legalization/.

[762] Michael Hartman, "Cannabis Overview," *NCSL*, July 6, 2021, https://www.ncsl.org/research/civil-and-criminal-justice/marijuana-overview.aspx.

[763] Robert Channick, "Illinois recreational cannabis sales set record in December and hit $1.38 billion for the year, more than doubling 2020," *Chicago Tribune*, January 4, 2022, https://www.chicago tribune.com/business/ct-biz-illinois-cannabis-sales-record-20220104-5y2qd2wnlvfrpnm25ibgohje3m-story.html.

[764] Elisabeth Garber-Paul and Ryan Bort, "The United States of Weed," *Rolling Stones*, map first published 2019, updated regularly, accessed October 13, 2021, https://www.rollingstone.com/feature/cannabis-legalization-states-map-831885/.

solution — legalize cannabis."[765] INCB is simply out of touch, as exemplified by Dr. Naidoo's statement, and his successor's echo, that of **Werner Sipp**.

Even more hopefully, Gustavo Petro, Colombia's new president who took office in August 2022, is openly calling for an end to the War on Drugs, the legalization of cocaine and marijuana, and a new international convention regarding drugs.[766] "It is time for a new international convention that accepts that the drug war has failed, which has left a million murdered Latin Americans during these 40 years," he said. "The War on Drugs strengthened the mafias and weakened the states.... Are we going to expect that another million Latin Americans will be murdered and that the number of deaths from overdoses in the United States will rise to 200,000 every year? Or rather, will we exchange failure for a success that allows Colombia and Latin America to live in peace?"[767]

---

[765] "An end to the UN as we know it?" *Cannabis News Network*, video, March 15, 2015, Commission on Narcotic Drugs, Vienna, Austria, YouTube, https://youtu.be/40vsGUxCbjc, 44 seconds in and minute 1:41, respectively.

[766] Alexander Lekhtman, "Colombia's New President Wants to End the Drug War. Can he Succeed?" *Filter*, August 9, 2022, https://filtermag.org/colombia-president-drug-war/amp/.

[767] Ibid.

Chapter 22 – U. S. Congress Preserves and Protects Drug Prohibition

Competing with the United Nations' head-in-the-sand approach to drug policy, *federal law in the U.S. still outlaws marijuana production, use, and sale for any purpose, medical*[768] or otherwise. Even with an overwhelmingly favorable American public opinion regarding marijuana legalization in some form, 91 percent, the U.S. Congress remains unable to reconcile incongruities between state marijuana laws, federal law, and real-life drug use in America.[769]

The dichotomy between what American voters want and what politicians deliver causes a prohibition headache for marijuana users, growers, dispensers and elected officials. But many members of Congress were elected to office by championing fiery rhetoric about getting tough on drugs and locking up drug dealers and throwing away the key. Therefore, it is very difficult for pols to reverse field and abandon drug-policy positions that helped them win their coveted seats in the U.S. Congress in the first place. Politicians, better than any other set of professionals, know that voters fear drugs, love to hear feel-good, "tough on drugs," "tough on crime," and "save our kids" malarkey. Historically, it attracted votes without fail.

Despite dramatically changed public opinion regarding marijuana, politicians are still eternally tempted to go to the drug-war well for votes at election time and any time. Take as an example the 2020 Republican Party Platform on Drugs that promotes old, failed drug-policy ideas and punishment pitches. The Republican platform called for "jail time" for drug offenders, "drug-free schools and school drug-testing," the death penalty for drug kingpins, and noted that "Clinton surrendered [in the] Drug War."[770]

Even with recreational marijuana legal in California since 2018, picture politicians like Congressman **Doug LaMalfa** (R-CA) personally bulldozing cannabis farms in Sis-

768 Christina Majaski, "Is Medical Marijuana Legal Under Federal Law?" *LawInfo*, updated March 31, 2021, https://www.lawinfo.com/resources/criminal-defense/medical-marijuana/is-medical-marijuana-legal-under-federal-law.html.

769 Andrew Daniller, "Two-thirds of Americans support marijuana legalization," *Pew Research Center*, November 14, 2019, https://www.pewresearch.org/fact-tank/2019/11/14/americans-support-marijuana-legalization/.

770 "Republican Party on Drugs," *On The Issues*, 2020 Republican Platform, *Republican Platform*, adopted at GOP National Convention, August 12, 2000, https://www.ontheissues.org/celeb/ Republican_Party_Drugs.htm.

kiyou County, California. "California Attorney General Rob Bonta on Monday announced that the California Department of Justice's annual Campaign Against Marijuana Planting program, also known as CAMP, had eradicated nearly 1.2 million illegally cultivated cannabis plants this year."[771] Politicians keep snake oil sales, promo-
tions, and marijuana grandstanding in vogue at this late date, even in California.

Republicans and Democrats Mimic "Reefer Madness"

The political rhetoric regarding marijuana on the Democratic side of the aisle sounds
a little better, but not much. "The [2020] platform released last month states that
Democrats will 'reschedule' marijuana, which would allow scientists to study its medical benefits without making it fully legal. The platform voiced support for the legalization of medical marijuana and said that states should decide whether or not to allow
recreational use without the risk of Justice Department prosecutions."[772] But candidate
Biden in 2020 still opposed what America's majority wanted, legalized recreational
marijuana. Biden is still stuck in the past, supporting only marijuana decriminalization
and drug courts, incomplete and ineffective drug law reform.

Internationally, under President Biden, American policy regarding narcotics is still
a matter of war, not peace. **John A. Walsh**, Acting Assistant Secretary Bureau of International Narcotics and Law Enforcement Affairs (INL) and veteran drug warrior,
spoke at a Side Event of the 64th Session of the Commission on Narcotic Drugs on
April 15, 2021, and sounded much like a Republican reading from the Republican
Party Platform. Incidentally, INL is the money-muscle department that currently
manages a portfolio of more than $4 billion in more than ninety countries. Walsh said,
"The international community has entered a critical phase in the fight against illicit
narcotics. While we continue to fight traditional drug trafficking modalities, a new
illicit business model has taken shape.... *Today's synthetic drug crisis* is fueled by criminal organizations that exploit private sector platforms to enable their illegal activi-

[771] Andrew Sheeler, "California marijuana busts surge despite legalization as agencies target illicit growers," *The Sacramento Bee*, October 19, 2021, https://www.sacbee.com/news/california/california-weed/article 255103757.html.

[772] Leandra Bernstein, "Cannabis in the presidential race: Biden-Harris pledge to decriminalize marijuana," *Sinclair's Broadcasting Group*, September 17, 2020, https://wjla.com/news/nation-world/cannabis-in-the-presidential-race-biden-harris-pledge-to-decriminalize-marijuana.

ties. The anonymity and convenience of the internet, encrypted peer-to-peer messaging apps, and other communications technologies allow these criminal organizations to aggressively market and sell drugs directly to clients on a global scale...."""

Americans Want Marijuana Legal but Congress Just Says "No"

Normally, the first rule of politics in a democratic state is to follow the will of the voters. Marijuana policy is the peculiar exception to that rule. (An outright ban on civilian ownership of assault weapons is another. "Bans on assault weapons and high-capacity ammunition magazines have an approval rating of over 60 percent in the US, according to Pew."[773]) A clear majority of Americans, 60 percent of them, want recreational marijuana legalized, as 2021 polling by Pew Research Center reflected. When medical marijuana is added to the mix, 90 percent of Americans favor its legalization, yet medical marijuana remains illegal under federal law.[774]

Despite the obvious tangle of state marijuana laws and the head-on conflict between federal and state laws regarding it, a majority of the U.S. Congress has not yet voted to legalize recreational marijuana, or even medical marijuana. American politicians have become so accustomed to collecting votes making anti-drug speeches, it is very difficult for them to reverse field and support legalization. Like it or not, members of the U.S. Congress remain saddled with international, marijuana responsibilities imposed by UN drug-control conventions and politically addicted to pot prohibition and punishment — just as much as national representatives to the UN General Assembly.

Like the U.S. Congress, the UN and its drug-control agencies struggle with the simplest of drug-policy reform for the most benign controlled substance, a substance with many different names, including 1,200 slang terms for cannabis.[775] As early as

---

[773] Rani Molla, "Poll is clear: Americans want gun control," *Vox*, June 1, 2022, https://www.vox.com/policy-and-politics/23141651/gun-control-american-approval-polling.

[774] Ted Van Green, "Americans overwhelmingly say marijuana should be legal for recreational or medical use," *Pew Research Center*, April 16, 2021, https://www.pewresearch.org/fact-tank/2021/04/16/americans-overwhelmingly-say-marijuana-should-be-legal-for-recreational-or-medical-use/.

[775] *Wikipedia*, s.v. "List of names of cannabis," https://en.wikipedia.org/wiki/ List_of_names_for_cannabis, accessed March 17, 2023.

2010, Dr. Lester Grinspoon, a psychiatrist and retired professor at the Harvard Medical School, stated that he would stake his professional career on the notion that "cannabis is the least toxic psychoactive drug known to man."[776]

Finally, in March 2021 the CND approved a two-year-old cannabis rescheduling recommendation made by the World Health Organization regarding the medical use of cannabis.[777] One news reported: "The United Nations Commission on Narcotic Drugs (CND) on Wednesday accepted a World Health Organization (WHO) recommendation to remove cannabis and cannabis resin from Schedule IV of the 1961 Single Convention on Narcotic Drugs. The historic vote in Vienna could have far-reaching implications for the global medical cannabis industry, ranging from regulatory oversight to scientific research into the plant and its use as a medicine. The eagerly awaited approval of Recommendation 5.1 had a slim majority in favor with twenty-seven votes for, one abstention, and 25 votes against. The CND – the main drug policymaking body within the United Nations – turned down all five remaining recommendations."[778]

Nations Leading Obstruction of Drug Policy Reform at the United Nations

Because the vote to pass this minor marijuana matter passed by such a narrow margin, despite a two-year-old recommendation of the World Health Organization, it is worth noting the names of the countries dragging their feet on even the most modest reform of failed UN drug policy. Voting "no" on reform were the following countries: Afghanistan, Algeria, Angola, Bahrain, Brazil, Burkina Faso, Ivory Coast, Chili, China, Cuba, Egypt, Hungary, Iraq, Japan, Kazakhstan, Kenya, Kyrgyzstan, Libya, Nigeria, Pakistan, Peru, Russia, Togo, Turkey and Turkmenistan. Ukraine abstained.[779] Readers of this book living in those twenty-five countries, please let your leaders know that

[776] Madison Park, "Legal cannabis for the rest of us?" *CNN*, November 3, 2010, http://www.cnn.com/2010/HEALTH/11/01/marijuana.health.effects/index.html.

[777] Isabella Kwai, "U.N. Reclassifies Cannabis as a Less Dangerous Drug," *New York Times*, December 2, 2020, https://www.nytimes.com/2020/12/02/world/europe/cannabis-united-nations-drug-policy.html?referringSource=articleShare.

[778] Alfredo Pascual, "United Nations approves WHO recommendation to reschedule cannabis in historic vote," *MJBiz Daily*, updated December 3, 2020, https://mjbizdaily.com/united-nations-approves-who-recommendation-to-reschedule-cannabis-in-historic-vote/.

[779] Ibid.

global drug prohibition policy is a failure beyond measure, magnifying the drug problem and causing many other crises adversely affecting public health, security, freedom and human rights. People should not have to live under the yoke of drug prohibition.

Unfair Marijuana Arrests and Sadistic Deprivation of Medical Marijuana

In this author's estimation — positive, protracted marijuana reform is not nearly reform enough. Even after approval of the cannabis rescheduling amendment, UN marijuana scheduling, still, effectively criminalizes the consensual, recreational behavior of nearly 200 million people. And that is unfair and unnecessary. "Cannabis continues to be the most widely used drug worldwide. UNODC estimates that almost 4 percent... of the global population aged 15–64 years used cannabis at least once in 2019, the equivalent of some 200 million people..."[780]

It is unfair to drug users who get arrested because most marijuana users don't get caught. And marijuana criminalization is unfair because Blacks are about 3.73 times more likely than Whites to be arrested for marijuana, despite roughly equal usage rates, according to a U.S. study by the ACLU of 8.2 million marijuana arrests between 2001 and 2010.[781] In 2020, another ACLU work, confirmed that racial disparity based on analysis of marijuana possession arrests and attendant racial disparities from 2010 to 2018.[782] And a third ACLU study on the subject has, perhaps, the best title, "The War on Drugs in Black and White."[783]

In addition, depriving people of marijuana medicine is cruel and sadistic. The case of best-selling author Peter McWilliams is a good example. In 1996 Peter was diagnosed with non-Hodgkin's lymphoma and AIDS. He was wheelchair bound. To control the nausea caused by the medicines he took for cancer and AIDS, preventing him

---

[780] *The World Drug Report* 2021, Booklet 3, p. 19, https://www.unodc.org/res/wdr2021/field/WDR21_Booklet_3.pdf.

[781] "Marijuana Arrests by The Numbers," *ACLU*, 2022, https://www.aclu.org/gallery/marijuana-arrests-numbers.

[782] "A Tale of Two Countries: Racially Targeted Arrests in the Era of Marijuana Reform," *ACLU*, 2020, https://www.aclu.org/sites/default/files/field_document/marijuanareport_03232021.pdf.

[783] "The War on Drugs in Black and White," *ACLU*, 2013, https://www.aclu.org/report/report-war-marijuana-black-and-white.

from vomiting and expelling his medications, Peter consumed marijuana. And then what happened?

Author R.W. Bradford told the story. "[Peter McWilliams'] articulate advocacy of legalizing medical marijuana brought him to the attention of federal authorities, who got wind of Todd McCormick's attempt to grow marijuana for medicinal purposes and of Peter's involvement with it. And it came to pass that in the early morning of December 17, 1997, federal agents invaded [Peter's] home and business, and confiscated a wide array of his property (including his computers, one of whose hard disks contained the book he was writing). In July 1998 they arrested him on charges of conspiring to grow marijuana. His mother and brother put up their homes as bond and he was released from jail to await his trial. One of the conditions of his bail was that he smoke no marijuana. Unwilling to risk the homes of his mother and brother, [Peter McWilliams] obeyed the order. His viral load, which had fallen to undetectable levels, now soared to dangerous levels: 'Unable to keep down the life-saving prescription medications, by November 1998, four months after my arrest, my viral load soared to more than 256,000. In 1996 when my viral load was only 12,500, I had already developed an AIDS-related cancer.... Even so, the government would not yield. It continued to urine test me. If marijuana were found in my system, my mother and brother would lose their homes and I would be returned to prison,' Peter said."

"Last November, news came that would have crushed a lesser man: the judge in the case ruled that Peter could not present to the jury any information about his illness, the fact that the government's own research concludes that marijuana is virtually the only way to treat the illness, or that using marijuana for medical purposes was legal in California. Unable to defend himself against the government's charges, Peter concluded that he had no choice but to plea bargain. He agreed to plead guilty, in hopes that any incarceration could be served under house arrest, since sending him to prison, where he would not be able to follow his lifesaving regimen, would be tantamount to sentencing him to death. On June 11, there was a fire in his home, which destroyed the letters to the judge that he had acquired and the computer containing the book he was writing on his ordeal. Three days later, he died, apparently as a result of his inability to keep his medication down."[784] Another rendition of these facts by another writer called this scenario, correctly, "The Murder of Peter McWilliams."[785]

Shame on the judge, shame on the prosecutors, and shame on our narrow-minded, intolerant War on Drugs.

"Ain't Nobody's Business If You Do"

Peter McWilliams wrote *Ain't Nobody's Business If You Do,*[786] a great, down-to-Earth treatise on consensual "crime." The book takes up the prohibitions of alcohol, drugs, prostitution, homosexuality, gambling and much more, thematically holding that consensual behavior between consenting adults is not crime, despite our political leaders playing to popular prejudices and collecting votes thinking and legislating otherwise.

Publication of the outrages, intolerance, and prolific harms caused by the World War on Drugs, I believe, is the entry vestibule to a new, collective public opinion regarding drugs and how to better deal with them. By sharing and repeating these horrible stories perhaps public opinion will change regarding how to better control and regulate all drugs, as changed public opinion alcohol long ago in the United States and is now doing for marijuana, globally.

I Believe in the Evolution of Public Opinion

I believe, the way to advance the inevitable end of the dastardly World War on Drugs is to rally public opinion against it so powerfully that political leadership will have no choice but to follow. I believe the most powerful of all weapons, and perhaps the only weapon powerful enough to fire the Silver Bullet (drug legalization), is *Changed Public Opinion*. This book aims to do just that — change public opinion regarding the War on Drugs, to help us get past drug-legalization brain cramps and bring us back to a world and time of drug peace. I aim to accomplish this Project... "practically" and "in our lifetimes"... together, you and I.

---

[784] R.W. Bradford, "US: The Life and Death of Peter McWilliams," *Liberty Magazine*, August 2000, republished, *Media Awareness Project*, http://www.mapinc.org/drugnews/v00/n948/a03.html.

[785] Richard Cowan, "The Murder of Peter McWilliams," *The Antique Cannabis Book*, 2nd edition, Chapter 3, "Censored Medical Studies," information taken from *Marijuana* News, June 16, 2000, http://antiquecannabisbook.com/chap03/Doctors/Doctors-P3.htm.

[786] Peter Williams, *Ain't Nobody's Business If You Do* (Los Angeles: Prelude Press, 1993).

Chapter 23 - International Narcotic Control
Board Warnings

In June 2018, the INCB warned Canada that its actions regarding marijuana legalization conflicted with its drug treaty obligations.[787] Uruguay and the U.S. received similar warnings from INCB.[788]

Interestingly, neither Canada, Uruguay, nor the U.S. meaningfully replied to the warning. Despite national realities and parallel national actions, basically defying international law, no nation spoke up and said anything like: "Dear United Nations: The drug war just does not work. The drug war is lost. The drug war can never be won. The drug war will never end unless we just repudiate this antiquated public policy and substitute Drug Peace for Drug War."

Of course, the INCB marijuana warning was a nugatory act, because people want to use drugs regardless of what INCB has to say. And national sovereignty and national constitutions still matter. Eventually, at least in countries that are democratic States, politicians do what voters want. The power is in the people to end drug prohibition, and the people exert their power by forming, and sometimes changing, collective public opinion. If "We, the People" want the War on Drugs to continue, it will. If however, "We, the People" want the War on Drugs to discontinue, it will end. Frankly, I believe the same is true in nondemocratic countries as well, though marijuana legalization is off to a slow start in Russia, China, the Philippines, Brazil, and countries viewed as less democracy oriented. Universal laws of the Cosmos and contractual rights will eventually prevail, or as Michael T. Takac might hypothesize, "When the laws of society become so conflicted and adversarial to universal laws of nature and scientific contractual rights, either those societal laws must reform, and conform, or human life itself will be extinguished."[789]

---

[787] "International Narcotics Control Board expresses deep concern about the legalization of cannabis for non-medical use in Canada," *International Narcotics Control Board*, press release, June 21, 2018, https://www.incb.org/incb/en/news/press-releases/2018/incb-expresses-deep-concern-about-the-legalization-of-cannabis-for-non-medical-use-in-canada.html.

[788] Alan Travis, "UN drugs body warns US states and Uruguay over cannabis legalisation," *The Guardian*, March 3, 2015, https://www.theguardian.com/society/2015/mar/03/un-drugs-body-warns-us-states-and-uruguay-over-cannabis-legalisation.

[789] Michael T. Takac, *Scientific Proof of Our Unalienable Rights: a Road to Utopia* (Fremont, California: Robertson Publishing, 2019, 5th edition).

Chapter 24 – "Marijuana Majority" Leveraged to Reform Laws Regarding Other Drugs

Many people the world over have a fondness for marijuana, cannabis, ganja, and weed. The plant is given many names in many places over thousands of years. And again, marijuana is the most popular of the prohibited "bad drugs."

Because so many people choose to use marijuana, 200 million people in 2019 according to the *World Drug Report 2021*,[790] and because some nations now allow it, highly visible incongruities arise between drug-use commonality on the one hand and national drug laws and international drug treaties on the other. These incongruities reveal a huge crack in the drug-prohibition monolith, one large enough to enable leaders to use marijuana as Archimedes' lever to wedge the world free of drug prohibition, once and for all. And not only for marijuana — but for all commonly used, and sometimes abused, mind-altering substances that need control and regulation more than they need the drug-prohibition treatment.

Sadly, despite nations diverging from UN "single voice" drug-prohibition palaver, neither the "Home of the Brave" nor the "Land of the Free" have chosen to file a proposed amendment of the 1961 Single Convention on Narcotic Drugs. UN Secretary-General António Guterres sits poised on the edge of his chair awaiting such a filing, the key to turning the United Nations treaty amendatory machinery "On." The 1961 Single Convention, Article 47 provides: "Any Party may propose an amendment to this Convention. The text of any such amendment and the reasons therefor shall be communicated to the Secretary-General who shall communicate them to the Parties and to the Council." Performing that one act would distinguish any single, courageous nation that dared to break the ice, directly challenging the UN single-voice canon, and triggering the start of serious, concrete, drug-treaty-amendment discussion, globally.

What nation, or set of nations, will earn that honorable distinction?

---

[790] *The World Drug Report* 2021, Booklet 3, p. 19, Figure 6, Canna is Use Trends, https://www.unodc.org/res/wdr2021/field/WDR21_Booklet_3.pdf.

Part Eight - Public Opinion: A Weapon with the Power to Fire the Silver Bullet

Chapter 25 - Drug Legalization: "Not Practical" and "Not in Our Lifetimes"

Sweeping drug-policy reform is NOT on the table. "Radical" drug legalization is especially NOT on the table. The solution to societal problems must be crafted consonant within an immutable, global environment where recreational drug use (possession) and sale is outlawed. In other words, the antidote to any societal problem must be taken with the drug-prohibition poison pill.

Any new "stop the violence" initiative, whatever it is, must be attempted while the omnipresent poison pill continues to spoil societal systems. The new overdose prevention initiative must be taken with the poison pill. The solution to mass incarceration and private prisons must be crafted consonant with prohibition preservation. Reforms aimed to address policing problems, healthcare crises and persistent, systemic racism — all such reforms and solutions must be undertaken alongside drug-prohibition. Nearly all nations subscribe to UN drug-control international law (treaties), and thereby to its recreational poison-pill regimen. That regimen — the drug-prohibition paradigm — makes "harm reduction" a non sequitur, "drug control" an oxymoron, and "drug prevention and drug education" antithetical.

For sixty years, meaningful, systemic drug-policy reform (drug legalization) seemed unattainable, and reversion to times of past drug-peace and a drug-tolerant world seemed unimaginable and impractical during our lifetime.

Bruce DuMont, host of *Beyond the Beltway*, a U.S. nationally syndicated, weekly, television and radio show, proclaimed as much by his response to my answer to a question posed by him during his April 25, 2021 show. The show included discussion regarding the murder of a Black man named **George Floyd** by a white Minneapolis police officer named **Derek Chauvin**. Chauvin knelt on Floyd's neck while Floyd was handcuffed and helpless until life was wrung out of him. Justly, a jury convicted Chauvin of murder.

Bruce DuMont questioned me regarding the racial implications of that scenario, asking me: "Jim, if you were all powerful, what is the one thing you would do to end racism in American policing?"

"End the War on Drugs," I replied.

Bruce immediately interrupted me with a common, probable reaction of many viewers, listeners and leaders: "No, I mean something practical, something that can happen in our lifetime."

"Practical"... "In our lifetimes."[791]

Is not an end to our tragic, misconceived, failed and counterproductive World War on Drugs achievable during our lifetimes? Must someone other than you or I, or some life not yet in being, be the someone to wake up and smell the coffee? I believe we can end this miserable, misconceived World War on Drugs ourselves, in our lifetimes, practically — if we have a brain and use it. That's what I am asking of all of us by writing this book. That's what I am asking of each of you reading it

---

"I'm sometimes accused of drug trafficking. It's an activity that for the time being, historically, shall we say has been declared illegal. It's illegal at the moment, but in the long run and in the future, we're going to show that it will head for legalization."

— Pablo Escobar

---

[791] *Beyond the Beltway*, April 25, 2021, video, YouTube, https://youtu.be/HE51StBXKTg, Minutes 11, 16-18.

Appendix

Gierach Drug Policy Axioms

1. If drugs are bad, drug war is worse.

2. Drug prohibition is the most effective policy to put more drugs, uncontrolled and unregulated, everywhere.

3. We can have safe communities or drug prohibition, but not both.

4. UN Drug Treaties are the foundation and fountainhead for the World War on Drugs.

5. Everything in drug policy works in reverse; good drug policy is counterintuitive.

6. The harder we try to suppress drugs, the more they flourish.

7. An anti-drug ad is first and foremost a drug ad.

8. Drug cartels and street gangs want us to burn their seized drugs which is very helpful in protecting their exclusive control over drugs, drug markets and persons addicted to drugs.

9. Outlawing drug products makes something that grows on a plant in the ditch having no value, the most valuable commodity on the face of the Earth.

10. The 'good guys' and the 'bad guys' are both on the same side of the line of scrimmage, both in favor of drug prohibition. (Capone, Brownfield, Escobar, Botticelli, 'El Chapo' Guzman, Fedatov, Hoover, Emanuel…)

11. The fatal weakness of drug demand reduction strategies: It's easier to make a new addict than recover a confirmed one.

12. The fatal weakness of drug supply reduction strategies: The more we succeed, the more we fail. The more scarce the supply becomes, the higher the price and greater the incentive to produce. Prohibition engages laws of supply and demand, price and production, laws no less real or repealable than gravity.

13. Take the profit out of drugs; to take crime off our streets; and taxes off our backs.

14. Adult consensual behavior is not a crime; making it one is.

15. Freedom and self-discipline regarding substances is more powerful than any prohibition law, and all the King's horses and all the King's men.

16. Outlawing drugs is as effective as outlawing dandelions.

17. Protection from fentanyl is a matter of drug labeling, a potential positive side-effect of drug legalization and regulation.

18. The best line of defense against opioid overdose is the drug user and a contents label. Legalization allows that; prohibition does not.

Acknowledgements

A big thank you is in order here to Michael Krawitz, a veteran and respected medical cannabis drug policy reformer, who assisted me in posting my drafts of three proposed amendments of UN drug-control treaties on the UNODC website regarding NGO contributions preparatory to UNGASS 2016, preserving my work hopefully for posterity in perpetuity.

Also, a big thank you to Jack A. Cole who in 2004 asked me to become a speaker for Law Enforcement Against Prohibition (LEAP) and later a LEAP director, presenting me with an opportunity to expand my audience and reach. Likewise, thank you to my fellow LEAP directors, speakers, support staff and believers whose work, insight and courage put LEAP on the cutting-edge of drug policy reform internationally for years. Bless you all.

Thank you to Judge Jim Gray for connecting me with a great publisher, Histria Books; to Bill Fried, a LEAP right arm, manuscript reviewer and adviser; and to all manuscript reviewers — Michel Kazatchkine, Jack A. Cole, Peter Christ, Romesh Bhattacharji, Rodrigo Vélez, David Borden, Reverend Alexander E. Sharp and Dr. Alex Wodak. And big thanks to neighbor and friend Michael J. Cherskov and to Audrey Weinbrecht whose outstanding editing skills, knowledge, and judgment greatly contributed to this project.

And thank you to my wife who helped carry the ball with copyright permissions and licensing when I began to tire.

Finally, to the many kind people who urged me to continue down the road to the land of drug-policy reform over the decades with words of encouragement like those of an Indiana physician, Mona K. Stern, M.D., who I never met, but who wrote to simply advise, "Keep writing." I have.

Index

HISTRIA BOOKS

GAUDIUM

Gaudium Publishing
Books to challenge and enlighten

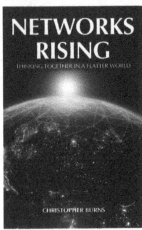
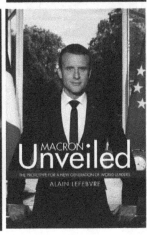

FOR THESE AND OTHER GREAT BOOKS VISIT
HISTRIABOOKS.COM